RECORDKEEPING IN INTERNATIONAL ORGANIZATIONS

Recordkeeping in International Organizations offers an important treatment of international organizations from a recordkeeping perspective, while also illustrating how recordkeeping can play a vital role in our efforts to improve global social conditions.

Demonstrating that organizations have both a responsibility and an incentive to effectively manage their records in order to make informed decisions, remain accountable to stakeholders, and preserve institutional history, the book offers practical insights and critical reflections on the effective management, protection, and archiving of records. Through policy advice, surveys, mind mapping, case studies, and strategic reflections, the book provides guidance in the areas of archives, records, and information management for the future. Among the topics addressed are educational requirements for recordkeeping professionals, communication policies, data protection and privacy, cloud computing, classification and declassification policies, artificial intelligence, risk management, enterprise architecture, and the concepts of extraterritoriality and inviolability of archives. The book also offers perspectives on how digital recordkeeping can support the UN's 2030 Agenda for Sustainable Development, and the accompanying Sustainable Development Goals (SDGs).

Recordkeeping in International Organizations will be essential reading for records and archives professionals as well as information technology, legal, security, management, and leadership staff, including chief information officers. The book should also be of interest to students and scholars engaged in the study of records, archives, and information management, information technology, information security, and law.

Jens Boel is a Danish archivist and historian. From 1995 to 2017 he was the Chief Archivist of the United Nations Educational, Scientific and Cultural Organization (UNESCO) and launched the organization's records management programme and history project.

Eng Sengsavang is currently a Reference Archivist at the United Nations Educational, Scientific and Cultural Organization (UNESCO) in Paris. She received her dual master's of Archival and Library Studies degrees from the University of British Columbia, Vancouver, Canada, in 2015.

ROUTLEDGE GUIDES TO PRACTICE IN LIBRARIES, ARCHIVES AND INFORMATION SCIENCE

Guidance for Librarians Transitioning to a New Environment
Tina Herman Buck and Sara Duff

Recordkeeping in International Organizations
Archives in Transition in Digital, Networked Environments
Edited by Jens Boel and Eng Sengsavang

Trust and Records in an Open Digital Environment
Edited by Hrvoje Stančić

https://www.routledge.com/Routledge-Guides-to-Practice-in-Libraries-Archives-and-Information-Science/book-series/RGPLAIS

RECORDKEEPING IN INTERNATIONAL ORGANIZATIONS

Archives in Transition in Digital, Networked Environments

Edited by Jens Boel and Eng Sengsavang

Routledge
Taylor & Francis Group

LONDON AND NEW YORK

First published 2021
by Routledge
2 Park Square, Milton Park, Abingdon, Oxon OX14 4RN

and by Routledge
52 Vanderbilt Avenue, New York, NY 10017

Routledge is an imprint of the Taylor & Francis Group, an informa business

British Library Cataloguing in Publication Data
A catalogue record for this book is available from the British Library

Library of Congress Cataloging-in-Publication Data
Names: Boel, Jens, editor. | Sengsavang, Eng, editor.
Title: Recordkeeping in international organizations : archives in
transition in digital, networked environments / edited by Jens Boel and
Eng Sengsavang.
Other titles: Recordkeeping in international organisations
Description: 1 Edition. | New York : Routledge, 2020. | Series: Routledge
guides to practice in libraries, archives and information science |
Includes bibliographical references and index.
Identifiers: LCCN 2020029938 (print) | LCCN 2020029939 (ebook) | ISBN
9780367365578 (hardback) | ISBN 9780367365585 (paperback) | ISBN
9780429347092 (ebook) | ISBN 9781000282764 (adobe pdf) | ISBN
9781000282849 (epub) | ISBN 9781000282801 (mobi)
Subjects: LCSH: International agencies–Management. | Electronic
records–Management. | Archives–Administration.
Classification: LCC JZ4850 .R413 2020 (print) | LCC JZ4850 (ebook) | DDC
025.1/975–dc23
LC record available at https://lccn.loc.gov/2020029938
LC ebook record available at https://lccn.loc.gov/2020029939

ISBN: 978-0-367-36557-8 (hbk)
ISBN: 978-0-367-36558-5 (pbk)
ISBN: 978-0-429-34709-2 (ebk)

Typeset in Bembo
by Taylor & Francis Books

CONTENTS

ILLUSTRATIONS

Figures

Tables

CONTRIBUTORS

Jens Boel is a Danish archivist and historian. From 1987 to 1993 he was a Research Fellow employed by the Government of Greenland with the task of repatriating Greenlandic archives and helping to establish the National Archives of Greenland. He was UNESCO's Reference Archivist from 1993 to 1995 and its Chief Archivist from 1995 to 2017. Jens chaired the Section of International Organizations of the International Council on Archives (ICA) for eight years. He is a member of the Editorial Steering Committee for the UNESCO Courier. He was the Director of the Transnational Team of the InterPARES Trust (ITrust) Project from 2013 to 2019.

Paola Casini works as Data and Information Manager at the Directorate General for Communication in the European Commission. Her previous experience includes roles as Chief Archivist at the United Nations in New York, and archivist at the European Economic and Social Committee and the North Atlantic Treaty Organization (NATO) in Brussels. She holds an MA in Political Science from the University of Florence, Italy, and a PhD in Archives and Information Management from the University of London, UK. Her expertise in archives, data, and information management in international organizations crosses academia, policy, and communications.

Ineke Deserno was appointed as the NATO Archivist in February 2010. Ineke arrived at NATO having accumulated 15 years of professional experience managing the corporate records and archives of the United High Commissioner for Refugees (UNHCR), the International Olympic Committee (IOC), and the World Health Organisation (WHO). Her approach to archives and information management was shaped by her education in three major national traditions in the field. She holds a master's of History and Archival Studies from the Radboud

Universiteit Nijmegen and Rijksarchief School, The Netherlands, a post-graduate degree in archives and records management from the University of British Columbia, Canada, and a PhD from Monash University, Australia.

Elaine Goh received her PhD in Library, Archival and Information Studies from the University of British Columbia, Canada. She is currently Manager of Information Management at the British Columbia College of Nursing Professionals in Vancouver, Canada. Her previous positions include Assistant Director of Records Management at the National Archives of Singapore. Concurrently with her doctoral program, Elaine was a graduate research assistant for the InterPARES Trust project from 2013 to 2016. Her research interest focuses on the interaction of law, records management, and organizational culture.

Stephen Haufek has been working in archives and records management at the United Nations since 2006. He started as an Audio-Visual Archivist at the International Criminal Tribunal for the former Yugoslavia, after completing a master's degree in the Preservation and Presentation of the Moving Image from the University of Amsterdam. He is currently the Chief of the Archives Unit in the Archives and Records Management Section in the United Nations Secretariat at UN headquarters in New York.

Darra L. Hofman, JD, MSLS, is a doctoral candidate at The University of British Columbia iSchool, where she specializes in archival science. Her research centres on the intersection of records, technology, and human rights, with a focus on privacy. She is a recipient of an Izaak Walton Killam Pre-Doctoral Fellowship and a Joseph-Armand Bombardier Canada Graduate Scholarships Doctoral Scholarship.

Julia Kastenhofer completed her undergraduate studies in History at the University of Vienna, Austria. She holds master's degrees in Archives and Records Management from University College London, UK, and in Global History from the University of Vienna. Her work experience in archives and records management includes positions at the International Atomic Energy Agency in Vienna and the Historical Archives of the European Union in Florence, Italy. At the time the research in this paper was conducted, she was a member of the InterPARES Trust project within the Transnational Team. She currently works as a Records Manager at the Inter-American Development Bank in Washington DC, USA.

Shadrack Katuu completed his undergraduate degree in Kenya, master's studies in Canada, and doctoral studies in South Africa. He is currently an Information Management Officer with the United Nations Mission in Iraq. He was previously an Information Management Officer at the United Nations Mission in South Sudan; head of the Records Unit at the International Atomic Energy Agency in Vienna, Austria; and before that, an archives/records officer at the International Monetary Fund in Washington DC, USA. He has previously held positions as

Manager of Information Systems in Nelson Mandela's post-presidential office at the Nelson Mandela Foundation and as Information Analyst at the South African History Archive in Johannesburg, South Africa. Shadrack has also served as full-time lecturer at the University of Botswana, as well as guest-lectured at several universities in Barbados, Canada, South Africa, and the USA. He is a Research Fellow at the Department of Information Science at the University of South Africa.

Giovanni Michetti is Associate Professor of Archival Science at Sapienza University of Rome. His main research interests are records management, description models, and digital preservation. He has been involved in national and international research projects on digital preservation, including ERPANET, CASPAR, and InterPARES. He is the Chair of the committee "Archives and Records Management" in the Italian Standards Organization (UNI). He is also the Italian representative in different ISO working groups on records management. He has authored the Italian versions of the Encoded Archival Description and the OAIS Reference Model.

Grant Mitchell has been the Manager of the Library and Archive Services at the International Federation of Red Cross and Red Crescent Societies (IFRC) in Geneva, Switzerland, since 1996. He was a records manager and archivist at the Insurance Corporation of British Columbia in Vancouver, Canada, from 1987 to 1996. Grant has a Master's of Archival Studies degree from the University of British Columbia, Canada.

Weimei Pan is an assistant professor in the School of Management at Tianjin Normal University, China, where she currently teaches courses on diplomatics and electronic records management. She earned her PhD from the University of British Columbia in 2019, where she focused on the management of records as evidence and information in the context of cloud-based services in China. Her research interests include diplomatics, records management, archival education, and the protection and demonstration of records as legal evidence. Her current research focuses on the management of electronic records so that they can be admitted in litigations in the Chinese context and diplomatics in China.

Dieter Schlenker has been the Director of the Historical Archives of the European Union since January 2013. Previously he worked for the United Nations Educational, Scientific and Cultural Organization (UNESCO), first as archivist at the Paris Headquarters, then as head of the Information and Knowledge Management Unit in Bangkok, Thailand. Previously, he worked as Records Manager at Ford Company European Headquarters in Cologne and at the UN Food and Agriculture Organization (FAO) headquarters in Rome. Describing himself as "an archivist by profession and heart," Dieter holds an Archivist Diploma from the Archival School of the Vatican Secret Archive and a PhD in Modern History from the University of Heidelberg, Germany.

Eng Sengsavang is the Reference Archivist at the United Nations Educational, Scientific and Cultural Organization (UNESCO) in Paris, France. She has previously worked for the North Atlantic Treaty Organization (NATO) in Brussels, Belgium, and interned at the United Nations Archives and Records Management Section (UNARMS) in New York, USA. She holds a dual master's degree in Archival Studies and Library and Information Studies from the University of British Columbia, Canada. Eng served as a Graduate Research Assistant and Consultant for the InterPARES Trust research project from 2014 to 2019.

FOREWORD

The InterPARES research project began in January 1999 under my direction at the University of British Columbia, funded by the Social Sciences and Humanities Research Council of Canada. It took its name from Latin "*inter pares*" (i.e., among peers) to convey the idea that the research would involve equal contributions of academics and professionals in an international multidisciplinary context. Inter-PARES then became an acronym for International research on Permanent Electronic Records in Electronic Systems. Its greatest achievement in the 20 years of its life was the creation of a network of researchers where none existed before, a network that has extended to 500 individuals in 42 countries on 6 continents.

The goal of the first two phases of InterPARES (1999–2006) was to develop the body of theory and methods necessary to ensure that digital records produced in databases and office systems, as well as dynamic, experiential, and interactive systems in the course of artistic, scientific, and e-government activities, could be created in accurate and reliable form and maintained and preserved in authentic form, both in the long and the short term, for the use of those who created them and of society at large, regardless of technological obsolescence and media fragility. The theory, methods, recommendations, and products of these two phases were and still are used worldwide. However, in 2007, the research team realized that several organizations with scarce financial and human resources were not adequately served by the outcomes of the project to date. Thus, InterPARES began a third phase, whose goal was to enable public and private archival organizations and programmes with limited resources to preserve over the long term authentic records that satisfy the requirements of their stakeholders and society's needs for an adequate record of its past. It did so by building on the products of the first two phases of InterPARES, namely:

- Policy Framework: A set of principles guiding the development of policies for records creating and preserving organizations;

- Creator Guidelines: Recommendations for making and maintaining digital materials for individuals and small communities of practice;
- Preserver Guidelines: Recommendations for digital preservation for archival institutions;
- Benchmark and Baseline Requirements: Authenticity requirements for assessing and maintaining the authenticity of digital records;
- File Format Selection Guidelines: Principles and criteria for adoption of file formats, wrappers, and encoding schemes;
- Terminology Database: Including a glossary, a dictionary, and ontologies;
- Two Records and Archives Management Models: The Chain of Preservation (COP) Model (based on the lifecycle concept) and Business-driven Record-keeping (BDR) Model (based on the continuum model);
- Two books outlining new theories, methods, and suggested practices.

The most important outcomes of the third phase of InterPARES (2007–2012) were Cost-benefit Models, Ethical Models, Education Modules, and Metadata Applications Profiles. However, many of the studies helped individual organizations and were used by similar ones to address common problems, such as the selection for preservation of legacy files.

By the end of InterPARES 3, the archival profession found itself confronted with a new challenge, cloud computing. Thus, the team began a fourth phase of InterPARES (2013–2019), which was named InterPARES Trust (ITrust). Its goal was to generate the theoretical and methodological frameworks that would support the development of integrated and consistent local, national, and international networks of policies, procedures, regulations, standards, and legislation concerning digital records online, to ensure public trust. As the team realized that findings would be highly dependent on context, it decided that culture had to be a key criterion for organizing the research groups. Thus, the international alliance of researchers was constituted of a North American team, a Latin America team, a European team, an African team, an Asian team, an Australasian team, and a Transnational team (comprising organizations that were not under the jurisdiction of a given country).

ITrust addressed five research domains: infrastructure, security, control, access, and legal issues. The international alliance also engaged in studies in five cross-domains: policy, social issues, education, terminology, and resources. The researchers used primarily archival and diplomatics methods of analysis, but they also used resource-based theory, because it studies the technologic, managerial, and relational means of maximizing competitive advantage; risk management, because it studies vulnerabilities and ways to mitigate them; design theory, because it studies policy in situations with unknown variables; digital forensics, because it studies the authenticity of digital materials that do not reside in the systems in which they were produced and kept; human-computer interaction; aero-spatial, cybercrime, and telecommunication law; and organizational theory.

Several of the ITrust outcomes and products are generally applicable regardless of cultural, legal, administrative, or social context. Examples are: a model of preservation in the cloud, Preservation as a Service for Trust (PaaST); a model for technological authentication using blockchain (the TrustChain); a checklist for contracts with cloud providers; papers on open government and open data; and many others. These outcomes and products are published in Luciana Duranti and Corinne Rogers, eds., *Trusting Records in the Cloud* (Facet Publishers and the Society of American Archivists, London and Chicago 2019). However, some findings, recommendations, products, and outcomes are specific to the context of a team and, for this reason, some of the teams (e.g., Europe, Africa, Latin America) are publishing them separately, targeting the interested audience. This volume presents the products of the ITrust Transnational Team. Though they were developed for the "transnational" community, most of them can also be useful, in whole or in part, in other contexts. It is my privilege to introduce the work of my "transnational" colleagues as presented in this book.

The fourth iteration of InterPARES is now complete. The products of all four projects are widely used internationally and none of them appears to be out of date. They can be found at www.interpares.org and https://interparestrust.org/trust/research_dissemination.

Luciana Duranti

INTRODUCTION

The value of recordkeeping[1] in international organizations

Jens Boel and Eng Sengsavang[2]

In 2020 the world is facing a pandemic, which is profoundly disrupting ways of life and work all over the globe. Among the immediate and long-term consequences are the overwhelming and accelerating presence and use of digital technologies. The digital transformation was already a fact before the pandemic. As two of the authors of this book point out: "Far from being just a tool, technology has become the glue – if not the objective – of many educational, professional, and scientific initiatives."[3] With the universal need for social distancing and teleworking, and the development and increased use of tracking applications, digital technologies are omnipresent in the lives of people everywhere.

The COVID-19 crisis will most likely lead to a partial withdrawal from economic globalization in order to strengthen the resilience of countries to external shocks. Assertions of national sovereignty are poised to return with a vengeance. This raises the question of how to rebuild multilateralism, since the world is facing multiple challenges that require multilateral action. Among the most obvious of these challenges are climate change, biodiversity, poverty, and increasing inequalities; but in fact, issues persist in all major areas of human life. Interrogations about the functioning of international organizations[4] are therefore critical to questions about, and solutions to, how the world should act and look like in the years to come.

To a large extent, the power of international organizations is symbolic, and many of their actions are expressed through words and images, rather than by military or financial resources. Their influence and work exist through reports on the state of human rights, the sciences, biodiversity, cultural heritage, communication, education, and so forth, as well as through declarations, recommendations, and conventions. This is even the case, although to a lesser degree, for those international organizations that implement a substantial part of their work through physical presence on the ground (like UNHCR and UNRWA) or by financial or military means (such as the IMF and NATO). Now even the international conferences and gatherings of experts that are needed to prepare such documents have become immaterial and have lost their physical presence. The virtual networking of the international community has become more important than ever before.

The evidence of the work of international organizations – their records – has become digital over the past few decades, co-existing in parallel with an older, analogue world, challenging our understandings of and approaches to records. Recently, the digital nature of records has increased exponentially. This is also the case with regard to the management of these records, the recordkeeping. The transformation of recordkeeping processes to a networked environment is critical to understand because the way the records are understood and managed today pre-conditions the state of the historical archives tomorrow.

The archives of international organizations are the evidence of what representatives of countries, civil society activists, and international staff have thought and argued in the melting pots of civilizations and cultures across the world in the twentieth and early twenty-first centuries. These archives are important, if perhaps still under-used, for anyone interested in contemporary history, politics, and culture. They speak not just to histories of international cooperation in almost every possible domain; the records also provide insight into national, local, and community histories. Far from simply being institutional, the archives of international organizations are also marked by the traces of countless individuals, from great thinkers and leaders of the era, to otherwise obscure international civil servants and bureaucrats who laboured to make a difference, to the individuals and communities who worked with and were impacted by international organizations. One of the founders of the International Council on Archives, Archivist of the United States, Solon J. Buck, wrote during that short interval between the end of the Second World War and the beginning of the Cold War, when so many dreams of human community across borders flourished:

> Should we not, therefore, think of all the archives of all the nations of the world, together with the archives of all the international agencies of all sorts, as constituting the archives of mankind, the official record of human experience in organized living?[5]

International organizations' archives were already then considered by leading archivists to be an essential part of "the instructive traces of life."[6]

The intensely networked environment almost all of us live in places recordkeeping in international organizations in front of a number of developments and questions that are widely relevant. While computing networks were being invented as early as the 1950s,[7] what is new is the extent to which they are increasingly woven into our lives. As such, this book is a first attempt to take a holistic look at the current challenges facing international organizations in digital, networked environments, and to make suggestions on how to address them through strategies for the future. In this sense, the book is a unique anthology bringing together studies – some of which have previously been published or presented in other contexts – on a confluence of topics that has not been widely explored together: recordkeeping in a pervasively networked environment within international organizations. We are profoundly indebted to our colleagues across the world; without a strong, international professional network, this book would not have been possible.

From this perspective, the purpose of this book is double: to study how recordkeeping in international organizations has been impacted by the extensively networked environment, and to provide, through case studies and professional experience, some reflections and advice. By doing so, we hope not only to offer insights into the specificities, strengths, and challenges of transnational approaches to recordkeeping, but also to demonstrate how recordkeeping is critical to the successful functioning of international organizations. Our target audiences are practitioners, students, and scholars with an interest in information management and/or international organizations. We also believe that the topics and research questions addressed have relevance well beyond readers who are particularly interested in this environment.

In her foreword to this book, Luciana Duranti explains the goals and methodology of the InterPARES Trust (ITrust) project. Our selection of topics largely originates from a number of studies conducted for or related to InterPARES Trust (Chapters 3–6 and Chapters 7 to 9). Other studies have been selected based on the availability of scholarship with dimensions related to international organizations (Chapters 1 and 2). For these reasons, we do not pretend to be comprehensive in our coverage of topics. The research domains and cross-domains described by Luciana Duranti set the context of the studies carried out by members of the Transnational Team between 2013 and 2019. As editors, we wish the present book to reflect the most relevant themes and results emerging from the studies, from the perspectives of practitioners, students, and scholars. We are grateful to all the authors who have enabled us to do exactly that.

The Transnational Team included members working in different types of international organizations, including intergovernmental organizations (IGOs) and nongovernmental organizations (NGOs). However, the majority, though not all, chapters in this book focus on IGOs. We hope that further studies of specific challenges facing recordkeeping for NGOs and multinational businesses will be the topic of future research.

The book opens, in Chapter 1, with Dieter Schlenker's reflections on the interaction between new technologies and developments in archival education and training, standardization, access, and research. In Chapter 2, Paola Casini describes and analyses the current status of data protection in the EU institutions, while looking ahead to the challenges posed by artificial intelligence and big data. Subsequent chapters consider issues at the crossroads between cloud computing, the records of international organizations, and inviolability and extraterritoriality. Chapter 3 by Elaine Goh and Eng Sengsavang examines the benefits and barriers to cloud computing use within international organizations, promoting a risk-analysis approach to cloud adoption. In Chapter 4, Darra Hofman discusses the meaning of "extraterritoriality" for international organizations and shows how cloud computing adds further complexity to the challenge of maintaining archival inviolability. Weimei Pan and Grant Mitchell present, in Chapter 5, a case study of the establishment of a cloud computing contract in the International Federation of Red Cross and Red Crescent Societies.

The next two chapters consider approaches to modelling information management functions on a system-wide level. In Chapter 6, Giovanni Michetti and Stephen Haufek develop a mind map of functions in a holistic information system within international organizations, on the basis of an "ontology of functional activities for archival systems" and a survey conducted for this book. Shadrack Katuu discusses, in Chapter 7, the potential relevance of enterprise architecture for intergovernmental organizations (IGOs). The next chapters turn to the topic of security classified records in international organizations. In Chapter 8, Ineke Deserno and Eng Sengsavang discuss the challenges, principles, and policies of managing, protecting, and providing access to classified records. Finally, in Chapter 9, Shadrack Katuu and Julia Kastenhofer analyse declassification procedures within IGOs.

On the basis of the studies presented in the preceding chapters, we discuss in the Conclusion how and to what extent recordkeeping in international organizations can help reach the goals and targets set by the United Nations' 2030 Agenda for Sustainable Development and the Sustainable Development Goals (SDGs), in particular Goal 16, "Promote peaceful and inclusive societies for sustainable development, provide access to justice for all and build effective, accountable and inclusive institutions at all levels." Among the targets that underpin this goal are "Develop effective, accountable and transparent institutions at all levels and ensure public access to information and protect fundamental freedoms." How and to what extent can recordkeeping in international organizations help reach this goal and these targets? We will discuss this question in the Conclusion, considering the studies presented in the chapters, and relevant UN strategies that impact recordkeeping concerns.

While each of the chapters in the book focuses on a different topic, common themes recur. Among them are the cross-cutting issues of transparency and accountability, principles that are critical to recordkeeping goals and processes. From the perspective of international organizations, this theme is highly relevant. The historian Paul Kennedy referred to the UN as "The Parliament of Man,"[8] and, indeed, the United Nations system, together with dozens of other existing international organizations, is at the heart of democracy as a global concept. Disseminating information is often at the core of their work and the very existence of international organizations; therefore, transparency and accountability are essential for them in order to maintain their ethical and symbolic power. This moral authority also means that international organizations are doubly accountable, in their actions and working methods, for abiding by the standards, values, and ethical imperatives that they help to set for the world. International organizations are accountable to a number of different groups: member states and governments, partners and other international organizations, individuals and communities who are beneficiaries of their programmes, and the worldwide public. But accountability works both ways: international organizations have carved a role for themselves as major standard-setters of ethical principles by which others – governments, organizations, and public and private entities – are to be made accountable. As non-commercial, multilateral fora with largely indirect relationships to national policy-setting, international organizations publish principles, guidelines, conventions, and recommendations, for which they request commitments from member states and other entities.

The work of international organizations in creating standards founded on the principles of transparency and accountability will continue to be relevant for the development of advanced technologies such as big data, the Internet of Things, robotics, blockchain, and artificial intelligence (AI), to name a few. Recordkeeping practices and policies are central to ensuring that ethical standards and practices are incorporated wherever data and records are used, processed, or generated by these technologies. This is perhaps most evident in challenges related to personal data and the interplay between access to information and privacy needs.

With widespread technology, forgetting has become the exception, and remembering the default, as Viktor Mayer-Schönberger points out in his thought-provoking book "*Delete.*"[9] The pervasive and tacit collection of personal data through our interactions on the Internet and social media, and through devices such as mobile phones and electronic appliances connected to the "Internet of Things," has become a basic fact of life. This enhances or creates numerous challenges for data privacy and data protection, security, and records security classification, among other issues. For example, as discussed in Chapter 2 (in relation to AI) and Chapter 3 (in relation to cloud computing), the "accumulation of technological, economic and political power in the hands of the top five players – Google, Facebook, Microsoft, Apple and Amazon – affords them undue influence in areas of society."[10] For AI, this includes the "collect[ion] of personal data for ... profit, surveillance, security and election campaigns."[11]

In the realm of cloud computing, the mass quantities of data and information that we entrust to private companies, and that are generated within remote, commercially owned systems, must be closely monitored. The growing worldwide use of cloud computing requires that organizations demand specific contract terms with cloud providers to ensure that data is managed according to standards not only of security and confidentiality, but also of integrity, authenticity, and reliability of data (Chapters 3, 4, and 5). To a large extent, the safe processing and protection of individuals' and organizations' data rests on fair and accountable guarantees outlined in cloud contracts with providers.

International organizations have worked to address these pressing concerns. The European Union (EU) has led the way in efforts to provide a policy framework protecting the rights of individuals and their data, most recently through the EU General Data Protection Regulation (GDPR). Chapter 2 focuses on how the accompanying Regulation 2018/1725, which "fully assimilates"[12] GDPR within the EU institutions, impacts the work of information management, and carries social and ethical implications. Further studies could analyse the impact of GDPR on recordkeeping processes within different types of international organizations, including IGOs and NGOs. As the legal scholar and GDPR specialist Christopher Kuner notes, "the GDPR contains numerous references to [international organizations] but does not state whether it applies to them."[13] This has led to competing positions and a lack of clarity on its applicability to international organizations.[14] Yet the processing and transfer of personal data is a necessary part of the daily work of international organizations; for those within the humanitarian sector in particular, "the misuse of personal data may have life and death consequences."[15] Therefore, a number of international organizations "have already adopted their own internal data protection rules."[16]

For example, within their own walls, UN organizations have committed to the Principles on Personal Data Protection and Privacy, which aim to "set out a basic framework for the processing of personal data by, or on behalf of, the United Nations System Organizations in carrying out their mandated activities."[17] The Principles have been endorsed by some 31 UN member organizations,[18] meaning that they are now obliged to adhere to "accountable processing of personal data" and the "right to privacy" in the management of personal data held by them.[19] Privacy is also an issue when it comes to managing other types of confidential information produced or received by international organizations, as discussed in Chapters 8 and 9. Classified records may hold highly sensitive military, national security, or political information, for example. Such records should be accountably managed through clearly defined organizational policy frameworks that ensure they are protected and handled within a holistic information lifecycle. An essential aim of these policies should be to eventually declassify and make the records available to the public, after they are no longer sensitive.

The issue of access to information is inseparable from issues of transparency, accountability, and data privacy. The digital environment opens an immense democratic opportunity at a global level thanks to the tremendously powerful possibilities for sharing information and knowledge – provided that the "digital divide" can be addressed. In recent years, there has been a growing awareness within international organizations that they should introduce or further develop access to information policies, very much in line with Freedom of Information policies established by many countries, starting with Sweden in 1766. Within the UN system, this new focus is reflected by the 2017 study and report of the Special Rapporteur on "Access to Information in International Organizations."[20]

Archivists of international organizations were from an early date conscious of the importance of providing access to the archives, not only for members of the Secretariat of the various organizations, but for a wider public. UNESCO, for example, opened an archives reading room in 1960 and created a publicly available database of its official documents as early as 1972.[21] In 1976, archivists from some of the most significant international organizations gathered in Washington, DC to create one of the very first sections of the International Council on Archives, namely the Section of International Organizations (ICA/SIO). Access to the archival holdings of international organizations became one of the priority activities of this new section. A major breakthrough happened in 1984 when UNESCO began publishing a three-volume *Guide to the Archives of International Organizations*.[22] Against this background, as discussed in Chapters 1, 8, and 9, in the late 1980s and early 1990s international organizations began to recognize the importance of access to their own records. A distinct movement towards transparency and openness resulted in the establishment of public archives for the first time within international organizations such as the IMF and NATO. In the mid-1990s, the ICA/SIO took the initiative to create an updated guide on the archives of intergovernmental organizations and the result was published in 1999, both as a website and as a UNESCO document.[23]

While the studies in this book relate to questions that are also pertinent to national environments, studying information management issues in a wider ecosystem at the international level offers an added dimension. Globalization has changed our world in profound ways, creating new interdependencies and both magnifying and flattening cultural differences. Within international organizations, the complex interplay of different languages, cultural environments, and political challenges has obliged international staff and national representatives, in particular, to work beyond sometimes competing political interests, towards shared ends for the improvement of the human condition in almost every imaginable area. While the complexity of challenges and institutional responses can seem overwhelming, holistic models can help us to better understand how recordkeeping and underlying information technologies contribute to supporting the missions of international organizations. To this end, the mind map of archival functions in Chapter 6 and approaches to enterprise architecture in Chapter 7 offer frameworks and high-level representations for managing complexity. These models can help to clarify and visualize connections, revealing how the work of information managers intersects with and supports that of practitioners and experts in other domains.

Finally, we would like to make a clarifying comment on the terminology used in this book. Although a number of terms are defined by the authors of the various chapters (see, for example, Chapters 8 and 9 for the definition of "security classified records"), several fundamental concepts, in particular the notions of records, documents, data, and information, may occasionally be used with variations in meanings by different authors. This situation reflects a real plurality within the professional community, which we cannot simply ignore or instantly make disappear. As editors, we refer to the *Multilingual Archival Terminology*, a tool developed jointly by the International Council on Archives and InterPARES Trust, and described as "an international source for the terminology and definitions used by many traditions to express shared archival concepts."[24] As a rule, the authors themselves define the terms they are using, whenever a doubt may arise. Our working principle has been to aim at striking a balance between diversities – whether cultural or across communities of practice or scholarly discourses – and the need for a common, conceptual understanding.

In studying global challenges through the lens of networked recordkeeping environments in international organizations, we hope that this book contributes to vital discussions, debates, and actions on how best to move forward together in an era defined in large part by our relationships to digital records and information technologies. By so doing, we also hope to draw attention to the question of how recordkeeping within international organizations can act as a critical ingredient in our efforts to improve global conditions by supporting the vision set out in the UN 2030 Agenda for Sustainable Development.

Notes

1 In this Introduction, we base the spelling and definition of "recordkeeping" on that found in the International Council on Archives' *Multilingual archival terminology*: "The systematic creation, use, maintenance, and disposition of records to meet administrative, programmatic, legal, and financial needs and responsibilities," Richard Pearce Moses, 2005, cited in InterPARES Trust & International Council on Archives, *Multilingual archival terminology*, n.d., 'Recordkeeping [definition no. 1]', viewed 3 June 2020, www. ciscra.org/mat/mat/term/293. We take a broad interpretation of this definition to include not just records management and archival functions, but also the increasingly overlapping functions of information management.

2 The author is responsible for the choice and the presentation of the facts contained in the publication and for the opinions expressed therein, which are not necessarily those of UNESCO and do not commit the Organization.

3 Giovanni Michetti & Stephen Haufek in this volume, p. 139.

4 *Encyclopedia Britannica* defines an international organization as an "institution drawing membership from at least three states, having activities in several states, and whose members are held together by a formal agreement. The Union of International Associations, a coordinating body, differentiates between the more than 250 international governmental organizations (IGOs), which have been established by intergovernmental agreements and whose members are states, and the approximately 6,000 nongovernmental organizations (NGOs), whose members are associations or individuals." In Karen Mingst, 2016, 'International organization', *Encyclopedia Britannica*, viewed 8 May 2020, www.britannica.com/topic/international-organization#ref267908.

5 Solon J Buck, 1947, 'The archivist's "One World,"' *American Archivist*, vol. 10, no. 1, p. 12.

6 UNESCO's Director-General, Jaime Torres-Bodet, used this expression when he, on 21 August 1950, addressed the first congress of the International Council on Archives. See Emma Rothschild, 2008, 'The archives of universal history', *Journal of World History*, vol. 19, no. 3, p. 381.

7 The development of SAGE, or the Semi-Automatic Ground Environment Air Defense System (1951–1963) for the U.S. military, is often considered to be the first computer network – see Lincoln Laboratory, Massachusetts Institute of Technology, 2020, 'SAGE: Semi-Automatic Ground Environment Air Defense System', viewed 30 May 2020, www.ll.mit.edu/about/history/sage-semi-automatic-ground-environment-air-defense-system. Hu, however, argues that the concept of cloud computing originated in 1922 based on a design of "computer" grids – human mathematicians – connected through telegraphs – see Tung-hui Hu and Project Muse, 2015, *A prehistory of the Cloud*, MIT Press Ltd, Cambridge, pp. ix–x.

8 Paul Kennedy, 2006, *The Parliament of Man: the United Nations and the quest for world government*, London, Allen Lane.

9 Viktor Mayer-Schönberger, 2009, *Delete. the virtue of forgetting in the digital age*, Princeton University Press, p. 2.

10 European Parliament, 2020 March, *The ethics of artificial intelligence: issues and initiatives*, viewed 5 May 2020, www.europarl.europa.eu/RegData/etudes/STUD/2020/634452/EPRS_STU(2020)634452_EN.pdf, p. 12.

11 Ibid.

12 Paola Casini in this volume, p. 29.

13 Christopher Kuner, 2020, 'The GDPR and international organizations', *AJIL Unbound*, vol. 114, pp. 15–19, viewed 14 May 2020, DOI: https://doi.org/10.1017/aju.2019.78.

14 Ibid.

15 Ibid.

16 Ibid.

17 UN High-Level Committee on Management, 2018 October 11, *Personal data protection and privacy principles*, viewed 7 May 2020, www.unsceb.org/CEBPublicFiles/UN-Principles-on-Personal-Data-Protection-Privacy-2018.pdf.

18 UN Privacy Policy Group, n.d., *List of member organizations that prepared and endorsed the Personal Data Protection and Privacy Principles*, viewed 7 May 2020, www.unsceb.org/CEBPublicFiles/UNPPGMembersList_Revised.pdf.

19 UN High-Level Committee on Management, 2018, p. 1.

20 United Nations, 2017, *Report of the Special Rapporteur to the General Assembly on access to information in international organizations*, www.ohchr.org/EN/Issues/FreedomOpinion/Pages/InformationIntOrganizations.aspx.

21 UNESCO Computerized Documentation System (CDS) 1987, *CDS/ISIS simplified retrieval manual*, UNESCO Integrated Documentation Network, viewed 15 May 2020, https://unesdoc.unesco.org/ark:/48223/pf0000092555.locale=en, p. 4. For historical background on UNESCO's Computerized Documentation Service as of 1968, see also UNESCO documents COM/IACODLA/71/5 (1971): https://unesdoc.unesco.org/ark:/48223/pf0000000509/PDF/000509engb.pdf.multi and COM/IACODLA/73/5 (1973): https://unesdoc.unesco.org/ark:/48223/pf0000004972/PDF/004972engb.pdf.multi.

22 UNESCO, 1984–85, *Guide to the archives of international organizations*, Paris. Only the first part of the Guide was published as a book (in 1984); the subsequent two parts were published as UNESCO documents, in 1985, with the codes PGI.85/WS/18 and PGI.85/WS/19, respectively.

23 UNESCO, 1999, *Guide to the archives of intergovernmental organizations*, CII.99/WS/2, Paris, https://unesdoc.unesco.org/ark:/48223/pf0000115937.locale=en. The original UNESCO Archives website has since moved, but efforts are currently underway to reconstruct this portion of the website.

24 International Council on Archives, 2012, *Multilingual archival terminology*, viewed 31 May 2020, www.ica.org/en/online-resource-centre/multilingual-archival-terminology. The editors accept the following definitions: *Data*, "The smallest meaningful units of information," Luciana Duranti, cited in InterPARES Trust & International Council on Archives, 2012. *Multilingual archival terminology*, 'Data [definition no. 1]', viewed 31 May 2020, www.ciscra.org/mat/mat/term/134; *Document*, "An indivisible unit of information constituted by a message affixed to a medium (recorded) in a stable syntactic manner. A document has fixed form and stable content," InterPARES 2, 2020, 'The InterPARES 2 Project Glossary,' viewed 31 May 2020, www.interpares.org/ip2/display_file.cfm?doc=ip2_glossary.pdf&CFID=21477057&CFTOKEN=20719449; *Information*, "Recorded data," International Council on Archives, 1999, cited in InterPARES Trust & International Council on Archives, 2012. *Multilingual archival terminology*, 'Data [definition no. 1]', viewed 31 May 2020, www.ciscra.org/mat/mat/term/202; and *Record*, "Information created, received, and maintained as evidence and information by an organization or person, in pursuance of legal obligations or in the transaction of business," International Organization for Standardization, 2001, cited in InterPARES Trust & International Council on Archives, 2012. *Multilingual archival terminology*, 'Record [definition no. 1]', viewed 31 May 2020, www.ciscra.org/mat/mat/term/60/1292.

References

Buck, SJ 1947, 'The archivist's "One World",' *American Archivist*, vol. 10, no. 1.

European Parliament 2020, *The ethics of artificial intelligence: issues and initiatives*, March, viewed 5 May 2020, www.europarl.europa.eu/RegData/etudes/STUD/2020/634452/EPRS_STU(2020)634452_EN.pdf.

Hu, T & Project Muse 2015, *A prehistory of the cloud*, MIT Press, Cambridge.

International Council on Archives 2012, *Multilingual archival terminology*, viewed 31 May 2020, www.ica.org/en/online-resource-centre/multilingual-archival-terminology.

InterPARES Trust & International Council on Archives 2012, *Multilingual archival terminology*, viewed 31 May 2020, www.ciscra.org/mat/mat.

InterPARES 2 Project 2020, 'The InterPARES 2 Project Glossary,' viewed 31 May 2020, www.interpares.org/ip2/display_file.cfm?doc=ip2_glossary.pdf&CFID=21477057&CFTOKEN=20719449.

Kennedy, P 2006, *The Parliament of Man: the United Nations and the quest for world government*, Allen Lane, London.

Kuner, C 2020, 'The GDPR and international organizations', *AJIL Unbound*, vol. 114, pp. 15–19, viewed 14 May 2020, doi:10.1017/aju.2019.78.

Lincoln Laboratory, Massachusetts Institute of Technology 2020, 'SAGE: Semi-Automatic Ground Environment Air Defense System', viewed 30 May 2020, www.ll.mit.edu/about/history/sage-semi-automatic-ground-environment-air-defense-system.

Mayer-Schönberger, V 2009, *Delete: the virtue of forgetting in the digital age*, Princeton University Press.

Mingst, K 2016, 'International organization', *Encyclopedia Britannica*, viewed 8 May 2020, www.britannica.com/topic/international-organization#ref267908.

Rothschild, E 2008, 'The archives of universal history', *Journal of World History*, vol. 19, no. 3, pp. 375–401.

UNESCO 1984–85, *Guide to the archives of international organizations*, Paris.

UNESCO 1999, *Guide to the archives of intergovernmental organizations*, CII.99/WS/2, Paris, viewed 15 May 2020, https://unesdoc.unesco.org/ark:/48223/pf0000115937.locale=en.

UNESCO Computerized Documentation System (CDS) 1987, *CDS/ISIS simplified retrieval manual*, UNESCO Integrated Documentation Network, viewed 15 May 2020, https://unesdoc.unesco.org/ark:/48223/pf0000092555.locale=en.

United Nations 2017, *Report of the Special Rapporteur to the General Assembly on access to information in international organizations*, www.ohchr.org/EN/Issues/FreedomOpinion/Pages/InformationIntOrganizations.aspx.

United Nations High-Level Committee on Management 2018 October 11, *Personal data protection and privacy principles*, viewed 7 May 2020, www.unsceb.org/CEBPublicFiles/UN-Principles-on-Personal-Data-Protection-Privacy-2018.pdf.

United Nations Privacy Policy Group n.d, *List of member organizations that prepared and endorsed the Personal Data Protection and Privacy Principles*, viewed 7 May 2020, www.unsceb.org/CEBPublicFiles/UNPPGMembersList_Revised.pdf.

1

ENDURING CHALLENGES, NEW TECHNOLOGIES

Some reflections on recordkeeping in international organizations

Dieter Schlenker[1]

Introduction

This chapter presents an overview of the current status of recordkeeping in international organizations and the challenges facing the archival community in this specific sector. It presents some reflections on recordkeeping practices, their developments, and future perspectives on a transnational environment. Moreover, it looks at recent innovative approaches and refers to relevant standards, norms, and tools that evolve around international archival practice. Finally, the chapter offers some critical reflections and observations on developments in archival access and research, grounded both in disciplinary theory and methodology, as well as the author's experience as an archival professional and practitioner.

Since the establishment of the first entity that could be defined as an international organization, the Commission Centrale pour la Navigation du Rhin (CCNR), by the Congress of Vienna in 1815, the landscape of international organizations has seen a constant growth. Particularly with the establishment of the United Nations in the aftermath of the Second World War, the number and variety of international and regional organizations have expanded greatly. In the long list of international organizations, non-governmental organizations (NGOs) currently largely outnumber intergovernmental organizations (IGOs), although both continue to flourish worldwide. The European Union, as a regional political union of states that developed from a unique community model, holds a particular position in transnational cooperation. International organizations have evolved around activities determined by their member states and their mission statement. They respond to multi-faceted dynamics and the requirements of modern, globalized societies. Their political aims cover a broad spectrum, ranging from political to economic and scientific to ecological, philanthropic, and cultural activity areas, thus integrating all fields of human interaction.

Intergovernmental organizations have been created on the basis of treaties, conventions, or other internationally recognized contractual arrangements signed by national governments. These organizations hold specific privileges and immunities that organizations operating on a national level do not. Non-governmental organizations are usually registered in the country that hosts their headquarters but have international missions and objectives. Both IGOs and NGOs may have a network of field or project offices in addition to their headquarters.

Working under international or European law and within the specifications of contracts with host countries, the records and archives of international organizations may be inviolable and exempt from the law of the territory where the organization's headquarters are located. The legal personality of international organizations impacts the management and preservation of their records and has consequences for all areas, from the storage locations of paper records to the hosting of storage servers for cloud services.[2] The main principles for records governance are the inviolability of the premises and archives, the protection of the physical archive and control of external access, and the fact that archival materials cannot be removed or altered by external entities or persons. This independence is crucial for archivists in international organizations to fulfil their responsibilities.[3]

Scholarly publications recognize the emergence of international organizations as a political feature characteristic of the twentieth century. Along with these organizations has come a new type of global actor, the "expatriate" official, a role that has received attention in numerous publications, fiction books, and autobiographies. Much less attention has been paid, however, to the birth of a new type of records manager and archivist in international organizations.[4]

While pursuing different objectives, international organizations record their actions and decisions in written documents that are managed by records and archives services. These organizations and their collaborators have an impact on the lives of billions of people under global initiatives such as the Sustainable Development Goals of the United Nations, or in supranational regional blocs that unite, for example, the European Union (EU), the Association of Southeast Asian Nations (ASEAN), or the African Union (AU). Their stakeholders comprise national governments and citizens, as well as other partners and associates in public and private bodies.

Since its establishment in 1945 as a specialized UN agency, the United Nations Educational, Scientific, and Cultural Organization (UNESCO) has taken responsibility for archival development and the global archival community. Through various important initiatives, UNESCO has been a key contributor to the professionalization and internationalization of archivists. Its first act in this direction was the establishment of the International Council on Archives (ICA) in 1948, which became the reference point for the archival community in the coming decennia and continues to be the main international hub for archivists to this day. Via the International Council on Archives, UNESCO has been undertaking activities for the promotion of access, the effective use of archives in member states, and the development of archival methods through education and training worldwide.

As a first methodological activity, UNESCO, in close cooperation with the ICA, initiated the Records and Archives Management Program (RAMP) with a series of studies to advance the global archival profession in 1979.[5] Subsequently, UNESCO introduced a 1992 cultural heritage programme for the documentary sector: "Memory of the World," which links memory and heritage, thus highlighting the unique character of (mainly archival) documents as possessing a heterogeneous memory with differences in terms of creation, structure, materiality, and intention.[6] In November 2011, UNESCO endorsed the ICA's "Universal Declaration on Archives," the first universal statement from the United Nations recognizing the unique global value of archives for humankind.[7]

But how do archives and archivists in international organizations see themselves and how can they best be described? Do they require a definition beyond a list of the characteristics of the classical denominations of space, administration, and material, but within an international political and legal context? Do these archives apply methods other than those deriving from cultural and social sciences and taught at universities or archival schools as part of media, information, or knowledge management studies?[8]

This chapter seeks to address the above questions, along with various other questions regarding international archival practice. Recordkeeping in international organizations is based on classical historical, technical, and legal aspects of archives, yet in practice it adds a specific transnational character with its methodology and a particular character in the cultural, educational, and linguistic spheres. The chapter is intended as a companion to the research articles in this publication and focuses on the topics of archival education and training, standardization, and access and research.

Archival education and training

Archivists have a long professional tradition and a broad methodological basis to draw upon. In some European countries, archival methods were taught at state-run advanced training schools attached to national or state archives, while in others archival science was taught at universities. Sometimes, both models existed in parallel. To the present day, these two models persist, with curricula for archival education defined at a national level. Maria Guercio stated in 2010 that "the archival schools and educational programs in the Library and Information Schools vary in different countries and depend on the juridical contexts and on the national traditions."[9] The long tradition of archival education in Europe did not evolve on the basis of a common culture or uniform political aim, but in heterogeneous organizational structures, disconnected one from another.[10]

The education that archivists receive varies from continent to continent, from country to country, and from university to university. In countries where archival methods have evolved around public institutions, education focuses on the history of administration. In countries where the records preserved date from the ancient period and cover a range of civilizations, the emphasis is placed on philological disciplines and ancient languages. Lastly, the structure of a programme also depends on other factors, such as the focus of the programme of the specific university or school, trends in the information management sector, technological developments, the profile of educators, and the resources available. These different approaches towards archival education are summarized by Luciana Duranti as four models: the historical model, which places archival science within the discipline of history; the philological model or the traditional European model, which focuses on diplomatic studies and palaeography as the main elements of the curricula; the managerial model (the most recent one), which considers archival theory as falling within the domain of information management and information; and finally the scientific/ scholarly model, which is mainly taught in university courses.[11]

At first, only a few archival schools and universities opened their courses to an international public. This began to change during the pioneer age, when courses were first established within a region. For instance, the University of New South Wales, established in 1973, was the first Australian university to educate archivists from neighbouring countries as well as those from Australia. Archival education was seen as critical for the development of the profession in the whole region as no other such courses existed at the time. While the course was designed around the needs of Australian national archivists, the target audience was extended to staff members of national archives from cross-regional countries in Oceania, South-East Asia, and Africa.[12]

UNESCO also played an important role in the development of archival education. Through the ICA, it launched a major project in the mid-1960s in Africa, establishing two regional archival training centres attached to universities, one in Dakar, Senegal, for francophone countries and one in Accra, Ghana, for anglophone countries. This project, followed by various other UNESCO initiatives, including expert missions and RAMP studies, led to the emergence of the first national education and training programmes in Africa. A recent inventory prepared by the Africa Group of the InterPARES Trust research programme identified education and training institutions in 38 of 54 countries in Africa.[13]

International organizations evolved under international law, and their privileges and immunities were defined through specific agreements with their host countries. As a consequence, the educational requirements for archivists in international organizations were different from those of a traditional archival education. Looking at the models proposed above, the historical and philological approaches are certainly the less applicable models for international organizations.

The specific linguistic and cultural requirements for an international work environment are often acquired through either a background in diplomacy or international relations, or through practice and experience. When hiring an archivist, international organizations usually require work experience in an international environment without specifying how archivists would acquire such international experience and for what purposes. Fluency in either English or French with a good knowledge of the other is another common requirement, as is an understanding of and experience in applying international archival standards and tools. Finally, intercultural personal skills are frequently listed as a requirement in vacancies. As archives services in international organizations have developed a certain degree of autonomy in terms of their internal rules, procedures, and workflows, personal qualities, such as openness, creativity, and flexibility are important in addition to the required technical knowledge and skills.

In international organizations, archivists are often first confronted with archival practices of different archival "schools" or "cultures," including specific methods, tools, processes, and technical vocabulary. During the early years of international organizations after the Second World War, archival processes and workflows were often established by librarians. Some of the first generations of registry clerks and archivists were educated and worked as librarians. This explains the use of the Universal Decimal Classification (UDC) system in the historical archives of some international organizations, such as UNESCO and the Council of the European Union. A particular challenge posed by these records is the fact that files were dismantled and recomposed according to UDC subject classifications after being transferred to the archives, which caused the loss of provenance-related information and the original context of the documents within the subject matter file.

Globalization demands integration and harmonization, and this is also the case for the field of archival education, especially regarding the challenging environment of digital records and archives management. A promising project entitled "Digital Pre-servation Europe" was launched in 2016 to develop a common curriculum in digital curation. This approach could serve as a common framework and guidance for trans-national accreditation among academic institutions in the field of archival science. Such a common curriculum could evolve into a modular international curriculum. This framework considers on-the-job training for the design, implementation, and man-agement of records management systems to be insufficient.[14]

Considering the digital skillset required in international archives, it can be argued that archivists with a traditional or limited education will not acquire the relevant knowledge,[15] or must learn on the job. Even today, there is a lack of educational opportunities in the digital field and very few archivists in international organiza-tions would consider themselves digital archivists. This may change with the recent establishment of the first digital archivist positions in some international organiza-tions. Looking at post-graduate digital archives programmes in Europe and North America, we can once again cite Maria Guercio:

> This evolution is characterized by some common elements: the fragmentation of the contents to be provided (also due to more options for the students and by the need for more technological skills in an advanced curriculum), the uncertainty of the programs' persistency and the general trend to transform the specific education for records managers, archivists (and librarians) into generic curricula in information studies.[16]

While we have seen that archival education is not particularly adapted to prepare archivists for an international work environment, the situation in the training sector is much more promising. This is, again, mostly thanks to the efforts of the ICA and its various specialized sections that provide regular opportunities for networking and training. The ICA hosts a specific Section of International Organizations (ICA/ SIO), which has, since its inception in 1976, played a key role in bringing archivists from international organizations together and providing opportunities for training and methodological exchange.

The role of the ICA sections at international level is similar to that of national associations for archivists; however, both international and national archivists participate in these ICA sections. An example of the exchange of information and discussions among these different professional groups occurred when the Swedish mentoring system was introduced in the early 2000s after a series of retirements necessitated the transmission of knowledge to the incoming junior staff. The resulting system of mentorships found its way to the international archival community through the activities of the ICA Section of Professional Associations (ICA/ SPA), which then drew up international guidelines for a similar system.[17]

In short, training opportunities for international archivists should be transversal, concentrate on normalization and standardization, digital conservation, the practical application of international standards and guidelines, the development of online finding aids, and include audiovisual archives.[18]

Standardization and archives

Regarding the standardization of archives, we should consider the 2011 words of Vera Maria Medina Da Fonseca: "Although younger archivists cannot imagine it, until recently (the early 1980s) the idea of creating standards for describing archival documents was considered by many professionals around the world not only strange, but also impossible."[19]

This statement is valid for both the general archival community and international organizations. The standardization of archival methods and processes is a key element in forming an archival community that is well educated and trained to work in international organizations. Standardization facilitates the work of archives operating at a transnational and global level and provides a common methodological framework.

For a long time, archivists argued against standardization due to a view of archival material and archival descriptions as unique, complex, and incomparable. Archival inventories were consulted individually without being considered on a wider scale, unlike the standardized catalogues used by librarians.[20] The fact that archives could also apply standardized and harmonized working methods had yet to be demonstrated.

We must remember that standards are the result of negotiation and therefore reflect the perspectives and approaches of those involved in the process. As with other negotiated processes and decisions, the preparation of international archival standards is entrusted to a group of specialists representing and serving archival communities worldwide. As a process of negotiated codification of professional knowledge, archival standards bear certain biases in terms of language and interpretations of terms and concepts and should, therefore, not be considered as neutral tools.[21]

The process of creating an archival international standard was launched under UNESCO and ICA leadership during the 1980s and led to the introduction of the General International Standard Archival Description (ISAD(G)) in 1994. This work by the ICA raised the interest of the main organization in charge of setting global standards, the International Standards Organization (ISO) in Geneva. The introduction of the ICA standard ISAD(G), the International Standard Archival Authority Record (ISAAR(CPF)), and the International Standard for Describing Institutions with Archival Holdings (ISDIAH), along with the ISO records management standard ISO 15489, were milestones in international archival practice. Archivists in international organizations have profited considerably from these developments.

With their standardization efforts, the ICA continued the Society of American Archivists' work in the development of archival standards from the late 1970s. At the 1982 ICA Congress, held in Kingston, two resolutions regarding the development of national standards for the arrangement and description of archival documents were adopted. The first set of rules was published by the United Kingdom and Ireland's professional archivist association as the Manual of Archival Description (MAD) in 1985 and was followed by the Rules for Archival Description (RAD) in Canada in 1990. The proposal to develop international standards of description was created by Canadian archivists, who called for a meeting of international experts on archival description to be held during the ICA's Ottawa Congress in 1988. In order to create what would become the first international standard for archivists, ISAD(G), the ICA established an Ad-Hoc Commission on Descriptive Standards (ICA/DDS) to prepare the final ISAD(G) text in 1990, which was published in 1994.[22]

The international archival profession advanced with this new "standards culture."[23] Within ISO, a network of national standards institutes from 163 countries with its secretariat in Geneva, the Technical Committee 46 (Documentation and Information), Sub Committee 11 (Archives and Records Management), TC 46/SC11, works on archives and records management standards. As of 2011, it consisted of 110 active experts from 27 countries, 12 additional observer countries, and a liaison member in the ICA.[24] The work of ISO also became relevant to the InterPARES Trust research project on records in the cloud, which identified the ISO standard 14721 on Space Data and Information Transfer Systems – Open Archival Information System (OAIS) Reference Model as relevant for digital long-term preservation using cloud services.[25]

An interesting development related to cloud services, standardization, and its potential impact on usage by international organizations based in Europe, is provided by the Italian project "Cloud for Europe."[26] EU institutions must house their archival storage devices in an EU member state, which is not necessarily the host country. International organizations may decide on a similar approach for their archives, and "Cloud for Europe" could therefore be a viable common solution.[27]

The records management standard ISO 15489 is ISO's most concrete success in the field of records and archives management thus far. For international organizations, the availability of ISO 15489 helped in different ways. Perhaps most significantly, it helped elevate the status and authority of the records management profession within international organizations, overturning the conception of records and archives services as low-profile internal administrative services dealing primarily with mail and pouch, registry, and logistics. The emergence of standards and, in particular, the digital agenda have challenged this outdated conception.[28]

With the emergence of the digital era and the need to implement digital records management, the profession earned further recognition and focus within organizations. Unlike national archives, records and archives services in international organizations are always embedded in operational organizations whose main business is not archives. The value of the profession is therefore measured by operational needs, accountability, and transparency rather than considerations of collective or institutional memory. This is why, with the emergence of related legislation regarding the right to information, the availability of standardized processes, and the automation of processes, records management has become the more valued sector, usually prevailing over the archival branch of the profession. This development is reflected in vacancy announcements and organizational charts of records and archives services.

The process of prioritization of records management in international organizations was also fostered by the European Commission's 2009 Model Requirements for the Management of Electronic Records (MOREQ). This model has become the relevant guide for the implementation of digital records management systems in many international organizations. It provides a detailed overview of the services that a state-of-the-art digital records management system should provide in order to comply with international standards and business requirements.[29]

Once launched, standardization gained traction in the archival profession and facilitated efficient communication, sharing, and collaboration among professionals. Archivists in international organizations became instrumental drivers in this process and started to use and apply the new standards to their work in a coherent way. For the first time, international standards offered a way for archives to choose a coherent approach, rather than applying either the methods of the host country, the individual archivist or head archivist's methods, the method used by the archivist's teachers or mentors (as with the librarians establishing archival services), or a combination of the above. Ever since, international organizations have included knowledge of and experience applying international standards as hiring requirements for archivists.

In 2000, standardization was recognized as one of the ICA's priorities and the new Section on Professional Standards and Best Practices, later renamed the Committee on Best Practices and Standards, was formed. International organizations' archives became laboratories for transnational cooperation and the harmonization of archival methods, thus overcoming the "obvious difficulties of dealing with different archival traditions and different climates – physical, cultural and political, difficulties in language and terminology."[30]

The experience of librarians, particularly with regard to authority records, became increasingly relevant in 1993 when the ICA began working on the standard on archival authority records, ISAAR(CPF). The standard was published in 1996 and presented at the ICA's 13th International Congress on Archives in Beijing. During the review process for both the ISAD and ISAAR standards, the data exchange formats Encoded Archival Description (EAD) and Encoded Archival Context (EAC-CPF) were released and the ICA released two further complementary standards: the International Standard for Describing Institutions with Archival Holdings (ISDIAH) and the International Standard for Describing Functions (ISDF), presented during the Congress in Kuala Lumpur in 2008.[31]

After the release of the aforementioned standards, the ICA, under the auspices of UNESCO, commissioned the development of an open-source, descriptive database system based on these international standards: the ICA-Access to Memory (ICA-AtoM) database developed by Artefactual. AtoM was initially developed as a follow-up to the CITRA (Conférence Internationale de la Table ronde des Archives) in Cape Town in 2003, an international archives meeting on the topic of archives and human rights, and was an initiative of the ICA Working Group on Archives and Human Rights (which in 2019 became the ICA Section on Archives and Human Rights). "The idea was to provide a platform in which information on archives documenting human rights violations all over the world could be made available through the Internet."[32] The tool led to the creation of the first global open-source software for archival description. The UNESCO Archives was the first archives service of an international organization to introduce the software in 2008.

Another opportunity offered by international standardization was cross-institutional research in interoperable databases. Europeana's "Archives Portal Europe" is an ambitious project promoting interoperability on a transnational level. It includes archival descriptions from archives on every level (from local to international). Descriptions are accessible on one platform and ingested by the participating archives via the use of the standardized EAD/EAC archival data exchange formats for the ISAD/ISAAR standards.[33]

The ongoing work on the conceptual model aims to reconcile all previous ICA descriptive standards with the Records-in-Contexts (RiC) standard and will need to demonstrate whether it can aid in the development of a common understanding of archival principles and the applicability of standards in all segments of archival work.[34] This is particularly true considering the effect of standards on archival memory:

> Archives – hence our memory – rely on the use of technical standards in order to be managed, accessed and preserved. Therefore, it is fundamental to investigate the nature of technical standards along with their biases in order to understand how they affect our documentary heritage, i.e., our memory. In a sense, standards shape our memory just like any container does when we pour some water in it.[35]

Access and research

As institutions that are described as society's memory and conscience, archives hold a control function over the past, contribute to the shaping of the future, and support society through the preservation of authentic and complete records with accessibility as the long-term goal.[36]

Until the emergence of the right-to-information movements, access to archives of international organizations mainly targeted the scholarly community. Search and retrieval tools in archives were therefore developed for a knowledgeable and professional cohort of users. In international organizations, where archival research may require considerable effort in terms of travel and multilingual skills, the target audience for physical attendance in archival reading rooms was rather limited.

With the emergence of the global Freedom of Information movements, another target audience for some archives of international organizations appeared. This was particularly true in the European Union, where the Access to Documents Regulation 1049 of 2001 granted European citizens the right to access EU institutions' records.[37] In EU institutions, the transparency regulation added a new role for records managers and archivists as managers of public document registers.[38] The public's right to access documents also required the implementation of efficient digital records management and retrieval systems.[39]

Particular challenges faced by records managers and archivists of international organizations regarding access to records include multilingual and geographic barriers, as well as the broad thematic spread of requests, diverse archival and administrative cultures, heterogeneous records classification systems, disclosure and access rules, and limited cross-organizational cooperation. Efficient systems of access to records are required as a global community of non-expert citizens cannot be expected to use traditional finding aids for specialized researchers. Simplicity and user-friendliness are key, instead of in-depth professional preparation. Furthermore, the ability of global users to access archives during opening hours and via phone consultations is affected by time differences, linguistic and cultural barriers, and the costs of use.[40]

The call for enhanced protection of personal data and privacy emerged in response to the right-to-information regulations. In the European Union, both types of regulations were published in 2001; the data protection rules were recently further strengthened due to the 2016 General Data Protection Regulation (GDPR) and the 2018 Regulation 1725/2018 on data protection in EU institutions.[41]

Beyond data protection, various other institutional rules restrict public access to international organizations' records, especially access to classified records discussing defence and military, political, trade, commercial, or industrial secrecy. International organizations also apply independent disclosure rules for their archives and, as a consequence, researchers may encounter very different access provisions or, in certain cases, the closure of archives to the public due to the absence of staff, budget, or rules and procedures.

This leads us to the question of appraisal and selection, which is the basic condition for access to international organizations' archives. Applying modern archival appraisal and selection techniques with a schedule of file destruction, the common understanding is that 5–10% of written records are made available to the public as historical archives.[42] Archivists are particularly concerned with maintaining the provenance and context of archival documents, which is particularly relevant, since, during long years of inaccessibility to the public, these records serve primarily internal administrative and legal purposes. Reflections on the value of historical documents is often partly driven by administrative prerogatives, while developing a selection approach based on the potential needs of future researchers and archives users is less straightforward.[43]

The Internet and information technology have challenged archives' traditional practices regarding access. Instead of a physical reading room, Internet users of our contemporary digital information society request access from wherever they are located and at any time. They expect archives to provide efficient, user-friendly web platforms for inventory consultation, ideally in database format. Furthermore, the expectation towards online availability of digital copies of archival material has grown. The new digital reading room requires sophisticated, standardized solutions for access. Users also expect records inventories to be digital, comprehensible, and even multilingual.

In response to the new community of digital users, digitization of paper archives has become key in making holdings available online. Some archival collections are being digitized, either in their entirety as with the League of Nations' archives or partially, as with the UN and specialized agency archives, including UNESCO. EU institutions have a rather unique approach to digitization. Instead of digitizing selected holdings on a project basis, the Archives Regulation of 2015 prescribes that all archival documents must be digitized before they are opened to the public after 30 years. Public access to the digital copies of these archival materials is then granted and they are made available through a central online database managed by the Historical Archives of the European Union in Florence.[44]

While the primary scope of digitization is online access to these documents, the originals also benefit from a preservation standpoint as they are no longer available for reading room consultation. At the same time, archives continue to maintain their reading rooms onsite, though fewer readers may visit once holdings are made available online. The professional community must therefore reflect on the consequences of the digitization of international organizations' archives on archives services, methods, tools, skills, and strategies, particularly in regard to the challenge of making the digitized mass of records available online.[45]

To provide refined search features in archival databases, the use of standardized vocabularies has gained importance. While libraries have advanced in this field with standardized, multilingual thesauri, keywords, and controlled vocabularies, this is not always the case in international organizations' archives. The consistent use of authority records based on the ISAAR(CPF) standard, in particular, is at an early stage. The introduction of several automated processes in archival description and classification is also a work in progress. Such tools would automatically add metadata to archival documents in order to allow for mass treatment and description of archival holdings and therefore accelerate and ease access to holdings that otherwise may remain closed for a long time as a backlog of unprocessed records. Auto-classification operates on semantic analysis of text by categorizing documents against the existing taxonomies and vocabularies of a given organization. Such auto-indexing has proven particularly valuable when it comes to cases where human indexing document-per-document is not feasible and where machines deliver speed with acceptable quality, such as big data and documents on a large scale.[46]

Some archivists may already be noticing that researchers are losing the necessary skills for using onsite finding aids. With the availability of dynamic online databases, researchers may expect all relevant information to be laid out in a simple search engine-like application in their preferred language or at least in English. Researchers may even go as far as only consulting online resources, omitting those which are not digitally available. The effect is two-fold; the complex context of archival documents is certainly lost in this approach to search and retrieval, and archival research becomes inadequate, limited to just the contents of documents, while lacking information about the conditions of their creation and contextualization. Furthermore, the archivist working in an online environment who has prepared a specific inventory or is responsible for reference services has to adapt to new digital tools to continue providing research support. The democratization of online access to archives has thus numerous consequences on the work of archivists.[47]

In response to the growing community of digital users, international organizations' archives should invest in developing their communication and outreach strategies. This is particularly relevant in view of their widespread and diverse audience. In an era of the Internet, social media, and financial restrictions, the question is no longer why there is a need for communication and outreach but rather how to communicate in the most user-friendly, cost-effective, and efficient ways, even in the naturally conservative field of archives.

Developing a communication strategy for archives in a transnational environment is paramount and helps formulate an organization's key messages to its target audience. Communication supports the operations, functions, and services of archives and helps international organizations achieve their strategic goals. The goal of long-term preservation, making unique archival heritage available and ensuring citizens' right to access public records, must be clearly stated, regularly reviewed, and adapted according to evolving communication environments. Websites should include practical information, news, online exhibitions, and other useful resources. Databases hosting archival inventories should be available online to the public, as should digitized copies of paper archives and digital-born archives housed on digital platforms.

Conclusion

International organizations' archives are undergoing important changes and must confront numerous challenges to their traditional nature, role, and mission, especially as regards the digital environment. The digital society questions traditional understandings of archives by engendering trends in social media, open data, big data, the right to information, privacy and data protection laws, e-government, and cybersecurity.[48] Globalization and digitization have helped raise the profile of records management and archives within international organizations. Particularly in the digital sphere, records managers and archivists must continue to claim their strategic roles within international organizations, upgrade their positions within the organization, develop their professional attitudes, skills, and knowledge, and address the values and norms relevant for overall information management policies.

Notes

1 The author is responsible for the choice and the presentation of the facts contained in the publication and for the opinions expressed therein, which are not necessarily those of the European University Institute and do not commit the Organization.
2 Luciana Duranti & Corinne Rogers (eds.), 2019, *Trusting records in the cloud – the creation, management, and preservation of trustworthy digital content*, Facet Publishing, London.
3 Weimei Pan & Grant Mitchell, 2016, *Case study: IFRCjobs, a SaaS recruiting tool – Final Report*, Technical Report TR02, InterPARES Trust, p. 9.
4 Hermann Lübbe, 2016, 'Archivarische Gewaltenteilung,' in M Lepper & U Raulff (eds.), *Handbuch Archiv: Geschichte, Aufgaben, Perspektiven*, JB Metzler, Stuttgart, p. 13.
5 Frank Evans, 1987, 'Promoting archives and research: a study in international cooperation', *The American Archivist*, vol. 50, no. 1, p. 48; RJ Cox, 1990, 'RAMP studies and related UNESCO publications: an international source for archival administration', *American Archivist*, vol. 53, no. 3, p. 488.
6 Marcel Lepper & Ulrich Raulff (eds.), 2016, *Handbuch Archiv: Geschichte, Aufgaben, Perspektiven*, JB Metzler, Stuttgart, p. VII.
7 United Nations Educational, Scientific and Cultural Organization (UNESCO), 2011, *The Universal Declaration on Archives, adopted by the 36th Session of the General Conference of UNESCO on 10th November 2011*, viewed 25 March 2020, www.ica.org/en/universal-declaration-archives.
8 Marcel Lepper & Ulrich Raulff, 2016, 'Erfindung des Archivs', in M Lepper & U Raulff (eds.), *Handbuch Archiv: Geschichte, Aufgaben, Perspektiven*, JB Metzler, Stuttgart, p. 1.
9 Cited in Maria Guercio, 2010, 'Innovation and curricula: an archival perspective on education of "digital curators"', *Comma*, vol. 1, p. 155.
10 Karsten Uhde, 2006, 'New education in old Europe', *Archival Science*, vol. 6, no. 2, p. 193.
11 Luciana Duranti, 2007, 'Models of archival education: four, two, one, or a thousand?', *Archives & Social Studies*, vol. 1, pp. 41–50.
12 Sigrid McCausland, 2011, 'Educating archivists in Australia and beyond: the contribution of the University of New South Wales archives course, 1973–2000', *Comma*, vol. 1, pp. 79–83.
13 Shadrack Katuu, 2018, *Curriculum alignments at institutions of higher learning in Africa: preparing professionals to manage records created in networked environments*, Final Project Report AF01, InterPARES Trust, pp. 9–10.
14 Maria Guercio, 2010, pp. 163–164; International Council on Archives (ICA) & International Records Management Trust (IRMT), 2016, *Digital preservation in lower resource environments: a core curriculum. understanding digital records preservation initiatives*, viewed 25 March 2020, www.ica.org/sites/default/files/Digital%20Preservation%20Initiatives%20Module_0.pdf.
15 Katuu, 2018, p. 7.
16 Guercio, 2010, p. 154.

17 Sara Naeslund Lems, 2010, 'The Swedish Mentor Scheme – a case study of trial and error and success', *Comma*, vol. 1, p. 142.
18 Joan Boadas i Raset, 2010, 'De quoi les citoyens ont-ils besoin? S'adapter ou disparaitre!', *Comma*, vol. 1, pp. 106–107.
19 Cited in Vitor Da Fonseca, 2011, 'The ICA description standards: the history of their creation and efforts to disseminate them', *Comma*, vol. 2, p. 49.
20 Ibid, p. 50.
21 Giovanni Michetti, 2015, 'Unneutrality of archival standards and processes', paper presented at Re-inventing Information Science in the Networked Society, 14th Symposium on Information Science (ISI 2015), 19–21 May, Zadar, Croatia, pp. 2–8, viewed 25 March 2020, https://zenodo.org/record/16421#.Xnsw5m5FyUk.
22 Da Fonseca, 2011, pp. 50–52.
23 Cited in Alan Bell, 2011, 'Standards and standards culture: understanding the nature and criticisms of standardisation', *Comma*, vol. 2, p. 25.
24 Barbara Reed, 2011, 'The ISO standards process and implications of ISO for ICA standards', *Comma*, vol. 2, pp. 123–124.
25 Jessica Bushey et al., 2016, *Checklist for cloud service contracts*, Project NA14, InterPARES Trust, p. 10.
26 Agenzia per l'Italia digitale, 2016, *Cloud for Europe: realization of a research and development project (pre-commercial procurement) on "Cloud for Europe"*, viewed 25 March 2020, www.agid.gov.it/cloudforeurope.
27 Stefano Allegrezza et al., 2018, *The impact of the Italian legal framework for cloud computing on electronic recordkeeping and digital preservation system*, Final report EU35, InterPARES Trust, pp. 5–6.
28 Bell, 2011, p. 38.
29 Bushey et al., 2016, p. 10.
30 Cited in Marion Beyea, 2011, 'Introduction: ICA and standards', *Comma,* vol. 2, p. 1.
31 Da Fonseca, 2011, pp. 53–57.
32 Cited in United Nations Educational, Scientific and Cultural Organization (UNESCO), n.d., *About ICA-AtoM and UNESCO*, viewed 25 March 2020, https://atom.archives.unesco.org/about.
33 Archival Portal Europe Foundation, 2019, *Archives Portal Europe*, viewed 25 March 2020, www.archivesportaleurope.net/.
34 Daniel Pitti, Bill Stockting & Florence Clavaud, 2016, 'An introduction to "Records in Contexts": an archival description draft standard', *Comma*, vol. 1, p. 173.
35 Cited in Michetti, 2015, p. 21
36 Hans-Christian Ströbele, 2018, 'Eröffnungsvortrag', Verband deutscher Archivarinnen und Archivare (VDA) (ed.), Verlässlich, richtig, echt – Demokratie braucht Archive! 88. Deutscher Archivtag in Rostock, *Tagungsdokumentationen zum Deutschen Archivtag*, vol. 23, pp. 15–17; Lepper & Raulff, 2016, p. 7.
37 European Communities, *Regulation (EC) No 1049/2001 of the European Parliament and of the Council of 30 May 2001 regarding public access to European Parliament, Council and Commission documents*, viewed 25 March 2020, https://eur-lex.europa.eu/eli/reg/2001/1049/oj.
38 Adrian Cunningham & Margaret Phillips, 2005, 'Accountability and accessibility: ensuring the evidence of e-governance in Australia', *Aslib Proceedings*, vol. 57, no. 4, p. 303.
39 Hans Hofman, 2012, 'Rethinking the archival function in the digital era', *Comma*, vol. 2, pp. 26–28; Fiona Gill & Catriona Elder, 2012, 'Data and archives: the Internet as site and subject', *International Journal of Social Research Methodology*, vol. 15, no. 4, p. 271.
40 Joan Boadas i Raset, 2010, p. 105.
41 European Communities, *Regulation (EC) No 45/2001 of the European Parliament and of the Council of 18 December 2000 on the protection of individuals with regard to the processing of personal data by the Community institutions and bodies and on the free movement of such data*, viewed 25 March 2020, https://eur-lex.europa.eu/eli/reg/2001/45/oj; European

Union, *Regulation (EU) 2016/679 of the European Parliament and of the Council of 27 April 2016 on the protection of natural persons with regard to the processing of personal data and on the free movement of such data, and repealing Directive 95/46/EC (General Data Protection Regulation)*, viewed 25 March 2020, https://eur-lex.europa.eu/eli/reg/2016/679/oj; European Union, *Regulation (EU) 2018/1725 of the European Parliament and of the Council of 23 October 2018 on the protection of natural persons with regard to the processing of personal data by the Union institutions, bodies, offices and agencies and on the free movement of such data, and repealing Regulation (EC) No 45/2001 and Decision No 1247/2002/EC*, viewed 25 March 2020, https://eur-lex.europa.eu/eli/reg/2018/1725/oj.
42 Nicolas Berg, 2016, 'Geschichte des Archivs im 20. Jahrhundert', in M Lepper & U Raulff (eds.), *Handbuch Archiv: Geschichte, Aufgaben, Perspektiven*, JB Metzler, Stuttgart, p. 68.
43 Joan Boadas i Raset, 2010, p. 106.
44 European Union, *Council Regulation (EU) 2015/496 of 17 March 2015 amending Regulation (EEC, Euratom) No 354/83 as regards the deposit of the historical archives of the institutions at the European University Institute in Florence*, viewed 25 March 2020, https://eur-lex.europa.eu/eli/reg/2015/496/oj.
45 Gill & Elder, 2012, p. 271.
46 Gesa Buettner, 2017, 'Auto-classification in an international organization: report from a feasibility study', *Comma*, vol. 2, no. 2, pp. 15–25.
47 Gaël Chenard, 2014, 'Les lecteurs qu'on mérite', *Comma*, vol. 1, p. 195.
48 Hans Hofman, 2012, 'Rethinking the archival function in the digital era', *Comma*, vol. 2, p. 25.

Bibliography

Agenzia per l'Italia digitale 2016, *Cloud for Europe: realization of a research and development project (pre-commercial procurement) on "Cloud for Europe"*, viewed 25 March 2020, www.agid.gov.it/cloudforeurope.

Allegrezza, S, Bezzi, G, Caravaca, M, Guercio, M, Pescini, I & Brizio, T 2018, *The impact of the Italian legal framework for cloud computing on electronic recordkeeping and digital preservation system*, Final report EU35, InterPARES Trust.

Archival Portal Europe Foundation 2019, *Archives Portal Europe*, viewed 25 March 2020, www.archivesportaleurope.net/.

Bell, A 2011, 'Standards and standards culture: understanding the nature and criticisms of standardisation', *Comma*, vol. 2, pp. 25–38.

Berg, N 2016, 'Geschichte des Archivs im 20. Jahrhundert', in M Lepper & U Raulff (eds.), *Handbuch Archiv: Geschichte, Aufgaben, Perspektiven*, JB Metzler, Stuttgart, pp. 57–76.

Beyea, M 2011, 'Introduction: ICA and standards', *Comma*, vol. 2, pp. 1–24.

Boadas i Raset, J 2010, 'De quoi les citoyens ont-ils besoin? S'adapter ou disparaitre!', *Comma*, vol. 1, pp. 103–108.

Buettner, G 2017, 'Auto-classification in an international organization: report from a feasibility study', *Comma*, vol. 2, no. 2, pp. 15–25.

Bushey, J, Demoulin, M, How, E & McLelland, R 2016, *Checklist for cloud service contracts*, Project NA14, InterPARES Trust.

Chenard, G 2014, 'Les lecteurs qu'on mérite', *Comma*, vol. 1, pp. 195–204.

Cox, RJ 1990, 'RAMP studies and related UNESCO publications: an international source for archival administration', *American Archivist*, vol. 53, no. 3, pp. 488–495.

Cunningham, A & Phillips, M 2005, 'Accountability and accessibility: ensuring the evidence of e-governance in Australia', *Aslib Proceedings*, vol. 57, no. 4, pp. 301–317.

Da Fonseca, V 2011, 'The ICA description standards: the history of their creation and efforts to disseminate them', *Comma*, vol. 2, pp. 49–58.

Duranti, L 2007, 'Models of archival education: four, two, one, or a thousand?', *Archives & Social Studies*, vol. 1, pp. 41–62.

Duranti, L & Rogers, C (eds.) 2019, *Trusting records in the cloud – the creation, management, and preservation of trustworthy digital content*, Facet Publishing, London.

Engvall, T, Liang, V & Anderson, K 2015, *The role of the archivist and records manager in an open government environment in Sweden*, Project EU11, InterPARES Trust.

Evans, F 1987, 'Promoting archives and research: a study in international cooperation', *The American Archivist*, vol. 50, no. 1, pp. 48–65.

Gill, F & Elder, C 2012, 'Data and archives: the Internet as site and subject', *International Journal of Social Research Methodology*, vol. 15, no. 4, pp. 271–279.

Guercio, M 2010, 'Innovation and curricula: an archival perspective on education of "digital curators"', *Comma*, vol. 1, pp. 151–167.

Hofman, H 2012, 'Rethinking the archival function in the digital era', *Comma*, vol. 2, pp. 25–34.

International Council on Archives (ICA) & International Records Management Trust (IRMT) 2016, *Digital preservation in lower resource environments: a core curriculum. Understanding digital records preservation initiatives*, viewed 25 March 2020, www.ica.org/sites/defa ult/files/Digital%20Preservation%20Initatives%20Module_0.pdf.

Katuu, S 2018, *Curriculum alignments at institutions of higher learning in Africa: preparing professionals to manage records created in networked environments*, Final Project Report AF01, InterPARES Trust.

Lepper, M & Raulff, U 2016, 'Erfindung des Archivs', in M Lepper & U Raulff (eds.), *Handbuch Archiv: Geschichte, Aufgaben, Perspektiven*, JB Metzler, Stuttgart, pp. 1–8.

Lübbe, H 2016, 'Archivarische Gewaltenteilung', in M Lepper and U Raulff (eds.), *Handbuch Archiv: Geschichte, Aufgaben, Perspektiven*, JB Metzler, Stuttgart, pp. 9–17.

McCausland, S 2011, 'Educating archivists in Australia and beyond: the contribution of the University of New South Wales archives course, 1973–2000', *Comma*, vol. 1, pp. 79–87.

Michetti, G 2015, '*Unneutrality of archival standards and processes*', paper presented at Reinventing Information Science in the Networked Society, 14th Symposium on Information Science (ISI 2015), 19–21 May, Zadar, Croatia, viewed 25 March 2020, https:// zenodo.org/record/16421#.Xnsw5m5FyUk.

Naeslund Lems, S 2010, 'The Swedish Mentor Scheme – a case study of trial and error and success', *Comma*, vol. 1, pp. 141–148.

Pan, W & Mitchell, G 2016, *Case study: IFRCjobs, a SaaS recruiting tool – final report*, Technical Report TR02, InterPARES Trust.

Pitti, D, Stockting, B & Clavaud, F 2016, 'An introduction to "Records in Contexts": an archival description draft standard', *Comma*, vol. 1, pp. 173–188.

Reed, B 2011, 'The ISO standards process and implications of ISO for ICA standards', *Comma*, vol. 2, pp. 123–130.

Ströbele, HC 2018, 'Eröffnungsvortrag', Verband deutscher Archivarinnen und Archivare (VDA) (ed.), Verlässlich, richtig, echt – Demokratie braucht Archive! 88. Deutscher Archivtag in Rostock, *Tagungsdokumentationen zum Deutschen Archivtag*, vol. 23, pp. 15–20.

Uhde, K 2006, 'New education in old Europe', *Archival Science*, vol. 6, no. 2, pp. 193–203.

United Nations Educational, Scientific and Cultural Organization (UNESCO) 2011, *The Universal Declaration on Archives, adopted by the 36th Session of the General Conference of UNESCO on 10th November 2011*, viewed 25 March 2020, www.ica.org/en/universa l-declaration-archives.

United Nations Educational, Scientific and Cultural Organization (UNESCO) n.d., *About ICA-AtoM and UNESCO*, viewed 25 March 2020, https://atom.archives.unesco.org/a bout.

Legislation

European Communities, *Regulation (EC) No 1049/2001 of the European Parliament and of the Council of 30 May 2001 regarding public access to European Parliament, Council and Commission documents*, viewed 25 March 2020, https://eur-lex.europa.eu/eli/reg/2001/1049/oj.

European Communities, *Regulation (EC) No 45/2001 of the European Parliament and of the Council of 18 December 2000 on the protection of individuals with regard to the processing of personal data by the Community institutions and bodies and on the free movement of such data*, viewed 25 March 2020, https://eur-lex.europa.eu/eli/reg/2001/45/oj.

European Union, *Council Regulation (EU) 2015/496 of 17 March 2015 amending Regulation (EEC, Euratom) No 354/83 as regards the deposit of the historical archives of the institutions at the European University Institute in Florence*, viewed 25 March 2020, https://eur-lex.europa.eu/eli/reg/2015/496/oj.

European Union, *Regulation (EU) 2016/679 of the European Parliament and of the Council of 27 April 2016 on the protection of natural persons with regard to the processing of personal data and on the free movement of such data, and repealing Directive 95/46/EC (General Data Protection Regulation)*, viewed 25 March 2020, https://eur-lex.europa.eu/eli/reg/2016/679/oj.

European Union, *Regulation (EU) 2018/1725 of the European Parliament and of the Council of 23 October 2018 on the protection of natural persons with regard to the processing of personal data by the Union institutions, bodies, offices and agencies and on the free movement of such data, and repealing Regulation (EC) No 45/2001 and Decision No 1247/2002/EC*, viewed 25 March 2020, https://eur-lex.europa.eu/eli/reg/2018/1725/oj.

2

DATA PROTECTION IN THE EUROPEAN UNION INSTITUTIONS FROM AN INFORMATION MANAGEMENT PERSPECTIVE

Paola Casini[1]

Introduction

The traces we leave through our lives on the web and social media, while working, chatting, or dealing with everyday activities such as paying bills, streaming videos, reading the news, and listening to music, render us continuously prey to identity theft, hacking, and even government surveillance. There exists an abstract belief in privacy, and most people who leave traces of their activities or provide personal information online feel they have at least some control over this information.[2] Personal data[3] is perceived, through the numerous cultural differences present in the European Union (EU) member states, in different ways. A great deal is at stake for individuals, groups, and societies if privacy is misunderstood, misused, or mismanaged. It has become clear for information managers that due to continuous technological innovations, it is crucial to understand the many facets of this complex topic.

Although European information managers consider data as naturally linked to data protection law, other issues such as records retention, security, and privacy must increasingly be addressed in the context of European regulations concerned with trans-border data flows.[4] Furthermore, through their involvement in discussions about big data[5] and open data,[6] information managers have realized that challenges arise from working in an age of digital abundance, faced with an explosive increase in records creation, and the consequent need to find ways of securing, preserving, and providing access to records on an unprecedented scale.[7]

The General Data Protection Regulation (GDPR) has created, since its publication in 2016 and especially since entering into force in May 2018, widespread concern among organizations, both private and public, regarding their ability to match the demanding requirements set by the regulation. This concern is particularly acute among recordkeeping professionals, who understand well the volume of effort that will be required in order to achieve compliance.[8] The European Union institutions are not exempt from this situation. They constitute an exceptional test bed to understand how the increased requirements of GDPR might affect records management practices. Since 2001, the European Union institutions have been subject to a specific regulation on data protection (Regulation (EC) No. 45/2001)[9] applicable to their particular environment.

Since 25 May 2018, the date of enforcement of GDPR, European Union institutions enjoyed a "grace period" during which GDPR was fully applicable to Member States, but not to European Union institutions, which were still bound by the less stringent 2001 regulation. This exception ended on 11 December 2018 with the entry into force of the new Regulation (EU) 2018/1725, hereafter referred to as R. 2018/1725 or the Regulation, meaning that data protection in the European Union institutions is fully assimilated to GDPR.

This chapter will address the challenges faced by information managers working in the European Union institutions to embed several fundamental principles established by the new regulation in their routine information management practices, such as processing for archival purposes, transparency, data minimization, and data retention. The chapter will also offer guidance in these areas.

Throughout the chapter, I use the preferred term of "information managers" instead of archivists or record managers,[10] since the European Union institutions are elements of a wide information governance system, which "include not only the compliance and privacy issues that are familiar to records managers and archivists, but also matters such as information security, which are more usually associated with managing computer systems."[11] Yeo further suggests:

> In practice, interpretations of information governance can vary from one organization – or one type of organization – to another, but it is often viewed in terms of risk management; information governance programmes generally seek to identify and mitigate the risks that would arise if issues relating to information security, privacy, confidentiality or legal compliance are inadequately addressed … It usually emphasises threats rather than opportunities, and is most likely to be effective in highly regulated organizations where compliance, accountability and risk mitigation are seen as essential.[12]

We are in fact in the presence of an organization, the European Union, wherein privacy *and* freedom of information laws are in force, making the organization's information subject to those laws, and hence potentially discoverable in the event of litigation.[13]

In this chapter, I also do not define data and information, which have extensively been discussed by other authors,[14] and simply agree with the fact that:

> Data protection laws, the open data movement and the burgeoning world of data analytics all rest on assumptions that data is meaningful. The idea that data can or should be reliable and authentic is also posited on a belief that data convey meaning and are not merely material aggregations of bits and bytes.[15]

In the following pages, I concentrate on the European Union, which might be characterized as a technocratic machine[16] or as an "unfinished adventure"[17]; and the European Union institutions,[18] for which "data and information have become the most important assets."[19] Information governance and data protection have been high on the European Union agenda.[20] The former European Commission President Jean-Claude Juncker stressed that "only a strong and united Europe can master the challenges of global digitisation. It is because of our single market that we can set standards for big data, artificial intelligence, and automation."[21] The current Commission President, Ursula von der Leyen, follows her predecessor's footsteps. In her Political Guidelines, she provides a vision for the future development of the European Union digital strategy.[22] She announces "a Europe fit for the digital age," in which she wants:

> Europe to strive for more by grasping the opportunities from the digital age within safe and ethical boundaries. Digital technologies, especially Artificial Intelligence (AI), are transforming the world at an unprecedented speed. They have changed how we communicate, live and work. They have changed our societies and our economies.[23]

The Digital Single Market strategy is not new; it was adopted in May 2015[24] and it is at the origin of the new data protection and digital technologies rules. It focuses on the removal of barriers for European citizens and businesses when using online tools and services. The strategy is meant to improve access to digital goods and services by consumers and businesses; create an environment where digital networks and services can prosper by providing high-speed, secure, and trustworthy infrastructures and services; and establish "digital" as a driver for growth, notably by enhancing digital skills.

However, if we consider that, according to the 2018 Digital Economy and Society Index Report's findings, 43% of Europeans still have low or no digital skills,[25] then we should agree with Zygmunt Bauman: we are still in that fuzzy blurred situation that he defines as "liquid modernity." According to Bauman, we have moved away from a "heavy" and "solid," hardware-focused modernity to a "light" and "liquid," software-based modernity. This passage has brought profound changes to all aspects of the human condition.[26] "The frozen time of factory routine, together with the bricks and mortar of factory walls, immobilized capital as effectively as it bound the labour it employed. It all changed, though, with the advent of software capitalism and 'light' modernity."[27] We do not know yet when this liquefaction will end and if this interregnum will last long enough. Bauman believed there is a way to survive liquidity. Indeed, the realization that we live in a liquid society requires new tools to be understood and perhaps overcome.

In this liquid society, information managers will seek tools that can help us to understand and contextualize complex data aggregations, and discover interrelationships among data sets. They will:

Probably look to tools enhanced by artificial intelligence, retain information on a large scale, and perhaps even aim to keep everything. Even when total retention appears unaffordable, or when privacy laws impose limits on what can be retained, future information managers will keep much more information than their predecessors.[28]

Information managers should be aware that some of their routine activities, such as records selection, transfer to a repository, and making information available to users are all considered processing under R. 2018/1725.[29] Furthermore, R. 2018/1725 enforces the principle that processing can take place only when it is really necessary. This concept is new and can be seen as a challenge for the information management profession.

The principles discussed in this chapter, which form the backbone of data protection, are presented following the structure of article 4 of R. 2018/1725, which includes the following points: (a) lawfulness, fairness, and transparency; (b) purpose limitation; (c) adequate, relevant, and limited data ("data minimization"); (d) "accuracy"; (e) "storage limitation"; and (f) appropriate security of personal data ... against accidental loss, destruction, or damage ("integrity and confidentiality").

Although information managers are familiar with the concepts of transparency and accountability, accuracy, confidentiality, security and integrity, and their ethical and legal aspects,[30] some of the implications of such principles are nevertheless less obvious in the context of R. 2018/1725.

Transparency and accountability

In R. 2018/1725, the principle of transparency requires that any information and communications relating to the processing of personal data is accessible and easy to understand, and that clear and plain language is used. This principle concerns, in particular, information to individuals on the identity of the controller,[31] the purposes of fair and transparent processing, and citizens' rights to obtain confirmation and communication on personal data concerning them. Individuals should be made aware of risks, rules, safeguards, and rights in relation to the processing of personal data and how to exercise their rights in relation to such processing.[32]

The principle of transparency means – among other things[33] – that EU institutions and their services need to publish clear, user-friendly information on their reasons for processing personal data, and help individuals to access this information. According to Article 31(1) of R. 2018/1725, controllers need to maintain a record of processing activities under their responsibility. The record is considered an internal tool to help implement R. 2018/1725, as it supports the analysis of the implications of any data processing, whether existing or planned. It facilitates the factual assessment of the risk of the processing activities performed by a controller on individuals' rights, and the identification and implementation of appropriate security measures to safeguard personal data – both key components of the principle of accountability[34] contained in R. 2018/1725.

The record must be in writing (including in electronic form), clear and intelligible, and must contain specific information about every processing activity carried out. It must include the name and contact data of the controller, and if necessary state other organizations with whom the controller has established common purposes and means of the processing; and clearly indicate the Data Protection Officer and the purposes for which the EU institutions process personal information.[35] When the EU institutions share data with a foreign country or an international organization outside the EU, they have to clearly refer to their agreements or memoranda of understanding in the record. The EU institutions need to describe the technology, applications, and software used for data processing in their general description of the technical and organizational measures taken in order to secure personal data. They also need to clearly state when they outsource processing activities to third-party providers (processors) while remaining fully responsible as controllers. The record can contain any additional information that is considered of importance by the Data Protection Officer of the activities carried out, for example, an indication of the legal basis for data processing. For the European Data Protection Supervisor, records represent prerequisites for compliance and effective accountability measures.[36] Records help the Data Protection Officers to perform their tasks of monitoring compliance, informing, and advising the controller or the processor.

Data Protection Officers[37] are certainly key players in data protection in the EU institutions. They assist the controller in all issues related to the protection of personal data, supervise the activities, and collaborate with the records' creators. The Data Protection Officers inform and advise the controllers and their assistants of their obligations under R. 2018/1725, and inform individuals of their rights. They also monitor compliance by ensuring the correct internal application of the Regulation and by handling queries and complaints. They should also provide advice as regards the data protection impact assessment and cooperate with the supervisory authority. The EU institutions have, however, an advantage over public authorities and private bodies of the member states, which must now appoint a Data Protection Officer under the GDPR. Indeed, while the appointment of a Data Protection Officer has not been considered compulsory by national entities prior to the GDPR, it has been a legal requirement for all EU institutions, regardless of their size and core activities, for over 17 years.[38]

Archiving purposes and data minimization

One of the most interesting aspects of R. 2018/1725 for information managers concerns the concept of "archiving purposes in the public interest." Recital 25 does not fully explain the meaning of this concept, but states that it "should be considered compatible lawful processing operations." Article 13 is dedicated to "processing for archiving purposes in the public interest, scientific or historical research purposes or statistical purposes." The first paragraph of this article lays down rules that are common both for processing of personal data "for archiving purposes in the public interest" and for "scientific or historical research purposes or statistical purposes." These processing activities are subject to appropriate safeguards to protect the rights and freedoms of individuals. The safeguards need to ensure that technical and organizational measures are in place and that they respect the principle of data minimization, i.e. they must ensure that a controller collects only the strict minimum amount of personal data necessary to fulfil the purpose of the processing. The measures may also include pseudonymization[39] or other means, which do not or no longer allow for the identification of individuals.

The European Data Protection Supervisor, however, warns controllers against the interpretation of this concept as a blanket permission to store everything for an extended period of time for archiving, scientific research, and historical or statistical purposes. Instead:

> In each case, [the controller] must have an appropriate legal basis for the processing and assess the necessity and proportionality of any data storage. In addition, [the controller] must also think of safeguards you can apply – e.g. aggregating personal data kept/disclosed for research purposes, banning re-identification in the conditions for granting access for research purposes.[40]

Although not a new concept, data minimization needs some reflection.[41] This principle was already established in Regulation 45/2001, which indicated that personal data should be collected and processed only if it is really necessary, and should be "kept in a form which permits identification of individuals for no longer than is necessary for the purpose for which the data was collected."[42] If interpreted in a strict sense, this principle could have led to the destruction of records containing personal data. Instead, EU lawmakers have acknowledged that "personal data may be stored for longer periods insofar as the personal data will be processed solely for archiving purposes in the public interest, scientific or historical research purposes," under the condition that it "safeguard[s] the rights and freedoms of the data subject."[43]

The principle of data minimization and the obligation of taking appropriate safeguards in order to protect individuals' rights are therefore common to both "processing for archiving purposes in the public interest" and processing for "scientific or historical research purposes or statistical purposes," with differences according to the area of application. Pseudonymization of records is, for example, commonly applied as an appropriate measure in health research, where it is important to preserve the correlation of different health data regarding patients, but their identity is irrelevant. In another case, an EU institution that holds records in the public interest has to preserve the integrity of its records selected for permanent preservation, whether the records are sensitive (e.g., medical records[44]) or not with regards to the individuals' interest.

Information managers are accustomed to enforcing the principle of data minimization when they select records that contain personal data for permanent preservation through the application of retention schedules. They furthermore enforce laws concerning access to records within the framework of public access to documents legislation[45] and in conformity with archival policies,[46] and are bound by ethical codes for the non-disclosure of personal data.[47] In ensuring that access to records is managed appropriately and that correct organizational and technical safeguards are in place, EU institutions comply with article 80 of R. 2018/1725, which gives the right to individuals to access the data that concern them.[48]

Accuracy, confidentiality, and integrity principles

When it comes to accuracy, controllers must make all reasonable efforts to ensure that the data is accurate, since decisions based on wrong information may have negative impacts on individuals, and may expose the EU institutions to liability. In practice, accuracy refers to the fact that a certain statement [record] containing personal data is accurately recorded; all people involved in such statement or record should be able to complement the information recorded and provide their own view on the matter.[49]

To the familiar concept of "confidentiality" as a standard practice to protect confidential information from unauthorised access,[50] R. 2018/1725 adds the principles of integrity and availability. Confidentiality is therefore measured following a risk-based approach: the higher the risk, the more rigorous the measures that controllers need to take in order to manage the risk. R. 2018/1725 does not define the security measures that business owners should put in place. It requires them to have a level of security that is "appropriate" to the risks presented by their processing. Before deciding what measures are appropriate, they need to assess their information risk through a formal risk management methodology. The chosen measures must enable the owners to restore access and availability to personal data in a timely manner in the event of a physical or technical incident, and this means having appropriate processes in place to test the effectiveness of their measures, and undertake any required improvements.

Taking into account the ever-increasing use of digital and/or online data processing systems, often based on cloud services and smart devices, security risks for personal data are associated today to a great extent with the security risks of the underlying IT networks and system components.[51] Furthermore, the "security principle" stated in article 33 of R. 2018/1725 also requires the controller and the processor[52] to consider risk analysis, organizational policies, and physical and technical measures. The controller and the processor can consider the state of the art[53] and costs[54] of implementation when deciding what measures to take, but these measures must be appropriate both to the circumstances and to the risk posed by the processing.

Closely associated to security, R. 2018/1725 creates through its article 34 a system of notification of personal data breaches.[55] This includes breaches that are the result of both accidental and deliberate causes. When a personal data breach is likely to result in a risk to the rights and freedoms of natural persons, the controller shall notify the personal data breach to the European Data Protection Supervisor without undue delay, and no later than 72 hours after the incident. Information managers are responsible for the security of personal data in their care and, in accordance with existing professional practices, safeguard their integrity and authenticity and protect them from unauthorized access, alteration, loss, damage, or destruction. They should also be aware that the level of security must be proportionate to the nature of the data and the harm that could arise from a security breach. In the event of a serious breach arising from the processing (e.g., storage, access, communication), European Union institutions must consider whether the breach is likely to cause significant damage to individuals' interests. If so, notification of the breach should be considered under the terms of article 35, which states, "when the personal data breach is likely to result in a high risk to the rights and freedoms of natural persons, the controller shall communicate the personal data breach to the data subject without undue delay." However, in case this would involve "disproportionate effort," which can happen when a breach concerns a large number of records containing thousands of personal data, article 35(3) point (c) offers the alternative of "a public communication or similar measure whereby the data subjects are informed in an equally effective manner." This could result in a notice on the website or a communication via a mailing list.

As mentioned above, articles 4b and 4e speak of the principles of "purpose limitation" and of "storage limitation." It is clear that the principle of storage limitation has a direct correlation to records disposal, one of the key record-keeping functions. Only a very small percentage of documents created or received by the European Union institutions, in the course of their activities, ends up in archival institutions. The principle imposes on the European Union's institutions the obligation to publish general criteria on records' appraisal, selection, elimination, and permanent preservation, and to explain their decisions to retain those records containing personal data.[56] Both principles allow, however, derogations for archiving purposes in the public interest and for historical research purposes, subject to measures, which safeguard the individuals' rights and freedoms.

The issue of data integrity has already started to be publicly discussed and will certainly nourish European jurisprudence[57] in the future. The principle of data integrity in the Regulation implies not only that administrative malpractice leading to data loss constitutes a clear breach of the Regulation, it also hints at further technological developments. The quality and integrity of data become of paramount importance for the performance of AI systems, where it is essential to guarantee that processed personal data does not contain socially constructed biases, inaccuracies, errors, and mistakes. The requirements must be addressed prior to processing any given data set, as feeding malicious data into an AI system may change its behaviour, particularly with self-learning systems. To this end, processes and data sets must be documented at each phase of planning, testing, and deployment.[58]

Individuals' rights: access, rectification, and erasure

It is essential to highlight that one of the main goals of R. 2018/1725 is to grant individuals control over their personal data. For this reason, the Regulation provides individuals with a comprehensive set of rights regarding their own personal data, such as the right to know which data is processed and why, and rights to access, erase, and transfer their data.[59]

The European Union institutions have consequently put in place mechanisms to allow individuals the widest possible control over their data. The individuals' right to information has reached a higher significance than in the previous legal framework. It must be seen as a central instrument for the enforcement of the right to informational self-determination.[60] The right to information has three main components: first, the person has the right to a confirmation that the controller has his/her data; second, the person is entitled to extensive information about the processing of his/her personal data; third, the person has the right to claim a copy of his/her own personal data. The information obligations of the controller and the right to information of the person concerned complement each other. They are, so to speak, two sides of the same coin. Articles 14 and 15 stipulate, on the one hand, an active duty to inform the person concerned of the processing of personal data, while, on the other hand, they enounce the individual right of access. However, the exercise of the right of access in no way depends on whether or not the controller has duly fulfilled their duties of information.[61]

As noted earlier, the European Data Protection Supervisor explicitly encourages controllers to make the information about the processing publicly available.[62] This represents a novelty compared to Regulation 45/2001. Another novelty is the obligation to state the contact details of the Data Protection Officer, which the European Data Protection Supervisor, in its Opinion 5/2017, links to the "increased transparency of the Data Protection Officer function."[63] The use of plain language for privacy statements, the requirement to reply to individuals' requests in principle within one month, and the fact that controllers' replies must be free of charge are complementing features of the same obligation. Additionally, privacy statements must be available where data is collected, which implies in most cases their online publication.

Consequently, as provided in recital 37 and Article 17 of R. 2018/1725, individuals should have the right of access[64] to personal data that have been collected concerning them, and can exercise their right easily and at reasonable intervals, in order to be aware of, and verify the lawfulness of, the processing.[65] Additionally, individuals have the right to know the purposes of the processing, the categories of personal data, and other information regarding the processing of their personal data. As in the case of the obligation to inform, access to data is not only an individual right but also an obligation of the data controller. In fact, the European Union institutions should put in place data protocols governing data access, which should outline who can access data and under which circumstances. Only duly qualified personnel with the competence and need to access individuals' data should be allowed to do so.[66]

Article 18 of R. 2018/1725 also gives individuals the right to obtain the rectification of their personal data if it is inaccurate and/or incomplete. The controller has to comply with such requests without undue delay. Information managers must, however, guarantee records' integrity and records' evidential value. The Regulation recognizes records' evidential value and balances the responsibility of controllers to maintain the records' integrity, and the individual's right to have their personal data rectified or completed by "providing a supplementary statement." In practical terms, original records are not altered; instead, they are simply complemented by addenda.

The individual right that is always debated in information managers' circles is the "right to be forgotten." Within the European Union, the concept was first stated in 2014, in the decision by the Court of Justice of the European Union in the Google Spain case.[67] The EU Court of Justice has decided that, under certain conditions, individuals have the right to request search engines to remove search results from their search index. In its reasoning, the Court admitted that search engines and search results can establish a detailed profile of an individual, since the information could not have been easily discovered without a search engine. It thus constitutes a possibly serious interference of individuals' fundamental rights to privacy. As a consequence, the Court ordered Google Spain to remove two reports on insolvencies indexed through search results regarding a Spanish citizen, with no impact on the newspaper's analogue and digital records. Following this Court decision, individuals can now request their personal data to be delinked from search engines. The decision by the EU Court of Justice in the Google Spain case was grounded on Directive 95/46/EC, which did not explicitly include a "right to be forgotten."

By contrast, R. 2018/1725 uses these words in the title of article 19, "Right to erasure ('right to be forgotten')." It must, however, be noted that the Regulation does not make any reference to delinking, but to the actual erasure of personal data. Article 19 grants individuals a de facto right to obtain from the controller the erasure of personal data concerning them without undue delay. This right can apply where "the personal data is no longer necessary in relation to the purposes for which they were collected," or where individuals withdraw consent on its processing. However, this right is subject to different restrictions, and it shall not apply if processing is necessary for archiving purposes in the public interest, and if erasure "is likely to render impossible or seriously impair the achievement of the objectives of that processing."

From an information management point of view, the right to be forgotten as stated by the EU Court of Justice (i.e. not erasure, but delisting of personal data) can be enforced by European Union institutions without prejudice to record-keeping principles. Delinking or delisting, or in other ways preventing the use of search engines to search for names in records, should not affect the integrity of records, nor does it endanger their permanent preservation. Lastly, in its most recent judgement on Internet search engines, processing of data on web pages, and the territorial scope of the right to de-referencing, the EU Court of Justice[68] coined the new term "de-referencing" for what was previously known as delisting. The Court ruled this time in favour of Google by stating that de-referencing by Google should be limited to EU Member States' versions of its search engine. Furthermore, when Google receives a request for de-referencing related to published sensitive data, a balance must be sought between the fundamental rights of the person requesting such de-referencing and those of Internet users potentially interested in that information. This can be interpreted as the first attempt by the Court to strike a balance between these rights so far as the Union is concerned.

R. 2018/1725 also grants individuals the right to obtain from the controller restrictions on processing (Art. 20) and the right to object to processing of their personal data (Art. 23). Such rights share the same ultimate goal of granting individuals control over the processing of their personal data. However, the restriction of processing does not prevent the storage of personal data (Art. 20(2)). Moreover, individuals have the right to object to the processing of personal data concerning themselves, even if the processing "is necessary for the performance of a task carried out in the public interest." In that case, "the controller shall no longer process the personal data" (Art. 23(1)). However, the controller can continue processing personal data, if they can demonstrate "compelling legitimate grounds for the processing which override the interests, rights and freedoms of the data subject" (Art. 23(1)). This provision might apply to the processing of records in the public interest. R. 2018/1725 unfortunately does not determine which kind of personal data processing activities can be considered as being "in the public interest."[69] Nevertheless, from recent judgements, it is safe to say that "public interest" covers "matters which are capable of giving rise to considerable controversy, which concern an important social issue, or which involve a problem that the public would have an interest in being informed about."[70]

We have mentioned above that the recent Google case concerns sensitive data, which are dealt with in Article 10 of R. 2018/1725. For the most part, the provisions of Article 10 are not new. Regulation 45/2001 already prohibited the processing of special categories of personal data, with some exemptions. Regulation 2018/1725 has enlarged the categories of personal data deserving special protection by adding "genetic data, biometric data for the purpose of uniquely identifying a natural person."[71] It provides special protection to certain categories of personal data, the processing of which could create significant risks to individuals' fundamental rights and freedoms. It forbids the processing of personal data revealing racial or ethnic origin, political opinions, religious or philosophical beliefs, or trade union membership, and the processing of genetic data, biometric data for the purpose of uniquely identifying a natural person, data concerning health, or data concerning a natural person's sex life or sexual orientation. However, the Regulation allows for some derogations from this provision. The prohibition to process such sensitive data does not apply in cases where "processing is necessary for archiving purposes in the public interest" and for historical research, and the prohibition must be based on law and proportionate to the aim pursued. Moreover, it must "respect the essence of the right to data protection and provide for suitable and specific measures to safeguard the fundamental rights and the interests of the data subject."[72]

Data protection by design

In order to implement data protection principles that safeguard the individual's interests and rights, the Regulation foresees in Article 27 that controllers must "implement appropriate technical and organizational measures, such as pseudonymisation" when they plan the means for processing personal data. This is what R. 2018/1725 refers to as "data protection by design." Article 27 further requires that controllers "implement appropriate technical and organisational measures for ensuring that, by default, only personal data which are necessary for each specific purpose of the processing are processed." The technical measures should be foreseen in the development of new information systems and in the creation of web tools.

For some, Article 27 might deliver the promises as outlined by the European Data Protection Supervisor almost a decade ago,[73] as it requires data controllers to use technical and organizational measures that by design and default implement the principles of data protection. However, Article 27 has inspired detractors from the privacy engineering community and from some lawmakers[74] for not offering guidance about privacy engineering in practice, or for exposing a tension between principles that seek to uphold the rights of individuals versus principles like data minimization that attempt to eliminate or reduce data storing and sharing. The language of Article 27 probably suffers from several drafting attempts, and does not suggest technical and organizational measures other than pseudonymization; and, in the name of technological neutrality, it avoids any mention of specific privacy engineering techniques, which only heightens the confusion over what it requires. Some solutions to these obvious tensions have been provided by the extensive guidance published by the European Union Agency for Cybersecurity (ENISA) about Privacy-Enhancing Technologies (PETs) and Privacy Management tools,[75] which tries to align with current privacy engineering methods and practices and proposes future solutions for information specialists. Commonly, privacy technology seeks on the one hand to minimize any disclosure of personal data to controllers and relies on cryptographic protocols to ensure this outcome, and on the other hand assumes that individuals will at one point lose control over their data and have to place some trust in controllers. In the latter case, privacy engineering builds tools that help users make good decisions about data sharing, while satisfying informed consent requirements (e.g., preference languages, cookie consent management).[76]

Automated decision-making and its ethical implications

Finally, we should touch upon algorithms, artificial intelligence (AI), and big data as they are all closely linked to data protection. Harari and other scholars and cultural commentators notice that governance and decisions made by algorithms, which were once made by people, increasingly shape important parts of our lives.[77] This includes bank loans, job searches and recruiting,[78] predictions about health,[79] surveillance, and even politicians' choices. As decisions based on AI technologies and machine learning become the norm, they raise critical questions about the right to challenge automated decision-making. The principles contained in the EU regulations on data protection include appropriate safeguards for individual rights, such as the right to information, the right to transparent decision-making, the ability to change the collected data, and the derived possibility to challenge the assumption that information processing decisions are all ethically right. It is currently difficult to see how this is conceivable in an automated context.[80] However, this should not be impossible,[81] and the fact that data protection rules recognize that decision-making based on algorithms is not neutral or simply technical is a positive advancement. Although we usually see privacy in terms of personal control over data or data processes, individuals should not be left alone to take the responsibility for processes that are difficult or even impossible to understand or manage.

Privacy is not just personal. It requires trusted stronger actors working on behalf of individuals to implement mechanisms about what is acceptable in terms of sharing personal data. We can learn a great deal from social media, as the majority of Internet users use online social networks at least daily or almost daily.[82] People are very willing to share insights and information about themselves on social media, yet they still require privacy.[83] A recent Eurobarometer enquiry shows that more than six in ten users are concerned about not having complete control over the information they provide online.[84] Respondents who feel they have partial or no control over the information they provide online were asked how concerned they were about this. Overall, 62% say they are concerned, with 16% who are very concerned. It is therefore understandable that the majority of social network users have tried to change the default privacy settings of their profile.[85]

Although experiences of privacy are certainly personal, privacy has to be defended as a common good. Privacy is not just a personal experience of border, security, and breaches, but a collective responsibility, a fundamental ethical principle. It is evident, therefore, that individuals' rights to control personal data and the processing of such data should be carefully addressed in the context of big data and AI. Control requires awareness of the use of personal data and real freedom of choice. These conditions, which are essential to the protection of fundamental rights, can be met through different legal and technical solutions, which we have examined in the previous pages. They should take into account the technological context, but even more, individuals' lack of knowledge. The complexity and obscurity of big data, algorithms, and AI applications should therefore prompt decision-makers to consider the notion of control, which goes beyond individual control. They should adopt a broader idea of control over the use of data, according to which individual control evolves in a more complex process of impact assessment[86] of the risks related to the use of data.[87]

The guidelines on big data issued by the Council of Europe in 2017[88] move in this direction and focus on the ethical and social consequences of data use for the protection of individuals with regard to automatic processing of personal data. Therefore, the challenge rests with all actors to embed the principles of transparency[89] in all automated decision-making processes and to make clear the terms by which decisions are taken. The recent "Guidelines for the ethical use of AI" and the "Recommendations for boosting European sustainability, growth and competitiveness"[90] by the European High-level Group have been described either as "an act of genius, or slow suicide."[91] European Union and AI experts remain divided about which rules are needed. On the one hand, European leaders are convinced that ethical guidelines will be enablers of innovation and consumers will demand "trustworthy AI" once it reaches the market, while critics believe that an ethics-first approach combined with restrictive regulations will prevent European competitiveness on the global market.[92] Webb points to the fact that the future of artificial intelligence is already controlled by just nine tech titans: Google, Microsoft, Amazon, Facebook, IBM, and Apple in the United States; and Baidu, Alibaba, and Tencent in China. These companies fund the majority of research and earn the lion's share of patents. While doing this, they gain access to personal data in ways that are not transparent. In Webb's view, Europe's attempt to solve the problem with strict regulations is a mistake, as AI is progressing so fast that any regulations created today will quickly become outdated. Policymakers should instead work towards setting AI on a path that defends democratic values.

Conclusion

Many international organizations and data protection authorities believe that there is a need for a platform to engage, share best practices, and raise awareness of the importance of ensuring strong safeguards for personal data. To this end, the European Data Protection Supervisor co-organizes, on a yearly basis, a workshop dedicated to the most common data protection issues (e.g., issues arising from the use of web services, such as tracking by third-party cookies), in which 40 different organizations participate. Issues arising from contractual arrangements with software providers, the challenges faced when contractual counterparts fail to implement the obligations they have committed to, or when they refuse to negotiate a data protection clause, are topics that the European Data Protection Supervisor has recently decided to investigate.[93] The costs and complexity of any negotiation with the big service providers[94] are felt as a common issue by international organizations and are an incentive to work together on this issue. Cooperation with national Data Protection Authorities and through the International Conference of Data Protection and Privacy Commissioners is also encouraged. At its 40th meeting in 2018,[95] the International Conference of Data Protection and Privacy Commissioners stated that machine learning technologies and artificial intelligence systems rely on the processing of large sets of personal data, and impact data protection and privacy. They also took into account the potential risks induced by the current trend of market concentration in the field of artificial intelligence, and stressed that artificial intelligence-powered systems, whose decisions cannot be explained, raise fundamental questions of accountability even beyond privacy and data protection law.

Undoubtedly, the current challenges triggered by the development of artificial intelligence and machine learning systems reinforce the need for the adoption of an international approach and standards, in order to ensure the promotion and protection of human rights in all digital developments at an international level. The Conference also endorsed guiding principles, among others the principle of fostering collective and joint responsibility, involving the whole chain of actors and stakeholders, for example with the development of collaborative standards and the sharing of best practices. This calls for common governance principles on artificial intelligence to be established, fostering concerted international efforts in this field, in order to ensure that AI development and use take place in accordance with ethics and respect human dignity. They must be created and enforced at an international level, since the development of artificial intelligence is a trans-border phenomenon and may affect all humanity.

None of the provisions and measures described in the chapter are silver bullets, and they come with problems and vulnerabilities, contradictions, and interpretations of what privacy means. They are likely to fuel the field for many years to come. Nevertheless, these approaches show that despite the current privacy models and practices, there is an international capability and intent to innovate technically as well as conceptually. After all, even more than through legal or technical compliance, we should ensure trust[96] in new technologies by showing respect for users' rights and freedoms.

Notes

1 The information and views set out in this article are those of the author and do not necessarily reflect the official opinion of the European Commission.
2 European Commission, 2019b, *Special Eurobarometer 487a, Summary, The General Data Protection Regulation, Fieldwork March 2019*, Survey requested by the European Commission, Directorate-General for Justice and Consumers and coordinated by the Directorate-General for Communication, p. 3: "Almost two-thirds of respondents (65%) who provide personal information online feel they have at least some control over this information."
3 Throughout the chapter "personal data" follows the definition in the R. 2018/1725. Personal data is "any information relating to an identified or identifiable natural person ('data subject'); an identifiable natural person is one who can be identified, directly or indirectly, in particular by reference to an identifier such as a name, an identification number, location data, an online identifier or to one or more factors specific to the physical, physiological, genetic, mental, economic, cultural or social identity of that natural person" (R. 2018/1725, art. 3(1)). It must also be noted that while in the GDPR, "Member States may provide for rules regarding the processing of personal data of deceased persons" (recital 27), R. 2018/1725 protects personal data only of living persons. For the sake of readability, the term "data subject" has frequently been replaced by "individual."
4 European Commission, 2017, *Communication from the Commission to the European Parliament and the Council, exchanging and protecting personal data in a globalised world – COM (2017) final*, viewed 5 October 2019, https://eur-lex.europa.eu/legal-content/EN/TXT/PDF/?uri=CELEX:52017DC0007&from=EN.
5 For information managers' interest in big data and its relevance for retention, see John McDonald & Valerie Léveillé, 2014, 'Whither the retention schedule in the era of big

data and open data?', *Records Management Journal*, vol. 24, no. 2, pp. 99–121. For educators' interest in big data see Richard Marciano et al., 2018, 'Archival records and
training in the age of big data', in *Re-envisioning the MLS: perspectives on the future of library
and information science education advances in librarianship*, vol. 44B, Emerald Publishing
Limited, Bingley, UK, pp. 179–199. Among the European organizations dealing with
big data and data protection, certainly the Council of Europe has done the groundwork:
Council of Europe, 2017, *Guidelines on the protection of individuals with regard to the processing of personal data in a world of big data*, viewed 5 October 2019, https://rm.coe.int/
16806ebe7a.

6 The legal basis on open data and reuse of public sector data for the European Union
member states is quite recent: 'Directive (EU) 2019/1024 of the European Parliament
and of the Council of 20 June 2019 on open data and the re-use of public sector
information', *Official Journal of the European Union*, L 172, 26.6.2019, pp. 56–83. For
what concerns the European institutions, the European Union Open Data Portal (EU
ODP) gives access to open data published by EU institutions and bodies. All the data
published on the catalogue are free to use and reuse for commercial or non-commercial
purposes: viewed 3 October 2019, https://data.europa.eu/euodp/en/home. For information management specialists' interest in open data, see Elizabeth Shepherd, 2013.
'Open government, open data: where is the records manager?', paper presented at the
ICA Annual Conference, Brussels, 23–24 November, viewed 3 October 2019, www.
ica.org/sites/default/files/AC2013_Shepherd%20paper.pdf.

7 Geoffrey Yeo, 2018, *Records, information and data: exploring the role of record-keeping in an
information culture*, Facet Publishing, London, p. 194.

8 Ehmann & Selmayr note that with the new data protection regulations, the motto often
used in data protection practice, "advancement through legal breach," has quickly
become "advancement through compliance." In Eugen Ehmann & Martin Selmayr,
2018, *Datenschutz-Grundverordnung*, 2nd edn, C.H. Beck, München, p. 144.

9 European Parliament & Council of the European Union, 2001a 'Regulation (EC) No
45/2001 of the European Parliament and of the Council of 18 December 2000 on the
protection of individuals with regard to the processing of personal data by the Community institutions and bodies and on the free movement of such data', *Official Journal of
the European Communities*, L 8/1.

10 Frans Smit, 2014, 'The metamorphosis of the records manager', *ARMA*, viewed 5
October 2019, www.slideshare.net/fpsmit/the-metamorphosis-of-the-records-mana
ger-arma-mrt-2014. Smit states that records managers should be able to participate in the
creation and implementation of information architecture. Their primary aim – to preserve information and keep this information accessible – requires that they should be
involved right from the start and should be able to speak the language of information
architects.

11 Yeo, 2018, pp. 68–69. Data Governance is defined through the European Commission
Digital Strategy, pp. 27–28, in European Commission, 2018a, *Communication to the
Commission. European Commission Digital Strategy. A digitally transformed, user-focused and
data-driven Commission, C (2018) 7118 final*, pp. 27–28, viewed 2 October 2019, https://
ec.europa.eu/info/sites/info/files/file_import/digitally-transformed_user-focused_data
-driven_commission_en.pdf.

12 Yeo, 2018, p. 69.

13 Ibid, p. 76.

14 For the many definitions of "data" and "information," please consult the International
Council on Archives' *Multilingual archival terminology*, viewed 2 October 2019, www.
ciscra.org/mat/mat. For the European Commission, "data is a reinterpretable representation of information in a formalized manner, suitable for communication, interpretation or processing." In European Commission, 2014, *Communication from the
Commission to the European Parliament, the Council, the European Economic and Social Committee and the Committee of the Regions, towards a thriving data-driven economy, COM(2014)
442 final*, p. 4, viewed 2 October 2019, https://eur-lex.europa.eu/legal-content/EN/

TXT/?qid=1404888011738&uri=CELEX:52014DC0442, quoting the definition from International Organization for Standardization, 2015, *Information technology – vocabulary ISO/IEC-2382*, viewed 2 October 2019, www.iso.org/obp/ui/#iso:std:iso-iec:2382:ed-1:v1:en.

15 Yeo, 2018, p. 116. At the European Commission, data governance is defined in the document *Data, information and knowledge management at the European Commission, C (2016) 6626 final*, viewed 2 October 2019, https://ec.europa.eu/transparency/regdoc/rep/3/2016/EN/C-2016-6626-F1-EN-MAIN.PDF.

16 Jürgen Habermas, 2015, *The lure of technocracy*, Polity Press, Cambridge, UK.

17 Zygmunt Bauman, 2004, *Europe: an unfinished adventure*, Polity Press, Cambridge, UK; Malden, MA.

18 According to Article 13 of the Treaty on European Union, the institutional framework comprises seven institutions: the European Parliament; the European Council; the Council of the European Union (simply called "the Council"); the European Commission; the Court of Justice of the European Union; the European Central Bank; and the Court of Auditors. In European Union, 2016, 'Consolidated version of the Treaty on European Union', *Official Journal of the European Union*, C 202, p. 22. The regulation is also applicable to other bodies such as the European External Action Service (EEAS); the European Economic and Social Committee (EESC); European Committee of the Regions (CoR); European Investment Bank (EIB); European Ombudsman; European Data Protection Supervisor (EDPS); and European Data Protection Board (EDPB). The complete list of all bodies and inter-institutional bodies, viewed 15 April 2020, https://europa.eu/european-union/about-eu/institutions-bodies_en.

19 Alexander Borek et al., 2014, *Total information risk management*, Morgan Kaufmann, Waltham, MA, cited in Yeo, 2018, p. 197.

20 In the chapter "The hour of European sovereignty," in JC Juncker, 2018, *State of the European Union*, p. 5, viewed 2 October 2019, https://ec.europa.eu/commission/sites/beta-political/files/soteu2018-speech_en_0.pdf. President Juncker states again the central role of the digital economy in his *Letter of Intent to President Antonio Tajani and to Chancellor Sebastian Kurz* prior to the European election of June 2019, p. 4, viewed 2 October 2019, https://ec.europa.eu/commission/sites/beta-political/files/soteu2018-letter-of-intent_en.pdf.

21 Juncker, 2018, p. 5. More on the EU role as global player in European Commission, 2017.

22 Ursula von der Leyen, 2019, 'Political guidelines for the next European Union 2019–2024, a Union that strives for more: my agenda for Europe', European Commission, viewed 2 October 2019, https://ec.europa.eu/commission/sites/beta-political/files/political-guidelines-next-commission_en.pdf.

23 Ibid, p. 13.

24 European Commission, 2015, *Communication from the Commission to the European Parliament, the Council, the European Economic and Social Committee and the Committee of the Regions. A digital Single Market Strategy for Europe, COM(2015) 192 final*, viewed 5 October 2019, https://Eurlex.europa.eu/legal-content/EN/TXT/?uri=COM%3A2015%3A192%3AFIN.

25 European Commission, 2018b, *Digital economy and society index report 2018. Human capital*, viewed 2 October 2019, https://ec.europa.eu/digital-single-market/en/human-capital.

26 Zygmunt Bauman, 2000b, *Liquid modernity*, Polity Press, Blackwell, Cambridge, UK.

27 Daniel Cohen, 1997, *Richesse du monde, pauvretés des nations*, p. 84, Flammarion, Paris, quoted in Zygmunt Bauman, 2000a, 'Time and space reunited', *Time & Society*, vol. 9, no. 2/3, p. 176.

28 Yeo, 2018, pp. 195–196.

29 "'Processing' means any operation or set of operations which is performed on personal data or on sets of personal data, whether or not by automated means, such as collection, recording, organization, structuring, storage, adaptation or alteration, retrieval,

consultation, use, disclosure by transmission, dissemination or otherwise making available, alignment or combination, restriction, erasure or destruction" (EU Regulation 2018/1725 art. 3(3)).

30 All codes of ethics of archivists, librarians, and record managers have chapters dedicated to the concepts of impartiality, fairness, equity, accuracy, transparency, and accountability, and the rights of stakeholders. Here are some eloquent examples:
International Council on Archives, 1996, *Code of ethics*, viewed 2 October 2019, www.ica.org/en/ica-code-ethics; the current International Federation of Library Associations and Institutions (IFLA), 2012, *IFLA Code of ethics*, IFLA, viewed 2 October 2019, www.ifla.org/publications/ifla-code-of-ethics-for-librarians-and-o ther-information-workers–short-version-; Archives and Records Association (UK and Ireland) (ARA), 2018, *Code of ethics*, ARA, viewed 5 October 2019, www.archives. org.uk/images/ARA_Documents/ARA_Code_Of_Ethics.pdf.
See also earlier studies, Thomas J Froehlich, 1997, *Survey and analysis of the major ethical and legal issues facing library and information services*, IFLA Publications, K.G. Saur, Munich.
It has to be noted that codes of ethics are called "codes of conduct" in the European Union General Data Protection Regulation. The GDPR has in fact given a new impetus to codes of conduct and encourages "the drawing up of codes of conduct intended to contribute to the proper application of the Regulation" (art. 40). The European Archives Group, a European Commission expert group composed of representatives from National Archives of European Union Member States, has drafted guidelines on the application of GDPR: European Archives Group, 2018, *Guidance on data protection for archive services*, viewed 2 October 2019, https://ec.europa.eu/info/files/guida nce-data-protection-archive-services_en. It must be stressed that these guidelines did not go through the approval procedure provided by art. 40 of the GDPR.

31 "'Controller' means the Union institution or body or the directorate-general or any other organisational entity which, alone or jointly with others, determines the purposes and means of the processing of personal data," art. 3(8) of R. 2018/1725. This role is closely linked to accountability and risk. Accountability and risk are two concepts familiar to information managers and associated with the role of "risk owner." The risk owner is the "person or entity with the accountability and authority to manage a risk." In International Organization for Standardization, 2018, *Information technology – Security techniques – Information security management systems – Overview and vocabulary*, ISO 27000:2018(en), term 3.71, International Organization for Standardization, Geneva. Risk is a key element in the R. 2018/1725, as it is mentioned 64 times. The controller shall be responsible for, and be able to demonstrate compliance with, paragraph 1 ("accountability"). Art. 4. Article 26, "responsibility of the controller," further speaks of risk linked to the processing of personal data and the "varying likelihood and severity for the rights and freedoms of natural persons."

32 Recital 20 and Section I, "Transparency and modalities," article 14 of R. 2018/1725.

33 It is interesting here to refer to the recently defined term of "transparency" for AI: "[Transparency] is closely linked with the principle of explicability and encompasses transparency of elements relevant to an AI system: the data, the system and the business models." European Commission Independent High-Level Expert Group on Artificial Intelligence, 2019b, *Ethics guidelines for trustworthy AI*, viewed 2 October 2019, https:// ec.europa.eu/digital-single-market/en/news/ethics-guidelines-trustworthy-ai. Transparency also plays a very important role in the "functionality of PETs, as well as [in] the underlying business models of the PETs developers/providers (which in many cases play a critical role in the privacy settings of a tool)". European Union Agency for Network and Information Security (ENISA), 2016b, *PETs controls matrix. A systematic approach for assessing online and mobile privacy tools. Final report*, p. 55, viewed 2 October 2019, www. enisa.europa.eu/publications/pets-controls-matrix/pets-controls-matrix-a-systematic-app roach-for-assessing-online-and-mobile-privacy-tools.

34 The European Data Protection Supervisor has developed the RACI matrix: "responsible, accountable, consulted, informed" – a framework for assigning tasks and

responsibilities. European Data Protection Supervisor, 2019b, *Accountability on the ground Part I: Records, registers and when to do Data Protection Impact Assessments*, v1.3, p. 4, viewed 5 October 2019, https://edps.europa.eu/sites/edp/files/publication/19-07-17_accounta bility_on_the_ground_part_i_en.pdf.

35 The Council has a dedicated webpage for all its records, viewed 28 April 2020: https:// www.consilium.europa.eu/en/general-secretariat/corporate-policies/data-protection/sea rch/; the European Parliament has a publicly available and accessible Register of Records of its data processing operations, viewed 28 April 2020: https://www.europarl. europa.eu/data-protect/index.do; for the European Commission, the Data Protection Officer's register is available at: https://ec.europa.eu/dpo-register/. The Registers of other European Union institutions and bodies are also published online, but have not been included here for reasons of brevity and space.

36 European Data Protection Supervisor, 2018b, *Position paper on role of Data Protection Officers of the EU institutions and bodies*, p. 15, viewed 2 October 2019, https://edps. europa.eu/sites/edp/files/publication/18–09–30_dpo_position_paper_en.pdf.

37 Articles 43, 44, and 45 R. 2018/1725 cover the designation, position, and tasks of the Data Protection Officer.

38 European Data Protection Supervisor, 2018b, p. 4.

39 "'Pseudonymization' means the processing of personal data in such a manner that the personal data can no longer be attributed to a specific data subject without the use of additional information; provided that such additional information is kept separately and is subject to technical and organisational measures to ensure that the personal data is not attributed to an identified or identifiable natural person," R. 2018/1725 art. 3(6). Unlike anonymization, pseudonymization preserves the correlation of different data relating to a person as well as the relation between different data records. Pseudonymized personal data maintain their nature of personal data, and are therefore subject to the provisions of the Regulation. The European Union Agency for Network and Information Security has conducted advanced research and has published useful recommendations: European Union Agency for Network and Information Security, 2018b, *Recommendations on shaping technology according to GDPR provisions. An overview on data pseudonymisation*, viewed 2 October 2019, www.enisa.europa.eu/publications/recommendations-on-shaping-tech nology-according-to-gdpr-provisions.

40 European Data Protection Supervisor, 2019b, p. 21.

41 In the foundational works of the Article 29 Working Party, data minimization is contextualized and its definition is interesting from an information management perspective: "data minimization: data processing systems are to be designed and selected in accordance with the aim of collecting, processing or using no personal data at all or as few personal data as possible." European Commission, Article 29 Data Protection Working Party, 2009, *The future of privacy*, WP 168, p. 14, viewed 3 October 2019, https://ec.europa.eu/justice/ article-29/documentation/opinion-recommendation/files/2009/wp 168_en.pdf.

42 Regulation 45/2001 – art. 4.1(e), European Parliament & Council of the European Union, 2001a, pp. 1–22.

43 Art. 4(1) point (e) of R. 2018/1725.

44 For staff medical files, the European Commission foresees elimination after 30 years from the date of termination of duties of the person concerned as per category 12.3.10 of the Commission Retention Lists: European Commission, 2019a, *Common Commission-level retention list for European Commission files. Second revision SEC(2019) 900*, viewed 2 October 2019, https://ec.europa.eu/info/sites/info/files/sec-2019-900_en.pdf and its annex: https://ec.europa.eu/transparency/regdoc/rep/2/2019/EN/SEC-2019-900-1-E N-ANNEX-1-PART-1.PDF.

45 Public access to documents of the Council of the European Union, the European Parliament, and the European Commission is regulated by Regulation 1049/2001, European Parliament & Council of the European Union, 2001b, 'Regulation (EC) No 1049/2001 of the European Parliament and of the Council of 30 May 2001 regarding public access to European Parliament, Council and Commission documents', *Official*

Journal of the European Communities, L 145, 31.5.2001, pp. 43–48. Other European Union institutions are regulated by specific decisions: Court of Justice of the European Union, 2020, 'Decision of the Court of Justice of the European Union, of 26 November 2019 concerning public access to documents held by the Court of Justice of the European Union in the exercise of its administrative functions', *Official Journal of the European Union*, C 45/02, pp. 2–7; European Central Bank, 2011, 'Decision of the European Central Bank of 9 May 2011 amending Decision ECB/2004/3 on public access to European Central Bank documents (ECB/2011/6)', *Official Journal of the European Union*, L 158/37; European Court of Auditors, 2009, 'Decision No 14–2009 amending Court Decision No 12–2005 regarding public access to Court documents', *Official Journal of the European Union* C 67/1.

Other bodies also have a very similar legal framework: European Economic and Social Committee, 2003, 'Decision of the European Economic and Social Committee of 1 July 2003 on public access to European Economic and Social Committee documents (2003/603/EC)', *Official Journal of the European Union*, L 205/19, of 14.08.2003; European Committee of the Regions, 2003, 'Bureau decision 64/2003 on public access to Committee of the Regions documents', *Official Journal of the European Union*, L 160, 28.6.2003, pp. 96–99.

46 Council of the European Union, 2003, 'Council Regulation (EC, Euratom) No 1700/2003 of 22 September 2003 amending Regulation (EEC, Euratom) No 354/83 concerning the opening to the public of the historical archives of the European Economic Community and the European Atomic Energy Community', *Official Journal of the European Union*, L 243/1, pp. 1–4.

47 International Council on Archives, 1996, article 7: "Archivists should respect both access and privacy, and act within the boundaries of relevant legislation."

48 The Charter of Fundamental Rights of the European Union considers both the protection of personal data and freedom of expression and information (which includes freedom to receive and impart information) as fundamental rights. European Union, 2012, 'Charter of fundamental rights of the European Union', *Official Journal of the European Union*, 26.10.2012, C 326/391; art.8 'Protection of Personal Data' and art. 11 'Freedom of Expression and information.'

49 European Data Protection Supervisor, 2019b, p. 21.

50 "Confidentiality" is defined in the European Commission as "the property that information is not disclosed to unauthorized individuals, entities or processes." In European Commission, 2015, 'Commission Decision (EU, Euratom) 2015/444 of 13 March 2015 on the security rules for processing EU classified information', *Official Journal of the European Union*, L 72/53, art. 34.

51 European Union Agency for Network and Information Security, 2018a, *Reinforcing trust and security in the area of electronic communications and online services. Sketching the notion of "state-of-the-art" for SMEs in security of personal data processing*, p. 8, viewed 3 October 2019, www.enisa.europa.eu/publications/reinforcing-trust-and-security-in-the-area-of-electronic-communications-and-online-services.

52 "'Processor' means a natural or legal person, public authority, agency or other body which processes personal data on behalf of the controller," R. 2018/1725, art. 3(12).

53 European Union Agency for Network and Information Security, 2016a, *Privacy enhancing technologies: evolution and state of the art. A community approach to PETs maturity assessment*, viewed 2 October 2019, www.enisa.europa.eu/publications/pets-evolution-and-state-of-the-art, p. 5. ENISA recognizes the lack of guidance about PETs, i.e. which PET to select for a given purpose and the need for a publicly available repository of PETs.

54 European Union Agency for Network and Information Security, 2018a, p. 16. "The cost of implementation is clearly linked to the state-of-the-art, as technical solutions also need to be applicable in practice. In that sense, costs should be interpreted both in terms of budget, as well as in terms of human resources required for implementation of specific security measures."

55 "'Personal data breach' means a breach of security leading to the accidental or unlawful destruction, loss, alteration, unauthorised disclosure of, or access to, personal data

transmitted, stored or otherwise processed," R. 2018/1725 art. 3(16). This definition is of paramount relevance for information managers, as the Regulation links data breaches to "integrity and confidentiality" (art. 4). Guidance to the European Union institutions can be found in European Data Protection Supervisor, 2018c, *Guidelines on personal data breach notification*, viewed 5 October 2019, https://edps.europa.eu/sites/edp/files/publica tion/18-12-14_edps_guidelines_data_breach_en.pdf.

56 The European Commission has published its retention schedules: European Commission, 2012, *Common Commission-level Retention List for European Commission files – First Revision Document SEC(2012)713*, viewed 2 October 2019, https://ec.europa.eu/info/sites/info/ files/sec-2012-713_en.pdf, with its latest revision SEC(2019) 900, https://ec.europa.eu/ info/sites/info/files/sec-2019-900_en.pdf, and its annex https://ec.europa.eu/transpa rency/regdoc/rep/2/2019/EN/SEC-2019-900-1-EN-ANNEX-1-PART-1.PDF.
The European Parliament, in its *Decision D(2013)44804*, established the framework for document management inside the institution, viewed 3 October 2019, www.europa rl.europa.eu/RegData/publications/des/2013/0001/EP-PE_DES(2013)0001_XL.pdf.
Unfortunately, the European Parliament Historical Archives have not published their retention schedules on their website. They are, however, accessible through the European Parliament public register of documents under several references. Each department has developed its own retention schedule, for example: European Parliament, 2008a, *Gestion des archives courantes et intermédiaires au sein du PE (Décision du Secrétaire général du 1.10.2008) Tableau de gestion des documents de la Direction Générale des politiques internes*, viewed 2 October 2019, www.europarl.europa.eu/RegData/publications/des/ 2013/0001/EP-PE_DES(2013)0001(PAR01)_XL.pdf; European Parliament, 2008c, *Gestion des archives courantes et intermédiaires au sein du PE (Décision du Secrétaire général du 1.10.2008) Tableau de gestion des documents de la Direction Générale personnel*, viewed 2 October 2019, www.europarl.europa.eu/RegData/publications/des/2013/0001/ EP-PE_DES(2013)0001(PAR02)_XL.pdf; European Parliament, 2008b, *Gestion des archives courantes et intermédiaires au sein du PE (Décision du Secrétaire général du 1.10.2008) Tableau de gestion des documents de la Direction Générale traduction*, viewed 2 October 2019, www.europarl.europa.eu/RegData/publications/des/2013/0001/EP-PE_DES(2013) 0001(PAR05)_XL.pdf.
While the decision to open the Council archives goes back to 1983 (Council of the European Union, 1983, 'Council Regulation (EEC, Euratom) 354/83 of 1 February 1983 concerning the opening to the public of the historical archives of the European Economic Community and the European Atomic Energy Community', *Official Journal of the European Communities*, L 43/1), the Council has yet to develop its retention policy.
Furthermore, the European Data Protection Supervisor has issued a special warning to European Union institutions regarding paper records and the need to use "special caution … if personal data is stored on paper due to its existence being hard to trace." European Data Protection Supervisor, 2018a, *Guidelines on the protection of personal data in IT governance and IT management of EU institutions*, p. 14, viewed 5 October 2019, http s://edps.europa.eu/sites/edp/files/publication/it_governance_management_en.pdf.

57 Data integrity is defined as "an obligation on organisations to take reasonable steps to ensure that data is reliable for its intended use, accurate, complete and current." In *Case C-362/14 Maximillian Schrems v Data Protection Commissioner, Opinion of Advocate General Bot*. The case makes reference to Commission Decision 2000/520, Annex I, on the adequacy of the protection provided by the safe harbour privacy principles and related frequently asked questions issued by the U.S. Department of Commerce, *Official Journal of the European Communities*, L 215, 25.8.2000, pp. 7–47.

58 European Commission Independent High-Level Expert Group on Artificial Intelligence, 2019b, p. 17. The European Union Agency for Cybersecurity defines data integrity as "the confirmation that data which has been sent, received, or stored are complete and unchanged." ENISA also makes reference at the ISO/IEC PDRT 13335–1 definition: "The property that data has not been altered or destroyed in an unauthorized manner."

ENISA Glossary, viewed 10 October 2019, www.enisa.europa.eu/topics/threat-risk-ma nagement/risk-management/current-risk/risk-management-inventory/glossary.
   For ISO, integrity is the "property of accuracy and completeness." In International Organization for Standardization, 2018, term 3.36.

59 For a thorough analysis of data subjects' information rights, correction rights, and restrictive rights see Mariusz Krzysztofek, 2018, *GDPR: General Data Protection Regulation (EU) 2016/679: post-reform personal data protection in the European Union*, pp. 135–178, European Monographs Series, vol. 107, Kluwer Law International, Alphen aan den Rijn, The Netherlands. For a very interesting point on erasure and the purpose of for- getting beyond privacy, see Viktor Mayer-Schönberger, 2018, 'Remembering (to) delete: forgetting beyond informational privacy', in F Thouvenin et al., *Remembering and forgetting in the digital age*, Springer, Cham, pp. 118–123, viewed 3 October 2019, http s://doi.org/10.1007/978-3-319-90230-2.

60 Ehmann & Selmayr, 2018, p. 425. German data protection law developed a new dimension in 1983 with the *Census Decision* of the German Federal Constitutional Court. In this decision, the Court held that the individual has a constitutional right to "informational self-determination." The decision prohibits the handling of personal data unless specific statutory authorization is given or the individual consents. In German Federal Constitutional Court, Abstract of the German Federal Constitutional Court's Judgment of 15 December 1983, 1 BvR 209, 269, 362, 420, 440, 484/83 [CODICES], viewed 2 October 2019, www.bundesverfassungsgericht.de/SharedDocs/Entscheidun gen/EN/1983/12/rs19831215_1bvr020983en.html. For a summary in English, see Kommers & Miller, 2012. Legislators have also tried to strengthen the bargaining power of individuals against data controllers. In Aurelia Tamò-Larrieux, 2018, *Designing for privacy and its legal framework*, Springer, Cham, viewed 5 October 2019, https://doi.org/ 10.1007/978-3-319-98624-1, p. 81.

61 Ehmann & Selmayr, 2018, pp. 426–427.

62 European Data Protection Supervisor, 2017b, *Guidance Paper on Articles 14–16 of the new Regulation 45/2001: transparency rights and obligations*, p. 14, viewed 10 October 2019, https://edps.europa.eu/sites/edp/files/publication/18-01-15_guidance_paper_arts_en_1. pdf.

63 European Data Protection Supervisor, 2017a, *Opinion 5/2017, Upgrading data protection rules for EU institutions and bodies*, viewed 5 October 2019, https://edps.europa.eu/sites/ edp/files/publication/17-03-15_regulation_45-2001_en.pdf, p. 12.

64 Access to data is a quite well-known right, as demonstrated by the fact that 65% of respondents have heard of this right. In European Commission, 2019b, p. 3.

65 Under R. 2018/1725, the processing of personal data is legitimate only if at least one of the specific circumstances listed in article 5 applies. For the European Union institutions article 5(a) the "public interest" is the first and most used criterion for lawful processing. The European Union has in fact the obligation to serve its citizens as per article 13 of the Treaty. In European Union, 2016, 'Consolidated version of the Treaty on European Union', *Official Journal of the European Union*, C 202, p. 22.

66 Controllers should design their systems in such a way that access to personal data is limited on a strict need-to-know basis. Personal data must be protected against access by unauthorized persons at all stages –whether at rest or in transit, using encryption where appropriate. In European Data Protection Supervisor, 2019c, *Accountability on the ground, Part II, Data Protection Impact Assessments & prior consultation*, viewed 10 October 2019, https://edps.europa.eu/sites/edp/files/publication/19-07-17_accountability_on_the_ ground_part_ii_en.pdf, p. 15. Also reflected by the European Commission, Independent High-Level Expert Group on Artificial Intelligence, 2019b, p. 17.

67 Court of Justice of the European Union, 2014, *Judgement of the Court Grand Chamber, Case C-131/12, Google Spain SL and Google Inc. v Agencia Española de Protección de Datos (AEPD) and Mario Costeja González. Request for a preliminary ruling from the Audiencia Nacional.*

68 Court of Justice of the European Union, 2019, *Judgment of the Court (Grand Chamber), 24 September 2019, (Reference for a preliminary ruling – Personal data – Protection of individuals with regard to the processing of such data – Directive 95/46/EC – Regulation (EU) 2016/679 – Internet search engines – Processing of data on web pages – Territorial scope of the right to de-referencing), in Case C-507/17, Request for a preliminary ruling under Article 267 TFEU from the Conseil d'État (Council of State, France), made by decision of 19 July 2017, received at the Court on 21 August 2017, in the proceedings Google LLC, successor in law to Google Inc., vs. Commission nationale de l'informatique et des libertés (CNIL).*

69 Council of Europe, 2018, *Case law of the European Court of Human Rights concerning the protection of personal data,* T-PD(2018)15, viewed 5 October 2019, https://rm.coe.int/t-pd-2018-15-case-law-on-data-protection-may2018-en/16808b2d36. Particularly interesting is the chapter on 'Balancing data protection with freedom of expression and the right to information,' and the tension expressed by some public authorities in the Member States regarding the difficulty of striking a balance between art. 8 and art. 11 of the Charter of Fundamental Rights of the European Union.

70 European Court of Human Rights, 2016, *Magyar Helsinki Bizottság v. Hungary[GC], No. 18030/11, Judgement of 8 November 2016,* para. 162.

71 R. 2018/1725 Article 10(1)

72 R. 2018/1725 Article 10(2)(j).

73 Peter Hastinx, 2010, 'Privacy by design: delivering the promises', *Identity in the Information Society,* vol. 3, pp. 253–255. For the groundwork on privacy by design see Ann Cavoukian, 2010, 'Privacy by design: the definitive workshop', *Identity in the Information Society,* vol. 3, no. 2 (August), pp. 247–251.
    The European Commission divulges article 25 of the GDPR – which corresponds exactly to art. 27 of R. 2018/1725 – to the users, viewed 3 October 2019, https://ec.europa.eu/info/law/law-topic/data-protection/reform/rules-business-and-organisations/obligations/what-does-data-protection-design-and-default-mean_en.

74 Ehmann & Selmayr, 2018, p. 549.

75 John Sabo, 2017, *Privacy engineering – tools and professional practice,* Organization for the Advancement of Structured Information Standards (OASIS), viewed 2 October 2019, www.oasis-open.org/committees/download.php/60849/.

76 The European Data Protection Supervisor has issued guidelines to EU institutions on the use of web services and tools, with a large portion dedicated to consent for cookies, server-side processing, tracking, and profiling. European Data Protection Supervisor, 2016, *Guidelines on the protection of personal data processed through web services provided by EU institutions,* viewed 5 October 2019, https://edps.europa.eu/sites/edp/files/publication/16-11-07_guidelines_web_services_en.pdf.

77 Yuval Noah Harari, 2019, *21 Lessons for the 21st century,* Penguin Vintage, London, pp. 85–88. Pasquale points to the key issue of algorithms and "black boxes," which contain them and are only accessible to very few people. This calls for effective oversight and greater transparency over automated decision-making. Frank Pasquale, 2015, *The black box society,* Harvard University Press, Cambridge, p. 191.

78 Jeffrey Dastin, 2018, 'Amazon scraps secret AI recruiting tool that showed bias against women', *Reuters,* October 10, viewed 5 October 2019, www.reuters.com/article/us-amazon-com-jobs-automation-insight/amazon-scraps-secret-ai-recruiting-tool-that-showed-bias-against-women-idUSKCN1MK08G.

79 Sharona Hoffman makes an interesting point on computerization, which, contrary to what it had promised, has not resolved the data accuracy problem, but instead has created many new error vulnerabilities. In Sharona Hoffman, 2016, *Electronic health records and medical big data,* Cambridge University Press, New York, p. 23.

80 It is even more perilous if we consider that the discrimination might not only target groups of populations, but "in the twenty-first century we might face a growing problem of individual discrimination." In Harari, 2019, p. 84.

81 Bryce Goodman & Seth Flaxman, 2017, 'European Union regulations on algorithmic decision-making and a "Right to Explanation"', ICML Workshop on Human

Interpretability in Machine Learning, *AI Magazine*, p. 50, viewed 10 October 2019, https://doi.org/10.1609/aimag.v38i3.2741.

82 A comparison of these results to those from 2015 shows the use of online social networks has increased considerably – and in particular daily or almost daily use. In European Commission, 2019b, p. 10.

83 More on this topic in Andrew D Selbst & Julia Powles, 2017, 'Meaningful information and the right to explanation', *International Data Privacy Law*, vol. 7, no. 4, pp. 233–242, viewed 5 October 2019, https://doi.org/10.1093/idpl/ipx022https://academic.oup.com/idpl/article/7/4/233/4762325.

84 European Commission, 2019b, pp. 13–14.

85 Ibid, p. 18.

86 R. 2018/1725 requires controllers to carry out a data protection impact assessment prior to the processing, when the processing "is likely to result in a high risk to the rights and freedoms of natural persons" (article 39(1)). Impact assessments are important tools for accountability, as they help controllers not only to comply with requirements of the Regulation but also to demonstrate compliance. Their aim is to identify and to assess the risk that could arise for the individual (as citizen, client, patient, etc.) from a new type of processing. If the nature of the data or the way of processing is likely to create a high risk for data subjects, an assessment is required. The European Data Protection Supervisor has published a list of the kind of processing operations that are subject to the requirement for a data protection impact assessment and also of those that are not: European Data Protection Supervisor, 2019a, *Decision of the European Data Protection Supervisor of 16 July 2019 on DPIA Lists issued under articles 39(4) and (5) of Regulation (EU) 2018/1725*, viewed 5 October 2019, https://edps.europa.eu/sites/edp/files/publication/19-07-16_edps_dpia_list_en.pdf; European Data Protection Supervisor, 2019b.

87 Mantelero proposes a technologically neutral model, which is a rights-based and values-oriented model. Alessandro Mantelero, 2018, 'AI and big data: a blueprint for a human rights, social and ethical impact assessment', *Computer Law & Security Review*, no. 34, pp. 754–772.

88 See Council of Europe, 2017.

89 Principle no. 3 "Artificial intelligence systems transparency and intelligibility should be improved … by investing in scientific research on explainable artificial intelligence; … by promoting algorithmic transparency and the auditability of systems, while ensuring meaningfulness of the information provided, and by guaranteeing the right to informational self-determination; notably by ensuring that individuals are always informed appropriately when they are interacting directly with an artificial intelligence system or when they provide personal data to be processed by such systems. … providing adequate information on the purpose and effects of artificial intelligence systems in order to verify continuous alignment with expectation of individuals and to enable overall human control on such systems." International Conference of Data Protection and Privacy Commissioners, Brussels, October 2018, *Declaration on Ethics and Data Protection in Artificial Intelligence*, viewed 5 October 2019, https://icdppc.org/wp-content/uploads/2018/10/20180922_ICDPPC-40th_AI-Declaration_ADOPTED.pdf. Transparency is also one of the seven key requirements for trustworthy AI in European Commission, Independent High-Level Expert Group on Artificial Intelligence, 2019b.

90 European Commission, Independent High-Level Expert Group on Artificial Intelligence, 2019a, *Policy and investment recommendations for trustworthy AI*, p. 6, viewed 2 October 2019, https://ec.europa.eu/digital-single-market/en/news/policy-and-investment-recommendations-trustworthy-artificial-intelligence.

91 Janosch Delcker, 2019, 'Europe silver bullet in global AI battle: ethics', *Politico*, March 14, pp. 14–15.

92 Margrethe Vestager, European Commissioner for Competition, supports European tech firms' complaints that the lack of access to data is putting them at a disadvantage to global competitors. She affirms that "it is not enough that you want to do AI in a way that corresponds to basic values – you also need the raw material." In Delcker, 2019.

Philippe Legrain and Hosuk Lee-Makiyama explore the possibilities offered by AI for better EU policy-making and for monitoring legal compliance, also in the field of data protection. In Philippe Legrain & Hosuk Lee-Makiyama, 2019, *Ever cleverer Union. How AI could help EU institutions become more capable, competent, cost-effective and closer to citizens*, p. 34, viewed 5 March 2020, www.opennetwork.net/ever-cleverer-union/; Amy Webb, 2019, *The big nine: how the tech titans and their thinking machines could warp humanity*, PublicAffairs, New York.

93 European Data Protection Supervisor, 2019d, *EDPS investigates contractual agreements concerning software used by EU institutions*, Press Release, EDPS/2019/02.

94 To this end, the International Conference established a permanent working group. This working group is in charge of promoting understanding of and respect for the principles of the Declaration by all relevant parties involved in the development of artificial intelligence systems, including governments and public authorities, standardization bodies, artificial intelligence systems designers, providers and researchers, companies, citizens, and end users of artificial intelligence systems. The Conference thus endeavours to proactively support an active public debate on digital ethics, aiming at the creation of a strong ethical culture and personal awareness in this field.

95 International Conference of Data Protection and Privacy Commissioners, 2018, Declaration on ethics and data protection in Artificial Intelligence, p. 2.

96 The Independent High-level Expert Group notes that although "'Trust' is usually not a property ascribed to machines, this document [the Ethics Guidelines for Trustworthy AI] aims to stress the importance of being able to trust not only in the fact that AI systems are legally compliant, ethically adherent and robust, but also that such trust can be ascribed to all people and processes involved in the AI system's life cycle." European Commission Independent High-Level Expert Group on Artificial Intelligence, *Policy and investment recommendations for trustworthy AI*, p. 38, viewed 2 October 2019, https://ec.europa.eu/digital-single-market/en/news/policy-and-investment-recommendations-trustworthy-artificial-intelligence.

Bibliography

Archives & Records Association (UK and Ireland) 2018, *Code of ethics*, viewed 2 October 2019, www.archives.org.uk/images/ARA_Documents/ARA_Code_Of_Ethics.pdf.

Bauman, Z 2000a, 'Time and space reunited', *Time & Society*, vol. 9, no. 2/3, pp. 171–185.

Bauman, Z 2000b, *Liquid modernity*, Polity Press, Cambridge.

Bauman, Z 2004, *Europe, an unfinished adventure*, Polity Press, Cambridge.

Borek, A, Parlikad, AK, Webb, J & Woodall, P 2014, *Total information risk management*, Morgan Kaufmann, Waltham, MA.

Cavoukian, A 2010, 'Privacy by design: the definitive workshop', *Identity in the Information Society*, vol. 3, no. 2 (August), pp. 247–251.

Cohen, Daniel 1997, *Richesse du monde, pauvretés des nations*, Flammarion, Paris.

Council of Europe 2017, *Guidelines on the protection of individuals with regard to the processing of personal data in a world of big data*, viewed 5 October 2019, https://rm.coe.int/16806ebe7a.

Dastin, J 2018, 'Amazon scraps secret AI recruiting tool that showed bias against women', *Reuters*, October 10, viewed 5 October 2019, www.reuters.com/article/us-amazon-com-jobs-automation-insight/amazon-scraps-secret-ai-recruiting-tool-that-showed-bias-against-women-idUSKCN1MK08G.

Delcker, J 2019, 'Europe silver bullet in global AI battle: ethics', *Politico*, March 14, viewed 16 May 2020, www.politico.eu/article/europe-silver-bullet-global-ai-battle-ethics/.

Ehmann, E & Selmayr, M 2018, *Datenschutz-Grundverordnung*, 2nd edn, C.H. Beck, München.

European Archives Group 2018, *Guidance on data protection for archive services*, viewed 2 October 2019, https://ec.europa.eu/info/files/guidance-data-protection-archive-services_en.

European Commission 2011, *Special Eurobarometer 359. Attitudes on data protection and electronic identity in the European Union. Report.* Fieldwork: November–December 2010, viewed 2 October 2019, http://ec.europa.eu/commfrontoffice/publicopinion/archives/ebs/ebs_359_en.pdf.

European Commission 2012, *Common Commission-level retention list for European Commission files – First Revision SEC(2012)713*, viewed 2 October 2019, https://ec.europa.eu/info/sites/info/files/sec-2012-713_en.pdf.

European Commission 2014, *Communication from the Commission to the European Parliament, the Council, the European Economic and Social Committee and the Committee of the Regions, towards a thriving data-driven economy, COM(2014) 442, final*, viewed 2 October 2019, https://eur-lex.europa.eu/legal-content/EN/TXT/?qid=1404888011738&uri=CELEX:52014DC0442.

European Commission 2015, *Communication from the Commission to the European Parliament, the Council, the European Economic and Social Committee and the Committee of the Regions. A digital Single Market Strategy for Europe, COM(2015) 192 final*, viewed 5 October 2019, https://eur-lex.europa.eu/legal-content/EN/TXT/?uri=COM%3A2015%3A192%3AFIN.

European Commission 2016, *Communication to the Commission. Data, information and knowledge management at the European Commission, C(2016) 6626 final*, viewed 2 October 2019, https://ec.europa.eu/transparency/regdoc/rep/3/2016/EN/C-2016-6626-F1-EN-MAIN.PDF.

European Commission 2017, *Communication from the Commission to the European Parliament and the Council, exchanging and protecting personal data in a globalised world, COM(2017) final*, viewed 5 October 2019, https://eur-lex.europa.eu/legal-content/EN/TXT/PDF/?uri=CELEX:52017DC0007&from=EN.

European Commission 2018a, *Communication to the Commission. European Commission Digital Strategy. A digitally transformed, user-focused and data-driven Commission, C (2018) 7118 final*, viewed 2 October 2019, https://ec.europa.eu/info/sites/info/files/file_import/digitally-transformed_user-focused_data-driven_commission_en.pdf.

European Commission 2018b, *Digital economy and society index report 2018. Human capital*, viewed 2 October 2019, https://ec.europa.eu/digital-single-market/en/human-capital.

European Commission 2019a, *Common Commission-level retention list for European Commission files. Second revision SEC(2019) 900*, viewed 2 October 2019, https://ec.europa.eu/info/sites/info/files/sec-2019-900_en.pdf and its annex: https://ec.europa.eu/transparency/regdoc/rep/2/2019/EN/SEC-2019-900-1-EN-ANNEX-1-PART-1.PDF.

European Commission 2019b, *Special Eurobarometer 487a, summary, the General Data Protection Regulation, fieldwork March 2019*, viewed 2 October 2019, https://ec.europa.eu/commfrontoffice/publicopinionmobile/index.cfm/Survey/getSurveyDetail/surveyKy/2222.

European Commission, Article 29 Data Protection Working Party 2009, *The future of privacy*, WP 168, p. 14, viewed 3 October 2019, https://ec.europa.eu/justice/article-29/documentation/opinion-recommendation/files/2009/wp168_en.pdf.

European Commission, Independent High-Level Expert Group on Artificial Intelligence 2019a, *Policy and investment. Recommendations for trustworthy AI*, viewed 2 October 2019, https://ec.europa.eu/digital-single-market/en/news/policy-and-investment-recommendations-trustworthy-artificial-intelligence.

European Commission, Independent High-Level Expert Group on Artificial Intelligence 2019b, *Ethics guidelines for trustworthy AI*, viewed 2 October 2019, https://ec.europa.eu/digital-single-market/en/news/ethics-guidelines-trustworthy-ai.

European Data Protection Supervisor 2016, *Guidelines on the protection of personal data processed through web services provided by EU institutions*, viewed 2 October 2019, https://edps.europa.eu/sites/edp/files/publication/16-11-07_guidelines_web_services_en.pdf.

European Data Protection Supervisor 2017a, *Opinion 5/2017, Upgrading data protection rules for EU institutions and bodies*, viewed 5 October 2019, https://edps.europa.eu/sites/edp/files/publication/17-03-15_regulation_45-2001_en.pdf.

European Data Protection Supervisor 2017b, *Guidance Paper on Articles 14–16 of the new Regulation 45/2001: transparency rights and obligations*, viewed 10 October 2019, https://edps.europa.eu/sites/edp/files/publication/18-01-15_guidance_paper_arts_en_1.pdf.

European Data Protection Supervisor 2018a, *Guidelines on the protection of personal data in IT governance and IT management of EU institutions*, viewed 2 October 2019, https://edps.europa.eu/sites/edp/files/publication/it_governance_management_en.pdf.

European Data Protection Supervisor 2018b, *Position paper on role of Data Protection Officers of the EU institutions and bodies*, viewed 2 October 2019, https://edps.europa.eu/sites/edp/files/publication/18-09-30_dpo_position_paper_en.pdf.

European Data Protection Supervisor 2018c, *Guidelines on personal data breach notification*, viewed 5 October 2019, https://edps.europa.eu/sites/edp/files/publication/18-12-14_edps_guidelines_data_breach_en.pdf.

European Data Protection Supervisor 2019a, *Decision of the European Data Protection Supervisor of 16 July 2019 on DPIA Lists issued under articles 39(4) and (5) of Regulation (EU) 2018/1725*, viewed 2 October 2019, https://edps.europa.eu/sites/edp/files/publication/19-07-16_edps_dpia_list_en.pdf.

European Data Protection Supervisor 2019b, *Accountability on the ground Part I: records, registers and when to do Data Protection Impact Assessments*, v1.3, viewed 5 October 2019, https://edps.europa.eu/sites/edp/files/publication/19-07-17_accountability_on_the_ground_part_i_en.pdf.

European Data Protection Supervisor 2019c, *Accountability on the ground, Part II, Data Protection Impact Assessments & prior consultation*, viewed 10 October 2019, https://edps.europa.eu/sites/edp/files/publication/19-07-17_accountability_on_the_ground_part_ii_en.pdf.

European Data Protection Supervisor 2019d, *EDPS investigates contractual agreements concerning software used by EU institutions*, Press Release, EDPS/2019/02.

European Union Agency for Network and Information Security 2016a, *Privacy enhancing technologies: evolution and state of the art. A community approach to PETs maturity assessment*, viewed 2 October 2019, www.enisa.europa.eu/publications/pets-evolution-and-state-of-the-art.

European Union Agency for Network and Information Security 2016b, *PETs controls matrix. A systematic approach for assessing online and mobile privacy tools. Final report*, viewed 2 October 2019, www.enisa.europa.eu/publications/pets-controls-matrix/pets-controls-matrix-a-systematic-approach-for-assessing-online-and-mobile-privacy-tools.

European Union Agency for Network and Information Security 2018a, *Reinforcing trust and security in the area of electronic communications and online services. Sketching the notion of "state-of-the-art" for SMEs in security of personal data processing*, viewed 3 October 2019, www.enisa.europa.eu/publications/reinforcing-trust-and-security-in-the-area-of-electronic-communications-and-online-services.

European Union Agency for Network and Information Security 2018b, *Recommendations on shaping technology according to GDPR provisions. An overview on data pseudonymisation*, viewed 2 October 2019, www.enisa.europa.eu/publications/recommendations-on-shaping-technology-according-to-gdpr-provisions.

Froehlich, TJ 1997, *Survey and analysis of the major ethical and legal issues facing library and information services*, IFLA Publications, K.G. Saur, Munich.

Goodman, B & Flaxman, S 2017, 'European Union regulations on algorithmic decision-making and a "Right to Explanation"', paper presented at 2016 ICML Workshop on Human Interpretability in Machine Learning, New York, AI Magazine, vol. 38, no. 50, pp. 50–57.

Habermas, J 2015, The lure of technocracy, Polity Press, Cambridge, UK.

Harari, YN 2019, 21 Lessons for the 21st Century, Penguin Vintage, London.

Hastinx, P 2010, 'Privacy by design: delivering the promises', Identity in the Information Society, vol. 3, pp. 253–255.

Hoffman, S 2016, Electronic health records and medical big data, Cambridge University Press, New York.

International Conference of Data Protection and Privacy Commissioners 2018, Declaration on ethics and data protection in Artificial Intelligence, viewed 2 October 2019, https://icdppc.org/wp-content/uploads/2018/10/20180922_ICDPPC-40th_AI-Declaration_ADOPTED.pdf.

International Council on Archives 1996, Code of ethics, International Council on Archives, viewed 2 October 2019, www.ica.org/sites/default/files/ICA_1996-09-06_code%20of%20ethics_EN.pdf.

International Council on Archives 2012, Multilingual archival terminology, viewed 2 October 2019, www.ciscra.org/mat/mat.

International Federation of Library Associations and Institutions (IFLA) 2012, IFLA Code of Ethics for librarians and other information workers, viewed 2 October 2019, IFLA, www.ifla.org/publications/ifla-code-of-ethics-for-librarians-and-other-information-workers–short-version-.

International Organization for Standardization 2015, Information technology – vocabulary, ISO/IEC 2382:2015(en), International Organization for Standardization, Geneva, viewed 2 October 2019, www.iso.org/obp/ui/#iso:std:iso-iec:2382:ed-1:v1:en.

International Organization for Standardization 2018, Information technology – Security techniques – Information security management systems – Overview and vocabulary. ISO/IEC 27000:2018(en), International Organization for Standardization, Geneva.

Juncker, JC 2018, State of the European Union, European Commission, viewed 2 October 2019, https://ec.europa.eu/commission/sites/beta-political/files/soteu2018-speech_en_0.pdf.

Juncker, JC 2019, Letter of intent to President Antonio Tajani and to Chancellor Sebastian Kurz, European Commission, viewed 2 October 2019, https://ec.europa.eu/commission/sites/beta-political/files/soteu2018-letter-of-intent_en.pdf.

Kommers, DP & Miller, RA 2012, The constitutional jurisprudence of the Federal Republic of Germany, 3rd edn, Duke University Press, Durham.

Krzysztofek, M 2018, GDPR: General Data Protection Regulation (EU) 2016/679: Post-Reform Personal Data Protection in the European Union, European Monographs Series, vol. 107, Kluwer Law International, Alphen aan den Rijn, The Netherlands.

Legrain, P & Makiyama, HL 2019, Ever cleverer Union. How AI could help EU institutions become more capable, competent, cost-effective and closer to citizens, p. 34, viewed 5 March 2020, www.opennetwork.net/ever-cleverer-union/.

Mantelero, A 2018, 'AI and big data: a blueprint for a human rights, social and ethical impact assessment', Computer Law & Security Review, no. 34, pp. 754–772.

Marciano, R, Lemieux, V, Hedges, M, Esteva, M, Underwood, W, Kurtz, M & Conrad, M 2018, 'Archival records and training in the age of big data', in Re-envisioning the MLS: perspectives on the future of library and information science education advances in librarianship, vol. 44B, Emerald Publishing, Bingley, UK.

Mayer-Schönberger, V 2018, 'Remembering (to) delete: forgetting beyond informational privacy', pp. 118–123, in Thouvenin, F, Hettich, P, Burkert, H & Gasser, U, Remembering *and forgetting in the digital age*, Springer, Cham, viewed 3 October 2019, https://doi.org/10.1007/978-3-319-90230-2.

McDonald, J & Léveillé, V 2014, 'Whither the retention schedule in the era of big data and open data?', *Records Management Journal*, vol. 24, no. 2, pp. 99–121.

Pasquale, F 2015, *The black box society*, Harvard University Press, Cambridge.

Sabo, J 2017, *Privacy engineering – tools and professional practice*, Organization for the Advancement of Structured Information Standards (OASIS), viewed 2 October 2019, www.oasis-open.org/committees/download.php/60849.

Selbst, AD & Powles, J 2017, 'Meaningful information and the right to explanation', *International Data Privacy Law*, vol. 7, no. 4, viewed 5 October 2019, https://doi.org/10.1093/idpl/ipx022.

Shepherd, E 2013, '*Open government, open data: where is the records manager?*' paper presented at the ICA Annual Conference, Brussels, 23–24 November, viewed 3 October 2019, www.ica.org/sites/default/files/AC2013_Shepherd%20paper.pdf.

Smit, F 2014, 'The metamorphosis of the records manager', *ARMA*, viewed 5 October 2019, www.slideshare.net/fpsmit/the-metamorphosis-of-the-records-manager-arma-mrt-2014.

Tamò-Larrieux, A 2018, *Designing for privacy and its legal framework*, Springer, Cham, viewed 5 October 2019, https://doi.org/10.1007/978-3-319-98624-1.

von der Leyen, U 2019, 'Political guidelines for the next European Union 2019–2024, a Union that strives for more: my agenda for Europe', European Commission, viewed 2 October 2019, https://ec.europa.eu/commission/sites/beta-political/files/political-guidelines-next-commission_en.pdf.

Webb, A 2019, *The big nine: how the tech titans and their thinking machines could warp humanity*, PublicAffairs, New York.

Yeo, G 2018, *Records, information and data: exploring the role of record-keeping in an information culture*, Facet Publishing, London.

Legislation

Council of Europe 2018, *Case Law of the European Court of Human Rights concerning the protection of personal data*, T-PD(2018)15, viewed 5 October 2019, https://rm.coe.int/t-pd-2018-15-case-law-on-data-protection-may2018-en/16808b2d36.

Council of the European Union 1983, 'Council Regulation (EEC, Euratom) 354/83 of 1 February 1983 concerning the opening to the public of the historical archives of the European Economic Community and the European Atomic Energy Community', *Official Journal of the European Communities*, L 43/1.

Council of the European Union 2003, 'Council Regulation (EC, Euratom) No 1700/2003 of 22 September 2003 amending Regulation (EEC, Euratom) No 354/83 concerning the opening to the public of the historical archives of the European Economic Community and the European Atomic Energy Community', *Official Journal of the European Union*, L 243/1, pp. 1–4.

European Central Bank 2011, 'Decision of the European Central Bank of 9 May 2011 amending Decision ECB/2004/3 on public access to European Central Bank documents (ECB/2011/6)', *Official Journal of the European Union*, L 158/37.

European Commission 2000, 'Commission Decision 2000/520, of 26 July 2000 on the adequacy of the protection provided by the safe harbour privacy principles and related frequently asked questions issued by the U.S. Department of Commerce, *Official Journal of the European Communities*, L 215, 25.8.2000, pp. 7–47.

European Commission 2015, 'Commission Decision (EU, Euratom) 2015/444 of 13 March 2015 on the security rules for processing EU classified information', *Official Journal of the European Union*, L 72/53.

European Committee of the Regions 2003, 'Bureau Decision 64/2003 on public access to Committee of the Regions documents', *Official Journal of the European Union*, L 160, 28.6.2003, pp. 96–99, viewed 2 October 2019, https://eur-lex.europa.eu/legal-content/EN/TXT/?uri=uriserv:OJ.L_.2003.160.01.0096.01.ENG&toc=OJ:L:2003:160:TOC.

European Court of Auditors 2009, 'Decision No 14–2009 amending Court Decision No 12–2005 regarding public access to Court documents', *Official Journal of the European Union*, C 67/1.

European Court of Human Rights 2016, *Magyar Helsinki Bizottság v. Hungary[GC], No. 18030/11, Judgement of 8 November 2016*, viewed 3 October 2019, https://hudoc.echr.coe.int/eng#%22itemid%22:%22001-167828%22.

European Economic and Social Committee 2003, 'Decision of the European Economic and Social of 1 July 2003 on public access to European Economic and Social Committee documents (2003/603/EC)', *Official Journal of the European Union*, L 205/19, of 14.08.2003, viewed 2 October 2019, www.eesc.europa.eu/resources/docs/decision-on-public-access-to-eesc-documents.pdf.

European Parliament 2008a, *Décision du Secrétaire general. Gestion des archives courantes et inter-médiaires au sein du PE. Tableau de gestion des documents de la Direction Générale des politiques internes*, viewed 2 October 2019, www.europarl.europa.eu/RegData/publications/des/2013/0001/EP-PE_DES(2013)0001(PAR01)_XL.pdf.

European Parliament 2008b, *Décision du Secrétaire general. Gestion des archives courantes et intermédiaires au sein du PE. Tableau de gestion des documents de la Direction Générale traduction*, viewed 2 October 2019, www.europarl.europa.eu/RegData/publications/des/2013/0001/EP-PE_DES(2013)0001(PAR05)_XL.pdf.

European Parliament 2008c, *Décision du Secrétaire general. Gestion des archives courantes et inter-médiaires au sein du PE. Tableau de gestion des documents de la Direction Générale personnel*, viewed 2 October 2019, www.europarl.europa.eu/RegData/publications/des/2013/0001/EP-PE_DES(2013)0001(PAR02)_XL.pdf.

European Parliament 2013, *Decision D(2013)44804*, viewed 3 October 2019, www.europarl.europa.eu/RegData/publications/des/2013/0001/EP-PE_DES(2013)0001_XL.pdf.

European Parliament & Council of the European Union 2001a, 'Regulation (EC) No 45/2001 of the European Parliament and of the Council of 18 December 2000 on the protection of individuals with regard to the processing of personal data by the Community institutions and bodies and on the free movement of such data', *Official Journal of the European Communities*, L 8/1, pp. 1–22.

European Parliament & Council of the European Union 2001b, 'Regulation 1049/2001 of the European Parliament and of the Council of 30 May 2001 regarding public access to European Parliament, Council and Commission documents,' *Official Journal of the European Communities*, L 145/43, pp. 43–48.

European Union 2012, 'Charter of fundamental rights of the European Union,' *Official Journal of the European Union*, C 326, 26.10.2012, pp. 391–407.

European Union 2016, 'Consolidated version of the Treaty on European Union,' *Official Journal of the European Union*, C 202.

European Union 2019, 'Directive (EU) 2019/1024 of the European Parliament and of the Council of 20 June 2019 on open data and the re-use of public sector information,' *Official Journal of the European Union*, L 172.

Cases

Court of Justice of the European Union 2014, *Judgement of the Court Grand Chamber, Case C-131/12, Google Spain SL and Google Inc. v Agencia Española de Protección de Datos (AEPD) and Mario Costeja González. Request for a preliminary ruling from the Audiencia Nacional.*

Court of Justice of the European Union 2015, *Case C-362/14 Maximillian Schrems v Data Protection Commissioner, Opinion of Advocate General Bot.*

Court of Justice of the European Union 2019, *Judgment of the Court (Grand Chamber), Case C-507/17, Request for a preliminary ruling under Article 267 TFEU from the Conseil d'État (Council of State, France), made by decision of 19 July 2017, received at the Court on 21 August 2017, in the proceedings Google LLC, successor in law to Google Inc., vs. Commission nationale de l'informatique et des libertés (CNIL).*

Court of Justice of the European Union 2020, 'Decision of the Court of Justice of the European Union, of 26 November 2019 concerning public access to documents held by the Court of Justice of the European Union in the exercise of its administrative functions,' *Official Journal of the European Union*, C 45/02, pp. 2–7.

German Federal Constitutional Court 1983, *Abstract of the German Federal Constitutional Court's Judgment of 15 December 1983, 1 BvR 209, 269, 362, 420, 440, 484/83 [CODI-CES]*, viewed 2 October 2019, www.bundesverfassungsgericht.de/SharedDocs/Entscheidungen/EN/1983/12/rs19831215_1bvr020983en.html.

3

CLOUD COMPUTING DRIVERS, BARRIERS, AND RISK ANALYSIS FOR INTERNATIONAL ORGANIZATIONS

Elaine Goh and Eng Sengsavang[1]

Introduction

Cloud computing has become ubiquitous in our daily lives, and yet despite this, or because of it, it has also become invisible. This tendency can be attributed to the seamlessness of cloud service delivery on the one hand, and the remoteness of cloud computing physical infrastructure on the other hand. The OECD describes cloud services as "mark[ing] a paradigm shift in ICT provision, allowing businesses and individuals to access on-demand IT services over a network, without the need to make large up-front investments in physical ICT capital."[2] In cloud computing, the "physical ICT capital" and computing resources delivered over the Internet or over a private network are all outsourced, usually to commercial entities; access to this powerful computing resource happens remotely and appears deceptively "virtual." The average user interacts with cloud computing through a computer or mobile interface in the comfort of their own home or work environment, and is not acutely aware of the infrastructural realities of cloud computing. The infrastructure of the cloud is characterized by "miniature cities"[3] populated by server farms and underground networks of fibre-optic and submarine cables, which transport large amounts of data among sprawling server farms located across the globe. Cloud computing minimizes the need for users to interact with a given cloud provider, or with any of the underlying mechanisms, physical or virtual, behind the services and applications that are scalable and available at the user's fingertips.

Cloud computing was formally introduced as a term in 2006 by Eric Schmidt, then CEO of Google.[4] Schmidt referred to cloud computing as "a new business model" wherein users access data stored in the "cloud somewhere" through the use of multiple devices, including computers and mobile phones.[5] Today, individuals and businesses depend on cloud computing in multiple ways, some of which may not be immediately obvious. For example, email applications such as Gmail, Yahoo, or Hotmail, which offer free basic services while charging a premium for extra storage, are "freemium" services based on public clouds.[6] Data that individuals and organizations generate on social media platforms such as Instagram, Facebook, Twitter, and others are likewise hosted and stored on public clouds. Cloud-based collaboration tools such as Dropbox and Google Drive are ubiquitous, used in both personal and business contexts.

Organizations are also adopting cloud services in more official ways. Between 2014 and 2018, there was a 50% increase, on average, in the purchase of cloud computing services by large and small businesses, meaning that cloud computing services "registered the fastest increase in uptake" compared to other information technologies.[7] McAfee also notes that there has been a 15% increase in the use of cloud services by organizations from 2018 to 2019.[8]

Cloud computing is, moreover, influencing the development, use, and delivery of information technology. The OECD reports: "From 2010, adoption began to rise quickly due to the increased number of cloud providers (e.g., Google, IBM, Microsoft, and Oracle) followed by an associated decline in the price of such services."[9] A 2016 press release by Gartner claims that "Cloud will increasingly be the default option for software deployment. The same is true for custom software, which increasingly is designed for some variation of public or private cloud."[10] In the same year, a report by Forbes notes that "the vendors – who see the handwriting on the wall – are pushing a lot of this. They are all becoming cloud vendors."[11]

Foreseeably, the question for organizations with regard to cloud computing has evolved from "*Should* we adopt cloud computing?" to "*How* do we adopt cloud computing?" The importance of understanding the risks and opportunities that cloud computing presents over traditional models of computing is more relevant than ever. From a recordkeeping perspective, the potential impact that cloud computing may have on the integrity, confidentiality, availability, and security of organizational data and archives continues to be a serious concern. For international organizations, the adoption of cloud computing is further complicated by their unique legal status. International organizations face particular risks to their privileges and immunities that should be taken into account during the decision-making process when they consider adopting and using cloud computing.

Fortunately, several tools are available to support international organizations in the cloud computing evaluation and decision-making process. In this chapter, we consider the drivers and barriers of cloud computing adoption in international organizations, and promote a risk-based approach for implementing cloud services, including controls for mitigating risks. We also consider risks to the inviolability of the archives of international organizations posed by cloud computing.

What is cloud computing?

Cloud computing refers to a suite of computing technologies and services that may be described in multiple ways. A 2008 research study revealed that there were over

22 definitions of cloud computing.[12] Some definitions may emphasize either technologies or services over the other. For instance, Schubert et al. view cloud computing as "a concept comprising a set of combined technologies,"[13] while Wu & Buyya assert that cloud computing is not a new technology, but rather a new way of delivering computing resources.[14]

Cloud computing can be conceived of as both a set of combined technologies – many, indeed, pre-existing – *and* a set of services, all delivered over the Internet, or over a "dedicated network."[15] In this vein, ENISA describes cloud computing as "an on-demand service model for IT provision, often based on virtualization and distributed computing technologies."[16] A commonly cited definition that integrates many others is that provided by the National Institute of Standards and Technology (NIST), which describes cloud computing as:

> A model for enabling ubiquitous, convenient, on-demand network access to a shared pool of configurable computing resources (e.g., networks, servers, storage, applications, and services) that can be rapidly provisioned and released with minimal management effort or service provider interaction.[17]

This definition conveys both the vision of service delivery and the array of inter-dependent technologies, both physical and virtual ("networks, servers, storage, applications") that form the nebulous system known as "cloud computing."

Despite the different definitions of cloud computing postulated by various authors, recurring elements are also comprehensively addressed by NIST's "five essential characteristics" of cloud computing: on-demand self-service; broad network access; rapid elasticity; measured service; and resource pooling, which encompasses multi-tenancy, a shared computing resource that can be "controlled"[18] and "dynamically assigned"[19] based on the needs of the consumer.

Cloud computing service and deployment models

Three recognized cloud service types offered by cloud providers are software as a service (SaaS), platform as a service (PaaS), and infrastructure as a service (IaaS).

Software as a service (SaaS): The client rents computer applications and software running on a cloud provider's physical and virtual infrastructure.[20] The provider controls "networks, servers, operating systems, storage … even individual application capabilities, with the possible exception of limited user-specific application configuration settings."[21]

Platform as a service (PaaS): The client rents a computing platform owned and controlled by the cloud provider, to develop their own computing applications or software. NIST defines "platform" as "a development platform and/or deployment platform for cloud-enabled applications."[22] Examples of platforms include database management systems, libraries, middleware, and the programming environment of the cloud provider.[23]

Infrastructure as a service (IaaS): The client rents computing capabilities such as "processing, storage, networks, and other fundamental computing resources," which may be run on the cloud provider's computing infrastructure, including "operating systems and applications."[24] The client controls "operating systems, storage, and deployed applications," while the cloud provider controls the "underlying cloud infrastructure" (physical and virtual).[25]

NIST also defines four types of cloud deployment models: private cloud (used by a single organization); community cloud (used by a specific community); public cloud (open use by the public); and hybrid cloud (a combination of two or more cloud deployment models – private, community, or public – that are distinct but interoperable).[26] Private and community clouds may be "owned, managed, and operated" either by the client, a third party, or a combination thereof, and may be on or off premises, while public clouds are "owned, managed, and operated" by a third party and hosted on the premises of a cloud provider.[27]

Beyond these accepted cloud models, NIST (2018) cautions that the term "aaS" has been used as a "marketing term" that has resulted in confusion.[28] Organizations may mistakenly procure services that they believe to be cloud services, when in reality, such services do not meet the definition of cloud computing, or NIST's criteria for cloud service models. However, authors like Murugesan & Bojanova[29] and Miyachi[30] note that cloud technologies have become more complex and diverse, for example to include serverless computing, and argue that there is a need to expand the models initially defined by NIST. Some of these proposed models include the following:

- Analytics as a Service (AaaS), which involves the use of big data in the cloud to draw insights about data;
- Function as a Service (FaaS), which is based on serverless computing wherein application developers upload their codes in the cloud, and "infrastructure is deemed to be "transparent"[31];
- Security as a Service (SecaaS), which deploys and uses security applications through the cloud, such as intrusion detection, encryption, and virus and malware detection;
- Identity and Access Management as a Service (IAMaaS), which involves password management and authentication for cloud computing;
- Blockchain as a Service (BaaS), which involves the use of cloud-based tools for blockchain applications;
- Surveillance as a Service (SVaaS), a term used by Zuboff to refer to SaaS that tracks and collects the online behaviour of individuals. The behavioural data from SVaaS is "inferred," "presumed," and "deduced," and can reveal personal information about individuals.[32]

The use of "aaS" as a catchall term for various forms of specialized cloud-based computing services and technologies indicates that cloud services and technologies will evolve and expand, sometimes in unpredictable ways. This also supports the idea espoused by Hu that "the cloud is both an idea and a physical and material object."[33]

Cloud computing and international organizations

Several international organizations are engaged on a programmatic level in discussions on the implications of cloud computing for society. The United Nations (UN) has actively encouraged both governments and businesses in low- and middle-income countries to leverage the benefits of cloud technology.[34] While warning against the potential challenges that cloud computing poses to free and open-source software, and increased control of computing by a few "Internet giants," the United Nations Educational, Scientific and Cultural Organization (UNESCO) nevertheless recognizes the potential for cloud computing to balance "inequalities of access" by "significantly [lowering] investment requirements (e.g., in servers, software, and service contracts), creating dynamic opportunities for new users in developing countries."[35] The OECD has also issued several reports on contemporary digital trends that recognize the ascendency of cloud computing in the digital era.[36]

Cloud-dependent technologies are becoming more and more the norm, so that for international organizations, the adoption of cloud technologies is no longer simply a matter of conscious choice, but a matter of availability and interoperability of cloud-based versus non-cloud-based options on the market, with the former quickly overtaking the latter.

With IT markets becoming increasingly cloud-dependent, organizations must actively demand accountability and specific terms when selecting and negotiating with cloud providers, to ensure equity between provider and client, and to protect the integrity, confidentiality, availability, and security of their records. International organizations, many of which themselves are large entities, may work together as powerful coalitions that form a sizeable portion of the potential cloud market. This is notably true of the UN family of organizations. As a first step, international organizations should understand as fully as possible the potential impacts and consequences of moving to the cloud, in order to leverage the benefits of cloud computing, while minimizing the risks and the amount of control over their data and records conceded to a cloud provider.

Use of cloud computing in international organizations

The following sections draw from the 2019 UN Joint Inspection Unit (JIU) report, *Managing Cloud Computing Services in the United Nations System*, as well as from the InterPARES Trust (ITrust) study, *The Use of Cloud Services for Records Management Purposes in International Organizations*, conducted from 2013 to 2017. In particular, the discussion focuses on the study findings related to the uses, drivers, and barriers of cloud computing in international organizations.

Like other enterprises of different sizes and stripes, international organizations have begun to increase their use of cloud technologies. UN agencies and other international organizations are either already using or considering deploying public, private, or hybrid clouds for their own business operations. Although some international organizations fall onto either end of the spectrum of not using cloud services at all, or of adopting a "cloud-first approach," most use some form of cloud computing services.[37] Research conducted by the UN JIU on the use of cloud computing reveals that 22 out of 24 UN organizations surveyed use different cloud solutions.[38] However, UN organizations are at different stages of development and maturity levels in terms of adoption of cloud services.[39]

This finding is consistent with the results of a 2015 ITrust survey which found that, while the majority of international organizations use or have used cloud computing (83% of survey respondents), there are differences in the degree of use: the majority (55%) of respondents reported that their organization uses cloud computing in limited ways, while 24% use cloud computing only exceptionally, and 5% use cloud computing at a large scale.[40]

The JIU study reports that international organizations use IaaS and SaaS services most, while PaaS is used to a lesser, though still significant, extent, most often to develop websites and customize applications.[41] According to the study, 72% of international organizations who use cloud services employ Microsoft, primarily because of their reliance on the cloud-hosted SaaS suite Microsoft Office 365, including cloud-based email.[42] Given that Microsoft Office has become a de facto business software, it is hardly surprising that international organizations are compelled to use cloud services, which, in the case of UN organizations, has become an "operational reality."[43]

The uptake in cloud engagement is reflected in the major services offered by the UN International Computing Centre (ICC), which provides IT and communication services to all UN agencies, including consultancy services in cloud computing and cloud management and support for the implementation of private, public, and hybrid cloud solutions.[44] ICC operates four data centres – two located in Switzerland, and one each in the United States and Spain.[45] All have "United Nations jurisdiction for the safeguarding of privileges and immunities."[46]

The ICC is involved in a number of major cloud projects within the UN system. For example, it assisted the United Nations High Commissioner for Refugees (UNHCR) in the acquisition of IrisGuard, a biometric registration and identification system of Microsoft Azure, which is hosted in the cloud.[47] The IrisGuard system uses iris scan technology as part of the registration process for refugees, enabling easier access to cash assistance without the need for a bank card or physical travel to the UNHCR office.[48] Some UN organizations have also started the process of partnering with major cloud service providers. For example, in 2018, UN Environment partnered with Google to monitor environmental degradation specifically on freshwater ecosystems. This partnership is indicative of Google's expertise in cloud computing, big data, and satellite imagery.[49]

Drivers and barriers of cloud computing adoption in international organizations

Cloud computing offers international organizations a variety of choices and access to novel solutions, while at the same time, the very nature of its dynamic and open architecture poses risks, so that some of its most appealing attributes may also constitute barriers to its adoption. The following sections summarize the drivers and barriers of cloud computing for international organizations, drawing from the two studies mentioned above.

Drivers of cloud computing adoption for international organizations

Flexibility and ease of deployment

Flexibility and ease in deploying computing resources and application systems are cited as drivers for the adoption of cloud computing.[50] The notion of "flexibility" refers to several characteristics, either specific or vague, but generally is a concept linked to both the ease of setting up and using cloud technologies. Due to the virtual nature and online delivery of services, cloud computing requires neither physical set-up by the client, nor physical replacement of hardware and network infrastructures.[51] It is therefore seen to be a more user-friendly technology than traditional computing models.[52] Public cloud-based SaaS services such as Google Drive and Dropbox are often already used on an ad hoc, informal basis within organizations, as well as by individuals in their private lives.[53] The qualities of ease and flexibility may be especially attractive for organizations that struggle with internal IT services, due to inadequate IT capacity and resources, or a perception of poor IT services and lack of IT knowledge among staff.[54] However, the JIU cautions that the ease of using standardized, out-of-the-box cloud products could mean a corresponding lack of flexibility when it comes to customization.[55]

Enhanced availability and access

Enhanced availability refers to increased access to computing services at any time of day and from any location. Cloud computing offers "broad network access" largely through the "public Internet"[56] as well as through private networks; it is designed to be available globally, through any type of computing device, such as "mobile phones, tablets, laptops, and workstations."[57] Cloud computing appeals to international organizations that are composed of field offices scattered across various continents, whose work often relies on collaboration with multiple stakeholders and third parties. It is cited as a technology that offers global access and helps to reduce complexity and facilitate collaboration,[58] providing ready access to records that can be shared outside the organization, in a manner that is "expedient" and convenient.[59] In addition, some international organizations have decentralized reporting structures and systems of governance; field offices may operate relatively independently and make their own informed decisions on the selection of cloud services.[60] Cloud computing has the potential to provide the "backbone for ICT infrastructure of field offices" and to support the virtualization of office applications.[61]

Cloud computing may also be perceived as an especially viable technology for access to open data, historical archives, and "non-sensitive" records, in other words, for sharing and storing public and/or unclassified data and records.[62] Since public records represent a lower risk to data privacy and security, some organizations have started to use cloud computing by first deploying documents that have already been disclosed to the public.[63]

Service continuity

Related to enhanced availability is the capacity for cloud computing to assure service continuity in times of need. The operation of multiple data centres throughout the world for processing data "allow[s] for redundant facilities, multiple backup locations and worldwide support and systems 24 hours a day and seven days a week, facilitating business continuity ... that cannot be matched," even by the pooled resources of UN organizations.[64] Business and digital continuity are critical in times of calamity or urgency, such as "natural catastrophes,"[65] "power failures or other crisis,"[66] or when staff have to travel across different field offices on "short notice," and must access shared IT infrastructures and information services to conduct business.[67]

For example, UN Women shared that within a four-year time frame, they experienced a downtime of less than four hours in terms of the service delivery of their cloud-based email system.[68] In order to mitigate the risk of downtime in service interruption, UN Women has developed disaster recovery and business continuity plans. However, the effective implementation of these plans depends upon the reliability of cloud providers to fulfil their obligations as specified in the contract.[69]

Scalability and elasticity

Scalability is cited as one of the central drivers for international organizations to adopt cloud computing, and is often linked to the concept of elasticity.[70] The latter is one of NIST's "five essential characteristics" of cloud computing, wherein

> Capabilities can be elastically provisioned and released, in some cases automatically, to scale rapidly outwards and inwards commensurate with demand. To the consumer, the capabilities available for provisioning often appear to be unlimited and can be appropriated in any quantity at any time.[71]

For the client, scalability and elasticity mean the ability to easily scale up or scale down computing capabilities depending on their needs.[72] For example, some staff prefer to store data in a cloud-computing environment because they worry that traditional computing models only offer limited storage capacity.[73] By contrast, in cloud computing, more storage is easily provisioned and available for purchase on an as-needed basis.

Cost savings

Cost effectiveness has been cited as a major impetus for UN organizations to implement cloud computing, since they are "constantly under pressure to provide high-quality services and innovative solutions under a continued budget reduction."[74] Similarly, the UNHCR reported employing cloud computing as a means of "reducing the need for on-site equipment, allocated space, and dedicated human resources, and provide a more accessible and secure ICT service at a lower cost to the organization."[75]

The perception that cloud computing is an economical option is related to its scalability and shared computing resources, as well as to the fact that clients no longer need to invest in up-front costs.[76] Instead, organizations can deploy IT services and resources based on what they need and use, without bearing the capital cost of acquiring and maintaining hardware infrastructure, software upgrades, and other maintenance. Some also believe that cloud computing economizes on IT staff.[77]

Similar to the concept of a utility model, the "metering"[78] principle of cloud computing, wherein "each client is billed for their actual use of resources," was not a sudden phenomenon with the advent of cloud computing, but a gradual evolution of IT services. John McCarthy, who proposed this idea during a 1961 speech at the Massachusetts Institute of Technology (MIT) argues, "If computers of the kind I have advocated become the computers of the future, then computation may someday be organized as a public utility, just as the telephone system is a public utility."[79] However, the original utility model proposed by McCarthy differs from how cloud computing is being implemented today; as Hu describes it, cloud computing is no longer conceived of as a public utility, but as a private enterprise operating within a "private infrastructure,"[80] where individuals and corporations are united into a "set of gated communities."[81]

While cost-savings is one of the key drivers for international organizations to embark on cloud computing,[82] the savings may be "difficult to quantify"[83] and "some costs are sometimes hidden or overlooked."[84] In practical terms, the change from a capital investment to a privately owned metered service in the cloud also means a shift in budgeting allocation, becoming a perennial operational cost, rather than a capital cost. Studies in other contexts indicate the need for more transparency in terms of calculating and making a comparison between in-house storage versus storage of records and data in the cloud. For example, research conducted by McLeod & Gormly[85] as well as Oliver & Knight[86] on cloud computing in governmental, educational, and heritage and cultural institutions cautioned archivists and records managers to develop a more robust economic model, taking into account both technical and non-technical costs. This would enable organizations to make informed comparisons, rather than simply jumping onto the bandwagon or "taking a leap of faith"[87] that uses costs savings as a deciding factor for storing records and data in the cloud.

Security

The ability to provide timely security updates and to obtain greater economies of scale in security services within the cloud environment are other factors that propel UN organizations to implement cloud computing. Hodson argues that the benefits to security services through cloud computing "draw direct parallels with the business benefits of cloud computing: scale flexibility, cost savings and improved performance."[88] Cloud providers have the capacity and scale to provide a comprehensive suite of security services that can detect and respond to cyberattacks, including filtering, monitoring, and hardening of virtual machines, and the provision of identity management tools.[89] Some of these security tools also meet international and industry standards of certification and compliance in security. Organizations like the World Intellectual Property Organization (WIPO) perceive that major cloud providers can offer better security services as compared to an internal IT department, because the former has the scalability and capacity to invest in more robust cybersecurity tools.[90]

Innovation

Corporate cloud computing giants have the ability to invest in research and development efforts both on a large scale and in niche areas.[91] Based on their ability to dedicate substantial resources to the development of advanced technologies, such as data analytics, artificial intelligence, and blockchain, cloud providers are at the forefront of technology and are perceived as capable of offering innovative services.[92] International organizations such as the International Civil Aviation Organization (ICAO) are keen to tap into such services.[93]

A recent example is the launch in March 2020 of the "AWS Diagnostic Development Initiative." An Amazon blog post announces that the company is "committing an initial investment of $20 million to accelerate diagnostic research, innovation, and development to speed our collective understanding and detection of COVID-19 and other … diagnostic solutions to mitigate future infectious disease outbreaks."[94] The blog goes on to note that diagnostic science relies on "scalable compute power" that can be delivered by AWS, "along with industry-leading services like analytics and machine learning, so they can process and analyze large data sets and iterate quickly."[95] The reach of an empire such as Amazon is not limited to just hard capital; it also has the social capital to mobilize powerful networks, in this case an "outside technical advisory group consisting of leading scientists, global health policy experts, and thought leaders in the field of infectious disease diagnostics," including a member of the World Health Organization's Digital Health Technical Advisory Group.[96] Another example is a partnership between the Statistics Division of the UN Department of Economic and Social Affairs and ESRI, a private company dealing with geographic information systems. The partnership will produce a COVID-19 data-hub that includes "geospatial data web services" and "other data visualizations and analyses" for all UN member states to access data needed to monitor the spread of COVID-19 and to support their responses in dealing with the pandemic.[97] These examples show how innovation in cloud computing operates at the crossroads between technological, economic, and social spheres of influence.

Barriers to cloud computing adoption for international organizations

Vendor lock-in

While cloud computing offers organizations flexibility in using and selecting the appropriate level of resources and range of products to meet their business needs, there is a risk of vendor lock-in. Vendor lock-in may manifest in the use of proprietary file formats that can only be used in specific information systems, resulting in challenges for data migration and preservation, the use of customized codes and application programming interfaces (APIs), and application lock-in of infrastructure services such as access controls.[98] While vendor lock-in existed in ICT prior to the advent of cloud computing, in a cloud environment it is particularly challenging because users have no choice but to upgrade to a new version of a software and are forced to "either adapt their internal processes to the new features or consider a migration to a different platform and face the challenges and associated costs of a forced migration."[99] If the organization chooses to change service providers, it bears the costs of data mapping, to ensure that data is transferred into the new application, and of retraining staff.[100] The OECD notes that once an organization has selected a PaaS cloud service provider, the organization is essentially locked in because it has no choice but to migrate the data, software, and components into a new cloud platform, should it decide to change to a new service provider.[101]

One factor in vendor lock-in is the "market dominance of a handful of major providers" in the realm of cloud computing.[102] The UN JIU notes: "According to recent industry reports, the top five IaaS providers, led by Amazon Web Services (AWS), Microsoft Azure and Google Cloud Platform, account for about 80 per cent of all IaaS sales globally."[103] The OECD affirms that big "content providers" such as Amazon, Google, Facebook, and Microsoft have themselves become significant players in the development of global computing infrastructure, becoming builders not only of data centres, but also of the underground submarine cables that carry the inter-continental traffic of bulk data.[104] As Armbrust et al. point out, "a necessary … condition for a company to become a Cloud Computing provider is that it must have existing investments not only in very large datacenters, but also in large-scale software infrastructure and operational expertise required to run them."[105] Data centres also play an increasingly important role in the movement and processing of big data and the Internet of Things (IoT), and this has "added to the value and growth of data centres."[106]

The market for SaaS is also characterized by "a small number of large-scale providers – Microsoft and Google."[107] While there is more diversity of providers for specialized software, "independent SaaS providers and services rely on the infrastructure of the large IaaS providers … which results effectively in an even higher concentration of cloud data in the private data centres of the few biggest IaaS providers."[108] Increasingly, service providers push to integrate SaaS with mobile devices to increase their market share, as seen for example in Microsoft's "mobile first, cloud first" strategy.[109] Satya Nadella, the CEO of Microsoft, envisaged the converging of the cloud and mobile devices and of Microsoft "moving into a frontier of helping IT manage when employees want to bring whatever cloud service they need to get their work done."[110] Besides Microsoft, many other service providers have moved to only the SaaS platform. UNESCO has observed that human resources solutions by major service providers are all SaaS, and there is no support for on-premises solutions.[111]

Legal risks

There are also legal risks in implementing cloud computing services. The "transnational character of cloud computing services"[112] means that organizations have to take into account the different laws and jurisdictions of nation states when data is stored (data at rest) and when data moves across different jurisdictions (data in motion).[113] As noted by De Filippi & McCarthy, data by itself "does not have any nationality but merely inherits the law of the territory in which it is located."[114] Consequently, the same bits of information can be subjected to several national laws within a specific moment in time. There are also concerns of access to data by law enforcement and national security agencies from various countries. For example, the Clarifying Lawful Overseas Use of Data (CLOUD) Act of 2018 allowed the U.S. government to compel cloud service providers to "release data in their possession, custody or control" even if the data is stored outside the country.[115] Although the CLOUD Act operates in relation to other agreements and legal instruments, including mutual legal assistance treaties signed with other nation states, the Act provides an avenue for "cross-border data sharing in criminal matters."[116] Correspondingly, foreign governments can request data stored in the United States in cases "involving serious crimes when not targeting U.S. persons" and where the "United States has determined that the foreign nations' laws adequately protect privacy and civil liberties among other requirements."[117] The CLOUD Act has been perceived as a "massive overreach on the part of the U.S. government that contravenes the norms of international law,"[118] which is potentially a matter of concern for international organizations.

The mandate of international organizations is derived from specific legal treaties that clearly articulate the "regime of privileges and immunities" and protect international organizations from national courts.[119] Two types of privileges and immunities are jurisdictional immunities and inviolability of premises and archives.[120]

Jurisdictional immunity refers to "immunity from prosecution or jurisdiction," which allows international organizations to "function independently and without fear of judicial harassment on the territory of its host State."[121] The inviolability of archives and premises is established in the constitutional treaties and multilateral and host-seat agreements of most international organizations, such as the 1946 General Convention of the United Nations (Article II, Sections 3 and 4).[122] The purpose of inviolability is to preserve the independence[123] and privacy of international organizations and their member states.[124] The system of privileges and immunities prevents law enforcement agencies from entering the physical premises of international organizations and accessing their data and archives, which may also be stored outside the building, without first seeking the express consent of the respective international organization.

Besides legal issues governing the storage and processing of, and access to, data, there are concerns regarding contractual terms and conditions with service providers, which tend to tip in favour of the provider while leaving "little or no negotiation options" for the customer.[125] The contractual terms and conditions outline the commercial and legal terms between the customer and the service provider, as well as disclaimers by the provider.[126] The lack of clarity in contracts on issues such as disruption to business continuity in the event of bankruptcy, dissolution of services on the part of the service provider, perceived risks in the ownership of data,[127] and ownership and use of metadata generated in cloud services[128] can act as barriers for the deployment and use of cloud services.

Security risks

While cloud-based solutions can offer the benefits of a centralized security approach, as outlined on p. 68, service providers may not cater to specific security requirements, nor can they leverage information-sharing networks afforded by international organizations in terms of responding to cyber threats.[129]

One of the unintended consequences of adopting a SaaS such as Microsoft Office 365 is that organizations may become more vulnerable to targeted phishing attacks. This is because malicious actors are aware that access to cloud-based solutions provide them with more opportunities for access to data. In October 2019, a cybersecurity firm detected a spike in phishing attacks on the UN and other international organizations, some of which targeted users of mobile devices.[130] These attacks attempt to steal the login credentials of users by impersonating the Office 365 login page. Phishing has also become more sophisticated: although close to 70% of malicious emails were identified by Office 365, another 25% of phishing emails bypass its security settings.[131] Most recently, an increased threat has been posed by malicious actors who attempt to prey on people's fears about the COVID-19 pandemic by sending phishing emails and attachments that purportedly come from healthcare and humanitarian organizations such as the World Health Organization (WHO). These malicious actors also attempt to steal the login credentials of staff working in these organizations.[132] WHO has issued an advisory warning to the public to be wary of criminals "disguising themselves as WHO to steal money or sensitive information."[133]

The United Nations Commission on International Trade Law (UNCITRAL) argues that features of cloud computing, including multi-tenancy and network access, make cloud providers more vulnerable to cyberattacks, and thus organizations need to institute mitigation strategies to prevent data leaks, compromise of users' login credentials, and other security breaches.[134] Similarly, Hu states, "it is a cruel irony that the cloud – sold as a more secure way of protecting us from vulnerabilities – has introduced an entirely parallel set of vulnerabilities."[135] For example, the National Security Agency's PRISM surveillance system, based on cloud technologies, involved the installation of "optical splitters inside data centres."[136] As a result, the NSA was able to "automatically copy virtually all traffic sent over fibre-optic cables."[137] Due to the multitenancy structure of the cloud, it is possible for an organization's virtual machine to be within the same physical server as an adversary. These adversaries or threat actors can potentially exploit a vulnerability between virtual machines and compromise the confidentiality and integrity of an organization's information assets.[138] Some international organizations have also experienced cyber-attacks from adversarial countries; should they be forced to adopt cloud computing, international organizations will need to impose requirements for data to be stored in member countries that are supportive of their mandate.[139] Consequently, there is a need for UN organizations to conduct a risk assessment, including examining the level of threat and vulnerability and benchmarking it against their resources, capacity, and level of risk tolerance.

Loss of governance in ICT and information management

Another barrier to the implementation of cloud services is the loss of ICT governance that is associated with the "management of technology as opposed to the technology itself."[140] This lack of governance in ICT and information management can manifest in various ways, including in a lack of control when developing a defensible security posture,[141] lack of control over the activities of service providers who may subcontract work to third parties, or lack of a policy framework governing the adoption and use of cloud computing. Some service providers maintain control over their infrastructure and, as a result, the service-level agreements do not adequately address issues relating to security controls of their infrastructure, including a commitment by the provider to conduct regular vulnerability assessments of their systems.[142] There are also difficulties in maintaining control over the "production chain" comprised of third parties; "any interruption or corruption in the chain or lack of coordination of responsibilities between all the parties involved" can result in data integrity issues and compromise the confidentiality and security of the data and records.[143]

Some international organizations noted that their policy framework is outdated and lags behind the adoption and use of cloud computing technologies. In such cases, cloud services may be deployed without consideration of legal, privacy, security, and records management requirements. In some international organizations, business units have purchased SaaS and other systems directly from the service providers because they were dissatisfied with the services from their IT department.[144] Such a practice is indicative of what is known as shadow IT, or the use of a system "without having been reviewed, tested, approved, implemented or secured by the enterprise IT and/or information security functions."[145] Shadow IT may result in risks to compliance, due to a lack of stringent controls in the protection of data, as well as security and privacy risks. There is also the perception that because cloud service providers have a commercial interest, they are not invested in the business strategy of ensuring the long-term preservation of records for their clients.[146]

Application of a risk management framework in cloud computing

The UN recognizes that risk management is an integral component of its own activities and operations. At a macro level, UN organizations are "facing a risk climate growing increasingly more complex and prone to significant operational surprises."[147] Besides coping with changes in the external environment, such as rapid change in technology and globalization, UN organizations also face internal challenges, including a "wide range of mandates and limited resources, complex organizational structures and lengthy decision-making processes, many objectives, and lack of capacity, and reform backlogs."[148] Within the context of cloud computing, it is recognized that there is a need for a risk assessment prior to the signing of a contract with the service provider, and that assessment should be conducted on an "ongoing" basis "throughout the duration of the contract."[149]

Defining risk

This section discusses a risk-based approach to implementing a cloud-based system,[150] drawing upon ISO 31000:2018 Risk Management – Guidelines,[151] IEC 31010:2019 Risk Assessment Techniques,[152] and COBIT 5.[153] While ISO 31000 focuses on a framework of managing risks and does not confine itself to a particular industry or sector, COBIT 5 focuses on "IT-related risks" and "aims to create optimal value from IT by maintaining a balance between realising benefits and optimising risk levels and resource use."[154] As such, these two standards are complementary when assessing the level of threat and vulnerability in selecting and implementing a cloud computing service.

According to the ISO, risk is defined as the "effect of uncertainty on objectives"[155]; that uncertainty may be manifested through a variety of sources, including uncertainty in how events might occur and the consequences, uncertainty in terms of "how people or systems might behave,"[156] uncertainty in models to predict outcomes, or uncertainty resulting from the consequences of "systemic issues" that may result in "wide ranging impacts which cannot be clearly defined."[157] In the context of cloud computing, there is the element of uncertainty in how people, including IT staff, operate within such an environment, especially for organizations that have recently transitioned from an on-premise to a cloud-based system.

In COBIT 5, risk is defined as the "business risk associated with the use, ownership, operation, involvement, influence and adoption of IT within an enterprise."[158] The overall objective of risk management is to describe the various factors that lead to uncertain outcomes.[159] The implementation of cloud computing in organizations is more than just an IT solution, but can be positioned rather as a risk function requiring a risk management approach. Whereas a risk function focuses on the development of "efficient and effective core risk governance and management activities," the purpose of a risk management perspective is to develop the "process of identifying, analysing and responding to risk."[160]

Analysing an organization's external and internal context

Both ISO 31000 and COBIT 5 recognize the importance of analysing the organization's external and internal context as part of the process of developing a risk management framework. External context refers to the legal, political, financial, social, cultural, and technological factors, including technological changes[161] and the "threat landscape."[162] The transition made by service providers from an on-premise solution to the cloud is an example of how the technological context and market forces can result in a change in the IT roadmap and strategy of international organizations, which in turn has an impact on how records and data are managed and preserved. Recently, the COVID-19 pandemic has propelled an increase in the use of cloud services as organizations implement remote working. Some reports argue that increased usage during a pandemic does not negatively impact service availability, as service providers regularly conduct resilience planning and cloud services run on servers in different geographic locations to ensure business continuity.[163] However, other reports indicate that some organizations in Europe and Australia running on Azure encountered capacity issues in starting virtual machines.[164] Microsoft, while highlighting its commitment to service availability, implicitly acknowledged the need to prioritize resource capacities due to a surge in usage:

> As demand continues to grow, if we are faced with any capacity constraints in any region during this time, we have established clear criteria for the priority of new cloud capacity. Top priority will be going to first responders, health and emergency management services, critical government infrastructure organizational use, and ensuring remote workers stay up and running with the core functionality of Teams.[165]

The need for Microsoft to prioritize its resource allocation suggests that changes in the external context such as the COVID-19 pandemic can result in downtime in service availability, leading to additional costs as organizations are forced to pay more to scale up their computing power for a remote workforce.[166]

Video conferencing tools have also replaced face-to-face meetings because countries are tightening border controls, and social distancing is becoming the new normal to curb the spread of the virus. Concerns have been raised about privacy and security loopholes in some of these video conferencing tools. For example, Zoom, a cloud-based video and web conferencing tool, has been reported as a "bucket of red flags" in terms of privacy, as the tool gives meeting hosts the power to record calls, while the tool itself "collect(s) a potentially huge amount of personal data from accounts, calls made through the service and from scraping social profiles."[167] Zoom's privacy policy partly corroborates this report.[168] The policy states that a Zoom meeting host has the capability to record a meeting either on the host's computer or in the cloud hosted by Zoom. As such, Zoom advises that the meeting host "is responsible for obtaining any necessary consent."[169] In addition, there have been multiple reported cases of "Zoom-bombing," where uninvited guests attend and disrupt a meeting or a conference.[170] As part of analysing the external context, organizations need to take into account the need to facilitate communication among employees and with external stakeholders during a pandemic, and to carefully evaluate the threats and vulnerabilities associated with the use of cloud-based conferencing and other systems used to support telecommuting.

Internal factors refer to an organization's mission, vision, governance, strategic directions, organizational structure, organizational culture, its information assets, and systems. COBIT 5 addresses internal factors that are more focused on "organizational processes" that can support IT capacity and change management.[171] This includes the "strategic importance of IT in the enterprise,"[172] and "change management capability and risk management philosophy."[173] Within the context of UN organizations, one risk management philosophy is that enterprise risk management should be incorporated as part of the "organization's management systems and processes."[174] UN organizations opined that there was no need to create a separate organizational structure catering to risk management, because this would lead to the perception among staff that risk management is not their responsibility, resulting in "bureaucratic paperwork with little benefit."[175] Because many ICT departments in UN organizations are decentralized and are dispersed across regional and country offices, there is a recognition of the need to identify common elements for the development of an ICT governance framework.[176] One common element is the need for the "alignment of ICT with the business needs"[177] and for ICT to be an enabler for "achieving the organization's mandate and goals and for increasing effectiveness and efficiency."[178]

Establishing the risk criteria

The risk criteria take into account the organization's vision, business objectives, resources, and capacity, how uncertainty affects business objectives, and the likelihood of that uncertainty occurring,[179] as well as the level of risk appetite.[180] Risk appetite is defined as "the amount of risk, on a broad level, an entity is willing to accept in pursuit of its mission or vision."[181]

Conducting a risk assessment

There are three components in conducting a risk assessment: risk identification, risk analysis, and risk evaluation. Risk identification endeavours to "find, recognize and describe risks that might help or prevent an organization achieving its objective."[182] Risk analysis is a means of understanding the level of risk based on the likelihood and impact of a threat and includes examining existing controls.[183] The analysis is dependent on the assumptions made by various stakeholders, their biases, and the areas of exclusion.[184] The involvement of multiple stakeholders in different areas of expertise enables an organization to comprehensively identify risks and improve stakeholder engagement. Ultimately, the goal is for the organization to "achieve a common understanding of risk internally."[185] One component of risk analysis is to critically consider the "many interactions and dependencies between risks," which will affect decisions on how to treat the risks and help to implement a comprehensive treatment plan, rather than develop strategies that treat each risk factor separately.[186] Another component of risk analysis is to examine existing controls, assess whether these controls achieve the objectives, and identify gaps that can "reduce or eliminate control effectiveness."[187]

One risk factor in the cloud environment, as illustrated during the COVID-19 pandemic, is disruption in service availability from cloud service providers. There is a further dependency on the information architecture of the cloud system. If the organization adopts a "lifting and shifting" approach[188] in migrating data and architecture from an on-premise infrastructure to the cloud, instead of redesigning the architecture, that act in itself can hamper availability of service, regardless of whether the organization operates in a mass disruptive event such as a pandemic.

Another risk factor is that the organization may lack an effective backup strategy to restore vital systems and data in the cloud, which can negatively affect its ability to restart and resume business operations after an IT incident such as a ransomware or cyber attack. The organization may select a backup storage provider as a form of technical and organizational control to mitigate the risks of an IT disaster. However, the selection of a backup service provider may result in gaps in mitigating the risks, or it may introduce other risks. For example, if the organization selects the same service provider for the storage of backups as for the storage of their data and records, this will result in vendor lock-in. Alternatively, an organization may choose to store their backups in the same geographical location where their current data and records are stored. Such a measure does not adequately address the lack of an adequate backup and failover solution if there is a location-based service disruption. For international organizations, there may be constraints in terms of the choice of an alternative geographical zone for a backup solution due to restrictions linked to their privileges and immunities. For example, many international organizations will not store their data where national laws may put the inviolability of their archives and assets at risk.

Risk evaluation is the final step involving "comparing the results of the risk analysis with the established risk criteria to determine where additional action is required."[189] Essentially, this step entails examining the risk tolerance – the amount of risk that the management is prepared to take to meet their business objectives – in relation to the overall risk appetite of the organization.[190] ENISA has broadly identified three main categories of risk for organizations that adopt or implement cloud technology: policy and organizational, technical, and legal risks. Of the three main risks, technical risks were perceived to be the least challenging compared to policy and organizational as well as legal risks.[191]

Risk treatment

Risk treatment seeks to "select and implement options for addressing risk,"[192] which involves a variety of measures, including avoiding the risk, mitigating the risk, transferring or sharing the risk with another party, or accepting the risk.[193] An organization can transfer some of its risk by obtaining cyber insurance coverage against the financial impact from a security or privacy breach. However, an organization cannot transfer reputational risk because it is ultimately accountable for its own decisions.[194] Some international organizations have raised concerns about the reputational risk to the organization from the use of cloud computing, as there may be security issues or disputes regarding the use and disclosure of information.[195] Organizations should take into account the values and perceptions of the various stakeholders in considering risk treatment, and monitor and evaluate the selected treatment so as to "improve the quality and effectiveness of process design, implementation and outcomes."[196]

The risk management framework outlined in this section includes an understanding of the external and internal context, establishing the risk criteria, conducting a risk assessment, and weighing the various options for risk treatment. The selection, acquisition, and implementation of cloud services can be incorporated as part of an organization's risk management framework rather than viewing it strictly as an IT and/or a records management and information management initiative. The framework positions IT and records management as enablers and strategic resources for supporting the business to achieve its objectives, and acknowledges the varying perceptions of risks from stakeholders and the changing environment, while balancing these with the resources and priorities of the organization.

Conclusion

Cloud computing has the potential to offer international organizations considerable benefits related to its flexibility and ease of use, enhanced availability, service continuity, scalability, potential cost savings, security features, and access to technological innovations. At the same time, cloud computing poses serious risks, not only to an organization's information assets in relation to its independence, privacy, and privileges and immunities, but also other risks of a legal, reputational, security, and technological nature. Such risks are linked to the information architecture and market realities of cloud computing. Although some risks such as vendor lock-in exist even with traditional and on-premise solutions, the cloud environment is particularly challenging due to its multitenancy structure, the monopolization of a small but powerful group of dominant players, the interdependent layering of cloud services, and the hidden supply chains of subcontractors.

Due to their size, influence, and potential to collaborate, international organizations are well positioned – more than that, they have a responsibility – to demand specific rights and conditions when they select and negotiate with cloud providers. One positive step on the road to answering whether and how an international organization should adopt cloud computing, including an assessment of the cloud service options best suited to fit its specific needs, consists of understanding the benefits, barriers to adoption, and risks of cloud computing. A systematic approach to assessing risks, including the application of a risk management framework based on models such as ISO 31000:2018 and COBIT 5, provides an opportunity for international organizations to critically examine their needs, capacities, the changing environment, and the risks they will accept in return for defined benefits. The challenge of cloud computing adoption demands that international organizations go beyond an exclusively IT or records and information management framework, to arrive instead at an integrated, risk-based decision-making process that considers the needs and expertise of multiple stakeholders.

Notes

1   The author is responsible for the choice and the presentation of the facts contained in the publication and for the opinions expressed therein, which are not necessarily those of UNESCO and do not commit the Organization.
2   OECD, 2019, '1.1 Technology trends', in *Measuring the digital transformation: a roadmap for the future*, OECD Publishing, Paris, viewed 29 February 2020, www.oecd-ilibrary. org/sites/9789264311992-en/1/2/1/1/index.html?itemId=/content/publication/ 9789264311992-en&_csp_=32da5d2095ef596b16d96b0367b9d519&itemIGO=oecd& itemContentType=book.
3   Tung-Hui Hu & Project Muse, 2015, *A prehistory of the cloud*, MIT Press, Cambridge, p. 79.
4   Google Press Center, 2006, 'Conversation with Eric Schmidt hosted by Danny Sullivan: Search Engine Strategies Conference', 9 August, viewed 21 March 2020, www. google.fr/press/podium/ses2006.html.
5   Ibid.
6   OECD, 2019, '4.8 Roadmap: measuring cloud computing services', in *Measuring the digital transformation: a roadmap for the future*, OECD Publishing, Paris, viewed 29 February 2020, www.oecd-ilibrary.org/sites/9789264311992-en/1/2/4/8/index.html? itemId=/content/publication/9789264311992-en&_csp_=32da5d2095ef596b16d96b0 367b9d519&itemIGO=oecd&itemContentType=book.
7   OECD, 2019, '1.2 Digital transformations,' in *Measuring the digital transformation: a roadmap for the future*, OECD Publishing, Paris, viewed 29 February 2020, www.oec d-ilibrary.org/sites/9789264311992-en/1/2/1/2/index.html?itemId=/content/publica tion/9789264311992-en&_csp_=32da5d2095ef596b16d96b0367b9d519&itemIGO= oecd&itemContentType=book.
8   McAfee, 2019, *Cloud adoption and risk report*, viewed 29 February 2020, www.mcafee. com/enterprise/en-ca/solutions/lp/cloud-adoption-risk.html.

9   DeStefano, Kneller & Timmis, 2018, cited in OECD, 2019, '1.1 Technology trends',
    in *Measuring the digital transformation: a roadmap for the future*, OECD Publishing, Paris,
    viewed 29 February 2020, www.oecd-ilibrary.org/sites/9789264311992-en/1/2/1/1/
    index.html?itemId=/content/publication/9789264311992-en&_csp_=32da5d2095ef5
    96b16d96b0367b9d519&itemIGO=oecd&itemContentType=book.
10 Gartner, 2016, 'Gartner says by 2020, a corporate "no-cloud" policy will be as rare as
    a "no-internet" policy is today', viewed 29 February 2020, www.gartner.com/en/
    newsroom/press-releases/2016-06-22-gartner-says-by-2020-a-corporate-no-cloud-p
    olicy-will-be-as-rare-as-a-no-internet-policy-is-today.
11 Joe McKendrick, 2016, 'Is all-cloud computing inevitable? Analysts suggest it is',
    Forbes, 10 July, viewed 29 February 2020, www.forbes.com/sites/joemckendrick/
    2016/07/05/is-all-cloud-computing-inevitable-analysts-suggest-it-is/#2f0d36dbebf0.
12 Caesar Wu & Rajkumar Buyya, 2015, 'Cloud computing', in Caesar Wu & Rajkumar
    Buyya (eds.), *Cloud data centers and cost modelling: a complete guide to planning, designing
    and building a cloud data centre*, Morgan Kaufmann, Waltham, MA, p. 7.
13 Lutz Schubert, Keith Jeffery & Burkhard Neidecker-Lutz, 2010, *The future of cloud
    computing: opportunities for European cloud computing beyond 2010*, Public Version 1.0,
    http://cordis.europa.eu/fp7/ict/ssai/docs/cloud-report-final.pdf, in OECD 2014,
    Cloud computing: the concept, impacts and the role of government policy, viewed 21 March
    2020, www.oecd-ilibrary.org/docserver/5jxzf4lcc7f5-en.pdf?expires=1584811770&id=
    id&accname=guest&checksum=37B01C8B7C4578E547A87644F454ABB5.
14 Wu & Buyya, 2015.
15 San Murugesan & Irena Bojanova, 2016, 'Cloud computing: an overview', in Sam
    Murugesan & Irena Bojanova (eds.), *Cloud computing. In Encyclopaedia of cloud comput-
    ing*, John Wiley & Sons, West Sussex, p. 6.
16 ENISA, 2012, *Cloud computing: benefits, risks and recommendations for information security*
    Rev. B, viewed 28 March 2020, https://resilience.enisa.europa.eu/cloud-security-a
    nd-resilience/publications/cloud-computing-benefits-risks-and-recommendations-for-
    information-security, p. 4.
17 Peter Mell & Timothy Grance, 2011, *The NIST definition of cloud computing*, report,
    National Institute of Standards and Technology, U.S. Department of Commerce,
    viewed 8 March 2020, https://nvlpubs.nist.gov/nistpubs/Legacy/SP/nistspecialpublica
    tion800-145.pdf, p. 2.
18 Mell & Grance, 2011, p. 7.
19 Ibid, p. 5.
20 Eric Simmon, 2018, 'Evaluation of cloud computing services based on NIST SP
    800–145', viewed 29 February 2020, https://nvlpubs.nist.gov/nistpubs/SpecialPublica
    tions/NIST.SP.500-322.pdf. See also VV Arutyunov, 2012. 'Cloud computing: its
    history of development, modern state and future considerations', *Scientific and Technical
    Information Processing*, vol. 39, no. 3.
21 Simmon, 2018, p. 9
22 Mell & Grance, 2011, p. 3.
23 Ibid.
24 Ibid.
25 Ibid.
26 Ibid.
27 Ibid.
28 Simmon, 2018, p. 1.
29 S Murugesan & I Bojanova, 2016, 'Cloud computing: an overview', in Sam Mur-
    ugesan & Irena Bojanova (eds.), *Encyclopaedia of cloud computing*, John Wiley & Sons,
    West Sussex.
30 Christine Miyachi, 2018, 'What is cloud? It is time to update the NIST definition?',
    IEEE Cloud Computing, May/June, vol. 5, no. 3.
31 Philipp Leitner et al., 2019, 'A mixed-method empirical study of Function-as-a-Service
    software development in industrial practice', *Journal of Systems and Software*, vol. 149, p. 340.

32   Shoshana Zuboff, 2019, *The age of surveillance capitalism: the fight for a human future at the new frontier of power*, PublicAffairs, New York, p. 79.
33   Hu & Project Muse, 2015, p. ix.
34   United Nations Conference on Trade and Development, 2014, *Information economy report, 2013: The cloud economy and developing countries*, viewed 28 March 2020, http://unctad.org/en/PublicationsLibrary/ier2013_en.pdf.
35   United Nations Educational, Scientific and Cultural Organization (UNESCO), 2011, *UNESCO and the use of the Internet in its domains of competence*, viewed 28 March 2020, www.unesco.org/new/fileadmin/MULTIMEDIA/HQ/ED/ICT/pdf/useinternet domains.pdf.
36   See OECD, 2014 and OECD, 2019.
37   JT Flores Callejas & P Dumitriu, 2019, *Managing cloud computing services in the United Nations system*, report JIU/REP/2019/5, United Nations Joint Inspection Unit, p. iv.
38   Ibid, p. 10.
39   Ibid.
40   Elaine Goh & Eng Sengsavang, 2016, *Survey results on the use of cloud services for records management purposes by international organizations*, InterPARES Trust Research Report, viewed 22 March 2020, https://interparestrust.org/assets/public/dissemination/TR01_20160928_RMinIOs_TRWorkshop7_SurveyReport_Final.pdf, p. 8.
41   Callejas & Dumitriu, 2019, p. 11.
42   Ibid, p. 8.
43   Ibid, p. iii.
44   Ibid, p. 44.
45   International Computing Centre, n.d. 'Worldwide Data Centres – United Nations Jurisdiction', viewed 13 September 2020, www.unicc.org/data-centres/.
46   Callejas & Dumitriu, 2019, p. 44.
47   International Computing Centre, 2019, 'ICC assists UNHCR with migration of Iris-Guard to Microsoft Azure', November 14, viewed 29 February 2020, www.unicc.org/in-focus/2019/11/14/icc-assists-unhcr-with-migration-of-irisguard-to-microsoft-azure/.
48   Charlie Dunmore, 2015, 'Iris scan system provides cash lifeline to Syrian refugees in Jordan', United Nations High Commissioner for Refugees, March 23, viewed 22 March 2020, www.unhcr.org/news/latest/2015/3/550fe6ab9/iris-scan-system-provides-cash-lifeline-syrian-refugees-jordan.html.
49   UN Environment Programme, 2018, 'UN Environment and Google announce ground-breaking partnership to protect our planet', July 16, viewed 22 March 2020, www.unenvironment.org/news-and-stories/press-release/un-environment-and-google-announce-ground-breaking-partnership.
50   Callejas & Dumitriu, 2019, p. 19; Goh & Sengsavang, 2016, p. 12.
51   Goh & Sengsavang, 2016, p. 11.
52   Ibid, p. 7.
53   Unpublished comments by interviewees AR1, AR3, IT1 from InterPARES Trust project, *The use of cloud services for records management purposes in international organizations (TR01)*. See Eng Sengsavang & Elaine Goh, 2017a, *Final report TR01: the use of cloud services for records management purposes in international organizations*, viewed 28 March 2020, https://interparestrust.org/assets/public/dissemination/TR01_20170515_Cloud ServicesInternationalOrganizations_FinalReport.pdf.
54   Sengsavang & Goh, 2017b, *Interview analysis: the use of cloud services for records management purposes in international organizations*, InterPARES Trust Project Report, viewed 7 March 2020, https://interparestrust.org/assets/public/dissemination/TR01_20160928_RMinIOs_TRWorkshop7_SurveyReport_Final.pdf, p. 7.
55   Callejas & Dumitriu, 2019, pp. 13, 19.
56   Ibid, p. 16.
57   Ibid.
58   Ibid; Sengsavang & Goh, 2017b, pp. 8–9.

59 Ibid.
60 Ibid, p. 8.
61 Ibid.
62 Ibid, p. 9.
63 Ibid.
64 Callejas & Dumitriu, 2019, p. 17.
65 Sengsavang & Goh, 2017b, p. 9.
66 Callejas & Dumitriu, 2019, p. 17.
67 Sengsavang & Goh, 2017b, p. 9.
68 Callejas & Dumitriu, 2019, p. 17.
69 Ibid.
70 Ibid, p. 16.
71 Mell & Grance, 2011, p. 2.
72 Ibid, p. 4.
73 Sengsavang & Goh, 2017b, p. 9.
74 Internet Governance Forum, 2017, 'Managing cloud computing in the United Nations', December 17, viewed 7 March 2020, www.intgovforum.org/multilingual/content/igf-2017-day-1-room-xxv-of29-managing-cloud-computing-in-the-united-nations-system.
75 United Nations High Commissioner for Refugees, 2017, *Global strategic priorities – Progress Report*, www.unhcr.org/5b2b75e37.pdf, p. 59.
76 Callejas & Dumitriu, 2019, pp. 8–9.
77 Sengsavang & Goh, 2017b, p. 9.
78 Mell & Grance, 2011, p. 4.
79 Simson L Garfinkel, 1999, *Architects of the information society: thirty-five years of the laboratory for computer science at MIT*, Hal Abelson (ed.), The MIT Press, p. 1.
80 Hu & Project Muse, 2015, p. 64.
81 Ibid, p. 61.
82 Ibid, p. 18; Goh &Sengsavang, 2016, p. 12; Sengsavang & Goh, 2017b, p. 8–9.
83 Callejas & Dumitriu, 2019, p. 18.
84 Ibid, p. 18.
85 Julie Mcleod & Brianna Gormly, 2017, 'Using the cloud for records storage: issues of trust', *Archival Science*, vol. 17, no. 4, pp. 349–370.
86 Gillian Oliver & Steve Knight, 2015, 'Storage as a strategic issue: digital preservation in the cloud', *D-LIB Magazine*, vol. 21, no. 3/4, March/April, www.dlib.org/dlib/march15/oliver/03oliver.html.
87 Ibid.
88 Christopher J Hodson, 2019, *Cyber risk management: prioritize threats, identify vulnerabilities and apply controls*, KoganPage, London, p. 29.
89 Ibid. See also ENISA, 2012.
90 Callejas & Dumitriu, 2019, pp. 18–19.
91 Ibid, p. 20.
92 Ibid.
93 Ibid.
94 Teresa Carlson, 2020, 'AWS launches initiative to accelerate COVID-19 diagnostics, research, and testing', *The Amazon Blog* online, March 20, viewed 29 March 2020, https://blog.aboutamazon.com/innovation/aws-launches-initiative-to-accelerate-covid-19-diagnostics-research-and-testing.
95 Ibid.
96 Ibid.
97 Financial Post, 2020, 'ESRI and United Nations team to provide countries with COVID-19 data responses', viewed 11 April 2020, https://business.financialpost.com/pmn/press-releases-pmn/business-wire-news-releases-pmn/esri-and-united-nations-team-to-provide-countries-with-covid-19-data-resources.

98 United Nations Commission on International Trade Law, 2019, *Notes on the main issues of cloud computing contracts*, viewed 12 April 2020, https://uncitral.un.org/sites/uncitral.un.org/files/media-documents/uncitral/en/19-09103_eng.pdf. See also Justice Opara-Martins, Reza Sahandi & Feng Tian, 2016, 'Critical analysis of vendor lock-in and its impact on cloud computing migration: a business perspective', *Journal of Cloud Computing*, vol. 5, no. 4, https://link.springer.com/content/pdf/10.1186/s13677-016-0054-z.pdf.

99 Callejas & Dumitriu, 2019, p. 26.

100 ENISA, 2012, p. 4.

101 OECD, 2014, 'Cloud computing: the concept, impacts and the role of government policy', *OECD Digital Economy Papers*, No. 240, OECD Publishing, Paris, http://dx.doi.org/10.1787/5jxzf4lcc7f5-en, p. 21.

102 Callejas & Dumitriu, 2019, p. 7.

103 Ibid.

104 OECD, 2019, '1.1 Technology trends', in *Measuring the digital transformation: a roadmap for the future*, OECD Publishing, Paris, viewed 29 February 2020, https://doi.org/10.1787/9789264311992-en.

105 Armbrust et al., 2009, 'Above the clouds: a Berkley view of cloud computing', *Electrical Engineering and Computer Sciences*, University of California at Berkeley, Technical Report No. UCB/EECS-2009-28, www.eecs.berkeley.edu/Pubs/TechRpts/2009/EECS-2009-28.html, p. 5.

106 Ibid.

107 Callejas & Dumitriu, 2019, p. 7.

108 Ibid.

109 Satya Nadella, 2014, 'Mobile first, cloud first press briefing', Microsoft, March 27, viewed 7 March 2020, https://news.microsoft.com/2014/03/27/satya-nadella-mobile-first-cloud-first-press-briefing/.

110 Ibid.

111 Callejas & Dumitriu, 2019, p. 14.

112 Rolf H Weber, 2015, 'Legal safeguards for cloud computing' in Anne SY Cheung & Rolf H Weber (eds.), *Privacy and legal issues in cloud computing*, Edward Elgar, Cheltenham, UK, p. 49.

113 Data at rest is defined as "stored data: residing on a disk and/or in a file," whereas data in motion is "data that is being transferred across a network." See E Conrad, S Misenar & J Feldman, 2016, 'Asset Security (Protecting Security of Assets)', in E Conrad, S Misenar & J Feldman (eds.), *CISSP Study Guide* (3rd edn), Syngress, p. 96.

114 Primavera De Filippi & Smary McCarthy, 2012, 'Cloud computing: centralization and data Sovereignty', *European Journal of Law and Technology*, vol. 3 no. 2, p. 8.

115 Stephen P Mulligan, 2018, 'Cross-border data sharing under the CLOUD Act', Congressional Research Service, April 23, viewed 7 March 2020, https://fas.org/sgp/crs/misc/R45173.pdf, p. 2.

116 Ibid, p. 23.

117 Ibid, pp. 2–3.

118 Julian Box, 2018, 'How the CLOUD Act will affect the way cloud providers serve their customers', International Association of Privacy Professionals (IAPP), July 13, viewed 7 March 2020, https://iapp.org/news/a/how-the-cloud-act-will-affect-the-way-cloud-providers-serve-their-customers/.

119 Paul Whimpenny & Donata Rugarabamu, 2017, 'Promoting cloud in a risk-averse organization', *Network World*, Jan 9, viewed 7 March 2020, www.networkworld.com/article/3150257/promoting-cloud-in-a-risk-averse-organization.html.

120 Ademola Abass, 2014, *Complete international law: text, cases and materials*, 2nd edn, Oxford University Press, Oxford, p. 191.

121 Ibid.

122   General Assembly of the United Nations, 1946, 13 February, 'Convention on the privileges and immunities of the United Nations', viewed 7 March 2020, https://trea ties.un.org/doc/Treaties/1946/12/19461214%2010-17%20PM/Ch_III_1p.pdf.

123   Leonard Díaz-González, 1991, '(Consolidated) fifth report on relations between states and international organizations (second part of the topic): status, privileges and immunities of international organizations, their officials, experts, etc.', UN Document A/CN.4/438. Extract from the *Yearbook of the International Law Commission* II, no. 1 (1991): pp. 91–112, viewed 7 March 2020, http://legal.un.org/ilc/documentation/english/a_cn4_438.pdf.

124   Wilfred C Jenks, 1961, *International immunities*, Stevens & Sons Limited, London.

125   European Data Protection Supervisor, 2018, *Guidelines on the use of cloud computing services by the European institutions and bodies*, 16 March, viewed 7 March 2020, https:// edps.europa.eu/sites/edp/files/publication/18-03-16_cloud_computing_guidelines_ en.pdf, p. 44.

126   S Bradshaw, C Millard & I Walden, 2018, 'Contracts for clouds: comparison and analysis of the Terms and Conditions of cloud computing services', *International Journal of Law and Information Technology*, vol. 19, no. 3, p. 192.

127   Unpublished comments by interviewees IT2, IT3, AR2, AR3, AR9 and AR10. See Sengsavang & Goh, 2017b.

128   Weimei Pan & Grant Mitchell in this volume, p. 120.

129   Callejas & Dumitriu, 2019.

130   Jeremy Richards, 2019, 'Phishing attack targeting United Nations and humanitarian organizations discovered by Lookout Phishing AI', *Lookout blog*, 24 October, viewed 7 March 2020, https://blog.lookout.com/lookout-phishing-ai-discovers-phishing-attack-targeting-humanitarian-organizations.

131   Warwick Ashford, 2019, 'A quarter of phishing emails bypass Office 365 security', April 10, viewed 7 March 2020, www.computerweekly.com/news/252461400/ A-quarter-of-phishing-emails-bypass-Office-365-security.

132   Raphael Satter, Jack Stubbs & Christopher Bing, 2020, 'Coronavirus: WHO sees rise in cyberattack attempts by hackers, official says', *Global News*, March 23, viewed 7 March 2020, https://globalnews.ca/news/6720754/coronavirus-who-cyberattack-ha ckers/.

133   World Health Organization, 2020, *Beware of criminals pretending to be WHO*, viewed 7 March 2020, www.who.int/about/communications/cyber-security.

134   United Nations Commission on International Trade Law, 2019.

135   Hu & Project Muse, 2015, pp. 68–69.

136   Ibid, p. 69.

137   Ibid.

138   Thomas Ristenpart et al., 2009, 'Hey you, get off of my cloud: exploring information leakage in third-party compute clouds', *CCS '09: Proceedings of the 16th ACM conference on computer and communications security*, pp. 199–212.

139   Unpublished comments by interviewees IT1 and AR6. See Sengsavang & Goh, 2017b.

140   Callejas & Dumitriu, 2019, p. 22.

141   An organization's security posture is "characterized by the maturity, effectiveness, and completeness of the risk-adjusted security controls implemented." See Cloud Security Alliance, 2009, *Security guidance for critical areas in cloud computing v2.1*, viewed 29 March 2020, www.cloudsecurityalliance.org/guidance/csaguide.v2.1.pdf, p. 25.

142   ENISA, 2012, p. 18.

143   Ibid, p. 22.

144   Unpublished comments by interviewees AR1, AR2. See Sengsavang & Goh, 2017b.

145   ISACA, 2009, *Shadow IT primer*, viewed 11 April 2020, www.isaca.org/bookstore/ bookstore-wht_papers-digital/whpshad, p. 4.

146   Ibid, p. 4; unpublished comments by interviewees AR2, AR8. See Sengsavang & Goh 2017b.

147   Terzi & Posta, 2010, p. 6.
148   Ibid.
149   United Nations Commission on International Trade Law, 2019, p. 4.
150   The UN Special Interest Group on Information Security has issued a 2013 white paper on 'Use of cloud computing in the United Nations System: recommendations for risk mitigation', which is available through the UN intranet and is not accessible to the wider public. The paper identifies potential ICT risks with the adoption of public cloud and makes "recommendations for actions or policies which might be taken to reduce the identified risks to acceptable levels." See United Nations Development Programme Executive Board, United Nations Population Fund and the United Nations Office for Project Services, 2018, pp. 11–12.
151   International Organization for Standardization, 2018, *ISO 31000 Risk management – Guidelines*, International Organization for Standardization, Geneva.
152   International Organization for Standardization, 2019, *IEC 31010 Risk management – Risk assessment techniques*, International Organization for Standardization, Geneva.
153   ISACA, 2013, *COBIT 5: For risk*, ISACA, Illinois. COBIT 5 is a framework developed by the Information Systems and Audit Control Association (ISACA) to help organizations "in achieving their objectives for the governance and management of enterprise information technology (IT)." See ISACA, 2013, p. 9.
154   Ibid.
155   International Organization for Standardization, 2018, p. 1.
156   International Organization for Standardization, 2019, p. 10.
157   Ibid.
158   ISACA, 2013, p. 17.
159   Ibid, p. 100.
160   Ibid, p. 12.
161   International Organization for Standardization, 2018, p. 6.
162   ISACA, 2013, p. 61.
163   Paul Krill, 2020, 'COVID-19 stress tests cloud services', *InfoWorld*, March 24, viewed 12 April 2020, www.infoworld.com/article/3534051/covid-19-stress-tests-cloud-services.html.
164   See Mary Foley, 2020, 'European users reporting they're hitting Azure capacity constraints', *ZDNET*, March 24, viewed 2 April 2020, www.zdnet.com/article/european-users-reporting-theyre-hitting-azure-capacity-constraints/. See also Aaron Tilley, 2020, 'One business winner amid coronavirus lock-downs: the cloud', *Wall Street Journal*, March 27, viewed 2 April 2020, www.wsj.com/articles/one-business-winner-amid-coronavirus-lockdowns-the-cloud-11585327905.
165   Microsoft Azure, 2020, 'Our commitment to customers and Microsoft cloud services continuity', *Microsoft blog*, March 31, viewed 2 April 2020, https://blogs.microsoft.com/latinx/2020/03/31/our-commitment-to-customers-and-microsoft-cloud-services-continuity/.
166   KPMG, 2020, 'COVID-19: what the CIO and CISO can do to help', KPMG, March 31, viewed 2 April 2020, https://assets.kpmg/content/dam/kpmg/ca/pdf/2020/03/what-the-cio-and-ciso-can-do-to-help-en.pdf.
167   Kate O'Flaherty, 2020, 'Zoom's a lifeline during COVID-19: this is why it's also a privacy risk', March 25, viewed 2 April 2020, www.forbes.com/sites/kateoflahertyuk/2020/03/25/zooms-a-lifeline-during-covid-19-this-is-why-its-also-a-privacy-risk/#181563d128ba.
168   Zoom CEO Eric Yuen published a blog post on 1 April 2020 partly as a result of extensive media coverage on Zoom's lack of security and privacy controls. Mr. Yuen announced a 90-day "feature freeze" so that his company can focus on security and privacy issues, including "conducting a comprehensive review with third-party experts and representative users." He also announced an update on Zoom's privacy policy on 29 March. Eric Yuen, 2020, 'A message to our users', *Zoom Blog* online, April 1, viewed 2 April 2020, https://blog.zoom.us/wordpress/2020/04/01/a-message-to-our-users/.

169 Zoom, 2020, 'Privacy policy', March 29, viewed 2 April 2020, https://zoom.us/privacy.
170 The FBI has issued an advisory stating that they have "received multiple reports of conferences being disrupted by pornographic and/or hate images and threatening language" and provided tips on how to "mitigate teleconference hijacking threats." Kristen Setera, 2020, 'FBI warns of teleconferencing and online classroom hijacking during COVID-19 pandemic', FBI Boston online, March 30, viewed 2 April 2020, www.fbi.gov/contact-us/field-offices/boston/news/press-releases/fbi-warns-of-telec onferencing-and-online-classroom-hijacking-during-covid-19-pandemic.
171 ISACA, 2013, p. 87.
172 Ibid, p. 61.
173 Ibid, p. 62.
174 Terzi & Posta, 2010, p. 16.
175 Ibid.
176 Yishan Zhang & Nikolay Chulkov, 2011. *Information and communication technology (ICT) governance in the United Nations system organizations*, report JIU/REP/2011/9, United Nations Joint Inspection Unit, viewed 12 April 2020, www.unjiu.org/sites/ www.unjiu.org/files/jiu_document_files/products/en/reports-notes/JIU%20Products/ JIU_REP_2011_9_English.pdf, p. 6.
177 Ibid, p. 5.
178 Ibid, p. 9.
179 International Organization for Standardization, 2018, pp. 10–11.
180 ISACA, 2013, p. 87.
181 Ibid, pp. 48–49.
182 International Organization for Standardization, 2018, p. 11.
183 See International Organization for Standardization, 2018 and ISACA, 2013.
184 International Organization for Standardization, 2018.
185 International Organization for Standardization, 2019, p. 14.
186 Ibid, p. 22.
187 Ibid, p. 20.
188 R Mogull et al., 2017, *Security guidance for critical areas of focus in cloud computing v4.0*, Cloud Security Alliance, viewed 12 April 2020, https://downloads.cloudsecurityallia nce.org/assets/research/security-guidance/security-guidance-v4-FINAL.pdf, p. 74.
189 International Organization for Standardization, 2018, p. 12.
190 ISACA, 2013, p. 102.
191 ENISA, 2016, March, *Exploring cloud incidents*, viewed 12 April 2020, www.enisa. europa.eu/publications/exploring-cloud-incidents, p. 6.
192 International Organization for Standardization, 2018, p. 13.
193 ISACA, 2013, p. 90.
194 Ibid, p. 81.
195 Unpublished comments by interviewees AR2 and AR9. See Sengsavang & Goh, 2017b.
196 International Organization for Standardization, 2018, p. 14.

Bibliography

Abass, A 2014, *Complete international law: text, cases and materials*, 2nd edn, Oxford University Press, Oxford.

Armbrust, M, Fox, A, Griffith, R, Joseph, AD, Katz, RH, Konwinski, A, Lee, G, Patterson, DA, Rabkin, A, Stoica I & Zaharia, M 2009, 'Above the clouds: a Berkley view of cloud computing', *Electrical Engineering and Computer Sciences*, University of California at Berkeley, Technical Report No. UCB/EECS-2009–2028, www.eecs.berkeley.edu/Pubs/ TechRpts/2009/EECS-2009-28.html.

Arutyunov, VV 2012, 'Cloud computing: its history of development, modern state and future considerations', *Scientific and Technical Information Processing*, vol. 39, no. 3.

Ashford, W 2019, 'A quarter of phishing emails bypass Office 365 security', April 10, viewed 7 March 2020, www.computerweekly.com/news/252461400/A-quarter-of-phishing-emails-bypass-Office-365-security.

Box, J 2018, 'How the CLOUD Act will affect the way cloud providers serve their customers', International Association of Privacy Professionals (IAPP), July 13, viewed 7 March 2020, https://iapp.org/news/a/how-the-cloud-act-will-affect-the-way-cloud-providers-serve-their-customers/.

Bradshaw, S, Millard, C & Walden, I 2018, 'Contracts for clouds: comparison and analysis of the Terms and Conditions of cloud computing services', *International Journal of Law and Information Technology*, vol. 19, no. 3, p. 192.

Callejas, JT Flores & Dumitriu, P 2019, *Managing cloud computing services in the United Nations system*, report JIU/REP/2019/5, United Nations Joint Inspection Unit.

Carlson, T 2020, 'AWS launches initiative to accelerate COVID-19 diagnostics, research, and testing', *The Amazon Blog* online, March 20, viewed 29 March 2020, https://blog.aboutamazon.com/innovation/aws-launches-initiative-to-accelerate-covid-19-diagnostics-research-and-testing.

Chang, H 2015, 'Data protection regulation and cloud computing', in Anne SY Cheung and Rolf H Weber (eds.), *Privacy and legal issues in cloud computing*, Edward Elgar, Cheltenham, pp. 26–42, doi:10.4337/9781783477074.00009.

Cloud Security Alliance 2009, *Security guidance for critical areas in cloud computing v2.1*, viewed 29 March 2020, www.cloudsecurityalliance.org/guidance/csaguide.v2.1.pdf.

Conrad, E, Misenar, S & Feldman, J 2016, 'Asset security (protecting security of assets)', in E Conrad, S Misenar & J Feldman (eds.), *CISSP Study Guide*, 3rd edn, Syngress.

Cubitt, S, Hassan, R & Volkmer, I 2011, 'Does cloud computing have a silver lining?', *Media, Culture & Society*, vol. 33, no. 1, pp. 149–158.

De Brandeberes, E 2010, 'Immunity of international organizations in post–conflict international administrations', *International Organizations Law Review*, vol. 7, no. 1, doi:10.1163/157237310X523812.

De Filippi, P & McCarthy, S 2012, 'Cloud computing: centralization and data sovereignty', *European Journal of Law and Technology*, vol. 3, no. 2, pp. 1–18.

Díaz-González, L 1991, '(Consolidated) Fifth report on relations between States and international organizations (second part of the topic): status, privileges and immunities of international organizations, their officials, experts, etc.', UN Document A/CN.4/438. Extract from the *Yearbook of the International Law Commission* II, no. 1, pp. 91–112, viewed 18 December 2014, http://legal.un.org/ilc/documentation/english/a_cn4_438.pdf.

Dunmore, C 2015, 'Iris scan system provides cash lifeline to Syrian refugees in Jordan,' United Nations High Commissioner for Refugees, March 23, viewed 22 March 2020, www.unhcr.org/news/latest/2015/3/550fe6ab9/iris-scan-system-provides-cash-lifeline-syrian-refugees-jordan.html.

ENISA (European Network and Information Security Agency) 2012, 'Cloud computing: benefits, risks and recommendations for information security' Rev. B, viewed 28 March 2020, https://resilience.enisa.europa.eu/cloud-security-and-resilience/publications/cloud-computing-benefits-risks-and-recommendations-for-information-security.

ENISA (European Network and Information Security Agency) 2016 March, 'Exploring cloud incidents,' viewed 12 April 2020, www.enisa.europa.eu/publications/exploring-cloud-incidents

European Data Protection Supervisor 2018, 'Guidelines on the use of cloud computing services by the European institutions and bodies,' March 16, viewed 7 March 2020,

https://edps.europa.eu/sites/edp/files/publication/18-03-16_cloud_computing_guide
lines_en.pdf.

Financial Post 2020, 'ESRI and United Nations team to provide countries with COVID-19
data responses', viewed 11 April 2020, https://business.financialpost.com/pmn/press-relea
ses-pmn/business-wire-news-releases-pmn/esri-and-united-nations-team-to-provide-
countries-with-covid-19-data-resources.

Foley, M 2020, 'European users reporting they're hitting Azure capacity constraints',
ZDNET, March 24, viewed 2 April 2020, www.zdnet.com/article/european-users-rep
orting-theyre-hitting-azure-capacity-constraints/.

Fox, R & Hao, W 2018, *Internet infrastructure: networking, web services, and cloud computing*,
CRC Press, Taylor & Francis Group, Boca Raton.

Garfinkel, S 1999, *Architects of the information society: thirty-five years of the laboratory for computer
science at MIT*, edited by H Abelson, The MIT Press.

Gartner 2016, 'Gartner says by 2020, a corporate "no-cloud" policy will be as rare as a "no-
internet" policy is today', 22 June, viewed 29 February 2020, www.gartner.com/en/
newsroom/press-releases/2016-06-22-gartner-says-by-2020-a-corporate-no-cloud-policy-
will-be-as-rare-as-a-no-internet-policy-is-today.

General Assembly of the United Nations 1946, 13 February, 'Convention on the privileges
and immunities of the United Nations', viewed 7 March 2020, https://treaties.un.org/
doc/Treaties/1946/12/19461214%2010-17%20PM/Ch_III_1p.pdf.

Goh, E & Sengsavang, E 2016, 'Survey results on the use of cloud services for records.
management purposes by international organizations', InterPARES Trust Research
Report, viewed 22 March 2020, https://interparestrust.org/assets/public/dissemination/
TR01_20160928_RMinIOs_TRWorkshop7_SurveyReport_Final.pdf.

Google Press Center 2006, 'Conversation with Eric Schmidt hosted by Danny Sullivan:
Search Engine Strategies Conference', 9 August, viewed 21 March 2020, www.google.
fr/press/podium/ses2006.html.

Hodson, CJ 2019, *Cyber risk management: prioritize threats, identify vulnerabilities and apply controls*, KoganPage, London.

Hu, T & Project Muse 2015, *A prehistory of the cloud*, MIT Press, Cambridge.

International Computing Centre n.d., 'Worldwide Data Centres – United Nations Jurisdiction', viewed 13 September 2020, www.unicc.org/data-centres.

International Computing Centre 2019, 'ICC assists UNHCR with migration of IrisGuard to
Microsoft Azure', November 14, viewed 29 February 2020, www.unicc.org/in-focus/
2019/11/14/icc-assists-unhcr-with-migration-of-irisguard-to-microsoft-azure/.

International Organization for Standardization 2018, *ISO 31000 risk management – Guidelines*, International Organization for Standardization, Geneva.

International Organization for Standardization 2019, *IEC 31010 Risk management – Risk
assessment techniques*, International Organization for Standardization, Geneva.

Internet Governance Forum 2017, 'Managing cloud computing in the United Nations',
December 17, viewed 7 March 2020, www.intgovforum.org/multilingual/content/
igf-2017-day-1-room-xxv-of29-managing-cloud-computing-in-the-united-nations-system.

ISACA 2009, *Shadow IT primer*, viewed 11 April 2020, www.isaca.org/bookstore/book
store-wht_papers-digital/whpshad.

ISACA 2013, *COBIT 5: For risk*, ISACA, Illinois.

Jenks, WC 1961, *International immunities*, Stevens & Sons, London.

KPMG 2020, 'COVID-19: what the CIO and CISO can do to help', KPMG, March,
viewed 2 April 2020, https://assets.kpmg/content/dam/kpmg/ca/pdf/2020/03/what-the-
cio-and-ciso-can-do-to-help-en.pdf.

Krill, P 2020, 'COVID-19 stress tests cloud services', *InfoWorld*, March 24, viewed 12 April 2020, www.infoworld.com/article/3534051/covid-19-stress-tests-cloud-services.html.

Kunz, JL 1947, 'Privileges and immunities of international organizations', *American Journal of International Law*, vol. 41, no. 4, pp. 828–862.

Leitner, P, Wittern, E, Spillner, J & Waldemar, H 2019, 'A mixed-method empirical study of Function-as-a-Service software development in industrial practice', *Journal of Systems and Software*, vol. 149, pp. 340–359.

McAfee 2019, *Cloud adoption and risk report*, viewed 29 February 2020, www.mcafee.com/enterprise/en-ca/solutions/lp/cloud-adoption-risk.html.

Mcleod, J & Gormly, B 2017, 'Using the cloud for records storage: issues of trust', *Archival Science*, vol. 17, no. 4, pp. 349–370.

McKendrick J 2016, 'Is all-cloud computing inevitable? Analysts suggest it is', *Forbes*, July 10, viewed 29 February 2020, www.forbes.com/sites/joemckendrick/2016/07/05/is-all-cloud-computing-inevitable-analysts-suggest-it-is/#2f0d36dbebf0.

Mell, P & Grance, T 2011, *The NIST definition of cloud computing*, report, National Institute of Standards and Technology, U.S. Department of Commerce, viewed 8 March 2020, https://nvlpubs.nist.gov/nistpubs/Legacy/SP/nistspecialpublication800-145.pdf.

Microsoft Azure 2020, 'Our commitment to customers and Microsoft cloud services continuity', *Microsoft blog*, March 3, viewed 2 April 2020, https://blogs.microsoft.com/latinx/2020/03/31/our-commitment-to-customers-and-microsoft-cloud-services-continuity/.

Miyachi, C 2018, 'What is cloud? Is it time to update the NIST definition?', *IEEE Cloud Computing*, vol. 5, no. 3, May/June.

Mogull, R, Arlen, J, Gilbert, F, Lane, A, Mortman, D, Peterson, G & Rothman, M 2017, *Security guidance for critical areas of focus in cloud computing v4.0*, Cloud Security Alliance, viewed 12 April 2020, https://downloads.cloudsecurityalliance.org/assets/research/security-guidance/security-guidance-v4-FINAL.pdf.

Mulligan, SP 2018, 'Cross-border data sharing under the CLOUD Act', Congressional Research Service, April 23, viewed 7 March 2020, https://fas.org/sgp/crs/misc/R45173.pdf.

Murugesan, S & Bojanova, I 2016, 'Cloud computing: an overview', in S Murugesan & I Bojanova (eds), *Encyclopedia of cloud computing*. John Wiley & Sons, West Sussex, UK.

Nadella, S 2014, 'Mobile first, cloud first press briefing', Microsoft, March 27, viewed 7 March 2020, https://news.microsoft.com/2014/03/27/satya-nadella-mobile-first-cloud-first-press-briefing/.

OECD 2014, 'Cloud computing: the concept, impacts and the role of government policy', *OECD Digital Economy Papers*, No. 240, OECD Publishing, Paris, http://dx.doi.org/10.1787/5jxzf4lcc7f5-en, p. 21.

OECD 2019, *Measuring the digital transformation: a roadmap for the future*, OECD Publishing, Paris, viewed 29 February 2020, https://doi.org/10.1787/9789264311992-en.

O'Flaherty, K 2020, 'Zoom's a lifeline during COVID-19: this is why it's also a privacy risk', March 25, viewed 2 April 2020, www.forbes.com/sites/kateoflahertyuk/2020/03/25/zooms-a-lifeline-during-covid-19-this-is-why-its-also-a-privacy-risk/#181563d128ba.

Oliver, G & Knight, S 2015, 'Storage as a strategic issue: Digital preservation in the cloud', *D-LIB Magazine*, vol. 21, no. 3/4, March/April,www.dlib.org/dlib/march15/oliver/03oliver.html.

Opara-Martins, J, Sahandi, R & Tian, F 2016, 'Critical analysis of vendor lock-in and its impact on cloud computing migration: a business perspective', *Journal of Cloud Computing*, vol. 5, no. 4, viewed 25 March 2020, https://link.springer.com/content/pdf/10.1186/s13677-016-0054-z.pdf.

Reed, C 2015, *Information in the Cloud: ownership, control and accountability*, Edward Elgar Publishing, doi:10.4337/9781783477074.00014, pp. 139–159.

Richards, J 2019, 'Phishing attack targeting United Nations and humanitarian organizations discovered by Lookout Phishing AI', *Lookout blog*, 24 October, viewed 7 March 2020, https://blog.lookout.com/lookout-phishing-ai-discovers-phishing-attack-targeting-humanitarian-organizations.

Ristenpart, T, Tromer, E, Shacham, H & Savage, S 2009, 'Hey you, get off of my cloud: exploring information leakage in third-party compute clouds', *CCS '09: Proceedings of the 16th ACM conference on computer and communications security*, pp. 199–212.

Satter, R, Stubbs, J & Bing, C 2020, 'Coronavirus: WHO sees rise in cyberattack attempts by hackers, official says', March 23, viewed 7 March 2020, https://globalnews.ca/news/6720754/coronavirus-who-cyberattack-hackers/.

Sengsavang, E & Goh, E 2017a, *Final report TR01: the use of cloud services for records management purposes in international organizations*, InterPARES Trust Project Report, viewed 28 March 2020, https://interparestrust.org/assets/public/dissemination/TR01_20170515_CloudServicesInternationalOrganizations_FinalReport.pdf.

Sengsavang, E & Goh, E 2017b, *Interview analysis: the use of cloud services for records management purposes in international organizations*, InterPARES Trust Project Report, viewed 7 March 2020, https://interparestrust.org/assets/public/dissemination/TR01_20170515_CloudServicesIO_InterviewAnalysis_Final.pdf.

Setera, Kristen 2020, 'FBI warns of teleconferencing and online classroom hijacking during COVID-19 pandemic', FBI Boston online, March 30, viewed 2 April 2020, www.fbi.gov/contact-us/field-offices/boston/news/press-releases/fbi-warns-of-teleconferencing-and-online-classroom-hijacking-during-covid-19-pandemic.

Simmon, E 2018, 'Evaluation of cloud computing services based on NIST SP 800–145', viewed 29 February 2020, https://nvlpubs.nist.gov/nistpubs/SpecialPublications/NIST.SP.500-322.pdf.

Terzi, C & Posta, I 2010, *Review of enterprise risk management in the United Nations system: Benchmarking Framework*, report JIU/REP/2010/4, United Nations Joint Inspection Unit, viewed 12 April 2020, www.unjiu.org/sites/www.unjiu.org/files/jiu_document_files/products/en/reports-notes/JIU%20Products/JIU_REP_2010_4_English.pdf.

Tilley, A 2020, 'One business winner amid coronavirus lock-downs: the cloud', *Wall Street Journal*, March 27, viewed 2 April 2020, www.wsj.com/articles/one-business-winner-amid-coronavirus-lockdowns-the-cloud-11585327905.

United Nations Commission on International Trade Law 2019, 'Notes on the main issues of cloud computing contracts', viewed 12 April 2020, https://uncitral.un.org/sites/uncitral.un.org/files/media-documents/uncitral/en/19-09103_eng.pdf.

United Nations Conference on Trade and Development 2014, *Information economy report, 2013: the cloud economy and developing countries*, viewed 28 March 2020, http://unctad.org/en/PublicationsLibrary/ier2013_en.pdf.

United Nations Development Programme Executive Board, United Nations Population Fund and the United Nations Office for Project Services 2018 March 28, *Report of UNDP on the recommendations of the Joint Inspection Unit in 2017*, pp. 11–12.

United Nations Educational, Scientific, and Cultural Organization (UNESCO) 2011, *UNESCO and the use of the Internet in its domains of competence*, viewed 28 March 2020, www.unesco.org/new/fileadmin/MULTIMEDIA/HQ/ED/ICT/pdf/useinternetdomains.pdf.

United Nations Environment Programme 2018, 'UN Environment and Google announce ground-breaking partnership to protect our planet', July 16, viewed 22 March 2020, www.unenvironment.org/news-and-stories/press-release/un-environment-and-google-announce-ground-breaking-partnership.

United Nations High Commissioner for Refugees 2017, *Global strategic priorities – progress report*, viewed 22 March 2020, www.unhcr.org/5b2b75e37.pdf.

Weber, RH 2015, 'Legal safeguards for cloud computing', in Ann SY Cheung & RH Weber (eds.), *Privacy and legal issues in cloud computing*, Edward Elgar, Cheltenham, UK.

Whimpenny, P & Rugarabamu, D 2017, 'Promoting cloud in a risk-averse organization', *Network World*, Jan 9, viewed 7 March 2020, www.networkworld.com/article/3150257/promoting-cloud-in-a-risk-averse-organization.html.

World Health Organization 2020, 'Beware of criminals pretending to be WHO,' viewed 7 March 2020, www.who.int/about/communications/cyber-security.

Wu, C & Buyya, R 2015, 'Cloud computing', in C Wu & R Buyya (eds.), *Cloud data centers and cost modelling: a complete guide to planning, designing and building a cloud data centre*, Morgan Kaufmann, Waltham, MA.

Yuen, Eric 2020, 'A message to our users', *Zoom Blog* online, April 1, viewed 2 April 2020, https://blog.zoom.us/wordpress/2020/04/01/a-message-to-our-users/.

Zhang, Y & Chulkov, N 2011, *Information and communication technology (ICT) governance in the United Nations system organizations*, report JIU/REP/2011/9, United Nations Joint Inspection Unit, viewed 12 April 2020, www.unjiu.org/sites/www.unjiu.org/files/jiu_document_files/products/en/reports-notes/JIU%20Products/JIU_REP_2011_9_English.pdf.

Zoom 2020, 'Privacy policy', March 29, viewed 2 April 2020, https://zoom.us/privacy.

Zuboff, S 2019, *The age of surveillance capitalism: the fight for a human future at the new frontier of power*, PublicAffairs, New York.

4

EXTRATERRITORIALITY AND INTERNATIONAL ORGANIZATIONS[1]

Darra L. Hofman[2]

Introduction

International organizations (IOs) occupy a legally unique position. The International Law Commission[3] defines an IO as "an organization established by a treaty or other instrument governed by international law and possessing its own international legal personality." It should be noted, however, that "international organizations" is a broad and disputed term; as Klabbers writes in *An Introduction to International Organizations Law*, "what exactly is an international organization? ... The short answer is, quite simply, that we don't know."[4] Thus, while this chapter speaks about international organizations, extraterritoriality, and cloud computing in relatively general terms, it is important to remember that "international actors do not purposely set out to create an international organization following some eternally valid blueprint ... their aim will be to create an entity that allows them to meet their ends."[5] Thus, the precise privileges and immunities of a particular international organization, the functions of that organization and its archives, and the best use of the cloud for that organization will depend on the particular aims and context of the organization.

First, however, we must determine the subject under consideration. Determining what is meant by "international organizations" is more challenging than it might seem. Determining the particular rights, privileges, and immunities of a particular organization is even further challenging. As Lindbolm explains, the answers one arrives at to a number of questions of international law will depend upon the theoretical and methodological approach one takes to those problems. For example, "[w]hile there is a common understanding that the expressions 'subject of law' and 'legal personality' have to do with rights, obligations and legal capacity, it is not possible to deduce a fixed set of powers or capacities from the fact that an entity is a legal person."[6]

Most authors define "international organizations" as those "established by a treaty or other instrument governed by international law and possessing its own international legal personality. International organizations may include as members, in addition to States, other entities."[7] Thus, according to these authors, "international organizations" are limited to what might be called "intergovernmental organizations" (IGOs), and that is how this term will be used in this chapter. However, it is worth acknowledging that this is not the only perspective; we will address briefly some of the competing understandings of "international organizations" and the different types of organizations that operate internationally.

The term "intergovernmental organization" "refers to an entity created by treaty, involving two or more nations, to work in good faith, on issues of common interest. In the absence of a treaty an IGO does not exist in the legal sense."[8] IGOs are the archetypical international organizations with regard to extraterritoriality. However, that does not mean that legal questions concerning IGOs are simple to answer. Consider Sognnæs' classification: IGOs can roughly be divided into three different categories. There are the global organizations, such as the United Nations (UN), regional organizations, like the North Atlantic Treaty Organization (NATO), and supranational organizations. The latter is characterized by the ability to possess authority at the expense of the State's own authority. The European Union (EU) is the prime example.[9]

However, no classification, including Sognnæs', is universally accepted. As compared to Sognnæs, Schermers & Blokker, in their foundational work on international institutional law, argue that the EU "has no international legal personality of its own. It therefore has no status, and does not exist, in international law."[10] Thus, there exists controversy around the boundaries of the category of organization most clearly classified as "international organizations," IGOs. Nonetheless, IGOs, which are creations of treaty and have long been recognized as having legal personality, have the clearest relationship to extraterritoriality in the sense of privileges and immunities, discussed in greater detail below.

Not everyone agrees with limiting "international organizations" to IGOs, however. Judge argues that "[i]t is usual to distinguish between three main types of 'international organization,' namely: intergovernmental organizations, international non-governmental organizations, and multinational enterprises."[11] Indeed, Wiessner & Willard, taking a policy-based approach, find that there exists a large number of potential non-state participants in international relations, if not necessarily subjects of international law:

> Besides the traditional nation-state, whether independent or associated with another actor, the world of social and decision processes includes intergovernmental organizations, non-self-governing territories, autonomous regions, and indigenous and other peoples, as well as private entities such as multinational corporations, media, nongovernmental organizations, private armies, gangs and individuals. An actor with actual or potential influence is a candidate for participation in the decision process.[12]

The second large category of international actors – again, there is debate as to whether or not they qualify as "international organizations" – is non-governmental organizations (NGOs), specifically international non-governmental organizations, INGOs. Defining non-governmental organizations, however, is more challenging than their intergovernmental counterparts:

> To this day, there is no consensus around a universal definition of NGO ... NGOs are created without the involvement of States and without States as their members. They are rather established at the initiative of individuals. Besides the non-governmental interference, general features of NGOs are their non-profit making aim, volunteer work and the fact that they often have their grounds in goals of humanitarian value. To illustrate, one can mention Amnesty International and Greenpeace.[13]

NGOs, then, are an enormously diverse group of organizations, whose reach can be local, regional, national, or international. They can be created through a number of mechanisms and fulfil a number of mandates. The legal status of NGOs is developing rapidly,[14] with Lapaš referring to "advanced NGOs," as well as "trans-governmental organisations" as "IGO-like entities," to which privileges and immunities might be accorded.[15] The status of NGOs with regard to privileges and immunities, including the inviolability of the archives, remains unsettled.

Finally, there are international organizations, like the International Federation of Red Cross and Red Crescent Societies (IFRC) and the International Committee of the Red Cross (ICRC) that defy neat categorization. As Sognnæs explains with regards to the ICRC:

> The ICRC was originally a private organization established under the Swiss Civil Code by the initiative of individuals. Despite still having its roots in Swiss law, the organization now operates in over 80 countries with employment beyond the Swiss borders. The fact that the individual, national based organization operates under an international mandate has resulted in debates regarding the categorization of the organization, whether it is an IGO or an NGO.[16]

In short, then, while there is general agreement that IGOs are "international organizations," insofar as they have legal personality and rights, privileges, and immunities under international law, there is no such agreement regarding NGOs. Thus, the primary subject of consideration for this chapter will be IGOs; henceforth, "international organizations" and "IOs" will refer primarily to IGOs. The fact that IOs are established by instruments and governed by international law puts them within very particular juridical contexts, leading to unique challenges and opportunities with regard to records and archives. The juridical context of a particular IO encompasses international law, including the privileges and immunities particular to IOs; the contractual terms of the IO's establishing instrument;

and potentially the law of the IO's host state(s). Thus, determining how best to manage records throughout their lifecycle to support an IO's mandate, to meet its legal obligations, and to protect its rights requires analysis and a sophisticated understanding of the laws applying to the archives of the IO hosted in a particular jurisdiction. The introduction of cloud computing has added to the jurisdictional complexity of IOs' archives. For IOs considering cloud-based recordkeeping, a full understanding of the protections and limits of extraterritoriality is necessary to ensure that the organization's records and archives are protected as fully as possible.

The juridical context of international organizations

> [The] interplay of internal and external sovereignty that defines the modern state is not only constitutive for the power to enact, to enforce, and to speak the law within a specific territory. It is also a condition of possibility for the protection of human rights and for the internal division of sovereignty that defines the rule of law.[17]

Establishing the juridical-administrative context of records is both critical for making decisions about those records and a matter of some complexity. An organization must know which jurisdiction(s) have authority over its records in order to determine its legal obligations regarding retention, data privacy, access to information, and other regulated aspects of archives and recordkeeping. This can be challenging for any creating body. International organizations, however, occupy a unique position of marked juridical and legal complexity. As Klabbers observes, "the law of international organisations is still somewhat immature. We lack a convincing theory on the international legal personality of international organisations, to name just one thing."[18] Indeed, "[h]istorical usage of international legal personality for international organisations typically has meant no more than an empty legal fiction that enabled institutions to participate in the international legal system."[19]

Understanding the source and nature of the international legal personality[20] of an international organization, however, can help us understand the obligations and needs of the organization as a record-creating body:

> Having international personality for an international organisation means possessing rights, duties, powers and liabilities, etc. (all in the Hohfeldian sense) as distinct from its members or its creators on the international plane and in international law. What these rights, etc. are and how they are established is a subsequent question.[21]

Part of the challenge in determining the rights, duties, powers, and liabilities of international organizations flows from the fact that they are not sovereign. International law, after all, has historically dealt with the relationships between sovereigns; "Bentham … described it as 'that branch of jurisprudence … [exclusively concerned with] mutual transactions between sovereigns as such.'"[22] International organizations, however, are not sovereigns. A sovereign is "[a] person, body, or state vested with independent and supreme authority."[23] Instead, international organizations occupy a unique interstitial space between what Klabbers describes as "the two poles that have dominated theories about (and of) international law"[24]: "if a theory managed to explain a lot about sovereignty, it could not cope with considerations of community, and where it could cope with community, it was invariably at the expense of considerations of sovereignty."[25] In other words, Klabbers argues that international law has not found any satisfactory theory to address the paradox that IOs are created by and have obligations to the sovereignty of states while they at the same time have obligations to the broader international community in meeting their mandates, even when doing so might go against the interests of a particular state and its sovereignty. How to negotiate the interstitial space that IOs occupy – a space of legal personality, rights, and duties, but not of full sovereignty, and also a space of community mediation and disagreement – remains unresolved.

"[P]ublic international law has long been thought of as largely a law of coexistence … international law regulated the practical aspects of sovereign states living together on Planet Earth, dealing with such issues as the jurisdiction of states."[26] At the heart of the sovereignty pole is what Ford terms "the jurisdictional frame of mind"[27]: "Territorial jurisdiction categorizes the elements over which authority is to be exercised primarily by area, and secondarily, if at all, by type … It will always … be defined by area. … A jurisdiction is territorially defined."[28] Per Ford, territorial jurisdiction is so naturalized that:

> When the von Trapps reach Switzerland,[29] only the simplest child dares to ask, "Why don't the Nazis just cross the border to get them?" It is simply understood by those with a jurisdictions frame of mind … that they can't cross the line, that if they do their authority will vanish like Cinderella's carriage at the stroke of midnight. The logic of government is the logic of jurisdiction – question it and all that is solid melts into air.[30]

Despite how naturalized it has become, "jurisdiction" is not a given means of organizing legal authority. "'Jurisdiction' is a term first encountered in the early fourteenth century, initially referring to the administration of justice and soon meaning 'extent or range of administrative power,'"[31] yet many systems of law existed prior to then. Ford refers to jurisdiction as "a bundle of practices"[32] in which the lines on the map are "constantly being *made* real."[33] The controversy over the international legal personality of international organizations flows in part from the novelty of these organizations; while territorial sovereignty has largely been naturalized, making the practices to enact such sovereignty less visible, the practices that make international organizations real are quite young and still being refined and agreed upon. This "making real" becomes particularly apparent when the exercise of an international organization's rights and/or privileges challenges or limits the sovereignty of a state, be that state member or non-member.

Defining extraterritoriality

> We must remember that sovereign jurisdiction ... so far, is also the pre-condition of the unilateral enforcement of human rights, such as a fair trial, privacy, and non-discrimination. The challenge will be to sustain a measure of safety, freedom, and respect for human rights in cyberspace, based on a legality that cannot – however – be grounded in the monopolistic spatiality of territorial sovereignty.[34]

Extraterritoriality is perhaps one of the best examples of the complexity of the legal status of international organizations, and of the changes over time and across contexts in legal understanding and application. Extraterritoriality is challenging as a threshold matter simply because it is used to signify two separate concepts: extraterritorial exercise of jurisdiction and diplomatic immunity. Furthermore, the legal theory underpinning extraterritoriality in the sense of diplomatic immunity has changed over time, and there is significant confusion about the contexts and circumstances in which extraterritoriality-as-diplomatic-immunity applies. Because of both its complexity and its centrality to the inviolability of the archives, extraterritoriality, in both senses, must be understood if the larger questions of international organizations putting records and archives in the cloud is to be understood.

Extraterritorial exercise of jurisdiction

The complexity of "extraterritoriality" reflects, in part, the increasing complexity of international law; "international law has changed in fundamental ways during this period, in particular through the rise in recognition and importance of non-state actors."[35] Nonetheless, the literature on extraterritorial jurisdiction typically approaches the subject – at least initially – from the perspectives of states and sovereign entities.[36] In particular, the analysis of extraterritoriality typically starts, unsurprisingly, from the concepts of territoriality and jurisdiction.[37] "Jurisdiction" under public international law is generally defined as "the State's right under international law to regulate conduct in matters not exclusively of domestic concern ... Jurisdiction involves a State's right to exercise certain of its powers."[38] Some authors posit that jurisdiction can be independent from territory.[39] Hildebrandt notes that the potential for jurisdiction to be independent from territory has implications for cyberspace, citing authors such as John Perry Barlow, David Johnson, and David Post, who perceive that cyberspace is not a physical space.[40] Hildebrandt argues that concepts of geographical borders and territorial jurisdiction are not applicable in cyberspace, since the "assumption that the effects of any particular behaviour are restricted by physical proximity does not hold."[41] Szigeti goes so far as to argue that territorial jurisdiction as a concept is an illusion:

There is a general uncertainty in what counts as "territorial" and what counts as "extraterritorial" jurisdiction, and this is the result of the almost complete lack of geographical information in jurisdictional discourse. ... The lack of a geographical connection means that most jurisdictional conflicts are better described as conflicts between communities and their legal orders, without a territorial connection. Doctrines of jurisdiction in international law should be reformulated to reflect the illusory nature of the territorial-extraterritorial division.[42]

In short, then, Szigeti recommends legal reform to do away with the territorial/extraterritorial divide entirely. Even authors who accept the division between territorial and extraterritorial jurisdiction, however, acknowledge the fluidity and uncertainty of the space. Suda asserts that, "In practice, extraterritoriality refers to the exercise of direct authority over entities and behaviors in foreign jurisdictions. Such transborder claims of authority represent a violation of – or at least an exception to – the sovereign principle of territoriality."[43] Countries exercise extraterritorial jurisdiction in a number of domains: data protection, cybercrime, anti-corruption, and cross-jurisdictional transactions, for example, are all regulated by entities such as the United States and the European Union beyond the boundaries of those entities.[44] Further:

Extraterritoriality is employed when states have divergent policy preferences and practices. Hypothetically, if all countries have anti-corruption or anti-trust laws with equivalent provisions and enforce them to an equal extent, the US (or any other country) would not have an incentive to extend the reach of its foreign bribery regulation or competition policy. In this light, extraterritoriality can be considered a unilateral effort to manage differences in law and regulation across jurisdictions.[45]

Managing these differences through extraterritoriality is deeply problematic, however. Extraterritorial exercise of jurisdiction can lead to uncertainty for individuals and organizations in knowing to which laws they must adhere, challenges in interpreting the various meanings of legal terms of art[46] in different jurisdictions, expansive interpretations of legal instruments that lead to increased jurisdictional scope,[47] and the challenges of enforcing extraterritorial jurisdiction.[48] Indeed, Kuner notes that even "the term 'extraterritorial jurisdiction' ... seems to have different meanings in different legal systems," opting to use the term "exorbitant jurisdiction" instead.[49] Despite these challenges, Coughlan et al. argue that:

The rapidly growing volume and variety of transnational interactions between people, activities and events, which constitute the engine of globalization, ensure that the extraterritorial application of national legal powers cannot be avoided. Consequently, the scope, means and effectiveness of extraterritorial action must be examined and evaluated.[50]

Diplomatic immunity

Perhaps confusingly, "extraterritoriality" refers not only to the exercise of jurisdiction beyond the borders of a country, but also to certain immunities enjoyed by diplomats, foreign states, and international organizations, and to a theory justifying those immunities. *Black's Law Dictionary* defines extraterritoriality as "The freedom of diplomats, foreign ministers, and royalty from the jurisdiction of the country in which they temporarily reside."[51] Similarly, *The Oxford Dictionary of Law* defines extraterritoriality (sometimes termed "exterritoriality") as "A theory in international law explaining diplomatic immunity on the basis that the premises of a foreign mission form a part of the territory of the sending state."[52] *Encyclopaedia Britannica* explains that "extraterritoriality" represents "in international law, the immunities enjoyed by foreign states or international organisations and the official representatives from the jurisdictions of the country in which they represent."[53] Thus, while "extraterritoriality" encompasses, and is sometimes used to refer to, extraterritorial jurisdiction, its primary definitions relate to diplomatic privileges and immunities.

As Klabbers notes, "[o]ne of the classic branches of international law is the law of immunity"[54]; extraterritoriality is tied to the concept of diplomatic immunity with respect to states and not exclusively (or even specifically) to that of international organizations. Extraterritoriality as diplomatic immunity is arguably the "classic" meaning of "extraterritoriality" applicable to IOs. However, because both "extraterritoriality" and "extraterritorial jurisdiction" pose significant issues for IOs looking to use cloud computing for their records and archives, all meanings of the term must be considered.

The meaning of "extraterritoriality" more directly relevant to international organizations' archives and records, that of diplomatic immunity and inviolability of the archives, is problematic. Extraterritoriality was one of the three traditional arguments for diplomatic immunity:

> The theory of extraterritoriality assumes that a diplomat is always on the soil of the sending country. As a result, a diplomat is not subject to the receiving country's laws. The role of extraterritoriality theory in today's discourse is not entirely clear ... Many agree, however, that the theory sets forth an unjustifiably broad scope of diplomatic immunity.[55]

Understanding the particular privileges and immunities related to the extraterritoriality of any given entity is legally complex: "The actual scope of the immunities comprised in the doctrine of extraterritoriality depends, according to the circumstances, on principles of customary international law as applied in a particular country, on specific statutory or executive regulation, or on international agreements."[56] The dominant view, however, seems to be that extraterritoriality as a theory justifying diplomatic immunity has largely been rejected as a legal fiction in favour of "functional necessity."[57]

It must also be noted that there is a strong argument that the theory of extraterritoriality as justification for diplomatic privileges and immunities per se does not apply to international organizations. Unlike states and the diplomats whose privileges and immunities flow from those states, "International organisations have no territory of their own, and are not properly considered sovereigns either."[58] In other words, even if extraterritoriality as justification still carried weight in international law generally, the dominant argument holds that it is inapplicable to international organizations:

> [T]he theory of extraterritoriality [as a justification for diplomatic privileges and immunities] is not applicable [to international organisations]: besides the fact that also in relation to diplomatic missions the theory is seen as obsolete, for IOs it lacks relevance simply because they don't have territorial rights like states do.[59]

However, this does not mean that there are not important principles of immunity and inviolability that relate to IOs, even if they are not necessarily justified on the basis of "extraterritoriality." Extraterritoriality in the sense of privileges and immunities (rather than their theoretical justification) absolutely applies to IOs. As discussed in greater detail below, many legal scholars now justify IO privileges and immunities on the grounds of "functional necessity": without certain privileges and immunities, such as inviolability of the seat and the archives, an IO cannot fulfil its purpose. If an IO's archives are not protected against demands at the whim of the host state, the IO might well be unable to function, or at least unable to function independently. There are also significant issues to be understood regarding the inviolability of the archives of IOs in the context of the cloud, including inviolability of data and records that "travel" through a non-member state, the inviolability of data and records stored on commercial cloud services, and how best an IO can ensure that the inviolability of its archives includes those data and records that, due to the use of cloud computing, might be outside its physical custody. An understanding of these issues begins with an examination of the legal instrument(s) that establish(es) a particular IO.

The importance and limits of legal instruments[60]

> In most cases, the host agreement is but the basic document, which, implicitly or explicitly, in turn refers to or relies on, other sources of law. … The host arrangement of an international organisation … is not an entity or document as such, it is merely a term chosen … to be able to define the ensemble of instruments of law that regulate matters concerning the relationship between international organisations and their host states.[61]

Unlike a state, an IO cannot be presumed to have any particular rights, privileges, or immunities flowing from sovereignty. The existence of an IO, and therefore all of the rights attached thereto, extend from international law and its host country agreements, and dictates its relationship vis-à-vis states and other organizations. Muller notes that "the relationship between an international organisation and its host state is a bilateral one. Therefore, one would expect that the law regulating that relationship is mainly contained in bilateral instruments concluded between the organisation and the host state."[62]

Particularly now that the broader literature on extraterritoriality has made clear the extraterritorial theory of diplomatic immunity is largely a legal fiction, it is necessary to understand the theories underlying the privileges and immunities of IOs. An examination of a few illustrative cases makes it clear that these privileges and immunities are largely a matter of contract between IOs and the jurisdiction(s) in which they find themselves, and thus, are negotiated and contextual.

In examining IOs' legal instruments with regard to extraterritoriality, we chose three representative IOs: the International Monetary Fund (IMF), the International Atomic Energy Agency (IAEA), and the World Bank Group's International Bank for Reconstruction and Development (hereinafter World Bank[63]). There is starkly similar language throughout their constitutive agreements, including treaties, constitutions, and host agreements regarding the inviolability of their archives.

Thus, while most of the agreements considered below provide for the immunity of the IO's archives, that inviolability is not absolute, but rather, limited by "functional necessity."[64] In other words, the archives are inviolable insofar as necessary for the effective functioning of the IO in accordance with "the functions and purposes which have been laid down in its constitution."[65] Admittedly, "effective functioning" is a very broad – and arguably, problematic – idea. In practice, when the bounds of "effective functioning" have been the subject of litigation, the courts have considered the importance of archival inviolability to the independent functioning of the IO against the "duty [of the IO] to cooperate with the member states"; the court litigating such a case determines whether or not the refusal to provide access was justified in light of the particular facts of the case.[66] Generally, however, archival immunity is provided fairly broad support. For example, in *World Bank Group v Wallace,* [2016] 1 SCR 207 at para 71, the Supreme Court of Canada writes that "[s]hielding an organization's entire collection of stored documents, including official records and correspondences, is integral to ensuring its proper, independent functioning."

Indeed, although it may have become the most common justification for diplomatic immunity, Klabbers dissects the entire theory of functionalism. Klabbers argues that functionalism presents political, value-laden choices (such as whether a state may intervene in how an IO treats it employees) as apolitical, technical matters:

> [Functionalism] presents international organizations as neutral and a-political, solely functional entities, which do not compete with states over the good life but, instead, help to achieve it once it is decided what the good life shall be and which can serve the interests of all precisely by focusing on a specific function. Since the interests of all are being served, it follows that the functioning of organizations must be facilitated by the law.[67]

Nonetheless, "functionalism" remains the dominant theory; thus, in understanding the inviolability of a particular IO's archives, one must consider the constitution and host agreement of the organization, including functions and purposes (Table 4.1).

These provisions help illustrate the negotiated, contractual, and ultimately mutable nature of these privileges and immunities. As with many agreements governing IOs, each member country must separately accept the agreement, illustrating its ultimately contractual nature. As can be seen from the published member acceptances of the Agreement on the Privileges and Immunities of the [International Atomic Energy] Agency: Status List as of 30 September 2002,[68] many states condition their acceptance of the agreement on the modification or deletion of terms. A significant number of countries, in their agreements on the privileges and immunities of the IAEA, reject Sections 26 and 34 (referring disputes between the Agency and members to the International Court of Justice); Canada changes the terms to make explicit that Canadian nationals remain subject to Canadian law even while carrying out the Agency's mission. As Muller explains:

> The inviolability of an international organisation does not imply that it can ignore national legislation. National legislation of the host state is applicable unless the host arrangement says otherwise, and this is only the case if the functions of the organisation so require. In principle, the organisation must comply with the laws of the host state.[69]

This provides a useful contrast to the case of intergovernmental relations, where extraterritorial inviolability is not negotiated, but flows from the territorial rights of each state.

TABLE 4.1 International organizations' legal instruments with regards to extraterritoriality

International organization	Language from agreement
International Monetary Fund	"Immunity of the Archives: The archives of the fund shall be inviolable." *Articles of* Agreement of the International Monetary Fund, UNTS I-20, 22 July 1944, Article IX, Section 5.
International Atomic Energy Agency	"The archives of the Agency, and in general all documents belonging to it or held by it, shall be inviolable, wherever located." Statute of the International Atomic Energy Agency, UNTS I-3988, 23 October 1956, Article III, Section 5 (entered into force 29 July 1957).
World Bank Group – International Bank for Reconstruction and Development	"Immunity of Archives: The archives of the Bank shall be inviolable." Articles of Agreement of the International Bank for Reconstruction and Development, UNTS I-20, 22 July 1944, Article VII, Section 5 (as amended effective 27 June 2012).

One might note that none of the authorizing agreements referenced in Fig 4.1 provides a definition of what constitutes the "archives" of the organization. However, a broadly accepted definition can be found elsewhere:

> In its 1969 report on privileges and immunities, the Council of Europe supported the wide definition of the term "archives" as adopted by the Vienna Conference on Consular Relations in 1963. According to Article 1(k) of that Convention, the archives include: "all the papers, documents, correspondence, books, films, tapes and registers …, ciphers and codes, the card-indexes, and any article of furniture intended for their protection or safe-keeping."[70]

While the definition of "archive" provided by the Vienna Conference on Consular Relations (VCCR) is extensive, the boundaries of an "archive" were nonetheless more easily delineated in the purely paper past. However, existing law and practice concerning the archives of IOs provide reason to believe that cloud-based records are, likely, within the protections provided to any other records belonging to an IO's archives. After all, "it is not relevant whether [documents belonging to the archives] are within the seat or not."[71] However, cloud computing does complicate the privileges and immunities of IO archives and records, as discussed below.

For example, although the language of the IMF, IAEA, and the World Bank is very close, the immunity of their archives in a particular case would likely be interpreted through the lens of the functions and purposes of each organization. Whereas it might be justifiable for the IAEA to refuse access to a particular series of records, it might not be justifiable for the IMF to refuse access to a similar series of records in similar circumstances, because of the differing functions and purposes of the two organizations. They also highlight the importance of the host agreement in determining the rights and privileges of any particular IO's archives. That said, there exists a body of law and custom surrounding the inviolability of international organizations' archives, rooted in international law, including case law, conventions, and treaties that can provide some insight into how "extraterritoriality" may apply in the cloud-computing era.

Challenges of cloud computing in the territorial approach to law

> As the global economy has become more interconnected and the Internet ubiquitous, jurisdictional conflicts involving States, private actors, and regulatory agencies are becoming increasingly common. States also frequently assert their jurisdiction over conduct occurring outside their own territory, particularly with regard to conduct on the Internet.[72]

As Ascensio notes,

> Extraterritoriality raises many problems of both a legal and a practical nature. One of the most complex is to determine at what point a situation is located

in a given territory, in a context where boundaries are blurred by modern communication technology, the transnational structure of some corporations and economic and financial globalisation.[73]

How to resolve the issues of territoriality raised by cloud computing remains an open question; indeed, the dimensions of the very relationship between territoriality and cloud computing remain a matter of debate and, in some ways, rehearse precisely the general arguments about territoriality and jurisdiction discussed above.

Several authors assert that cloud-computing models are, basically, "location independent."[74] For example, Ryngaert & Zoetekouw assert that an entirely territorial model for extraterritoriality would have difficulty addressing crimes that occur solely online.[75] Examining the historical background to "jurisdictional alternatives to territory" and the challenges that virtual communities pose to territoriality, they conclude that the Internet presents unique issues that may "necessitate a paradigmatic shift in how we conceptualize spatiality … and the exercise of jurisdiction."[76] Andrews & Newman argue along the same lines as Ryngaert & Zoetekouw, finding that the cloud has revolutionized territorial law and that "from a legal perspective, the cloud embodies a new template for interactions."[77] Narayanan goes so far as to endorse a data protection framework structured similarly to the international laws of the sea, wherein data involved in transborder flows would be considered to be under no jurisdiction.[78]

Not all scholars agree, however, that cyberspace is beyond territory. Julie Cohen rejects the distinction between physical space and cyberspace, viewing humans as embodied beings who comprehend even the virtual through embodied experience, perceiving a "rich variety of entanglements between virtual and physical spaces that are real to the extent that they generate real consequences."[79] Currie & Scassa explore how the principles of territoriality continue to be applicable to the Internet; they ultimately envision supranational governance of the Internet.[80] Several authors attempt to offer solutions to issues of extraterritorial jurisdiction in cloud computing or on the Internet.[81] Cross-border data transfers have led to a renewed consideration of extraterritorial rights.[82] Clearly, cloud computing poses significant legal problems with regard to jurisdiction, but the law has yet to catch up with technology.[83]

One area in which the relationship between extraterritoriality and cloud computing is being tested extensively is privacy and data protection. This is perhaps unsurprising. "It has become a truism that data are routinely transferred internationally, and that data processing takes little account of national borders, largely because of the Internet. However, much data protection and privacy law scholarship is still inward-looking and constrained by national boundaries."[84] Kuner raised the problem of extraterritorial EU data privacy law under the old Data Privacy Directive (Directive 95/46/EC), arguing it was "cumbersome, expensive, slow," and "sends the wrong message to third countries."[85] Kuner further found that extraterritorial claims are unreasonable, as businesses and individuals cannot be expected to modify their online behaviour simply to comply with all data privacy laws in all jurisdictions.[86] Svantesson makes a comparable observation when describing a "conundrum" of extraterritoriality in data privacy law: while it is "reasonable" for states to protect data from foreign interference, it is "unreasonable" to expect Internet users to comply with every state law worldwide.[87] Of course, "the assertion of extra-territorial jurisdiction by States with respect to data protection and privacy related matters is far from novel and is likely to continue"[88]; statutes ranging from the Children's Online Privacy Protection Act of 1998 (United States of America) and the California Consumer Privacy Act of 2018 in the U.S. to the General Data Protection Regulation (GDPR) attempt to regulate both the intra- and extraterritorial impacts of cloud computing on individuals' personal information. Ultimately, as Greze notes, "in order to effectively realize the EU's aspiration to global jurisdiction in relation to data protection law and privacy law matters, both the territorial nature of enforcement jurisdiction and the principles of enforcement and recognition of foreign judgments must be grappled with."[89] Similarly, IOs must consider problems of enforcement when trusting their data and records to the cloud: what rights and recourse are available when archival materials pass into servers in the jurisdiction of a country with whom the IO has no host agreement? What privileges and immunities will be recognized? What risks arise?

In some ways, the structure of IOs anticipates the territorial complexities of cloud computing. As Muller notes, "all major international organisations now have a decentralized structure. Their offices are situated in host states around the world, and their legal status is largely regulated by bilateral and contractual arrangements."[90] Andrews & Newman,[91] writing about jurisdiction and cloud computing, argue that, "from a legal perspective, the cloud embodies a new template for interactions" and assert that all interactions in the cloud are contract-based. The interpretation and enforcement of those contracts are influenced by a nuanced, quickly changing body of international law. Similarly, the rights, duties, and powers of IOs are largely governed by a mix of host agreements, conventions, and international law. This complexity makes it challenging to generalize about the situation facing a particular IO in making use of cloud computing, but some general principles may be recognized.

Extraterritoriality and archival inviolability in practice

> [After inviolability of the premises and assets], [t]he second major element of the inviolability of an international organisation is the inviolability of its archives and all the documents in its possession. Without some degree of privacy, it is evident that the independence and effective functioning of international organisations cannot be guaranteed.[92]

International law has long recognized that it would be an absurdity to provide that the inviolability of a mission's archives and records would apply only to those records physically within the mission's premises. Indeed, Article 24 of the Vienna

Convention on Diplomatic Relations (VCDR), which sought to codify existing and generally accepted principles of diplomatic law, provides that "[t] he archives and documents of the mission shall be inviolable at any time and wherever they may be."[93] As Muller notes, the "at any time and wherever they may be" language is common in IO host agreements, whereas other agreements simply omit any reference to a territorial limitation on the extent of the privileges and immunities accorded an IO's archives.[94] Cloud computing, however, poses unique challenges with regard to protecting the inviolability of records beyond the IO's seat.

When an IO's data, records, and archives are held in the cloud, it can be challenging to determine the precise jurisdiction in which the archives are held, absent, for example, a contractual provision within the cloud service agreement with regard to where the data will be hosted. If an IO's archival records are hosted in a country with which the IO has no host agreement, it may have little or no recourse if its privileges and immunities are violated. It might find itself facing an adversary who says, as U.S. President Andrew Jackson apocryphally did, "[The courts] have made their decision, now let [them] enforce it."[95] Given the foregoing, the importance of the contract between IOs and their cloud service provider (s) cannot be overstated. The InterPARES Trust research project produced a "Checklist for Cloud Service Contracts" resource[96] that can serve as a jumping-off point for evaluating any agreements governing the provision of cloud services for IOs' data, records, and archives. However, the specific context, including the host agreements and legal contexts, of a given IO must be taken into consideration in determining if a cloud service agreement meets the needs of the IO.

Even if an IO has a satisfactory contract with the cloud service provider, it must take further steps to ensure its data, records, and archives in the cloud receive the full privileges and immunities to which they are entitled:

> Like the immunity from legal process and the inviolability of the premises of the organisation, it is of great importance that the host state authorities have some way of knowing to which object(s) the relevant immunity applies. Therefore, the archives should bear identification mark whenever possible.[97]

In the paper world, it is a relatively straightforward matter to identify archival records, such as by affixing seals or adding particular annotations. Doing so digitally is possible – for example, through the use of digital signatures – but less straightforward. Diplomatically, a digital signature can serve as a seal, but "because digital records might be converted to new formats, migrated to new media, emulated or virtualised in new environments due to ... technological obsolescence," care must be taken to ensure the ongoing availability and trustworthiness of the digital signature, particularly given that "digital signatures expire after a certain period."[98] Given that an IO's records may be hosted on servers with countless other organizations' and individuals' records, while being split from other records belonging to the IO, appropriate digital preservation measures to ensure ongoing identification must be taken, depending upon the technological needs and capacity of the IO.

This need becomes even more clear when one considers that the host state's duty to protect the archives imposes a positive duty to "prevent any interference with the archives by third parties, and ... to assist the organisation with evacuating its archives in times of crisis."[99] While cloud computing can provide some redundancy, it does not obviate the need for disaster recovery planning.

An illustration of the complexity of privileges, immunities, and jurisdiction in the cloud is provided by the Estonian Data Embassy. Estonia, of course, is a sovereign state, with the rights and powers, including diplomatic privileges and immunities, that come with such status. Estonia also employs digital technology extensively throughout its government. As one part of its plans to protect itself from "increasing, multifaceted uncertainties and disruptions: from cyberattacks and natural hazards, to legitimate threats to State sovereignty and territorial integrity,"[100] Estonia sought to establish an extraterritorial "Data Embassy" in which it could "systematically backup its information systems, databases and registries that are deemed critical to the continuity of the Republic of Estonia."[101]

Ultimately, doing so in a way that was sufficient to protect both Estonia and the host state (Luxembourg) required forging a new path. Existing embassies lacked the security capacity of a high-tiered data centre.[102] The uncertainty of the applicability of diplomatic privileges and immunities (and, specifically, of the Vienna Convention on Diplomatic and Consular Relations) outside of the clear boundaries of an embassy proved simply too risky.[103] Thus, a bilateral agreement had to be entered into between the two sovereigns in order to establish a legal framework for the Data Embassy, building on examples "whereby international organisations have drafted and exercised similar bilateral agreements for hosting data outside of their original jurisdiction".[104] In other words, even sovereigns feel the need for extra-legal protection in the untested, uncertain waters of extraterritorial cloud computing and diplomatic privileges and immunities.

Conclusion

Although extraterritoriality as a justification for diplomatic immunity has largely been pushed aside as a historical relic, it nonetheless remains important for researchers to understand the line of legal reasoning that it represents. In particular, for understanding the legal position of the archives of IOs, the contrast between the diplomatic immunity afforded the archives of a state and those of an IO is instructive; the negotiated, contractual nature of the immunity of IO archives cannot be overstated. Furthermore, as data flows across jurisdictions through cloud computing, novel problems – and solutions – will certainly continue to arise. As IOs navigate cyberspace and the thorny questions of their rights, privileges, and immunities therein, problems of jurisdiction and extraterritoriality will continue to loom large.

Ultimately, IOs use and likely will continue to utilize cloud computing for much the same reasons as other entities – cost efficiencies, accessibility, and convenience, which are no small considerations. However, they would be well advised to do so with an awareness that ensuring the continued inviolability of the archives in their physical custody will require awareness of the transjurisdictional nature of cloud computing. They need to take precautions to ensure that those privileges and immunities will persevere, even if their records are on an Amazon server on the other side of the globe. Given how much remains uncertain, international organizations will need to pay particular attention to the terms of contracts with their cloud service providers. The issue of international organizations and extra-territoriality – even in the analogue world of paper – raises a number of challenging, unanswered legal questions; cloud computing heightens both the complexity and urgency of these questions.

Notes

1 This chapter does not constitute legal opinion or legal advice. Those requiring legal advice should seek the assistance of competent counsel in their relevant jurisdiction(s).
2 This chapter stems from research originally performed by the author and Elissa How on behalf of InterPARES Trust. The contributions of Ms. How's research are immense and greatly appreciated.
3 United Nations, 2011, *Report of the International Law Commission* (UN GAOR, 66th Sess., Supp. 10 A/66/10, 2011), p. 54.
4 Jan Klabbers, 2015b, *An introduction to international organizations law* (3rd edn), Cambridge University Press, Cambridge, p. 6.
5 Ibid, p. 7.
6 Anna-Karin Lindblom, 2006, *Non-governmental organisations in international law*, Cambridge University Press, Cambridge/New York, p. 86.
7 United Nations, 2011, p. 54.
8 Bernard Koteen Office of Public Interest Advising, 'Intergovernmental organizations (IGOs)', Harvard Law School, viewed 13 April 2020, https://hls.harvard.edu/dept/op ia/what-is-public-interest-law/public-service-practice-settings/public-international-law/ intergovernmental-organizations-igos/.
9 Cecilia Sognnæs, 2014, 'International legal personality – an assessment of the International Committee of the Red Cross and its legal status,' Master's thesis, University of Oslo, p. 17–18.
10 Henry G Schermers & Niels Blokker, 2011, *International institutional law: unity within diversity*, 5th rev. edn, Brill Nijhoff, p. 977.
11 A Judge, 1978, 'Types of international organization: detailed overview', in *Yearbook of international organizations*, Union of International Associations.
12 Siegfried Wiessner & Andrew R Willard, 1999, 'Policy-oriented jurisprudence and human rights abuses in internal conflict: toward a world public order of human dignity', *American Journal of International Law*, vol. 93, no. 2, p. 323.
13 Sognnæs, 2014, p. 20.
14 Lindblom, 2006.
15 Davorin Lapaš, 2019, 'Diplomatic privileges and immunities for IGO-like entities', *International Organizations Law Review*, vol. 16, pp. 378–406.
16 Sognnæs, 2014, p. 11.
17 Mireille Hildebrandt, 2013, 'Extraterritorial jurisdiction to enforce in cyberspace? Bodin, Schmitt, Grotius in cyberspace', *University of Toronto Law Journal*, vol. 63, no. 2, doi:10.3138/utlj.1119, p. 204.
18 Klabbers, 2015b, p. 2.
19 James D Fry, 2018, 'Rights, functions, and international legal personality of international organizations', *Boston University International Law Journal*, vol. 36, no. 2, p. 221.

20   International legal personality and its role with regards to international organizations is a highly contested, complex concept. See, e.g., Fry, 2018. A full discussion of the nuances and controversies of international legal personality is beyond the scope of this chapter; presented herein is a simplified discussion of these issues as necessary to ground the discussion of extraterritoriality.

21   Chittharanjan Felix Amerasinghe, 2010, 'International legal personality revisited', in F Johns (ed.), *International legal personality*, Routledge, London, p. 244. "Hohfeldian" refers to an analytical system developed by Wesley Hohfeld (1879–1918), an American legal theorist whose analytical framework arranged eight fundamental legal concepts – right, no-right, privilege, duty, power, disability, immunity, and liability into relationships of opposites and correlatives. The opposites – right/no-right, privilege/duty, power/disability, and immunity/liability – exist in a relationship where, if someone has one thing, then they lack its opposite. If A has immunity, A lacks (does not have) liability. The correlative relationship applies to two people in a legal relationship: if A has a right, someone else has a corresponding duty. The correlative relationships are right/duty; privilege/no-right; power/liability; and immunity/disability.

22   Jeremy Bentham, 1843, cited in Ademola Abass, 2014, *Complete international law: text, cases, and materials*, Oxford University Press, Oxford, p. 5.

23   Bryan A Garner, 2000, *Black's law dictionary* (abridged 7th edn), West Group, St. Paul, MN, p. 1125.

24   Klabbers, 2015b, p. 4.

25   Ibid, p. 5.

26   Ibid, p. 16.

27   Richard T Ford, 1999, 'Law's territory: a history of jurisdiction', *Michigan Law Review*, vol. 97, no. 4, p. 851.

28   Ibid, p. 852.

29   In the film *The Sound of Music*, the von Trapp family escapes the Nazis by crossing the border into Switzerland.

30   Ford, 1999, p. 851.

31   Hildebrandt, 2013, p. 205.

32   Ford, 1999, p. 855.

33   Ibid, p. 856.

34   Hildebrandt, 2013, p. 224.

35   Alex Mills, 2014, 'Rethinking jurisdiction in international law', *British Yearbook of International Law*, vol. 84, no. 1, p. 187.

36   Hervé Ascensio, 2010, *Extraterritoriality as an instrument*. Contribution to the work of the UN Secretary-General's Special Representative on human rights and transnational corporations and other businesses, www.diplomatie.gouv.fr/en/IMG/pdf/Extraterritoriality_as_a_tool.pdf, p. 10; Robert J Currie & Teresa Scassa, 2011, 'New first principles? Assessing the internet's challenges to jurisdiction', *Georgetown Journal of International Law*, vol. 42, no. 4, pp. 1017–1082; Hildebrandt, 2013; Christopher Kuner, 2010a, 'Data protection law and international jurisdiction on the internet (part 1)', *International Journal of Law and Information Technology*, vol. 18, no. 2, pp. 176–193, http://papers.ssrn.com/sol3/papers.cfm?abstract_id=1496847; Christopher Kuner, 2010b, 'Data protection and international jurisdiction on the internet (part 2)', *International Journal of Law and Information Technology*, vol. 18, no. 3, pp. 227–247, http://papers.ssrn.com/sol3/papers.cfm?abstract_id=1689495; Yuko Suda, 2013, 'Transatlantic politics of data transfer: extraterritoriality, counter-extraterritoriality and counter-terrorism', *Journal of Common Market Studies*, vol. 51, no. 4, pp. 772–788.

37   Renee Berry & Matthew Reisman, 2012, 'Policy challenges of cross border cloud computing', United States International Trade Commission, viewed 12 April 2020, www.usitc.gov/research_and_analysis/documents/Final_Cloud_Computing_Seminar_61912_0.pdf; Currie & Scassa, 2011; Hildebrandt, 2013; Sarah Miller, 2009, 'Revisiting extraterritorial jurisdiction: a territorial justification for extraterritorial jurisdiction under the European Convention', *European Journal of International Law*, vol. 20, no. 4,

pp. 1223–1246, https://doi.org/10.1093/ejil/chp078; Vineeth Narayanan, 2012, 'Harnessing the cloud: international law implications of cloud-computing', *Chicago Journal of International Law*, vol. 12, no. 2, pp. 783–809; Cedric Ryngaert & Mark Zoetekouw, 2017, 'The end of territory? The re-emergence of community as a principle of jurisdictional order in the internet era', in U Kohl (ed.), *The net and the nation state: multidisciplinary perspectives on internet governance*, Cambridge University Press, Cambridge, pp. 185–201; Dan Jerker B Svantesson, 2014, 'The extraterritoriality of EU data privacy law – its theoretical justification and its practical effect on US businesses', *Stanford Journal of International Law*, vol. 50, no. 1, pp. 53–102; Steven R Swanson, 2011, 'Google set sail: ocean-based server farms and international law', *Connecticut Law Review*, vol. 43, no. 3, pp. 709–751.

38 FA Mann, 1964, *The doctrine of jurisdiction in international law*, A.W. Sijthoff, Leyden. p. 9.

39 Hildebrandt, 2013; Miller, 2009.

40 Hildebrandt, 2013, p. 202.

41 Ibid.

42 Peter D Szigeti, 2017, 'The illusion of territorial jurisdiction', *Texas International Law Journal*, vol. 52, no. 3, p. 369.

43 Yuko Suda, 2017, *The politics of data transfer: transatlantic conflict and cooperation over data privacy*, Routledge, New York, p. 219, doi:10.4324/9781315524856.

44 Ibid.

45 Raustiala, 2009 cited in Suda, 2017, p. 2.

46 A "term of art" is a word or expression that has a particularized meaning within a given context, profession, or discipline. As an example, in *Molzof v. United States*, 502 U.S. 301, 112 S. Ct. 711, 116 L. Ed. 2d 731 (1992), the relevant statute denied recovery of "punitive damages," which the trial court held included future medical expenses for the plaintiff. The appeals court overturned on the grounds that "punitive damages" is a term of art with an understood, agreed-upon meaning that did not extend to medical expenses. Because terms of art are typically specific to a particular legal system, their interpretation and use in international law can pose a problem of interpretation. As an example, Whitman (2004, p. 1160) writes that "our conceptions of privacy result from our juridified intuitions – intuitions that reflect our knowledge of, and commitment to, the basic legal values of our culture." In the dominant North American juridical context, privacy thus refers to "privacy as an aspect of liberty ... the right to freedom from intrusions by the state." This liberty-based North American concept of "privacy" is more analogous to the European concept of data protection than the concept of "privacy" found, for example, in the dignity-based French concept of "intimé." Intimé translates more closely to "intimacy" than to the English "privacy," particularly in the legalistic, data-protection idea of "privacy" commonly used. Whereas consent is decisive in the North American model of privacy, European jurisprudence has held that there are cases where the interest in human dignity is such that even if the data subject has consented, their private information cannot be used, because the usage is an offense to dignity.

47 Kuner, 2010a.

48 Svantesson, 2014.

49 Kuner, 2010b, p. 227.

50 SG Coughlan et al., 2006, *Global reach, local grasp: constructing extraterritorial jurisdiction in the age of globalization (Dalhousie Law School)*, Law Commission of Canada, p. 1.

51 Garner, 2000, p. 480.

52 J Law & E Martin, 2014, 'Extraterritoriality', *Oxford reference: a dictionary of law*, 7th edn, Oxford University Press, Oxford.

53 Encyclopaedia Britannica, 2009, 'Extraterritoriality', *Encyclopaedia Britannica*, 8th edn, Chicago.

54 Klabbers, 2015b, p. 130.

55 NM Bergmar, 2014, 'Demanding accountability where accountability is due: a functional necessity approach to diplomatic immunity under the Vienna Convention,' *Vanderbilt Journal of Transnational Law*, vol. 47, no. 2, p. 508.

56 Encyclopaedia Britannica, 2009, 'Extraterritoriality'.

57 K Ahluwalia, 1964, *The legal status, privileges and immunities of the specialized agencies of the United Nations and certain other international organizations*, Springer, Dordrecht.

58 Klabbers, 2015b, p. 131.

59 Dikker Hupkes, 2009, *Protection and effective functioning of international organisations*, Final Report International Institutional Law, Secure Haven Project, §4.2.

60 While this section looks at the plain language of the archives' inviolability texts in these agreements, it is important to remember that each organization's host agreement is much more complex than just the instrument. A full legal analysis would examine the relevant clauses in light of relevant facts, case law, conventions and treaties, customary law, and other relevant sources of law. Such analysis is beyond the scope of this chapter.

61 AS Muller, 1995, *International organisations and their host states: aspects of their legal relationship*, Kluwer Law International, The Hague/London/Boston, pp. 26–27.

62 Muller, 1995, p. 206.

63 The World Bank Group consists of five different organizations, each of which operates according to its own articles of agreements or other governing document. The World Bank Group and the International Monetary Fund both originated in the United Nations Monetary and Financial Conference (1–22 July 1944).

64 Muller, 1995, p. 206.

65 Ibid.

66 Ibid.

67 Jan Klabbers, 2015a, 'The EJIL foreword: the transformation of international organizations law', *European Journal of International Law*, vol. 26, no. 1, p. 16.

68 International Atomic Energy Agency, 2002, *Agreement on the privileges and immunities of the International Atomic Energy Agency*, IAEA Doc. INFCIRC/9/Rev.2/Add.13.

69 Muller, 1995, p. 208.

70 Ibid, p. 202.

71 Ibid, p. 205.

72 Kuner, 2010a, p. 147.

73 Ascencio, 2010, p. 1.

74 Berry & Reisman, 2012.

75 Ryngaert & Zoetekouw, 2017.

76 Ibid, p. 18.

77 Damon C Andrews & John M Newman, 2013, 'Personal jurisdiction and choice of law in the cloud', *Maryland Law Review*, vol. 73, no. 1, p. 327.

78 Narayanan, 2012.

79 Cohen, 2007, p. 203.

80 Currie & Scassa, 2011.

81 Andrews & Newman, 2013; Currie, 2006; Hildebrandt, 2013; Narayanan, 2012; Rynaert & Zoetekouw, 2014.

82 Coughlan et al., 2006.

83 Andrews & Newman, 2013.

84 C Kuner et al., 2017, 'The GDPR as a chance to break down borders', *International Data Privacy Law*, vol. 7, no. 4, p. 231, doi:10.1093/idpl/ipx023.

85 Christopher Kuner, 2009, 'Developing an adequate legal framework for international data transfers', in S Gutwirth (ed.), *Reinventing data protection*, Springer Science+Business, p. 263.

86 Christopher Kuner, 2014, 'The court of justice of the EU judgment on data protection and internet search engines: current issues and future challenges', in B Hess & CM Mariottini (eds.), *Protecting privacy in private international procedural law and by data*

protection, London School of Economics and Political Science, London, pp. 19–55, http://ssrn.com/abstract=2496060 or http://dx.doi.org/10.2139/ssrn.2496060.

87 Svantesson, 2014.

88 Benjamin Greze, 2019, 'The extra-territorial enforcement of the GDPR: a genuine issue and the quest for alternatives', *International Data Privacy Law*, p. 110, viewed 18 November 2019, doi:10.1093/idpl/ipz003.

89 Greze, 2019, p. 111.

90 Muller, 1995, p. 203.

91 Andrews & Newman, 2013, p. 327.

92 Muller, 1995, p. 202.

93 United Nations Monetary and Financial Conference, Bretton Woods, New Hampshire, July 1–22, 1944 Final Act and Related Documents, pp. 68–95, Department of State publication 2187, Conference Series 55; also, Department of State publication 2511, Treaties and Other International Acts Series 1502. Agreement signed at Washington, December 27, 1945; effective December 27, 1945.

94 Muller, 1995.

95 Paul F Boller & John H George, 1989, *They never said it: a book of false quotes, misquotes, and false attributions*, Oxford University Press, New York, p. 53.

96 Available at https://interparestrust.org/assets/public/dissemination/NA14_20160226_CloudServiceProviderContracts_Checklist_Final.pdf.

97 Muller, 1995, p. 205.

98 Hrvoje Stančić, 2016, 'Long-term preservation of digital signatures', paper presented at Tehnični in vsebinski problemi klasičnega in elektronskega arhiviranja, April 2016, Radneci, viewed 12 April 2020, https://bib.irb.hr/datoteka/810269.Stancic_H._Long-term_Preservation_of_Digital_Signatures_481-491.pdf.

99 Muller, 1995, p. 196.

100 Nick Robinson, Laura Kask & Robert Krimmer, 2019, 'The Estonian Data Embassy and the applicability of the Vienna Convention: An exploratory analysis', presented at ICEGOV2019 12th International Conference on the Theory and Practice of Electronic Governance, p. 392, Melbourne, VIC, Australia, April 2019, ACM, New York.

101 Robinson, Kask & Krimmer, 2019, p. 393.

102 Ibid.

103 Ibid.

104 Ibid.

Bibliography

Abass, A 2014, *Complete international law: text, cases, and materials*, Oxford University Press, Oxford.

Ahluwalia, K 1964, *The legal status, privileges and immunities of the specialized agencies of the United Nations and certain other international organizations*, Springer, Dordrecht.

Amerasinghe, CF 2010, 'International legal personality revisited', in F Johns (ed.), *International legal personality*, Routledge, London, pp. 239–262.

Andrews, DC & Newman, J 2013, 'Personal jurisdiction and choice of law in the cloud', *Maryland Law Review*, vol. 73, no. 1, pp. 313–384.

Ascensio, H 2010, *Extraterritoriality as an instrument*. Contribution to the work of the UN Secretary-General's Special Representative on human rights and transnational corporations and other businesses, www.diplomatie.gouv.fr/en/IMG/pdf/Extraterritoriality_as_a_tool.pdf.

Bergmar, NM 2014, 'Demanding accountability where accountability is due: a functional necessity approach to diplomatic immunity under the Vienna Convention,' *Vanderbilt Journal of Transnational Law*, vol. 47, no. 2, pp. 501–524.

Bernard Koteen Office of Public Interest Advising, 'Intergovernmental organizations (IGOs)', Harvard Law School, viewed 13 April 2020, https://hls.harvard.edu/dept/opia/what-is-public-interest-law/public-service-practice-settings/public-international-law/intergovernmental-organizations-igos/.

Berry, R & Reisman, M 2012, 'Policy challenges of cross border cloud computing', United States International Trade Commission, viewed 12 April 2020, www.usitc.gov/research_and_analysis/documents/Final_Cloud_Computing_Seminar_61912_0.pdf.

Boller, Paul F & George, John H 1989, *They never said it: a book of false quotes, misquotes, and false attributions*, Oxford University Press, New York, p. 53.

Coughlan, SG, Currie, RJ, Kindred, HM & Scassa, T 2006, *Global reach, local grasp: Constructing extraterritorial jurisdiction in the age of globalization (Dalhousie Law School)*, Law Commission of Canada, Canada.

Currie, RJ & Scassa, T 2011, 'New first principles? Assessing the internet's challenges to jurisdiction', *Georgetown Journal of International Law*, vol. 42, no. 4, pp. 1017–1082.

Denza, E 2018, 'Vienna Convention on Diplomatic Relations', *Audiovisual Library of International Law*, viewed 8 November 2018, http://legal.un.org/avl/ha/vcdr/vcdr.html.

Dikker Hupkes, SD 2009, *Protection and effective functioning of international organisations*, Final Report International Institutional Law, Secure Haven Project.

Encyclopaedia Britannica 2009, 'Extraterritoriality', *Encyclopaedia Britannica*, 8th edn, Chicago.

Ford, R 1999, 'Law's territory: a history of jurisdiction', *Michigan Law Review*, vol. 97, no. 4, pp. 849–930.

Fry, JD 2018, 'Rights, functions, and international legal personality of international organizations', *Boston University International Law Journal*, vol. 36, no. 2, pp. 221–248.

Garner, B 2000, *Black's law dictionary* (abridged 7th edn), West Group, St. Paul, MN.

Greze, B 2019, 'The extra-territorial enforcement of the GDPR: a genuine issue and the quest for alternatives', *International Data Privacy Law*, viewed 18 November 2019, doi:10.1093/idpl/ipz003.

Hildebrandt, M 2013, 'Extraterritorial jurisdiction to enforce in cyberspace? Bodin, Schmitt, Grotius in cyberspace', *University of Toronto Law Journal*, vol. 63, no. 2, pp. 196–224, doi:10.3138/utlj.1119.

International Atomic Energy Agency 2002, *Agreement on the privileges and immunities of the Agency: status list as of 30 September 2002*, IAEA Doc. INFCIRC/9/Rev.2/Add.13.

International Atomic Energy Agency 1967, *Agreement on the privileges and immunities of the International Atomic Energy Agency*, IAEA Doc. INFCIRC/9/Rev. 2, incorporated into the IAEA's governing statute (Statute of the Int'l Atomic Energy Agency, art. XV (1956)).

Judge, A 1978, 'Types of international organization: detailed overview', in *Yearbook of international organizations*, Union of International Associations.

Klabbers, J 2015a, 'The EJIL foreword: the transformation of international organizations law', *European Journal of International Law*, vol. 26, no. 1, pp. 9–82.

Klabbers, J 2015b, *An introduction to international organizations law*, 3rd edn, Cambridge University Press, Cambridge.

Kuner, C 2014, 'The court of justice of the EU judgment on data protection and internet search engines: Current issues and future challenges', in B Hess & CM Mariottini (eds.), *Protecting privacy in private international procedural law and by data protection*, London School of Economics and Political Science, London, pp. 19–55, http://dx.doi.org/10.2139/ssrn.2496060.

Kuner, C 2010a, 'Data protection law and international jurisdiction on the internet (part 1)', *International Journal of Law and Information Technology*, vol. 18, no. 2, pp. 176–193, http://papers.ssrn.com/sol3/papers.cfm?abstract_id=1496847.

Kuner, C 2010b, 'Data protection and international jurisdiction on the internet (part 2)', *International Journal of Law and Information Technology*, vol. 18, no. 3, pp. 227–247, http://papers.ssrn.com/sol3/papers.cfm?abstract_id=1689495.

Kuner, C 2009, 'Developing an adequate legal framework for international data transfers,' in S Gutwirth (ed.), *Reinventing data protection*, Springer Science+Business, pp. 263–273.

Kuner, C, Jerker, D, Svantesson, B, Cate, FH, Lynskey, O, Millard, C & Ni Loideain, N 2017, 'The GDPR as a chance to break down borders', *International Data Privacy Law*, vol. 7, no. 4, pp. 231–232, doi:10.1093/idpl/ipx023.

Kuner, C, Cate, FH, Millard, C & Svantesson, DJB 2013, 'The extraterritoriality of data privacy laws – an explosive issue yet to detonate', *International Data Privacy Law*, vol. 3, no. 3, pp. 147–148.

Lapaš, D 2019, 'Diplomatic privileges and immunities for IGO-like entities', *International Organizations Law Review*, vol. 16, pp. 378–406.

Law, J & Martin, E 2014, 'Extraterritoriality', *Oxford reference: a dictionary of law*, 7th edn, Oxford University Press, Oxford.

Lindblom, A 2006, *Non-governmental organisations in international law*, Cambridge University Press, Cambridge/New York.

Mann, FA 1964, *The doctrine of jurisdiction in international law*, A.W. Sijthoff, Leyden.

Miller, S 2009, 'Revisiting extraterritorial jurisdiction: a territorial justification for extra-territorial jurisdiction under the European Convention', *European Journal of International Law*, vol. 20, no 4, pp. 1223–1246, https://doi.org/10.1093/ejil/chp078.

Mills, A 2014, 'Rethinking jurisdiction in international law', *British Yearbook of International Law*, vol. 84, no. 1, pp. 187–239.

Muller, AS 1995, *International organisations and their host states: aspects of their legal relationship*, Kluwer Law International, The Hague/London/Boston.

Narayanan, V 2012, 'Harnessing the cloud: international law implications of cloud-computing', *Chicago Journal of International Law*, vol. 12, no. 2, pp. 783–809.

Nelson, CM 1989, 'Opening Pandora's box: the status of the diplomatic bag in international relations', *Fordham International Law Journal*, vol. 12, no. 3, pp. 494.

Putnam, TL 2009, 'Courts without borders: domestic sources of US extraterritoriality in the regulatory sphere,' *International Organization*, vol. 63, pp. 459–490.

Raustiala, K 2009, *Does constitution follow the flag? The evolution of extraterritoriality in. American law*, Oxford University Press, Oxford.

Reed, C & Cunningham, A 2014, 'Ownership of information in clouds,' in C Millard (ed.) *Cloud computing law*, Oxford Scholarship, Oxford, pp. 142–168, doi:10.1093/acprof:oso/9780199671670.003.0006.

Robinson, N, Kask, L & Krimmer, R 2019, '*The Estonian Data Embassy and the applicability of the Vienna Convention: An exploratory analysis*', paper presented at ICEGOV2019 12th International Conference on the Theory and Practice of Electronic Governance, pp. 391–396, Melbourne, VIC, Australia, April 2019, ACM, New York.

Ryngaert, C & Zoetekouw, M 2017, 'The end of territory? The re-emergence of community as a principle of jurisdictional order in the internet era', in U Kohl (ed.), *The net and the nation state: multidisciplinary perspectives on internet governance*, Cambridge University Press, Cambridge, pp. 185–201.

Schermers, HG & Blokker, NM 2011, *International institutional law: unity within diversity*, 5th rev. edn, Brill Nijhoff.

Sognnæs, C 2014, 'International legal personality – an assessment of the International Committee of the Red Cross and its legal status,' Master's thesis, University of Oslo.

Stančić, H 2016, '*Long-term preservation of digital signatures*', paper presented at Tehnični in vsebinski problemi klasičnega in elektronskega arhiviranja, April 2016, Radneci, viewed

12 April 2020, https://bib.irb.hr/datoteka/810269.Stancic_H._Long-term_Preservation_of_Digital_Signatures_481-491.pdf.

Suda, Y 2017, *The politics of data transfer: transatlantic conflict and cooperation over data privacy*, Routledge, New York, doi:10.4324/9781315524856.

Suda, Y 2013, 'Transatlantic politics of data transfer: extraterritoriality, counter-extra-territoriality and counter-terrorism', *Journal of Common Market Studies*, vol. 51, no. 4, pp. 772–788.

Svantesson, DJB 2014, 'The extraterritoriality of EU data privacy law – its theoretical justification and its practical effect on US businesses', *Stanford Journal of International Law*, vol. 50, no. 1, pp. 53–102.

Swanson, SR 2011, 'Google set sail: ocean-based server farms and international law,' *Connecticut Law Review*, vol. 43, no. 3, pp. 709–751.

Szigeti, PD 2017, 'The illusion of territorial jurisdiction,' *Texas International Law Journal*, vol. 52, no. 3, pp. 369–399.

United Nations 2011, *Report of the International Law Commission* (UN GAOR, 66th Sess., Supp. 10 A/66/10, 2011) p. 54.

United Nations Monetary and Financial Conference, Bretton Woods, New Hampshire, July 1–22, 1944 *Final Act and Related Documents*, pp. 68–95, Department of State publication 2187, Conference Series 55; also, Department of State publication 2511, Treaties and Other International Acts Series 1502. Agreement signed at Washington, December 27, 1945; effective December 27, 1945.

Whitman, JQ 2004, 'The two western cultures of privacy: dignity versus liberty', *Yale Law Journal*, vol. 113, no. 6, pp. 1151–1221.

Wiessner, S & Willard, AR 1999, 'Policy-oriented jurisprudence and human rights abuses in internal conflict: toward a world public order of human dignity', *American Journal of International Law*, vol. 93, no. 2, pp. 316–334.

Legislation

California. Californian Civil Code, as modified by the California Consumer Privacy Act of 2018 (Assembly Bill No 375), s 1798.140(c)(1).

Directive 95/46/EC of the European Parliament and of the Council of 24 October 1995 on the protection of individuals with regard to the processing of personal data and on the free movement of such data [1995] OJ L 281/31.

Regulation on the protection of natural persons with regard to the processing of personal data and on the free movement of such data, and repealing Directive 95/46/EC (Data Protection Directive). [2016] OJ L 119.

Regulation (EC) No 1049/2001 of the European Parliament and of the Council of 30 May 2001 regarding public access to European Parliament, Council and Commission documents. [2001] OJ L 145/43

Regulation (EC) No. 45/2001 of the European Parliament and the Council of 18 December 2000.

United States of America. Children's Online Privacy Protection Act 1998, 15 USC §§ 6501–6506, s1302(2)(a).

Cases

Shearson Lehman Brother *and* Another *v.* Maclaine, Watson & company Ltd. International
Tin Council Intervening. House of Lords, Judgement 3 December 1987, 1988 1 All ER
116.
World Bank Group v Wallace, [2016] 1 SCR 207.

5

CLOUD COMPUTING CONTRACT TERMS CHECKLIST FOR INTERNATIONAL ORGANIZATIONS

A case study[1]

Weimei Pan and Grant Mitchell[2]

Introduction

The International Federation of Red Cross and Red Crescent Societies (IFRC) has embraced cloud computing since 2012 as part of its efforts to optimize its IT budget, with the aim to enable more spending on mission-relevant projects, modernize IT services, and deliver higher-quality IT services. To maximize the benefits and mitigate the risks of cloud computing, a Cloud Computing Strategy and Roadmap have been developed to guide the transition into the cloud. These describe the target state as measured by the number of applications deployed in public cloud (i.e., Software as a Service (SaaS)), private cloud, and internal dedicated data centres; and the timeline and adoption plan of different cloud projects. When introducing a specific public cloud-based service, the IFRC conducts a comprehensive evaluation of the proposed services to ensure that commonly appreciated risks can be effectively avoided or mitigated. A series of templates, forms, checklists, and toolkits (e.g., sample questions to be asked to decide whether or not to move to the cloud, Request for Cloud Service Form, hosting security controls for different categories of information) have been formulated, which distil the experience the IFRC has accumulated in the use of cloud-based services, and which will guide the selection and introduction of more cloud-based services in the future.

IFRC*jobs* is one of the public cloud-based services adopted by the IFRC. It is an e-recruitment system delivered using SaaS, which aims to "introduce a new platform to provide an integrated e-recruitment solution for the Human Resource (HR) department to support the hiring process from staff request to the arrival of the person in the duty station."[3] IFRC*jobs* therefore attempts to offer an automated, streamlined, standardized, and modernized recruitment process. As a business application, IFRC*jobs* primarily fulfils three functions: it is a database storing recruitment data and records created in the conduct of recruitment activities; it is a business system enabling and supporting recruitment activities and transactions; and it is an electronic recordkeeping system maintaining recruitment records to protect their evidentiary capacity and to exploit the information contained therein for operational and strategic purposes.

In light of its features, IFRC*jobs* was identified as a case in the InterPARES Trust[4] project to study how records-related risks are addressed in the evaluation and introduction of cloud-based services in practice, and to provide empirical input to other InterPARES Trust studies. To this end, the IFRC*jobs* contract was evaluated against the InterPARES Trust Checklist for Cloud Service Contracts (hereafter the Checklist)[5] and the Retention & Disposition Functional Requirements,[6] both of which seek to guide the selection and introduction of cloud-based services so that records-related risks may be addressed. For example, a records-related risk could include failure to destroy metadata in accordance with the organization's retention and disposition schedule, or inability to export records in a usable and interoperable format at the end of the service. The tools help to identify gaps and discrepancies that exist between an organization's records requirements and the cloud computing terms and services offered by providers. The results of the analysis help to improve the usability of the Checklist and the Retention & Disposition Functional Requirements as practical tools for other organizations, and demonstrate how these tools may support the identification of records-related risks that must be addressed to protect records and data when organizations negotiate cloud-based service contracts.

The present chapter discusses in particular the evaluation of IFRC*jobs* against the Checklist.

Data collection and analysis

Major data collection for this study started in December 2014 and ended in February 2015. Two data collection methods were used: document analysis and semi-structured interviews.

Document analysis is "a systematic procedure for reviewing or evaluating documents – both printed and electronic (computer-based and Internet-transmitted) material."[7] Documents analysed included organizational policies, strategies, user manuals, and other guidelines, for example, the IFRC Data Protection Policy; ICT security policy; IFRC Cloud Computing Strategy and Roadmap; IFRC*jobs* user manual; Cloud Services Request Form; and Software and Hosting Agreements. Contractual documents between the IFRC and the cloud service provider were also analysed, including the Order Form, Terms and Conditions, and Service Level Agreement.

Ten interviews were conducted with staff from the Legal Department (2), Library and Archives Unit (1), IT Department (1), the Human Resources Department (5), and Risk and Audit Department (1). Interview guides were developed to ensure key topics were covered. Separate interview guides were developed for staff from each department.

While in general the interview questions prompted the interviewees to describe how the issues raised by the use of IFRC*jobs* were mitigated and how they utilize its benefits, the interview questions were geared towards the roles and responsibilities of each interviewee within IFRC and in the evaluation, adoption, implementation, and use of IFRCj*obs*. This ensured that a comprehensive understanding of IFRC*jobs* was obtained. For instance, the staff member from the IT department, who was also the project manager of IFRC*jobs*, was asked to discuss in greater detail IFRC's cloud strategy, the management of the IFRC*jobs* project, contract negotiation, and other issues related to the technology aspect of IFRC*jobs*; by contrast, the staff member from the Library and Archives Unit was asked to elaborate more on records management with IFRC*jobs* and other cloud-based applications within IFRC.

The evaluation and introduction of IFRC*jobs*

According to Interviewee 5, when IFRC started implementing a cloud strategy, they found that a purely private cloud solution was much more expensive and this was against their business case for fully reaping the benefits offered by cloud computing to modernize their IT infrastructure and spend the IT budget on more mission-relevant IT services. To balance these constraints, instead of a blanket ban on using public cloud-based SaaS for business processes and activities involving highly restricted and restricted data, assessments performed by the IFRC identified what applications are suitable for public cloud-based services, what applications are suitable for private cloud deployment, and what applications are recommended to remain internally dedicated.

The assessment as to whether the application is suitable for a public cloud-based SaaS, private cloud, or in-house server starts with an analysis and classification[8] of the data generated and stored in the application to be procured, the results of which are integral to the product selection cycle, as Interviewee 5 confirmed:

> It all boils down to the types of data we put in there. This is why data classification became one of the key things we consider ... not only in the cloud request form, but [throughout] the cycle of the product selection.

According to IFRC's Information Classification Standard, the classification of data is based on the potential operational and financial consequences the IFRC may face if there is unauthorized disclosure, alteration, or destruction of the data, which determines the sensitivity level of the data.[9] All information and data assets are classified in one of the following four categories: highly restricted, restricted, internal, and public, which will help determine what security controls need to be implemented so as to safeguard the information.[10] Generally, the more sensitive the data is, the riskier it is to have in the cloud.

Based on the sensitivity level of the data, a series of decisions have to be made by weighing the benefits and risks (i.e., the impact that the unauthorized disclosure, alteration, or destruction of that data would have on the IFRC). These decisions include:

- Do the sensitivity level and the potential risks associated with compromised data allow the data to be entrusted to the public cloud?
- If yes, what risks does the use of a cloud-based service pose to the data?
- And how can these potential risks be reduced or eliminated?[11]

Some of the risk mitigation measures include placing restrictions on the geographical locations of the data centres, restrictions on the geographical locations in which the service providers operate, examination of the security measures applied to data in transfer and at rest, measures for the backup of data, and the return and destruction of data.

As an international organization, the IFRC possesses an inviolability[12] status; yet it must negotiate for such inviolability with the government of each country in which it operates. Not every country will grant such inviolability to the IFRC. Taking this privilege into consideration, the IFRC, when making decisions on the use of cloud-based services, will have to determine – based on the sensitivity level of the data – whether the data should be stored in a country that has recognized the inviolability privilege of the IFRC or in a country that does not subject the IFRC to government interference.[13]

Once decisions have been made on whether a cloud-based service will be used and the geographical locations of the service providers' server farms/data centres, an assessment will be undertaken to evaluate the proposed applications that satisfy the geographical location requirements against functional requirements, non-functional requirements (i.e., IT requirements), legal requirements, and financial or other considerations. In particular, special attention will be paid to scrutinize whether security measures are in place to effectively control the potential risks associated with the use of a cloud-based service, as confirmed by the stated purpose of the Cloud Request Form – an important IFRC policy document used in the evaluation of cloud-based services "to uncover legal risks and communicate mitigation or plan of action to reduce or eliminate them."[14] For instance, some of the questions asked by the IFRC when selecting the application for e-recruitment included: Is there a risk of IFRC data being compromised while it is in transit (transfer over network/Internet) or at rest (storage in servers)? Is there a risk that IFRC data will not be properly removed from the cloud network infrastructure upon termination of cloud services? And is there a risk of data being transferred from one jurisdiction to another, therefore being subject to different national laws on data protection and privacy?[15]

Service providers that do not have robust measures to address these risks will be rejected, as IFRC cannot tolerate the level of risks accompanying the use of their services. Those left will enter contract negotiations with IFRC, in the course of which IFRC will take into account recommendations and comments received from the legal department and IT department to ensure that records-related risks are effectively treated.

An evaluation of IFRC*jobs* contract against the InterPARES Trust checklist for cloud service contracts

The contract between the IFRC and the service provider of IFRC*jobs* is comprised of the following documents: order form, terms and conditions (T&C), terms and conditions for other services, service level agreement (SLA), and documentation of the functionalities provided by the service provider. In addition to the formal contract, answers provided by the service provider to the questions on the Cloud Request Form are also used in the following evaluation of the IFRC contract against the InterPARES Checklist when no relevant information can be found in the formal contract.

Discussion

Gaps in the IFRCjobs contract

Overall, the IFRC*jobs* contract is rigorous and strong in terms of shielding the IFRC from the commonly recognized risks associated with the use of a public cloud-based service. Of the 69 questions on the Checklist, 43 questions[16] were positively addressed in the IFRC*jobs* contract (see Table 5.1). The remaining questions on the Checklist that were not addressed in the contract reveal the gaps and areas of risk of using cloud-based services for IFRC*jobs*. Issues raised by the questions not covered in the contract mainly relate to metadata, the ability to monitor and audit the cloud-based services, and the use of subcontractors.

Metadata-related functions

Metadata-related issues are consistently missing from the IFRC*jobs* contract; therefore, all questions on the Checklist concerning metadata (i.e., Q 2.6, Q 2.7, Q 2.8, Q 5.4, Q 5.5, Q 7.4, and Q 8.5) – including its ownership, access to it, its content and nature, its destruction, and the place where it is stored – were not addressed by the IFRC*jobs* contract. In fact, throughout the IFRC*jobs* contract, no such term as "metadata" appears. When IFRC staff were asked how metadata-related concerns were addressed in the introduction of cloud-based services, they responded that it is not necessary to make a distinction between data and metadata, and that metadata is considered a type of data and should therefore be addressed by contract clauses on data.[17] This response perhaps originates from a general lack of understanding of metadata specific to the records and archives management field and, therefore, there is an absence of appreciation by the cloud provider of the distinction between metadata and data, and of the critical role that metadata plays in record-keeping for organizations.

The international standard ISO 15489 defines metadata for records as "structured or semi-structured information, which enables the creation, management, and use of records through time and within and across domains"[18]; it should encompass information on: (a) the content of the record, (b) the structure of the record

TABLE 5.1 Examination of the IFRC*jobs* contract against the InterPARES Trust Checklist for Cloud Service Contracts

Question	Y	N	?	Notes re: IFRC*jobs* contract and the Checklist
1. Agreement				
1.1 Is the effective start date of the agreement clearly stated?	✓			The agreement shall commence on the effective date, which is the date the Order Form is signed.
1.2 Is there an explanation of circumstances in which the services could be suspended?	✓			E.g., where payment of fees is late by more than 30 days and the service provider has sent at least three written reminders to the IFRC, the service provider reserves the right to suspend the provision of the service, by giving the IFRC 14 days prior written notice.
1.3 Is there an explanation of circumstances in which the services could be terminated?	✓			E.g., when IFRC breaches a list of acceptable use policies, the service provider may terminate the user's access to the service.
1.4 Is there an explanation of notification, or an option to subscribe to a notification service, in the event of changes made to the terms governing the service?	✓			Amendments as agreed upon between the parties shall be in writing and shall be deemed to have been duly given if sent by registered post or acknowledged fax.
2. Data Ownership and Use				
2.1 Do you retain ownership of data that you store, transmit, and/or create with the cloud service?	✓			The service provider is a data processor and IFRC is a data controller. The service provider will only process personal data on behalf of, and in the name of, IFRC.
2.2 Does the Provider reserve the right to use your data for the purposes of operating and improving the services?	✓			Service provider may use the user's data for the purpose of the contract, and must keep confidential the user's data.

(continued)

TABLE 5.1 *Continued*

Question	Y	N	?	Notes re: IFRCjobs contract and the Checklist
2.3 Does the Provider reserve the right to use your data for the purpose of advertising?		✓		The service provider shall not at any time use IFRC's information to their private advantage. The term "private advantage" should be able to cover the advertising activity. Note: The way this question is phrased is not consistent with others. For this question, a "No" answer is required for the contract to be a good one, which is contrary to the rest of the questions in this Checklist, which usually require a "yes" answer for the contract examined to be a good one.
2.4 Does the Provider reserve the right to use, or make your data available as anonymized open data (through standard APIs)?			Not clear.	No information on this.
2.5 Does the Provider's compliance with copyright laws and other applicable intellectual property rights restrict the type of content you can store with the cloud service?	✓			It is specified that the IFRC should ensure that the data it supplies have been obtained fairly and lawfully.
2.6 Do the Provider's terms apply to metadata?			Not clear.	No information on metadata.
2.7 Do you gain ownership of metadata generated by the system during procedures of upload, management, download, and migration?			Not clear.	
2.8 Do you have the right to access these metadata during the contractual relationship?			Not clear.	

Question	Y	N	?	Notes re: IFRCjobs contract and the Checklist
3. Availability, Retrieval, and Use				
3.1 Are precise indicators provided regarding the availability of the service?	✓			
3.2 Does the degree of availability of the data meet your business needs?			Not clear.	These are assessments that should be carried out by IFRC based on the availability of the service and their own needs. Yet the answers are likely "yes"; otherwise, the IFRC would have experienced issues in their recruitment. Interviewees did not report such issues in the interview.
3.3 Does the degree of availability of the data allow you to comply with freedom of information (FOI) laws?			Not clear.	
3.4 Does the degree of availability of the data allow you to comply with the right of persons to access their own personal data?			Not clear.	
3.5 Does the degree of availability of the data allow you to comply with the right of authorities to legally access your data for investigation, control, or judicial purposes?			Not clear.	
3.6 Are the procedures, time, and cost for restoring your data following a service outage clearly stated?	✓	✓		Disaster recovery procedure is specified. But time and cost for restoring the data is not stated.
4. Data Storage and Preservation				
4.1 Does the Provider create backups of your organization's data?	✓			Full database backups are performed. Backup procedure, security measures at the off-site backups, and the retention period of backup are specified.
4.2 If your organization manages external records (e.g., customer data), does the Provider create backups of your customer's data?	✓			
4.3 Do the Provider's terms apply to any backup created?	✓			It is assumed so, as backup data is also owned by the IFRC.

(continued)

TABLE 5.1 *Continued*

Question	Y	N	?	Notes re: IFRCjobs contract and the Checklist
4.4 In the event of accidental data deletion, does the Provider bear responsibility for data recovery?	✓			In case of wrongful data deletion, data can be recovered from backups.
4.5 Are there procedures outlined to indicate that your data will be managed over time in a manner that preserves their usability, reliability, authenticity, and integrity?			Not clear.	If the focus of this question is on the ability of the service for long-term preservation – hence the term "over time" – then the answer is "No." The solution is a business system and a recordkeeping system. It is not a system for long-term preservation. If the focus of this question is on the ability of the service for protecting the usability, reliability, authenticity, and integrity of the data, then the answer may vary as different organizations may have different definitions of these characteristics and different standards for the protection of these characteristics. The question will be more answerable if it can be more specific, such as, does the system have access control?
4.6 Are there procedures to ensure file integrity during transfer of your data into and out of the system (e.g., checksums)?	✓			Encrypted access is enforced, and appropriate technical and organizational security measures have been implemented.
4.7 Is there an explanation provided about how the service will evolve over time (i.e., migration and/or emulation activities)?	✓			Different types of maintenance (i.e., releases, monthly patches, emergency patches, platform upgrade, and planned maintenance), including their content, frequency, and communication with the customer, have been specified.

Question	Y	N	?	Notes re: IFRCjobs contract and the Checklist
4.8 Does the system provide access to audit trails concerning activities related to evolution of the service?	✓			A standard quarterly review of service logs and reports can be provided to the IFRC upon written request. Any additional service reports will be provided as an optional service, available on demand, upon payment of an additional fee.
4.9 Will you be notified by the Provider of changes made to your data due to evolution of the service?	✓			Communication will be undertaken with the IFRC prior to the deployment of any type of maintenance or new release.
4.10 Can you request notification of impending changes to the system related to evolution of the service that could impact your data?			✓	
5. Data Retention and Disposition				
5.1 Are you clearly informed about the procedure and conditions for the destruction of your data?	✓			The service provider has implemented a secure disposal policy that is compliant with ISO 27001.
5.2 Will your data (and all their copies, including backups) be destroyed in compliance with your data retention and disposition schedules?	✓			The solution allows configuring data retention periods according to local legislation.
5.3 If so, will they be immediately and permanently destroyed in a manner that prevents their reconstruction, according to a secure destruction policy ensuring confidentiality of the data until their complete deletion?	✓	✓		Data can be permanently destroyed, but not immediately. Backups are performed on a data centre level rather than per client; thus, backups will not be overwritten until six months later.

(continued)

TABLE 5.1 Continued

Question	Y	N	?	Notes re: IFRCjobs contract and the Checklist
5.4 Is there information available about the nature and content of the associated metadata generated by the cloud service system?			Not clear.	No information about metadata.
5.5 Will the Provider destroy associated metadata upon disposition of your data?			Not clear.	
5.6 Will the Provider deliver and/or give access to audit trails of the destruction activity?			Not clear.	No information on these.
5.7 Will the Provider supply an attestation, report, or statement of deletion (if required by your internal or legal destruction policies)?			Not clear.	
6. Security, Confidentiality, and Privacy				
6.1 Does the system prevent unauthorized access, use, alteration, or destruction of your data?	✔			Appropriate technical, physical, and organizational measures have been implemented to protect data against unauthorized disclosure or access, accidental loss, or destruction.
6.2 Is your data secure during procedures of transfer into and out of the system?	✔			Encrypted access is enforced.
6.3 Does the system provide and give you access to audit trails, metadata, and/or access logs to demonstrate security measures?			Not clear.	No information on this.
6.4 Will you be notified in the case of a security breach or system malfunction?	✔			In the event of a data security breach, the Company will endeavour to notify the Customer as soon as the Company is made aware.

Question	Y	N	?	Notes re: IFRCjobs contract and the Checklist
6.5 Does the Provider use the services of a subcontractor?			Not clear.	The contract specifies that the service provider may at its sole discretion subcontract any of its obligations under the agreement. But the contract does not explicitly indicate whether the service provider uses a subcontractor or not.
6.6 Does the Provider offer information about the identity of the subcontractor and its tasks?			Not clear.	
6.7 Are subcontractors held to the same level of legal obligations as the Provider of the cloud service?			Not clear.	It is provided in the T&C that the service provider and all individuals assigned by it to perform services under the contract shall abide by a list of rules. However, it is not clear whether subcontractors should be considered as "individuals assigned by it."
6.8 Is a disaster recovery plan available or does the contract consider what happens in the event of a disaster?	✓			The disaster recovery procedure is described.
6.9 Does the Provider offer any information regarding past performance with disaster recovery procedures?			Not clear.	There is no information on the contract about the past performance of the disaster recovery procedures. But it is specified that the procedure is tested by the service provider once a year, which should guarantee its performance.
6.10 Does the Provider have a confidentiality policy in regard to its employees, partners, and subcontractors?			Not clear.	It is not clear whether the service provider has a confidentiality policy. The contract specifies that all individuals assigned by the service provider to perform service shall keep confidential any information known to them, and which has not been made public.
6.11 Do the Provider's terms include privacy, confidentiality, or security policies for sensitive, confidential, personal, or other special kinds of data you store with the Provider?	✓			The terms include privacy, confidentiality, or security policies that apply to all data the IFRC store with the Provider.

(continued)

TABLE 5.1 Continued

Question	Y	N	?	Notes re: IFRCjobs contract and the Checklist
6.12 Is it clearly stated what information (including personal information) is collected about your organization, why it is collected, and how it will be used by the Provider?			Not clear.	There is no information in the T&C or SLA on whether the service provider collects information about IFRC.
6.13 Does the Provider share this information with other companies, organizations, or individuals without your consent?		✓		The service provider shall not communicate at any time to any other personal (legal or natural), etc. any information known to it/them by reason of its/their association with IFRC which has not been made public, except with IFRC's consent. Note: The way this question is phrased is not consistent with others. For this question, a "No" answer is required for the contract to be a good one, which is contrary to the rest of the questions in this Checklist, which usually require a "yes" answer for the contract examined to be a good one.
6.14 Does the Provider state the legal reasons for which they would share this information with other companies, organizations, or individuals?			Not applicable.	It is only specified, as in the note to item 6.13, that the service provider shall not share the information to any other personal (legal or natural). Note: This should be a contingency question when the response to the previous question (6.13) indicates that the service provider would share information to other personnel for legal reasons.

Question	Y	N	?	Notes re: IFRCjobs contract and the Checklist
6.15 If the Provider shares this information with their affiliates for processing reasons, is this done in compliance with an existing privacy, confidentiality, or security policy?	✓			Assumed so. The service provider and any individuals assigned by it to perform service under the T&C shall assure compliance with applicable laws.
6.16 Is the Provider accredited with a third-party certification program?	✓			The service provider's platform is certified against ISO 27001 for the disposal of data and BS 25999 standard for Business Continuity.
6.17 Is the Provider audited on a systematic, regular, and independent basis by a third party in order to demonstrate compliance with security, confidentiality, and privacy policies?			Not clear.	Information on the procedures involved for obtaining and maintaining a third-party certification should be out of the scope of the contract between the service provider and its customer. The goal of a third-party certification is to provide a certain level of assurance with respect to certain activities of the certified institutions or organizations in order to save customers or organizations conducting their own examination and facilitate the conduct of business. Therefore, there is no need to look into the certification process but to assess the credibility of the certifying body.
6.18 Is such a certification or audit process documented?			Not clear.	
6.19 Do you have access to information such as the certifying or audit body and the expiration date of the certification?			Not clear.	
7. Data Location and Cross-border Data Flows				
7.1 Do you know where your data and their copies are located while stored in the cloud service?	✓			The locations of the primary and secondary data centre have been specified.
7.2 Does it comply with the location requirements that might be imposed on your organization's data by law, especially by applicable privacy law?	✓			

(continued)

TABLE 5.1 Continued

Question	Y	N	?	Notes re: IFRCjobs contract and the Checklist
7.3 Do you have the option to specify the location in which your data and their copies will be stored?	✓			Yes. Yet the IFRC has to choose from a list of locations where the service provider runs data centres.
7.4 Do you know where metadata are stored and whether they are stored in the same location as your data?			Not clear.	No information on this.
7.5 Will you be notified if the data location is moved outside your jurisdiction?	✓			The service provider can change the data centres within EEA during the term, provided that any new hosting centre provides at least the same level of services and security as the current data centres and will provide 30 days' notice in this event.
7.6 Is the issue of your stored data being subject to disclosure orders by national or foreign security authorities addressed?	✓			The service provider shall immediately notify the customer of any seizure of data by any relevant authorities. And if either party receives a disclosure request, it shall consult the other party on how to respond.
7.7 Does the Provider clearly state the legal jurisdiction in which the agreement will be enforced and potential disputes will be resolved?	✓			
8. End of Service – Contract Termination				
8.1 In the event that the Provider terminates the service, will you be notified?		✓		When customer breaches the acceptable use policy, the service provider may terminate the IFRC's access to the service.
8.2 Is there an established procedure for contacting the Provider if you wish to terminate the contract?	✓			With 20 business days' written notice.

Question	Y	N	?	Notes re: IFRCjobs contract and the Checklist
8.3 If the contract is terminated, will your data be transferred to you or to another Provider of your choice in a usable and interoperable format?	✓			Upon a written request by the customer within 30 business days of the expiry of the agreement, the service provider will return the customer data stored in the service provider's database in either CSV or XML format, free of charge. If the written request is made after the defined time length, or other formats are required, then the service provider can charge for such services.
8.4 Is the procedure, cost, and time period for returning/transferring your data at the end of the contract clearly stated?	✓			
8.5 At the end of the contract, do you have the right to access the associated metadata generated by the system?			Not clear.	No information on metadata.
8.6 At the end of the contract and after complete acknowledgement of restitution of your data, will your data and associated metadata be immediately and permanently destroyed, in a manner that prevents their reconstruction?		✓		The data will be destroyed permanently, but not immediately.
8.7 Is there an option for confirmation of deletion of records and metadata by the organization prior to termination of services with the Provider?			Not clear.	
8.8 Is there an option for the client to terminate the service agreement without penalty in the event that the Provider of the cloud service changes?	✓			

(e.g., its form, format), (c) its business context, (d) dependencies and relationships with other records and other metadata, (e) identifiers and other information needed to retrieve and present the record, and (f) the business actions and events involving the record throughout its existence.[19] As per ISO 15489, metadata is essential for the management of records, in particular the protection and demonstration of their evidentiary capacity – viz. authenticity, reliability, integrity, and usability, and should itself, therefore, be managed as a record.[20]

The significance of metadata for the management of records in the cloud increases in parallel with the increased risks to, and challenges of, protecting the trustworthiness of records stored and managed in the cloud. For instance, Blair identifies "preservation of metadata" as one of the key contractual provisions for information governance in the cloud[21]; and the standard Electronic Records as Documentary Evidence (CAN/CGSB-72.34–2017), issued by the Canadian General Standards Board to improve the admissibility and weight of electronic records in legal procedures, recommends:

> Admissibility of records held in a cloud environment is possible if the contract with the CSP [cloud service provider] includes clauses that allow access to the identity and recordkeeping metadata ... and the ability to verify the integrity of the system.[22]

Yet analysis of existing cloud service contracts shows that availability of metadata assigned to data is one of the major gaps in cloud service agreements,[23] corroborating the findings of the present analysis of the IFRC*jobs* contract. Bushey et al. explain that cloud service providers usually claim ownership of metadata on the basis that the metadata are generated for internal purposes – that is, to manage the cloud and ensure the use and quality of the service.[24] Indeed, analysis of the IFRC*jobs* contract shows that, in defining the ownership of data, the contract has restricted the scope of data owned by the IFRC to "personal data," and no explanation has been provided elsewhere in the contract on what personal data refers to. As a result, the IFRC could be denied access to and use of this metadata for recordkeeping purposes.

Of additional concern is the capacity of the metadata to be used for recordkeeping purposes if the procured cloud-based service is expected to function as a record-keeping system. Most cloud-based services are not designed with recordkeeping requirements in mind[25]; therefore, the metadata captured may not conform to an identified metadata standard for records in accordance with jurisdictional and/or organizational requirements. Due to these concerns, it is necessary that metadata-related questions on the Checklist are considered in the evaluation of cloud-based services and are positively addressed in cloud service contracts.

Monitoring and auditing functions

The ability for an organization to monitor and audit cloud-based services is addressed in the Checklist through questions on security measures (Q 6.3) and the destruction of data according to retention and disposition schedules, or at the end of a contract (Q 5.6, Q 5.7, Q 8.7). These monitoring and auditing functions originate from the need to verify, document, and prove the outcome of record-keeping activities. As recommended by ISO 15489–1: 2016:

> The creation, capture and management of records should be regularly monitored and evaluated with the involvement and support of records professionals, information technology professionals, legal professionals, auditors, business managers and senior managers as appropriate.[26]

Further, the standard explicitly states: "systems and processes provided by third-party providers should also be monitored and evaluated, using contractual requirements relating to the management of records as evaluation criteria."[27] The ability to obtain information (e.g., audit trails, access logs, and metadata) to monitor and evaluate the carrying out of recordkeeping policies, requirements, and procedures can help organizations account for their recordkeeping practices and prove the evidentiary capacity of their records.

With the use of cloud-based services, it appears that monitoring of activities undertaken by the service providers becomes more relevant and crucial. For instance, Ferguson-Boucher & Convery state that many of the risks generated by the use of cloud-based services can be mitigated through "audit and monitoring of the provider's services and infrastructure."[28] Assurance that the authenticity, reliability, and integrity of the data stored in the cloud are maintained is usually the focus of management of the data once they are in the cloud.[29]

However, as the present study and other studies show, the ability for organizations to monitor and audit activities in the cloud is often restricted because cloud service providers may wish to keep information concerning the operation of their services secret from competitors and hackers.[30]

Cloud computing subcontractors

The evaluation using the Checklist showed that there is no information in the IFRC*jobs* contract concerning the use of subcontractors (Q 6.5), the identity of subcontractors (Q 6.6), and whether subcontractors are held to the same level of legal obligations as the service provider (Q 6.7). The Terms and Conditions of IFRC*jobs* states that the service provider may, "at its sole discretion subcontract any of its obligations" under the contract, but the contract does not specify whether it has done so and, if yes, the identity of the subcontractor. The T&C provide that the service provider and all individuals assigned by it to perform services under the contract shall abide by a list of rules, including complying with all applicable laws, carrying out all duties with integrity, and keeping confidential the IFRC's information. This clause may provide the IFRC with some comfort. However, it is not clear whether subcontractors are considered as individuals assigned by the service provider.

The use of subcontractors is one of the commonly discussed risks of using cloud-based services, as organizations do not have any direct business relationships with cloud subcontractors who may hold and have access to their data,[31] and therefore subcontractors may not have any direct accountability towards cloud clients. Considering this, it is necessary that cloud service providers specify in the contract the use of subcontractors, their responsibilities, and whether they are held to the same level of obligations as the cloud service provider.

Suggested updates for the checklist

The examination of the Checklist against the IFRC*jobs* cloud contract also reveals ways in which the Checklist may be updated to improve its strengths as a tool for organizations wishing to address records-related risks when evaluating and adopting cloud-based services.

First, regarding the security of data, Q 6.4 on the Checklist asks if the user will be notified in the case of a security breach or system malfunction. Examination of the IFRC*jobs* contract reveals two other types of activities that may threaten the security of organizational data, which could be added to the Checklist: wrongful deletion or seizure of data by external parties. Furthermore, as existing questions in section 6 mainly concentrate on the outcome of the security measures, a question may be added to ask directly what security measures (e.g., technical, physical, or organizational) are in place.

Second, regarding the retention and disposition of data, a question may be added investigating whether there are circumstances under which the service provider will not destroy the data upon completion of the service or termination or expiry of the contract.

Third, regarding backups of the user's data created by the provider, in addition to Q 4.1, Q 4.2, and Q 4.3, further questions may be added investigating the backup procedure, security measures for the off-site backups, and the retention period of backups.

Fourth, Q 6.14 could be changed to a contingency question because it requires a positive answer to Q 6.13.

Fifth, information on the certifying body, certification/audit process, and expiration date of the certification (Q 6.17, Q 6.18, and Q 6.19) usually are out of the scope of the contract between the service provider and its customer. The goal of a third-party certification is to provide a level of assurance with respect to certain activities of the certified institutions or organizations, in order to save customers or organizations the effort of having to conduct their own examination, thereby facilitating the conduct of business. Rather, users can ask the service provider to keep them informed if there is any change to their certification status, such as when a certification has expired or is not renewed.

Sixth, consistency in the way the questions are phrased could be improved. For instance, the way Q 2.3 and Q 6.13 are phrased is not consistent with the other questions on the Checklist, to the extent that while a "Yes" answer to all other questions indicates that a risk has been addressed or mitigated in the cloud contract, a "No" rather than a "Yes" answer to Q 2.3 and Q 6.13 indicates positive coverage of an issue. This slight inconsistency may create confusion and increase complexity when presenting evaluation results.

Seventh, the consistency of the focus of the questions could be improved. While the majority of the questions are written to examine the presence of certain policies or procedures (e.g., Q 1.2, Q 1.3, Q 2.1, and Q 3.1) that are essential in order to mitigate the risks to data/records and as a result of which recordkeeping requirements can be satisfied, some questions (e.g., Q 2.5, Q 3.2, Q 3.3, Q 3.4, Q 3.5, Q 4.5, and Q 4.6) ask directly whether recordkeeping requirements have been satisfied. For instance, Q 4.5 asks if procedures are outlined to indicate that data will be managed over time in a manner that preserves their usability, reliability, authenticity, and integrity. It is unlikely for a cloud service provider to promise in the contract that the usability, reliability, authenticity, and integrity of the data will be preserved. To examine whether this requirement has been met, the user of the Checklist will first have to convert this requirement to various functionalities, procedures, and arrangements of the cloud service, and then examine if these are present within the examined cloud service. To improve this, the Checklist could pose specific questions about functions that would support the preservation of the required records qualities. For example, a question such as, "Does the system have access control?" would address in part the maintenance of the integrity of records.

Conclusion

Examination of the IFRC*jobs* contract against the Checklist met the objectives of improving both the Checklist and the IFRC's future cloud service contracts. Overall, the IFRC*jobs* contract is strong in terms of addressing the risks to data and records associated with the use of cloud services, with the majority of questions on the Checklist positively addressed in the contract. Yet, three weaknesses of the IFRC*jobs* contract have been identified: the absence of clauses on metadata; the lack of ability to monitor and audit the performance of recordkeeping activities; and ambiguities around the use, identification, and legal obligations of subcontractors. These gaps, in particular the first two, indicate the absence of records management considerations in the evaluation and introduction of cloud-based services. The analysis of the IFRC*jobs* contract against the Checklist was provided to the IFRC Legal Department as a guide for legal personnel to identify and address potential deficiencies during the drafting stage for future cloud service contracts.

The examination also identified seven areas of improvement[32] for the Checklist, in both the methodological design and content of questions. The contents of the Checklist could be expanded or modified in the following areas: notifications of wrongful deletion or seizure of data and records; technical, physical, and organizational measures for the security of data; circumstances in which the service provider may retain data or records upon termination of services or termination or expiry of the contract; backup procedures, security measures for off-site backups, and retention period of backups; and certification status of the cloud provider. The suggested improvements to the Checklist will enhance this useful tool designed to support organizations in addressing the commonly encountered risks in the use of cloud-based services.

Notes

1 This chapter is based on the final report of an InterPARES Trust project: Weimei Pan & Grant Mitchell, 2016, 'TR02 – Case Study: IFRCjobs, a SaaS recruiting tool.' After publication of the final report, the IFRC updated the cloud request form, drafted new standard clauses that apply to cloud service contracts, and in 2019, adopted a Policy on the Protection of Personal Data, which aims to ensure that "any personal data collected and used by, or on behalf of, the Federation is accurate and relevant, and that the personal data is not misused, lost, corrupted, or improperly accessed and shared." In the Policy on the Protection of Personal Data, some gaps in the IFRCjobs contract were addressed. For instance, the policy requires that all proposed transfers of personal data to third parties should be reviewed for compatibility with the principles outlined in the policy and the written transfer agreements should require that the third party, in addition to other conditions, only subcontract work with the IFRC's consent.

2 The author is responsible for the choice and the presentation of the facts contained in the publication and for the opinions expressed therein, which are not necessarily those of the International Federation of Red Cross and Red Crescent Societies and do not commit the Organization.

3 IFRC, 2013a, *Request for cloud services*, unpublished internal document, p. 4.

4 To learn more about the project, please visit https://interparestrust.org/.

5 The InterPARES Trust for Cloud Service Contracts is a product of project NA 14, Developing Model Cloud Computing Contracts. In this chapter, the final version is used for the evaluation. Therefore, the evaluation result is not applicable to any other versions of the Checklist.

6 The Retention & Disposition Functional Requirements is a product of project NA 06, Retention & Disposition in a Cloud Environment. In the original report of the IFRC-jobs project, a March 2015 version was used for the analysis. This content is not discussed in the present chapter.

7 Glenn A Bowen, 2009, 'Document analysis as a qualitative research method', *Qualitative Research Method*, vol. 9, no. 2, p. 27.

8 To clarify, "classification" here refers to classification of data based on the potential operational and financial consequences the IFRC may face if there is unauthorized disclosure, alteration, or destruction of the data.

9 IFRC, 2014, *Information classification standard*, unpublished internal document.

10 Ibid.

11 IFRC, 2013b, *IFRC ICT security policy*, unpublished internal document.

12 As a type of privilege and immunity enjoyed by international organizations, inviolability comprises four broad types: jurisdictional immunities, inviolability of premises and archives, freedom of communication, and immunity relating to financial matters. Among these four, inviolability of premises and archives means that the international organization is granted a heightened level of protection so that anyone external to the organization cannot enter its premises or access its archives unless given express permission or invited to do so.

13 IFRC, 2013b.

14 IFRC, 2013a, *Request for cloud services*. Unpublished internal document. p. 6.

15 Ibid.

16 Q 2.3 and Q 6.13 are considered positively addressed, though with "No" answers; explanations are provided both in the notes to these two questions in the table and in

the text. Q 5.3 and Q 8.6 are considered positively addressed, as the reason for the "No" part was accounted for in the contract. Q 6.9 is considered positively addressed, as a yearly test of the disaster recovery should achieve the purpose of guaranteeing its performance as asked in Q 6.9. Q 6.10 is considered positively addressed as well, as it is specified that all individuals assigned by the service provider to perform service shall keep confidential any information known to them, and which has not been made public. This should be the intended goal of the question of whether a confidential policy is in place. Q 6.14 is a contingency question not applicable to the IFRC contract, as it is already explained in the response to Q 6.13 that no information of the IFRC will be shared with any other person, both natural and legal. Thus, Q 6.14 is also considered positively addressed. Q 3.6 is not considered positively addressed since, although a disaster recovery procedure is specified, the time and cost for restoring data is not stated.

17 Interviewee 3 and Interviewee 4.
18 International Organization for Standardization, 2016, *Information and documentation – Records management – Part 1: Concepts and principles*, ISO 15489–1, International Organization for Standardization, Geneva, p. 2.
19 Ibid, pp. 5–6.
20 Ibid.
21 Barclay T Blair, 2010, 'Governance for protecting information in the cloud', *Information Management*, vol. 55, no. 5, pp. HT1–HT4.
22 Canadian General Standards Board, 2017, *Electronic records as documentary evidence (CAN/CGSB-72.34–2017)*, viewed 17 May 2020, http://publications.gc.ca/collections/collection_2017/ongc-cgsb/P29-072-034-2017-eng.pdf, p. 32.
23 Jessica Bushey, Marie Demoulin & Robert McLelland, 2015, 'Cloud service contracts: an issue of trust', *Canadian Journal of Information and Library Science*, vol. 39, no. 2, pp. 128–153.
24 Ibid, p. 136.
25 Blair, 2010, pp. HT1–HT4. Kirsten Ferguson-Boucher & Nicole Convery, 2011, 'Storing information in the cloud – a research project', *Journal of the Society of Archivists*, vol. 32, no. 2, pp. 221–239.
26 International Organization for Standardization, 2016, p. 9.
27 Ibid.
28 Ferguson-Boucher & Convery, 2011, p. 233.
29 Ibid.
30 Ibid.
31 Patrick Cunningham, 2016, 'Another walk in the cloud', *Information Management,* vol. 50, no. 5, pp. 20–24.
32 A copy of the cloud contract analysis table was provided to the Checklist creators during the InterPARES Trust project.

Bibliography

Blair, B 2010, 'Governance for protecting information in the cloud', *Information Management*, vol. 55, no. 5, pp. HT1–HT4.
Bowen, GA 2009, 'Document analysis as a qualitative research method', *Qualitative Research Method*, vol. 9, no. 2, pp. 27–40.
Bushey, J, Demoulin, M & McLelland, R 2015, 'Cloud service contracts: An issue of trust', *Canadian Journal of Information and Library Science*, vol. 39, no. 2, pp. 128–153.
Canadian General Standards Board 2017, *Electronic records as documentary evidence* (CAN/CGSB-72.34–2017), viewed 17 May 2020, http://publications.gc.ca/collections/collection_2017/ongc-cgsb/P29-072-034-2017-eng.pdf.
Cunningham, P 2016, 'Another walk in the cloud', *Information Management*, vol. 50, no. 5, pp. 20–24.

Duranti, L, Pan, W, Rowe, J & Barlauora, G 2013, 'Records in the Cloud (RiC) user survey report', viewed 18 November 2018, http://recordsinthecloud.org/assets/docum ents/RiC_Oct232013_User_Survey_Report.pdf.

Ferguson-Boucher, K & Convery, N 2011, 'Storing information in the cloud – A research project', *Journal of the Society of Archivists*, vol. 32, no. 2, pp. 221–239.

IFRC 2013a, *Request for cloud services*. Unpublished internal document.

IFRC 2013b, *IFRC ICT security policy*. Unpublished internal document.

IFRC 2014, *Information classification standard*. Unpublished internal document.

International Organization for Standardization 2016, *Information and documentation – Records management – Part 1: Concepts and principles*, ISO 15489-1:2016, International Organization for Standardization, Geneva.

6

MIND MAPPING FUNCTIONS FOR MANAGING INFORMATION, RECORDS, AND ARCHIVES

Giovanni Michetti and Stephen Haufek[1]

Introduction

New technology and socio-economic phenomena like globalization have dramatically changed the labour market, resulting in a request for new skills and professional figures able to cope with the change. This is more than true for the archival domain: the space in which archivists work, the tools they work with and the way they work have totally changed since the last century, to the point that the archival community is investigating whether the archivist's role and identity needs for a redefinition – rather: a reinterpretation – in light of these big changes.[2]

The need for redefinition and reinterpretation is true not only for archivists and records managers, but for the whole Library and Information Science domain, a space in which internal boundaries are more and more blurred while external boundaries keep on expanding and overlapping with other domains. Education and training have been affected by these phenomena. All around the world, universities and professional associations are struggling to be responsive to an increasing demand for new skills and competences. New courses are designed every day, advanced programmes are launched, novel professional figures are pushed into the market, and trendy terms are created – after all, jargon is an identifying feature of a professional community because mastering the language is a way to suggest that the underlying reality can be mastered, too. Interdisciplinarity is the rule, and technology is not optional anymore. Far from being just a tool, technology has become the glue – if not the objective – of many educational, professional, and scientific initiatives. This is perfectly understandable, because technology has been a major driver of globalization, so it makes sense to focus on it in order to try and understand this complex process. The overall result of globalization is a rich and stimulating environment, but such variety is also an issue because it makes it more difficult to create and possibly govern a consistent framework where all entities can interact smoothly.[3]

Standards play a major role in this integration process, since they establish uniform and agreed criteria, methods, processes, and practices. However, besides their value as technical tools, the fundamental value of standards "lies rather in their capacity to raise awareness and issues, and bring the community to discussion. Standards are a way by which a community – the archival community – identifies itself."[4] Codification of professional knowledge and development of standards through which that knowledge is applied, is a fundamental step in the professionalization process that leads an occupation to develop coherency as a group.[5] However, we should be aware of the political nature of standards: standardization is a very complex process in which many different factors need to be mediated and harmonized in order to create tools based on the consensus of the parties involved.

The best does not always win. In short, the most technically advanced solution does not necessarily become the dominant one. Standards are the result of a negotiation process wherein different perspectives and approaches of different stakeholders compete in a domain populated by uncertainty, chance, and human behaviour. As such, standards may well be qualified as social constructions. However, the widespread technocratic attitude tends to hide their very human nature, overstressing the technical aspects and presenting them as neutral instruments to achieve defined objectives.

Therefore, it is fundamental to investigate the main standards adopted worldwide in the records management and archival domain in order to get an overall picture of the concepts and values imbued in them. The globalized world is a complex network of interacting people, organizations, and governments bringing different cultures together and asking for their cooperation. Standards reflect such diversity.

In particular, several models have been developed in the records management area, including international standards designing a general framework of concepts and principles for records management (e.g., ISO 15489–1), standards defining the functional requirements of records management systems (e.g., ISO 16175-1, MoReq), standards focusing on the strategic dimension of records management (e.g., the ISO 30300 suite), national standards on design criteria for electronic records management software applications (e.g., DoD 5015.2), best practices, and a wide range of documents intended to support records management.

Similarly, standards and scientific literature related to the management of records in archival custody (i.e., non–current records) have explored the overall model of preservation (e.g., ISO 14721, InterPARES Chain of Preservation). Also, specific aspects related to preservation have been investigated (e.g., storage in ISO 11799, conversion and migration in ISO 13008), and models for archival description have been developed (e.g., ISAD, ISAAR, EAD, EAC).

However, there is a scarcity of literature on an overall model covering functions and activities that should be performed in a coherent system to manage records throughout their life. No standard is specifically designed to this aim. Organizations need to merge and integrate different authoritative sources in a consistent way in order to develop their records management and archival programmes so that all functions can interact smoothly.

The Ontology of functional activities for archival systems

Objectives

To identify the functions, objects, and agents addressed by the main international standards on records management and preservation, a research team consisting of Giovanni Michetti and Georg Gänser therefore developed a research project called "Ontology of functional activities for archival systems" (the Ontology) within the InterPARES Trust (ITrust) framework.[6] More precisely, the goal of the project was to create an ontology representing the functions and activities that are carried out on records from creation to long-term preservation, as they are described in the selected sources (see below).

The Ontology is designed to facilitate the representation of all the functionalities that should be performed by an *archival* system, where the term *archives* is meant to cover the entire lifespan of records, from creation to long-term preservation.[7] An ontological representation of the functional activities would provide archivists and records managers with a clear picture of the functions and activities that need to be implemented and performed within an organization. Such a model may aid in the analysis of archives and records management systems, through the identification of the performance areas and the gaps that need to be addressed. The model may also support the creation of comprehensive and consistent information systems. In this way, current, semi-current, and non-current records may be managed as a whole, or at least in a coherent way. The model may be used as a set of high-level guidelines by software producers, providing them with a sort of checklist to help improve their applications. The model may also be used as a high-level tool for audit and re-engineering actions. For example, based on such a systematic approach, documentary procedures may be redesigned and/or new procedures may be introduced in order to support existing and/or new activities.

Activities and results

The Ontology project was developed in three steps:

1. Identification of the sources;
2. Analysis of the sources;
3. Representation of the analysis.

First, the relevant standards and documents were identified, aiming to define a model that would represent the functions and activities needed to manage records from creation to long-term preservation. The research team created an annotated bibliography and then selected the sources that would form the foundation of the final model. The selection was based on a discretionary evaluation, so the list is not comprehensive. The aim was to focus on the most relevant sources to get an overall picture, not to be exhaustive. The following sources were selected and analysed:

- ARMA International. Generally Accepted Recordkeeping Principles. 2014
- Society of American Archivists. Core Archival Functions. 2016
- ISO 14641−1:2012 Electronic archiving − Part 1: Specifications concerning the design and the operation of an information system for electronic information preservation
- ISO 14721:2012 Space Data and Information Transfer Systems − Open Archival Information System (OAIS) − Reference Model
- ISO 15489−1:2016 Information and documentation − Records management − Part 1: Concepts and principles
- ISO/TR 15489−2:2001 Information and documentation − Records management − Part 2: Guidelines
- ISO/TR 15801:2017 Document management − Electronically stored information − Recommendations for trustworthiness and reliability
- ISO 16175−1:2010 Information and documentation − Principles and functional requirements for records in electronic office environments − Part 1: Overview and statement of principles
- ISO 16175−2:2011 Information and documentation − Principles and functional requirements for records in electronic office environments − Part 2: Guidelines and functional requirements for digital records management systems
- ISO 16175−3:2010 Information and documentation − Principles and functional requirements for records in electronic office environments − Part 3: Guidelines and functional requirements for records in business systems
- ISO 16363:2012 Space data and information transfer systems − Audit and certification of trustworthy digital repositories
- ISO 23081−1:2017 Information and documentation − Records management processes − Metadata for records − Part 1: Principles
- ISO 23081−2:2009 Information and documentation − Managing metadata for records − Metadata for records − Part 2: Conceptual and implementation issues
- ISO/TR 26122:2008 Information and documentation − Work process analysis for records
- ISO/IEC 27000:2016 Information technology − Security techniques − Information security management systems − Overview and vocabulary
- ISO/IEC 27001:2013 Information technology − Security techniques − Information security management systems − Requirements
- ISO/IEC 27002:2013 Information technology − Security techniques − Code of practice for information security controls
- ISO 30300:2011 Information and documentation − Management systems for records − Fundamentals and vocabulary

- ISO 30301:2011 Information and documentation – Management systems for records – Requirements
- ISO 30302:2015 Information and documentation – Management systems for records – Guidelines for implementation

As a second step, the research team analysed the selected sources and created statements based on their content. The team adopted an approach inspired by the Resource Description Framework.[8] The initial idea was to identify three classes of entities (Agents, Actions, and Objects) and the relationships among them, coherently with a consolidated approach in Information Science, where these entities are recognized as fundamental to interpret the meaning of the documentary objects, as shown in the diagrams below.

However, the picture quickly became dense and overcrowded with entities and relationships, so the research team decided to focus on Functions and Actions in order to limit the complexity of the model. For the same reason, the statements were merged, refined, and tweaked. For example, many triples extracted from the original sources would use different verbs like *encompass, include, imply*, to express a similar meaning. In such cases, the verb *involve* was chosen to represent any relation of inclusion or causation. The table below shows an example of some triples identified in ISO 15489–1.

Some labels were unified, as in the case of the terms "Record management," "Records management," "Management of records." Many choices were also made on the grounds of an attentive yet discretionary evaluation. In short, the statements taken as the basis for the creation of the model were the result of controlled interpretation.

The third step of the project was to create a representation of the statements. The team initially used a well-known standard, the Web Ontology Language (OWL),[9]

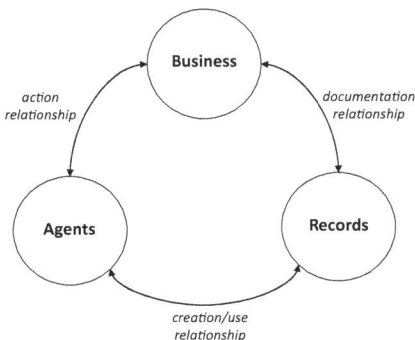

FIGURE 6.1 Types of metadata and their relationships. Adapted from ISO 23081–1: 2017 Information and documentation – Records management processes – Metadata for records – Part 1: Principles, Figure 1.

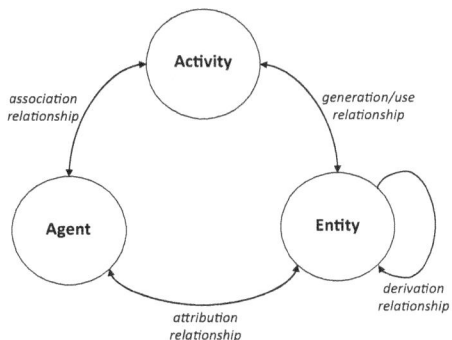

FIGURE 6.2 Structure of provenance records. Adapted from W3C, *PROV model primer. W3C Working Group note 30 April 2013*, viewed 10 October 2020, www.w3.org/TR/2013/NOTE-prov-primer-20130430/.

TABLE 6.1 Sample of triples extracted from ISO 15489–1

Subject	Predicate	Object
Record	Is evidence of	Business activity
Record	Is	Information asset
Information	Can be managed as	Record
Records management	Encompasses	Creating records [to meet requirements for evidence]
Records management	Encompasses	Capturing records [to meet requirements for evidence]
Records management	Encompasses	Protecting authenticity, reliability, integrity, and usability
Records management	Is supported by	Records systems
Metadata	Is	Data describing context, content, and structure of records
Metadata	Is	Data describing the management of records
Metadata	Is	Essential component of records

but the resulting representation was highly complex, so upon review the team decided to adopt a less advanced yet more effective approach for the purposes of the project – namely, rather than using a formal ontology, the team opted for a simple graphic representation. The figure below shows the top-level view of the ontology.

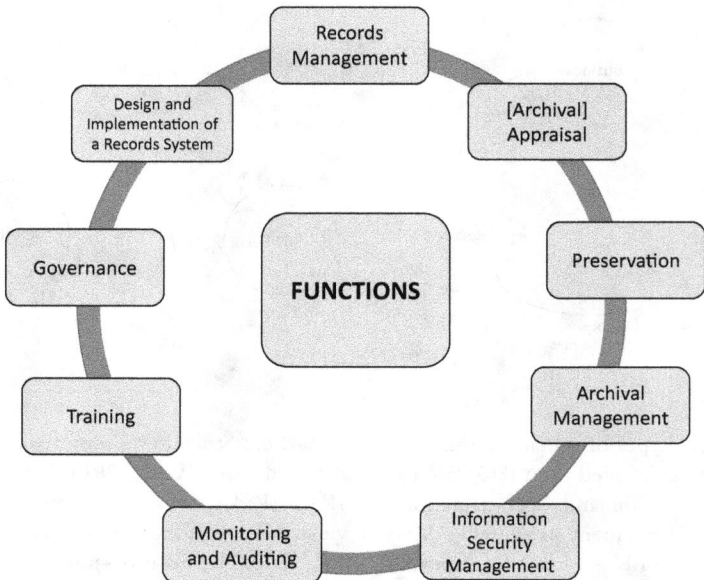

FIGURE 6.3 Ontology. Top-level view

This representation is very intuitive: the boxes represent the top-level functions that emerged from the analysis of the sources. Some of the functions (i.e., Records Management, Appraisal, Preservation, and Archival Management) describe the lifecycle of records from creation to preservation, whereas the other functions relate primarily to the context, rather than the objects. Each function can be opened to expose lower levels, subfunctions, and relationships in the network.[10]

From the Ontology to the mind map

The Ontology is a complex network of more than a hundred diagrams representing functions and activities related to records management and archives. However, such a model is the representation of the principles and statements found in international standards; therefore, it provides a picture of an abstract world. To be more precise, the model provides a theoretical picture that is far from being perfect: it represents the inconsistencies, the ambiguities, the errors, and the overlaps – in a word, the *issues* – that can be found in the international standards. Not surprisingly, the analysis has shown that ISO standards are not always internally consistent and do not make up a coherent system when considered together.

The next step, which was the starting point of this chapter, was to use the Ontology to examine the archives and records management systems within some specific organizations, that is, in the real world. In February 2019, Giovanni Michetti and Stephen Haufek, encouraged and supported by Jens Boel and Eng Sengsavang, started investigating the possibility of adopting the Ontology as a basis for a survey aimed at assessing how records and archives management are integrated within organizations, particularly international organizations. The analysis of the Ontology highlighted the existence of a gap between standards and practice, and confirmed the shift of the profession towards different and broader categories:

> Records managers have moved from a world in which they have been able to control and maintain information within an organisation's boundaries (albeit sometimes through server networks spread across the globe) to a world in which individuals may often create organisational records from beyond that organisation's boundaries through Web 2.0 technologies or business applications which are hosted and supported within a third party "Cloud". This makes the case for rethinking how information is captured, audited and managed for operational purposes, accountability and use over time. It also raises additional questions about information ownership … information rights legislation … and information reuse …. Within this context, many of the key information management questions relate to issues around information value, access, security and risk management over time.[11]

Records creation, receipt, use, appraisal, disposition, and preservation are indeed the traditional functions that still need to be carried out in order to manage records and archives properly, as depicted in the Ontology. However, technological advances, work practice changes, regulatory framework modifications, and social transformations have completely modified the picture in the past ten years: a different, more holistic approach is needed to cope with the diversity and complexity of the many factors that play a role on the documentary stage. This is especially true within international organizations because diversity and complexity may be considered part of their nature. It also seems to be confirmed by research in which Maik Schmerbauch examined all the vacancy announcements and postings for archives and records management jobs at international organizations in 2016: he found 27 post and job titles corresponding to 39 vacancies.[12]

Paper records have yielded to digital documents, permeating public and private activities and assuming a variety of forms and formats (for example, email messages, databases, social media posts, datasets), to the point that it is hard to recognize them as records and apply the traditional concepts and principles of records management. There is a plethora of interrelated digital objects that are not limited to a special class of information objects (i.e., digital records) and that need to be managed, not only to avoid being overwhelmed by the sheer abundance of information, but also to take advantage of the opportunities for exploiting information and making business processes more efficient. These too have undergone disruptive changes – for example, collaborative working has assumed a completely new meaning thanks to collaborative software and platforms. As a consequence, documentary objects are no longer just stored in records management repositories, but rather they are found in enterprise content management repositories, email servers, web servers, shared network drives, personal drives, cloud computing services, and myriad solutions now available. Again, the consequence is that these different solutions, environments, and outcomes need to be managed in an integrated way because, after all, we live and work in an integrated way.

For that reason, considering records and archives in isolation from larger discussions about information and data management could be problematic. Organizations are required to take into account a large number and a wide variety of stakeholders who are impacted by the decisions adopted in relation to information creation, use, management, and preservation. These include Audit, Compliance, Legal, Security, Information Technology, and Finance, all of which may have conflicting interests, yet are invested with some responsibility for managing information assets in organizations.

Simply managing records and archives seems insufficient, and to fill this perceived gap, the field of Information Governance has sprouted up and been offered as the solution for controlling all the different aspects – records and archives included – that make up the information assets of an organization. Information Governance is the framework for controlling information – records included – in a way that encourages compliance, increases efficiency, mitigates legal risks, and aligns to corporate governance policies.[13] It is important not to see it as a sort of Records Management 2.0 – Information Governance does not just deal with more and different types of documentary objects, players, and technologies, but rather it is about organizing such objects, players, and technologies in a comprehensive framework wherein regulatory requirements, organizational culture, and operational and security constraints are managed as a whole.

As a consequence, the Ontology elaborated in the ITrust project has not been considered as an adequate tool to investigate how information, records, and archives are managed by organizations – not only are the high-level functions strongly and specifically related only to records and archives, but also the activities listed at the lower levels design a model with a strong orientation, which is more apt to check conformity to a predefined paradigm than to let concepts and practices emerge from the ground so as to understand what is really going on within organizations with regard to their information assets.

For this reason, the Ontology has been analysed with the aim of re-arranging the functions and activities into a new set of top-level categories with a broader meaning, avoiding – unlike the Ontology – the definition of exact relationships linking such categories, and keeping in mind that the objects taken into consideration should not be limited to records. The result of the analysis has been a mind map – a simple yet effective representation of the main functions that are supposed to be related to information governance within an organization. The functions are:

- Creation (including Accession into an information/records system or an archives);
- Processing (including but not limited to Maintenance, Indexing, Appraisal, Disposition, Arrangement, Description, Digitization);
- Use and Re-use Management (entailing creation of new objects in a new context, with independent metadata);
- Preservation Management (including but not limited to Storage, Conservation, Migration, Preservation Planning);

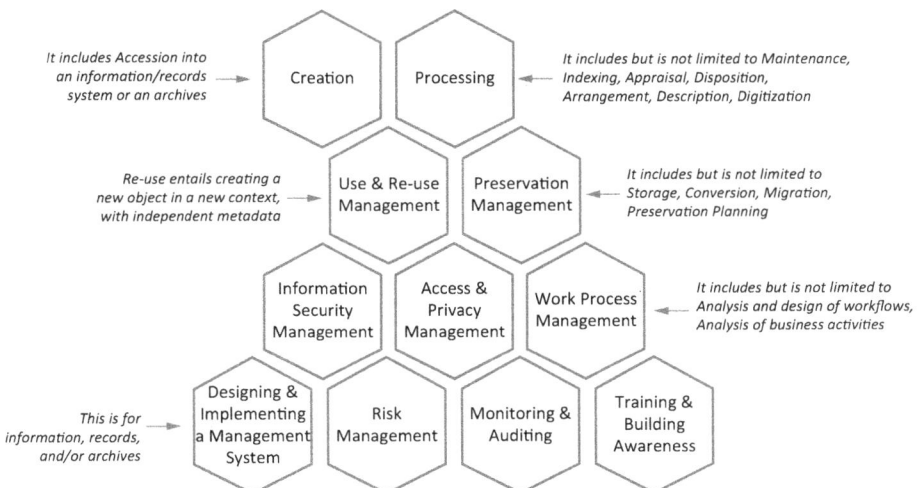

FIGURE 6.4 Mind map of functions to govern information, records, and archives

- Information Security Management;
- Access and Privacy Management;
- Work Process Management;
- Risk Management;
- Monitoring and Auditing;
- Designing and Implementing a Management System for information, records, and/or archives;
- Training and Building Awareness.

Feedback from international organizations

In order to assess how information, records, and archives management are integrated within organizations – and the extent to which the mind map accurately represented the functions that govern information, records, and archives – the authors designed and circulated a survey. It was developed specifically with information professionals from international organizations in mind as respondents (primarily records managers and archivists), although it was open to others as well. The intention of the survey was to gauge the extent to which key functions that are identified in international standards on information, records, and archives management are actually present in international organizations. Furthermore, it allowed us to assess the degree to which information, records, and archives management functions are integrated with each other; whether there are tools, policies, and/or frameworks that support their integration; and which organizational units are responsible for specific functions.

The first part of the survey focused on whether information, records, and archives management were, or should be, considered as components of one integrated programme or system. Specifically, it asked respondents if their organization (1) has an information governance framework that includes records and archives management, (2) has a system that manages the information lifecycle from creation through disposition, (3) has one integrated unit which is accountable for information, records, and archives management, and (4) has sufficient capacity for information, records, and archives management functions.

The responses overwhelmingly (>90%) supported the idea that information, records, and archives management should be considered as components of one integrated programme or system. This response substantiated our hypothesis that organizations believe that records and archives management need to be included in a larger discussion of information management that situates the records lifecycle within the entire information lifecycle.

Approximately 40% of the respondents stated that there was no information governance framework that includes records and archives management in their organization. The remaining 60% said there was one, or that one was being drafted, discussed, or in progress. We might be somewhat reassured that, on the one hand, there seems to be some notable movement (i.e., more than half) towards the development of an information governance framework in international organizations. However, there is clearly still a lot of work to be accomplished in this area.

Approximately 40% of the respondents stated that there was no system (or integrated systems) that manages the information lifecycle from creation through disposition, including the management of records and archives in accordance with best practice (e.g., application of retention schedules, access to records under organizational policy, arrangement and description of archives, digital preservation) in their organization. This response is interesting in that the numbers are similar to those above regarding an information governance framework. However, it is more meaningful in terms of the actual application of a framework. That is, having a framework may be considered more closely aligned with policies and standards, whereas having systems may be more closely aligned with processes and tools. Given that the answers to both questions (i.e., framework and systems) were similar, it suggests that those organizations with a framework (policies) are also those that have systems (processes and tools) to support them.

Approximately 60% of the respondents stated that accountability for information, records, and archives management is not integrated into one organizational unit – e.g., in an archives and/or records management unit or under the office of information and/or communications technology. Again, this response substantiates our hypothesis that accountability for information management activities is often spread across multiple stakeholders in an organization. Increasingly, different agents – including non-human agents such as technological systems that are responsible for ensuring compliance or triggering actions – are accountable throughout the information lifecycle.

In relation to capacity for information, records, and archives management functions, the majority of respondents (approximately 65%) noted that their organizations provide insufficient resources. This will of course not come as a great surprise to anyone who has worked in this field for any length of time. If anything, we were expecting an even higher number. Perhaps as the fields of information management and information technology have grown closer, resources are being distributed between them and increasing the capacity for information, records, and archives management functions.

The second part of the survey focused on the comprehensiveness of the mind map itself. Just under half (approximately 45%) of respondents did not think that the functions depicted in the mind map diagram addressed all the areas that need to be covered within a comprehensive information, records, and archives management ecosystem. On the one hand, this will suggest that more work is needed in this area, which was the intention – i.e., to create a model for information professionals in international organizations to discuss information governance. On the other hand, judging from the comments of those that stated that the mind map did not sufficiently cover all the information-, records-, and archives-related functions in their organizations, it would seem that they could all be resolved by better defining what is meant by the 11 functions detailed in the diagram. For example, various respondents raised concerns regarding the absence of "governance" in the diagram, whereas the authors' intention was that, taken together, the 11 functions depicted in the mind map are the basic elements of a governance framework. Similarly, respondents suggested that "retention management/scheduling" was missing, whereas we had understood that to be a key part of "Processing."

Responses on which of the 11 specific functions are addressed or need to be improved in respondents' organizations differ quite significantly. This is unsurprising given that different organizations have very different mandates and operational requirements, and therefore we can expect that different information management functions have been prioritized accordingly. However, from the survey results, we see that most organizations are addressing all 11 functions (although some just minimally), and at the same time all need to be improved (and in many cases quite dramatically).

In response to a question regarding the extent to which the 11 functions are addressed by separate organizational units, only 3 of 42 respondents said they were completely handled by separate units, and only one said they were handled by the same unit. As with the question on integration, the vast majority of international organizations have a distributed approach regarding the management of and accountability for information assets.

The third part of the survey focused on tools, with approximately 80% of respondents agreeing that the tools for managing the organization's data should be integrated in what could be described as a global content management ecosystem. However, from respondents' comments, it seems that little work has been done to achieve this in a meaningful or comprehensive way. Clearly the tools available to facilitate an integrated approach to information management have not caught up to the requirements for working in an integrated way.

The fourth part of the survey focused on standards, and particularly the importance of international standards. Approximately 80% of respondents agree that international standards help them carry out their activities in the fields of information, records, and/or archives management. This is both reassuring, but not surprising, especially given the community that completed the survey largely represents the international community. In particular, ISO 15489–1 and ISAD(G) were cited as relevant, with significant reference to OAIS.

Approximately 90% of respondents stated that an international, high-level standard, designing an integrated and comprehensive information, records, and archives management system would be useful. This is a very high number, and again speaks directly to the growing importance of information governance in the field previously dominated by records and archives management. Comments from respondents point to the perceived value of such a standard in relation to benchmarking, tools, software development, establishing best practices, and showing the value of information management vis-à-vis information technology.

The fifth and final part of the survey focused on the effectiveness of organizations' approaches to information, records, and archives management on the implementation of their mandates. Most respondents stated that their organization's approach was moderate. Only four out of 42 respondents rated it less than four on a scale of one to ten. Likewise, only five rated it higher than seven. Therefore 33 of 42 respondents rated their organization's effectiveness as between four and six on a scale of one to ten.

The results of the survey make it clear that the delivery of international organizations' mandates would be dramatically improved with a better information governance framework and would be more effectively attained if information, records, and archives are properly managed throughout their lifecycle, including the preservation stage.

Conclusion

The InterPARES Trust Ontology, from which the work of this chapter emerged, developed a model to represent the functions and activities related to records management and archives based on the key international and/or accepted standards that govern the work in that domain. However, in the spirit of interdisciplinarity and blurred boundaries that globalization and technology have promoted, and international organizations have helped facilitate, we attempted to widen the scope of the Ontology by mind mapping it to the field of information management more broadly. The mind mapping attempts, therefore, to represent the functions that are performed in an information management system, which includes, but does not end with, records and archives.

The impetus for this extension largely came from our questioning of the value to both individual users and organizations offered by a set of standards (i.e., those governing only the aspects of records and archives management), when the tools that are being developed and deployed to manage digital content increasingly attempt to manage it holistically and throughout its entire lifecycle. Our hypothesis was that there is a gap in the set of standards. To gather feedback on this, we proposed a set of questions to information, records, and archives professionals in international organizations via a voluntary survey circulated through professional networks. More than 90% of respondents to the survey stated that information, records, and archives should be managed as part of an integrated system. Additionally, almost the same percentage of respondents expressed a desire for an international standard designing a system to support their management.

The intention of the survey was to check the pulse of international organizations' capacity and capability for managing information, records, and archives in relation to the context of interdisciplinarity that globalization has created. However, the survey results should be seen as suggestive, not definitive. Considering that international organizations have different levels of maturity when it comes to their information, records, and archives management programmes, and that those with particularly weak programmes and/or no professional staff working in those areas were likely not to have responded, we can assume that the reality of the situation is worse than the survey suggested.

The primary value of the survey results is that they set a point of departure for further work in this area using the high-level functions detailed in the mind map as the model for establishing an information governance framework locally (i.e., within specific international organizations) or generally (i.e., as the basis for an international standard).

Notes

1 The views expressed herein are those of the author and do not necessarily reflect the view of the United Nations.
2 Giovanni Michetti, 2014, 'Knowledge, skills and competences: an Italian standard to design the archivist's profile within the European Qualifications Framework', in *Innovation and engagement in archival education*, paper presented at the 3rd Asia Pacific conference on archival education, 23–24 October 2013, Renmin University, China, International Council on Archives (ICA), Section on Archival Education and Training (SAE), p. 19, viewed 10 October 2020, www.ica-sae.org/proceedings/beijing2013/Proceedings_Beijing.pdf.
3 This paragraph is taken from Giovanni Michetti, 2016, 'Technical standards on professional profiles. An opportunity for library and archives convergence', in Jennifer Weil Arns (ed.), *Annual review of cultural heritage informatics. 2015*, Rowman & Littlefield, Lanham MD, p. 85.
4 Michetti, 2014, p. 35.
5 Susan Davies, 2003, 'Descriptive standards and the archival profession', *Cataloguing and Classification Quarterly*, vol. 35, no. 3–4, pp. 291–308.
6 The research project was designed by Giovanni Michetti and conducted from 2016 to 2018 by Giovanni Michetti and Georg Gänser. See https://interparestrust.org/assets/public/dissemination/TR05-FinalReport-20180526.pdf, viewed 10 October 2020.
7 "In a number of countries, a distinction is made between records and archives. Records may be defined as recorded information, regardless of form or medium, created, received and maintained by an agency, institution, organization or individual in pursuance of its legal obligation or in the transaction of business of any kind. Archives are a function of the records of an organization or person. They may be defined as non-current records permanently preserved, with or without selection, by those responsible for their creation or by their successors in function for their own use or by an appropriate archival repository because of their archival value. In countries like Belgium, France, Indonesia, Italy, the Netherlands, Yugoslavia and Spain, the term archives encompasses both records and archives. However, legal texts of some of these countries make a distinction between 'current' (or 'administrative' or 'dynamic') archives and 'historical' (or 'definitive') archives." UNESCO, 1985, *Archival and records management legislation and regulations: a RAMP study with guidelines,* prepared by Erik Ketelaar UNESCO, Paris, p. 6.
8 RDF (Resource Description Framework) is a data architecture, that is, a model to organize data. Its simple design is based on the triple: a statement consisting of a subject, a predicate, and an object, describing some elemental aspects of a resource. See www.w3.org/2001/sw/wiki/RDF, viewed 10 October 2020.
9 OWL is a formal language designed to represent knowledge about resources along with their interrelationships. See www.w3.org/OWL/, viewed 10 October 2020.
10 Some detailed diagrams can be found in Luciana Duranti & Corinne Rogers (eds.), 2019, *Trusting records in the cloud*, Facet, London, pp. 228–232.
11 Elizabeth Lomas, 2010, 'Information governance: information security and access within a UK context,' *Records Management Journal*, vol. 20, no. 2, p. 183.
12 The list of post and job titles covers a broad area of competences, ranging from Information Management Officer, through Document Management Assistant, to Digital Preservation Assistant. See Maik Schmerbauch, 2017, 'Requirements for archives and records management jobs in international organizations with focus on United Nations. A job analysis of the vacancy announcements in 2016', *Comma*, no. 2, pp. 125–133.

13 ARMA International defines Information Governance as "the overarching and coordinating strategy for all organizational information. It establishes the authorities, supports, processes, capabilities, structures, and infrastructure to enable information to be a useful asset and reduced liability to an organization, based on that organization's specific business requirements and risk tolerance." ARMA International, 2016, *Glossary of records management and information governance terms*, 5th edn.

References

ARMA International 2016, *Glossary of records management and information governance terms*, 5th edn, ARMA International, Overland Park, KS.

Davies, S 2003, 'Descriptive standards and the archival profession', *Cataloguing and Classification Quarterly*, vol. 35, no. 3–4, pp. 291–308.

Duranti, L & Rogers, C (eds.) 2019, *Trusting records in the cloud*, Facet Publishing, London.

International Organization for Standardization 2017, *Information and documentation. Records management processes. Metadata for records. Part 1. Principles*, ISO 23081–1:2017, International Organization for Standardization, Geneva.

Lomas, E 2010, 'Information governance: information security and access within a UK context', *Records Management Journal*, vol. 20, no. 2, pp. 182–198.

Michetti, G 2014, '*Knowledge, skills and competences: an Italian standard to design the archivist's profile within the European Qualifications Framework*', in *Innovation and engagement in archival education*, paper presented at the 3rd Asia Pacific conference on archival education, Renmin University, China. 23–24 October 2013, International Council on Archives (ICA), Section on Archival Education and Training (SAE), pp. 19–37, viewed 10 October 2020, www.ica-sae.org/proceedings/beijing2013/Proceedings_Beijing.pdf.

Michetti, G 2016, 'Technical standards on professional profiles. An opportunity for library and archives convergence', in J Weil Arns (ed.), *Annual review of cultural heritage informatics. 2015*, Rowman & Littlefield, Lanham, MD, pp. 84–106.

Schmerbauch, M 2017, 'Requirements for archives and records management jobs in international organizations with focus on United Nations. A job analysis of the vacancy announcements in 2016', *Comma*, vol. 2, pp. 125–134.

United Nations Educational, Scientific and Cultural Organization (UNESCO) 1985, *Archival and records management legislation and regulations: a RAMP study with guidelines*, prepared by E Ketelaar, UNESCO, Paris.

World Wide Web Consortium (W3C) 2020, *PROV model primer. W3C Working Group note 30 April 2013*, viewed 10 October 2020, www.w3.org/TR/2013/NOTE-prov-primer-20130430/.

7

USING ENTERPRISE ARCHITECTURE IN INTERGOVERNMENTAL ORGANIZATIONS[1]

Shadrack Katuu

Introduction

Modern institutions invest large amounts of resources to build technology platforms and business applications that will support organizational activities to fulfil their institutional mandates. These institutions operate hundreds of computer-based information systems or applications to support their activities. Each of these systems is aimed at improving the speed, efficiency, and quality of a number of business processes within the institution.[2]

However, the enormous number of systems gives rise to a high level of complexity for those actors responsible for implementing, integrating, operating, and further developing them.[3] There is the additional complexity of ensuring that all the various actors within an institution align their strategic and tactical perspectives for the common good. According to Kotusev, these actors are:

- Business executives who are responsible for strategic planning and making investment decisions;
- Information technology (IT) executives who are responsible for IT strategies and aligning them to business needs;
- IT project teams that are responsible for implementing IT projects in order to satisfy business requirements at the unit level; and
- Business unit managers who are responsible for running local routine business processes on a daily basis.[4]

The misalignment between business actors and IT actors caused by miscommunication often results in wasted IT investments, disappointment in IT, and reduced business performance.[5] Doucet et al. argue that enterprise architecture

(EA) has the potential to align strategy, business, and technology elements across the entire enterprise,[6] providing the context and standards for implementing best practices.[7] EA constitutes a collection of special documents (artefacts) that describe various aspects of an organization, particularly from an integrated business and IT perspective, that are intended to bridge the communication gap between business and IT stakeholders, facilitate information systems planning, and thereby improve business and IT alignment.[8] For this reason, researchers regard EA as a promising concept for business and IT stakeholders to cope with the complexity caused by multifarious technology ecosystems.[9]

Information professionals in general and records professionals in particular have not featured prominently in EA. This may be partly explained by the reality that records professionals have tried to fulfil their professional mandate using theories and methods developed for a paper rather than a digital environment.[10] Therefore, the research objective explores the extent to which archives and records professionals are aware of EA in their institutions. While a variety of institutions have implemented EA,[11] intergovernmental organizations (IGOs) are unique types of international organizations that are established by international agreement, that must have their own separate organs serving as secretariats, and that address issues or challenges that transcend national borders.[12]

This chapter outlines the development of the EA discipline and, within the context of IGOs, explores the extent to which actors (in general) and information professionals (in particular) are aware of EA.

This chapter draws from a research study conducted under the auspices of the InterPARES Trust project that explored the utility of an EA framework known as The Open Group Architecture Framework (TOGAF) within an institutional setting.[13] InterPARES Trust was the fourth phase of a multi-year project investigating the long-term preservation of authentic digital records.[14]

Literature review

This section traces the intellectual progress of the EA concept using an outline of its history and development. It offers a small sample of the varied framework models that have been developed throughout the course of EA's history. Next, the section briefly discusses one of these framework models, TOGAF, considered a de facto standard by EA practitioners; and an accompanying standard, ArchiMate.

Enterprise architecture definition

From a definitional perspective, the term "enterprise" covers many areas of systematic and purposeful human activity. However, in this context, the word most often refers to an institution or organization, parts of an institution or organization, or a group of institutions or organizations.[15] The term "architecture," when used in the context of abstracting the enterprise to identify scope, function, and relationships, includes the frameworks, methods, and artefacts that describe the design and function of enterprises in current and future states. Institutions often implement architectural activities at the enterprise, business unit, service, and system levels in a consistent manner.[16]

EA is an approach to improve the alignment between the organization's business and its information technologies. EA does this by capturing "the status of the organisations' business architecture, information resources, information systems, and technologies so that the gaps and weaknesses in their processes and infrastructures can be identified, and development directions planned."[17] According to Kotusev, EA constitutes a collection of special documents (artefacts) describing various aspects of an organization from an integrated business and IT perspective that are intended to bridge the communication gap between business and IT stakeholders.[18] These components are:

1.   Types of EA artefacts (different types of models, core diagrams, project-start architectures, etc.);
2.   Bases for EA artefacts (business strategy, operating model, business initiatives, etc.);
3.   Ways to structure EA artefacts (various frameworks);
4.   Process steps (architecture vision, business architecture, information systems architecture, migration planning, etc.);
5.   Objects of description (current state, future state, roadmaps, etc.);
6.   Scopes of description (entire enterprises or individual initiatives); and
7.   Ways to use EA artefacts (following roadmaps, implementing project-start architectures, etc.).[19]

Therefore, the artefacts become effective tools for cross-disciplinary communication.[20]

EA components are then organised in a five-step logic:

• Document the current state (or what is known as the "as-is" state);
• Describe the future state (or what is known as the "'should-be" or "to-be" state);
• Analyse the gaps;
• Develop a transition plan; and
• Implement the plan.[21]

In this way, EA deployment provides holistic views that address institution-wide integration through coherent principles, methods, and models.[22]

History and development of enterprise architecture

Kotusev argues that EA's history can be divided into three distinct phases: Business Systems Planning (BSP), early EA, and modern EA.[23]

According to Kotusev, the first EA phase featured BSP, a methodology initiated by IBM in the 1960s that lasted until the mid-1980s.[24] Kotusev argues that as a precursor, BSP resembled EA in several respects[25]:

- First, BSP activities were carried out by a dedicated group of experts (BSP study team) whose responsibilities included collecting data by interviewing managers and developing information systems plans in a top-down manner.
- Second, BSP information systems plans described the relationship between organization, business processes, data, and information systems using relationship matrices, information systems networks, flowcharts, and other techniques to model processes, systems, and data.
- Third, BSP was implemented in a stepwise manner starting from identifying business objectives, defining business processes and data, analysing the existing IT landscape, and developing a desired future information systems plan.
- Fourth, methodologies such as BSP used the notion of architecture as a "formal description of the relationship between business and IT," even though this idea was discussed under different titles, such as data architecture and information architecture.[26]

The second EA phase began in the mid-1980s with the emergence of the earliest EA frameworks.[27] By the time EA emerged, computer software developers and information system engineers had realized that they could only design suitable IT components if they "understood how the organisation works as defined by its processes, organisational structure and goals" within certain frameworks.[28] One such framework is Partnership for Research in Information Systems Management (PRISM), developed by a research project sponsored by about 60 global companies. A second framework is known as Zachman, developed by John Zachman, a marketing specialist at IBM.[29] Other frameworks include the National Institute of Standards and Technology (NIST) EA model and the Technical Architecture Framework for Information Management (TAFIM) methodology, both developed in the U.S.[30] The second EA phase lasted from the mid-1980s until the mid-1990s.

The third EA phase began in the mid-1990s and continues to this day with the development of numerous EA frameworks, including the following:

- Enterprise-developed frameworks such as the Generalised Enterprise Reference Architecture and Methodology (GERAM), Guide to the Enterprise Architecture Body of Knowledge (EABOK), and Reference Model of Open Distributed Processing (RM-ODP);
- Commercial frameworks such as the Architecture of Integrated Information Systems (ARIS), Integrated Architecture Framework (IAF), and Zachman Framework;
- Defence industry frameworks such as the Department of Defence Architecture Framework (DoDAF), France DGA Architecture Framework (AGATE), International Defence Enterprise Architecture Specification (IDEAS), Joint

Technical Architecture (JTA), NATO Architecture Framework, Technical Architecture Framework for Information Management (TAFIM), Technical Reference Model (TRM), and UK Ministry of Defence Architecture Framework (MODAF);

- Government frameworks such as the European Interoperability Framework (EIF), Federal Enterprise Architecture Framework (FEAF), Government Enterprise Architecture (GEA), NIST Enterprise Architecture (NIST), Standards and Architecture of eGovernment Applications (SAGA), Treasury Enterprise Architecture Framework (TEAF), and Treasury Information System Architecture Framework (TISAF).[31]

Figure 7.1 illustrates a few EA frameworks and shows how they have influenced each other over the years.

The Open Group Architectural Framework (TOGAF)

Researchers currently consider TOGAF to be the de facto industry standard for EA frameworks,[32] a technology architecture methodology based on the technical architecture framework for information management (TAFIM), developed by the United States Department of Defense.[33] Over the years, TOGAF has become a

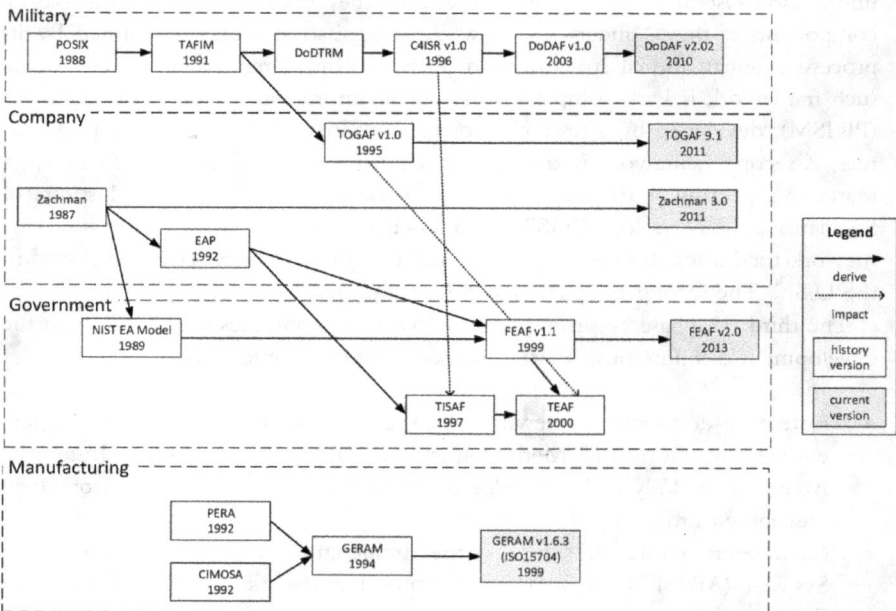

FIGURE 7.1 The development of EA frameworks in different domains
Source: Yiwei Gong & Marijn Janssen, 2019, 'The value of and myths about enterprise architecture', *International Journal of Information Management*, vol. 46, p. 3.

well-defined method for designing an information system in terms of building blocks and for showing how the building blocks fit and interact.[34]

TOGAF has three main pillars:

1. Architecture Development Method (ADM): Describes a method for developing and managing the lifecycle of an enterprise architecture and forms the core of TOGAF.[35]
2. Enterprise Continuum (EC): Provides methods for classifying architecture and solution artefacts, both internal and external to the Architecture Repository, as they evolve from generic foundation architectures to organization-specific architectures.[36]
3. Enterprise Architecture Domains (EAD): These are the areas of specialization that are commonly accepted by EA practitioners as subsets of an overall enterprise architecture.[37]

TOGAF organizes EA artefacts according to four major domains (business, data, applications, and technology) and proposes a metamodel providing more detailed technical classification of these domains.[38] Table 7.1 outlines the four interrelated areas of specialization, or architecture domains.

TABLE 7.1 Enterprise architecture domains

	Description	Key objective
Business architectures	This constitutes the business processes to meet goals, including business strategy, governance, organization, and key business processes.	How the business is organized to meet its objectives
Application architecture	This describes the design and interaction of specific applications. It provides a blueprint for the individual systems. In addition, it shows their relationship to the organization's core business processes as it exposes the frameworks for services as business functions for integration.	How information systems support the objectives of the business
Technical or technology architecture	This describes the hardware, software, and network infrastructure supporting the deployment of core, mission-critical applications and their interactions.	How the technology fits together
Data architecture	This describes how enterprise data stores are organized and accessed (i.e., the structure of an organization's logical and physical data assets and the associated data management resources).	The structure of the data assets

Sources: Pethuru Raj & Mohanavadivu Periasamy, 2011, 'The convergence of enterprise architecture (EA) and cloud computing', in Zaigham Mahmood & Richard Hill (eds.), *Cloud computing for enterprise architectures*, Springer, London, pp. 61–87; David Basten & D. Brons, 2012, 'EA frameworks, modeling and tools', in Frederik Ahlemann et al. (eds.), *Strategic enterprise architecture management: challenges, best practices, and future developments*, Springer Science & Business Media, Dordrecht, pp. 201–227.

In order to provide uniform representation for architectural descriptions within the TOGAF framework, modelling languages and notations such as ArchiMate, Unified Modelling Language (UML), and Business Process Model and Notation (BPMN) have been used.[39] However, ArchiMate best fits into the TOGAF framework because it was also developed by The Open Group as an "open and independent modelling language that is supported by different tool vendors and consulting firms."[40] ArchiMate provides concepts for creating a model that correlates to TOGAF's three architectures (layers):

1. A business layer (products and services offered to customers, the business processes that helped create the offering, and the actors that played a part in the business processes);
2. An application layer (application services, which support the business layer); and
3. A technology layer (infrastructure services that support the applications).[41]

ArchiMate provides a graphical representation of its language elements based on a UML class diagram, which could be quite complex but has been customized and limited to a small set of modelling constructs in the interest of simplicity of learning and use.[42] In this manner, ArchiMate provides a notation that enables enterprise architects to describe, analyse, and visualize the relationships among business domains in an unambiguous way.[43]

Enterprise architecture and intergovernmental organizations

This section traces the development of IGOs and discusses the extent to which EA is found in official IGO documentation.

What are IGOs?

In regular parlance, whenever one thinks of IGOs, the institutions that come to mind include those with global membership – such as those within the United Nations (UN) common system. Examples may include the United Nations Development Fund, United Nations Children's Fund, as well as specialized agencies and related organizations (such as the International Atomic Energy Agency, the World Trade Organization, the World Health Organization, the World Bank Group, and the International Monetary Fund). There are also many other IGOs that have regional representation.[44]

Volgy et al. define IGOs as "entities created with sufficient organisational structure and autonomy to provide formal, ongoing, multilateral processes of decision-making between states, along with the capacity to execute the collective will of their members (states)."[45] In order to distinguish an IGO from other types of international organizations, it must be established by an international agreement; must have its own separate organs; and must be established by international law.[46] The IGO addresses issues or challenges that transcend national borders while possessing own international legal personality.[47] This identity is separate from that of its members, which means that it can exercise certain powers, as well as enjoy certain rights and privileges.[48]

According to Abass, IGOs possess four types of privileges and immunities: "jurisdictional immunity, inviolability of premises and archives, freedom of communication, and immunity relating to financial matters."[49] Experts see the inviolability of premises and archives as enabling "privacy and the preservation of secrecy," which is at the foundation of the independence of IGOs and is required for the fulfilment of their purposes.[50]

EA implementation in IGOs

There are more than 300 IGOs throughout the world[51] and therefore one might expect a significant number of resources on the use of EA in IGOs. However, discussions on the utility of EA approaches are quite sparse. One of the rare sources discusses the interaction between civil and military partners to support peace-keeping, humanitarian relief, and development support.[52] Another source discusses EA principles used to facilitate the design and implementation of an information-sharing system between the U.S. government and IGOs for the exchange of unclassified content.[53] This section provides examples specific to three IGOs.

World Bank Group

The World Bank Group (WBG) is a family of five IGOs. Each institution has its own distinct purpose and set of founding documents, while all having a common commitment to reducing poverty, increasing shared prosperity, and promoting sustainable development.[54]

EA was adopted as a strategy at the World Bank in the 2008 financial year.[55] However, a decade later, a review team described EA as "an emerging tool used to support the design and implementation of strategic initiatives and significant process re-engineering."[56] The review's objective was to help the institution's senior management understand the existing EA approach, as well as provide "information that would be useful for deciding how to improve the implementation of EA in support of strategic initiatives and high-level end-to-end process re-engineering."[57] The review team noted that due to EA's limited mandate within the institution, "its contribution to business process design or other strategic initiatives" was not optimal, and EA tools were not consistently utilized.[58] For this reason, the team emphasized "the importance of connecting EA to all major business process improvement initiatives to ensure that business strategy, data, applications and technology are considered holistically."[59]

The International Atomic Energy Agency

The International Atomic Energy Agency (IAEA) is the world's central inter-governmental forum for scientific and technical co-operation in the nuclear field.

The IAEA promotes the safe, secure, and peaceful uses of nuclear science and technology.[60] In 2017, the IAEA's IT steering committee approved the use of EA principles "to help guide the design and deployment of IT systems" across the institution.[61] The IT steering committee noted that if EA guiding principles were properly followed they would "streamline and reduce the complexity of IT investment decisions and support IT governance decision-making by establishing relevant evaluation criteria."[62] So far, there are no published reports of more recent developments.

The UN Secretariat

The UN Secretariat is constituted by the Secretary-General and thousands of staff members who carry out the day-to-day work as mandated by the General Assembly and other principal organs.[63] By 2013, the UN Secretariat had instituted an Architecture Review Board.[64] However, a review team noted that EA implementation in the Secretariat was deficient, characterized by either incomplete, unapproved, or outdated policies, procedures, and guidelines.[65] The review team added that such inadequacies could lead to "inconsistencies between information requirements and application development, inefficient planning of ICT-enabled investment initiatives and irrelevant data accumulation."[66]

By 2014 the Secretariat had "completed the development of a road map for network infrastructure, information security and data privacy, content management, unified communication, identity management, principles and guidelines, and application architecture," in addition to establishing subcommittees for messaging systems and desktop management.[67] However, in a report on the progress of enterprise resource planning published in 2017, the UN Secretary-General noted that

[o]wing to historical constraints in information and communications technology (ICT), such as decentralised ICT units and challenging global connectivity, localised solutions were deployed to meet the needs of individual entities, often with little or no enterprise architecture.[68]

Observations regarding EA in IGOs

Although there are hundreds of IGOs, the search for sources on EA implementation revealed minimal information. This has made it difficult to identify the full extent to which IGOs have used EA. Even when there is information on EA initiatives within an IGO, reporting on approaches is scant and is mostly available from review processes, such as internal oversight and audit activities. In turn, most of the review processes noted either patchy implementation and/or a lack of impactful adoption of EA within the IGOs. For this reason, this study sought to survey several IGOs to see whether the observations above are borne out by the staff working in those institutions.

Research framework

Any research process involves the systematic investigation of a specific question or questions, which involves collating and integrating current knowledge on the topic by "designing a method to collect information to inform the research question; and finally developing new conclusions from the evidence."[69]

As the preceding section has demonstrated, there is scant information within IGOs regarding the extent to which they have implemented EAs. This chapter explores the awareness of EA by a specific category of actors within IGOs, information professionals.

Research motivation: information professionals and EA in IGOs

The data collected for this chapter explores the extent of information professionals' awareness of EA principles in general, the existence of the ISO technical report on EA, and TOGAF as a de facto standard.

Different categories of information professionals fulfil unique mandates within an enterprise. For instance, records professionals ensure the "efficient and systematic control of the creation, receipt, maintenance, use and disposition of records"[70] within a framework that ensures "defined roles and responsibilities, systematic processes, measurement and evaluation, as well as review and improvement."[71] However, in the modern age, most information professionals are confronted with highly complex technological ecosystems and have struggled to fulfil their professional mandate using theories and methods developed for a paper rather than digital environment.[72] Therefore, the challenge is how information professionals can best understand the complexity in a way that enables them to fulfil their professional mandate, which is the identification, capture, and management of information generated within an institution for as long as it is required.

As stated earlier, EA is a viable option to reduce technological complexity.[73] Therefore, ISO Technical Committee (TC) 46 Sub Committee (SC) 11, which is responsible for records management standards, has published a technical report titled *ISO/TR 21965:2019 Information and Documentation – Records Management in Enterprise Architecture.* [74] Work on ISO/TR 21965:2019 began in 2015 and was finally completed with the publication of the technical report in 2019.[75] ISO TC 46 SC 11 developed ISO/TR 21965:2019 as a common reference for records professionals and enterprise architects about "requirements for records processes and systems."[76]

The goal of the technical report is to establish records managers as key stakeholders in EA. The team is developing a technical report with three objectives:

- Explaining the core concepts and records management principles to enterprise architects;
- Explaining the core concerns of records management from an EA viewpoint;
- Explaining the alignment of the records management viewpoint and EA methods.[77]

The technical report uses two EA components or tools, ArchiMate and TOGAF.[78]

For the purposes of this study, the author divided information professionals within IGOs into two major categories: information technology, which has two subcategories, and information management, which has four subcategories. In both categories are professionals who engage in policy and strategy. In addition, information technology has an EA subcategory, while information management has subcategories for archives management, library and documentation management, as well as records management.

Research design

This study combined a descriptive survey research method and purposive sampling research technique. A descriptive survey primarily collects and arranges data, then identifies trends with the main purpose to "describe a particular phenomenon: its current situations, its properties and conditions."[79] In purposive sampling, the researcher selects samples based on their knowledge and opinion about their appropriateness and relevance to the topic.[80]

The author structured the survey into four components:

1. Information about the professional responsibilities of the respondents within individual IGOs;
2. Information about the extent to which EA principles and processes were used within individual IGOs;
3. Information about awareness of an ISO technical report on EA;
4. Information about the extent to which TOGAF is used within individual IGOs.

The author, using purposive sampling, contacted nine respondents from seven different IGOs, coded using the letters A to G. The author distributed the data collection instrument electronically through purposive sampling between August and October of 2018.

Research findings

This section reports the findings upon collection of the data. In keeping with the data collection instrument, there are four parts, plus an additional part that provides contextual information on the type of IGO included in the study.

Contextual information

The author drew contextual information from the survey, as well as from his knowledge of the IGO. Since the IGOs are anonymized, the contextual information provides only enough information to demonstrate the varied nature of the IGOs without revealing their identities. Three ingredients constitute the contextual information, namely:

- Age, or how long an IGO has existed;
- Jurisdictional coverage, i.e., whether it has a mandate that is regional (such as a continent or part of a continent) or global; and
- Number of staff working in the IGO.

Figure 7.2 shows that the ages of the IGOs span almost all categories. On the higher end, four IGOs (A, D, F, and G) have existed for more than 25 years. Two IGOs (B and C) have existed for 5–15 years. Finally, one organization has existed for less than five years.

Figure 7.3 shows that four IGOs (A, B, F, and G) have global jurisdiction, while the other three IGOs (C, D, and E) have regional jurisdiction. Figure 7.4 shows that IGOs span almost all the categories in terms of number of staff members. On the lower end, three IGOs (B, E, and G) have fewer than 500 staff members. Only one IGO (A) has between 500 and 3,000 staff members, while another IGO (C) has between 3,000 and 10,000 staff members. On the higher end, two IGOs (D and F) have more than 10,000 staff members.

Professional responsibilities

The second aspect in the data collected sought to reveal the professional responsibilities of the respondents within individual IGOs in the two main categories: information technology and information management. On the one hand, *information technology* deals with infrastructure such as hardware, software, peripheral equipment, as well as policies and practices that support the working of the infrastructure. While there are numerous subdisciplines, only two were targeted for this research study: policy and strategy, as well as EA. On the other hand, *information management* constitutes the management of the content generated and managed

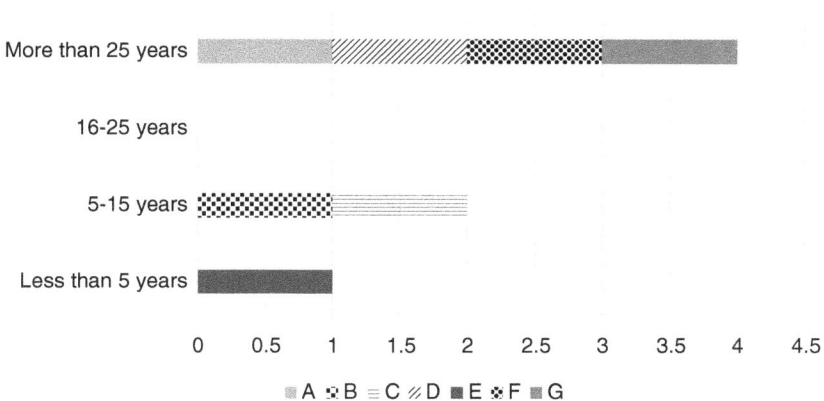

FIGURE 7.2 Research data – Age of the IGO

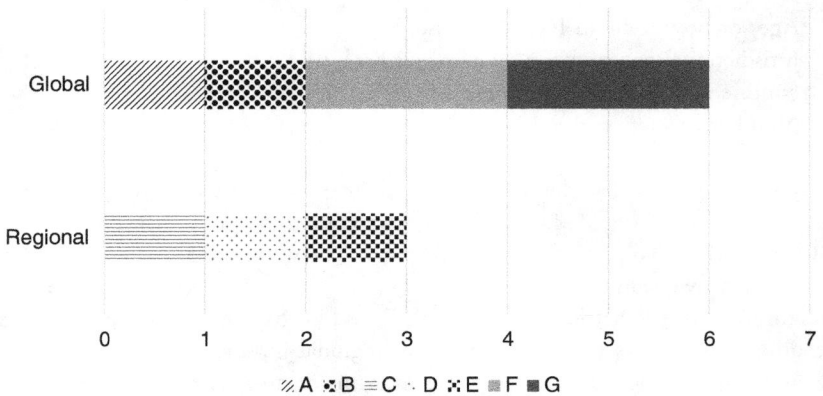

FIGURE 7.3 Research data – Jurisdiction of the IGO

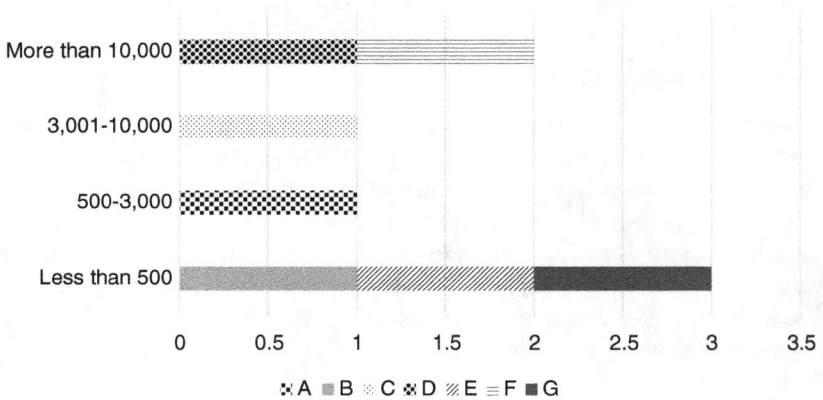

FIGURE 7.4 Research data – Number of staff members in the IGO

within an institution. For the purposes of this study, the author identified four subdisciplines: policy and strategy, archives management, library and documentation management, and records management. Figure 7.5 shows that the nine respondents were distributed across the categories ranging between 11% and 23%.

Extent to which EA principles and processes are pervasive in the IGO

Figure 7.6 shows that all nine respondents were distributed in three of the five categories. Most respondents were aware of EA and only varied in the extent to which they felt it was relevant to their IGO, i.e., five respondents stated it is relevant to a large extent, while three respondents stated it is relevant to a limited extent. Only one of the respondents was not aware of EA.

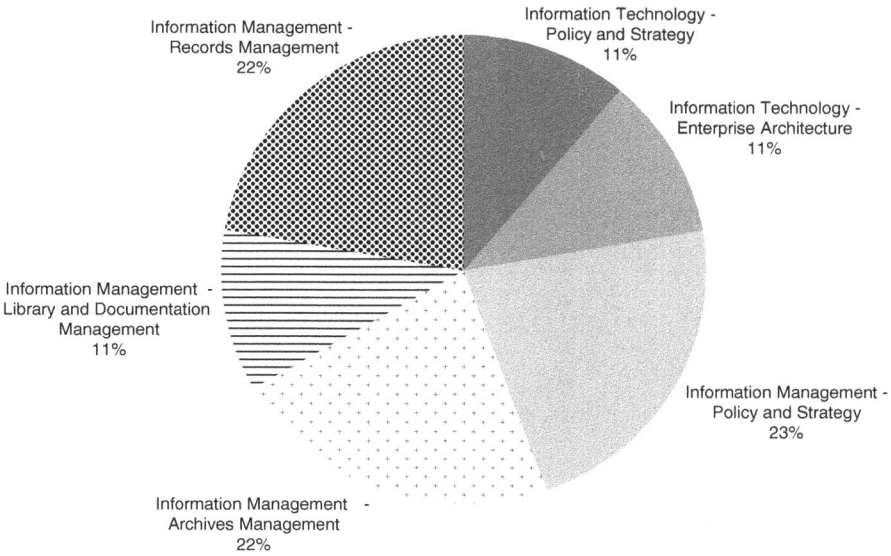

FIGURE 7.5 Research data – Professional responsibilities

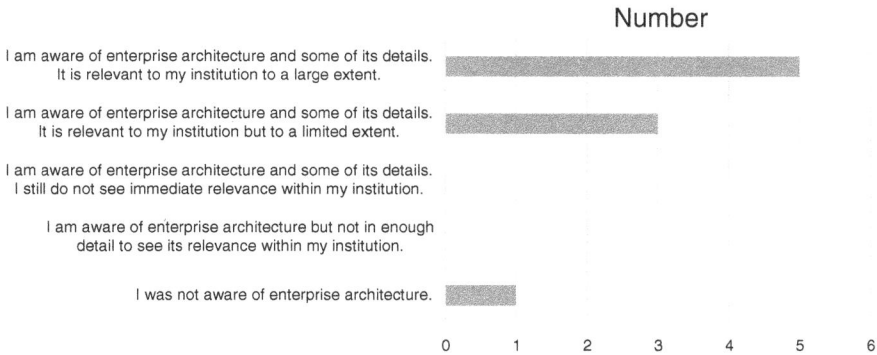

FIGURE 7.6 Research data – Pervasiveness of EA principles and processes

Awareness of the ISO technical report

Figure 7.7 shows that the respondents were distributed in four of the five categories of responses. Most of the respondents were aware that there was an ISO technical report on EA, ranging from those that saw a lot of relevance, those that saw only limited relevance, and those that were aware but had insufficient details. The rest of the respondents were not aware of the technical report.

Number

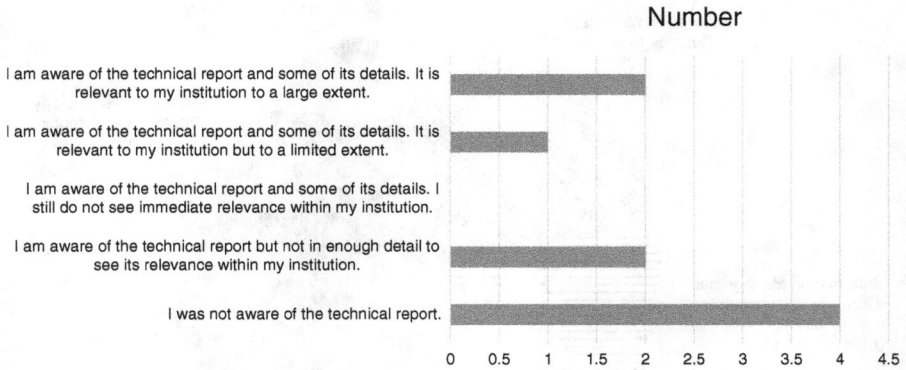

FIGURE 7.7 Research data – Awareness of ISO technical report

Awareness of TOGAF use within the IGO

Figure 7.8 shows that the respondents were distributed in four of the five categories of the possible responses. One-third of the respondents were not aware of TOGAF at all. Another one-third were aware of TOGAF, but there was not enough detail to see relevance within the IGO. The last one-third are divided between not seeing immediate relevance and only seeing limited relevance.

Discussion and concluding remarks

Doucet et al. argue that EA has the potential to align strategy, business, and technology elements across the entire enterprise, providing the context and standards for implementing best practices.[81] The deployment of EA is intended to align goals and perspectives of IT with those of the business. However, few institutions have adopted EA and even fewer use them extensively.[82] One of the reasons for not using EA extensively may be the large variety of frameworks. As discussed in the

Number

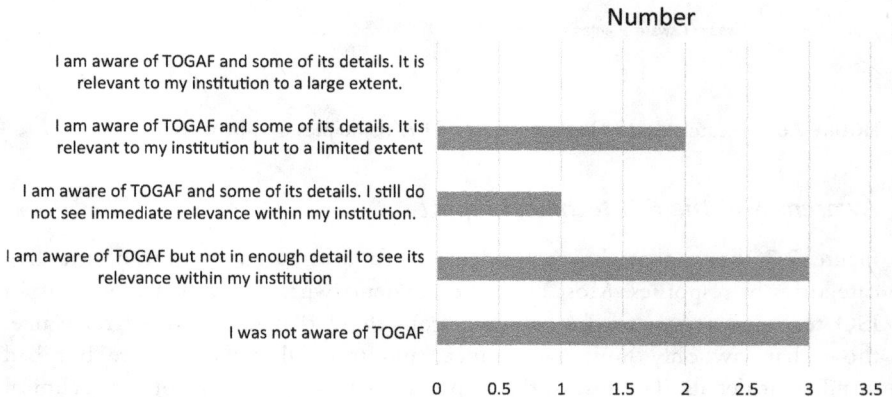

FIGURE 7.8 Research data – Extent to which TOGAF is used

preceding sections, over the last three decades EA practitioners developed more than two dozen frameworks, including Zachman, TOGAF, and FEA. These frameworks are popular because of their maturity. Zachman is the oldest; TOGAF and FEA allow free access to resources and information.[83]

This chapter provided an outline of the development of the EA discipline, as well as an overview of IGOs. In both discussions, the author illustrated the dearth of available sources on the implementation of EA within IGOs.

In order to begin to address this gap, a research framework was used to collect data from information professionals in seven different IGOs around the world, and the data was collected in five parts. Figures 7.2, 7.3, and 7.4 illustrated contextual information. Although there were only seven IGOs included in the data collection process, the IGOs are significantly different in their size, age, and jurisdictional coverage. Figures 7.5, 7.6, 7.7, and 7.8 demonstrated the varied nature of professional responsibilities, as well as differing levels of awareness of EA principles in general and the specifics related to the ISO technical report and TOGAF.

EA is well known among both information technology and information management professionals. However, respondents differed in their assessments of the relevance of EA within their institutions. In addition, there is a wide gap between those who are aware versus those who are not aware of the ISO/TR 21965:2019 report.[84] Those who are aware of the technical report provided different ratings on its relevance to their institutions. Although the work on the technical report started in 2015, the report was only published in 2019, which may explain the low awareness levels among respondents. While researchers consider TOGAF to be a de facto standard, there is still a question as to its immediate relevance among information technology and information management professionals. Again, this tallies with the few published studies that show that the adoption of TOGAF has been scant.[85]

It is commendable that the ISO has developed a technical report for EA that specifically uses TOGAF and ArchiMate to represent records management principles. Nonetheless, it should be only the beginning of a process that assists information professionals to explore the emerging opportunities in utilizing EA within their professional domains, through education and professional development opportunities.[86] This chapter is merely a first step in exploring EA principles and frameworks within the context of IGOs.

Notes

1 The author wishes to thank the editors and anonymous reviewers of this chapter for their constructive comments to improve the paper. The author gratefully acknowledges the thoughtful readings of previous iterations of the paper by Adrian Cunningham, William Underwood, Richard Marciano, Victoria Lemieux, and Mpho Ngoepe. The views expressed herein are those of the author and should neither be attributed to his current employer nor to any of his previous employers.
2 Gerold Riempp & Stephan Gieffers-Ankel, 2007, 'Application portfolio management: a decision-oriented view of enterprise architecture', *Information Systems and E-Business Management*, vol. 5, no. 4, p. 360.
3 Ibid.

4 Svyatoslav Kotusev, 2019a, 'Lecture 1: Introduction', viewed 28 March 2020, http://kotusev.com/lectures/Lecture%201%20-%20Introduction.pdf, p. 24.
5 Ibid, p. 26.
6 A discussion of the definition of "enterprise" is provided in Doucet et al. 2009, p. 27.
7 Gary Doucet et al., 2009, 'Coherency management: using enterprise architecture for alignment, agility, and assurance,' *Journal of Enterprise Architecture*, vol. 4, no. 2, p. 28.
8 Svyatoslav Kotusev, 2019b, 'Lecture 2: The concept of enterprise architecture', viewed 28 March 2020, http://kotusev.com/lectures/Lecture%202%20-%20The%20Concept%20of%20Enterprise%20Architecture.pdf, p. 3.
9 Riempp & Gieffers-Ankel, 2007, p. 359.
10 Ann-Sofie Klareld & Katarina L Gidlund, 2017, 'Rethinking archives as digital: the consequences of "paper minds" in illustrations and definitions of e-archives', *Archivaria*, vol. 83, no. 1, pp. 81–108; Terry Cook, 2007, 'Electronic records, paper minds: the revolution in information management and archives in the post-custodial and post-modernist era', *Archives and Social Studies: A Journal of Interdisciplinary Research*, vol. 1, pp. 399–443; Shadrack Katuu, 2018c, 'The utility of enterprise architecture to records and archives specialists', paper presented at the 2018 IEEE International Conference on Big Data (Big Data), Seattle, WA pp. 2702–2710.
11 Andreas Ask & Karin Hedström, 2011, 'Taking initial steps towards enterprise architecture in local government', in Kim Normann Andersen et al. (eds.), *Second International Conference on Electronic Government and the Information Systems (EGOVIS) Perspective Electronic Government and the Information Systems Perspective*, Toulouse, France, Springer International Publishing, AG, pp. 26–40; Endang Amalia & Hari Supriadi, 2017, 'Development of enterprise architecture in university using TOGAF as framework', in Hari Prasetyo et al. (eds.), *Proceedings of the 3rd International Conference on Engineering, Technology, and Industrial Application (ICETIA 2016)*, Surakarta, Indonesia, AIP Publishing, pp. 1–9.
12 Sander Dikker Hupkes, 2009, 'Protection and effective functioning of international organizations. Final report international institutional law; Secure Haven Project', Universiteit Leiden, viewed 17 May 2020, https://openaccess.leidenuniv.nl/handle/1887/14119, p. 10.
13 Shadrack Katuu, 2017, 'TR04: Assessing information systems: facing the challenges of managing records in transactional systems', in *2017 International Seminar – InterPARES Trust*, Cape Town, South Africa, InterPARES Trust Team Africa, viewed 28 March 2020, www.researchgate.net/publication/332845611_Assessing_information_systems_Facing_the_challenges_of_managing_records_in_transactional_systems; Shadrack Katuu, 2018a, 'TR04: Assessing information systems: a template of analysis – Final report', InterPARES Trust, viewed 28 March 2020, https://interparestrust.org/assets/public/dissemination/TR04FinalReportJuly2018.pdf; Shadrack Katuu, 2018b, 'Using enterprise architecture as a template of analysis', InterPARES Trust, viewed 28 March 2020, https://interparestrust.org/assets/public/dissemination/Katuu-CubaEnterprisearchitecture.pdf; Shadrack Katuu, 2019a, 'Enterprise architecture – a value proposition for records professionals', paper presented at the *2019 IEEE International Conference on Big Data*, Los Angeles, CA.
14 Luciana Duranti, 2019, 'Trusting records: 20 years of InterPARES research', InterPARES Trust, https://interparestrust.org/assets/public/dissemination/Duranti-20yearsofInterPARES-Cuba2019.pdf; Luciana Duranti & Corinne Rogers (eds.), 2019, *Trusting records in the cloud: the creation, management, and preservation of trustworthy digital content*, Facet Publishing, London.
15 Doucet et al., 2009, p. 27.
16 Ibid, p. 28; Gabriela Andaur et al., 2019, 'Open government' in Luciana Duranti & Corinne Rogers (eds.), *Trusting records in the cloud: the creation, management, and preservation of trustworthy digital content*, Facet Publishing, London, p. 52; Basma Makhlouf Shabou et al., 2019, 'Strategies, methods and tools enabling records governance in a cloud environment', 2019, in Luciana Duranti & Corinne Rogers (eds.), *Trusting records in the

cloud: the creation, management, and preservation of trustworthy digital content, Facet Publishing, London, pp. 102–105.

17 Dinh Duong Dang & Samuli Pekkola, 2017, 'Systematic literature review on enterprise architecture in the public sector', *Electronic Journal of e-Government*, vol. 15, no. 2, p. 130.

18 Kotusev, 2019b, p. 3.

19 Svyatoslav Kotusev, 2017, 'Conceptual model of enterprise architecture management', *International Journal of Cooperative Information Systems*, vol. 26, no. 3, pp. 12–13.

20 Hans Hofman, 2017, 'The use of models and modelling in recordkeeping research and development', in Sue McKemmish, Anne Gilliland & Andrew J Lau (eds.), *Research in the archival multiverse*, Monash University Publishing, Clayton, Australia, p. 633.

21 Purnomo Yustianto & Robin Doss, 2019, 'A unifying structure of metamodel landscape', *Journal of Modelling in Management*, vol. 14, no. 1, p. 136.

22 Tiko Iyamu & Leshoto Mphahlele, 2014, 'The impact of organisational structure on enterprise architecture deployment', *Journal of Systems and Information Technology*, vol. 16, no. 1, p. 2.

23 Svyatoslav Kotusev, 2016, 'The history of enterprise architecture: an evidence-based review', *Journal of Enterprise Architecture*, vol. 12, no. 1, p. 29.

24 Ibid.

25 Ibid, pp. 29–30.

26 Ibid, p. 30.

27 Ibid.

28 Frederik Ahlemann, Christine Legner & Daniel Schafczuk. 2012, 'Introduction', in Frederik Ahlemann et al. (eds.), *Strategic enterprise architecture management: challenges, best practices, and future developments*, Springer Science & Business Media, Dordrecht, pp. 1–33.

29 Kotusev, 2016, p. 30; Danny Greefhorst & Erik Proper, 2011, *Architecture principles: the cornerstones of enterprise architecture*, Springer, Amersfoort, The Netherlands.

30 Kotusev, 2016, pp. 31–32.

31 David Basten & Dorothea Brons, 2012, 'EA frameworks, modeling and tools', in Frederik Ahlemann et al. (eds.), *Strategic enterprise architecture management: challenges, best practices, and future developments*, Springer Science & Business Media, Dordrecht, p. 208.

32 Svyatoslav Kotusev, 2018a, 'Enterprise architecture: a reconceptualization is needed', *Pacific Asia Journal of the Association for Information Systems*, vol. 10, no. 4, p. 12.

33 Yiwei Gong & Marijn Janssen, 2019, 'The value of and myths about enterprise architecture', *International Journal of Information Management*, vol. 46, p. 3.

34 Pethuru Raj & Mohanavadivu Periasamy, 2011, 'The convergence of enterprise architecture (EA) and cloud computing', in Zaigham Mahmood & Richard Hill (eds.), *Cloud computing for enterprise architectures*, Springer, London, p. 72.

35 The Open Group, 2011c, 'Introduction to the ADM', viewed 28 March 2020, http://pubs.opengroup.org/architecture/togaf91-doc/arch/chap05.html.

36 The Open Group, 2011a, 'Enterprise continuum', viewed 28 March 2020, http://pubs.opengroup.org/architecture/togaf91-doc/arch/chap39.html.

37 The Open Group, 2011b, 'Introduction', viewed 28 March 2020, http://pubs.opengroup.org/architecture/togaf91-doc/arch/index.html.

38 Kotusev, 2018a, p. 6.

39 Svyatoslav Kotusev, 2018b, 'TOGAF-based enterprise architecture practice: an exploratory case study,' *Communications of the Association for Information Systems*, vol. 43, no. 1, p. 324.

40 Yustianto & Doss, 2019, p. 142; The Open Group, 2012, 'A pocket guide to Archimate® 2.1', The Open Group, viewed 28 March 2020, https://publications.opengroup.org/g137, p. 142.

41 Knut Hinkelmann et al., 2016, 'A new paradigm for the continuous alignment of business and IT: combining enterprise architecture modelling and enterprise ontology', *Computers in Industry*, vol. 79, p. 79.

42 Ibid.

43 The Open Group, 2012, p. 1.
44 Shadrack Katuu, 2019b, 'Managing classified records in inter-governmental organizations', in Noelle van der Waag-Cowling & Louise Leenen, *14th International Conference on Cyber Warfare and Security*, Stellenbosch University, South Africa, Academic Conferences and Publishing International, p. 179.
45 Thomas J Volgy et al., 2008, 'Identifying formal intergovernmental organizations', *Journal of Peace Research*, vol. 45, no. 6, p. 851.
46 AS Muller, 1995, *International organizations and their host states: aspects of their legal relationship*, Kluwer Law International, The Hague, Netherlands, p. 4.
47 Dikker Hupkes, 2009, p. 10.
48 Eng Sengsavang et al., 2016, 'TR01: Cloud services for international organizations – an annotated bibliography', InterPARES Trust, viewed 28 March 2020, https://interparestrust.org/assets/public/dissemination/TR_20161110_CloudComputingForInternationalOrganizations_AnnotatedBibliography_FINAL.pdf, p. 56.
49 Ademola Abass, 2014, 'International organizations', in *Complete international law: text, cases and materials*, Oxford University Press, New York, p. 191.
50 Sengsavang et al., 2016, p. 57; Abass, 2014, p. 199.
51 National Geographic, 2019, 'International organizations', *National Geographic*, viewed 28 March 2020, www.nationalgeographic.org/encyclopedia/international-organization/.
52 D Ooms, W van den Heuvel & B van de Walle, 2018, 'A conceptual framework for civil-military interaction in peace support operations', in K Boersma & B Tomaszewski (eds.), *ISCRAM 2018 Conference Proceedings – 15th International Conference on Information Systems for Crisis Response and Management*, Rochester Institute of Technology, Rochester, NY, pp. 1003–1015.
53 Nathan A Rao & Oscar W Simmons, 2013, *Koinonia: the requirements and vision for an unclassified information-sharing system*, Naval Postgraduate School.
54 World Bank Group, 2016, *The World Bank Group A to Z 2016*, World Bank Group, Washington DC, p. 189.
55 World Bank Group, 2017, 'Annual report: fiscal year 2017', World Bank Group – Internal Audit, viewed 28 March 2020, http://documents.worldbank.org/curated/en/741831513276556078/pdf/WBGIAD-FY17-Annual-Report-AC-Approved-120617-12112017.pdf, p. 15.
56 Ibid.
57 Ibid, p. 42.
58 Ibid, pp. 15, 42.
59 Ibid, p. 15.
60 International Atomic Energy Agency, 2019, 'Overview', International Atomic Energy Agency, viewed 28 March 2020, www.iaea.org/about/overview.
61 International Atomic Energy Agency, 2017, 'The agency's financial statements for 2017', International Atomic Energy Agency, viewed 28 March 2020, www-legacy.iaea.org/About/Policy/GC/GC62/GC62Documents/English/gc62-5_en.pdf, p. 189.
62 Ibid.
63 United Nations, 2019, 'About the UN: main organs', 28 March 2020, www.un.org/en/sections/about-un/main-organs/.
64 United Nations Architecture Review Board, 2013 'Enterprise architecture roadmap: report', viewed 28 March 2020, https://unite.un.org/sites/unite.un.org/files/app-desa-header/unitednations-ict-strategy.pdf.
65 United Nations Office of Internal Oversight Services, 2013, 'Activities of the Office of Internal Oversight Services for the period from 1 July 2012 to 30 June 2013', viewed 28 March 2020, https://oios.un.org/resources/ga_report/a-68-337-ar-parti.pdf, p. 9.
66 Ibid.
67 United Nations Office of Information and Communication Technology, 2015, 'ICT strategy', viewed 28 March 2020, https://unite.un.org/sites/unite.un.org/files/docs/unitednations-ict-strategy.pdf, p. 2.

68 United Nations General Assembly, 2017, 'Ninth progress report on the Enterprise Resource Planning Project: report of the Secretary General – United Nations General Assembly Seventy-Second Session agenda items 136 and 149 on 18th September', viewed 28 March 2020, https://undocs.org/A/72/397, p. 19.

69 Mary Hickson, 2008, *Research handbook for health care professionals*, Wiley-Blackwell, Chichester, UK, p. 3.

70 International Standards Organization, 2016a, *ISO 15489–1:2016 information and documentation – Records management – Part 1: Concepts and principles*, International Standards Organization, Geneva, viewed 28 March 2020, www.iso.org/iso/home/store/catalogue_tc/catalogue_detail.htm?csnumber=62542.

71 International Standards Organization, 2011, *ISO 30300:2011 information and documentation – Management systems for records – Fundamentals and vocabulary*, International Standards Organization, Geneva, viewed 28 March 2020, www.iso.org/iso/catalogue_detail?csnumber=53732.

72 Katuu, 2018c, p. 1.

73 Shadrack Katuu, 2019c, 'Using enterprise architecture as a template of analysis', InterPARES Trust, viewed 28 March 2020, https://interparestrust.org/assets/public/dissemination/Katuu-CubaEnterprisearchitecture.pdf.

74 International Standards Organization, 2016b, 'Records management in scope', viewed 28 March 2020, https://committee.iso.org/sites/tc46sc11/home/projects/published/records-management-in-scope.html.

75 International Standards Organization, 2015, 'Resolutions of the 31st ISO/TC 46/SC 11 archives/records management meeting, 1–4 June 2015, Beijing, China', viewed 28 March 2020, https://committee.iso.org/files/live/sites/tc46sc11/files/resolutions/N1522%20Resolutions%20of%20the%2031st%20ISOTC46SC11%20meeting%2004-06-2015%205-06.pdf.

76 International Standards Organization, 2016b.

77 Ibid.

78 Ibid.

79 Kerry Tanner, 2002, 'Survey research', in K Williamson (ed.), *Research methods for students, academics and professionals – Information management and systems*, Charles Sturt University, New South Wales, Australia, p. 91.

80 Martyn Denscombe, 2007, *The good research guide for small-scale social research projects*, 3rd edn, Open University Press, Berkshire, p. 17.

81 Doucet et al., 2009, p. 28.

82 Kotusev, 2018b, p. 324.

83 Basten & Brons, 2012, p. 209.

84 International Standards Organization, 2016b.

85 Kotusev, 2018b, p. 342.

86 Anneli Sundqvist, Tom Sahlen & Mats Andreasen, 2019, 'The intermesh of records management principles and enterprise architecture: a framework for information governance in the Swedish context', in Petra Bago et al. (eds.), *INFuture 2019: 7th International Conference – The Future of Information Sciences*, Zagreb, Croatia, Faculty of Humanities and Social Sciences, University of Zaghreb, pp. 75–85; Shadrack Katuu, 2020b, 'Exploring the challenges facing archives and records professionals in Africa: historical influences, current developments and opportunities', in Ray Edmondson, Lothar Jordan & Anca Claudia Prodan, *The UNESCO Memory of the World programme: key aspects and recent developments*, Springer Nature, Switzerland, pp. 275–292; Shadrack Katuu, 2020a, 'Enterprise resource planning: past, present and future', *New Review of Information Networking*, vol. 25, no. 1.

Bibliography

Abass, A 2014, 'International organizations', in *Complete international law: text, cases and materials*, Oxford University Press, New York, pp. 156–200.

Ahlemann, F, Legner, C & Schafczuk, D 2012, 'Introduction', in F Ahlemann, E Stettiner, M Messerschmidt & C Legner (eds.), *Strategic enterprise architecture management: challenges, best practices, and future developments*, Springer Science & Business Media, Dordrecht, pp. 1–33.

Amalia, E & Supriadi, H 2017, 'Development of enterprise architecture in university using TOGAF as framework', in H Prasetyo, MT Nugroho, N Hidayati, E Setiawan, T Widayatno, W Setiawan & F Suryawan (eds.), *Proceedings of the 3rd International Conference on Engineering, Technology, and Industrial Application (ICETIA 2016)*, AIP Publishing, Surakarta, Indonesia, pp. 1–9.

Andaur, G, Barnard, A, Deserno, I, Ditadi, CS, Flinn, A, Hurley, G, Katuu, S, Lowry, J, McLeod, J, Asma'Mokhtar, U, Sengsavang, E, Sexton, A & Suderman, J 2019, 'Open government', in L Duranti & C Rogers (eds.), *Trusting records in the cloud: the creation, management, and preservation of trustworthy digital content*, Facet Publishing, London, pp. 37–64.

Ask, A & Hedström, K 2011, 'Taking initial steps towards enterprise architecture in local government', in K Normann Andersen, E Francesconi, A Grönlund & TM van Engers (eds.), *Second International Conference on Electronic Government and the Information Systems (EGOVIS) Perspective Electronic Government and the Information Systems Perspective*, Springer International Publishing AG, Toulouse, France, pp. 26–40.

Basten, D & Brons, D 2012, 'EA frameworks, modeling and tools', in F Ahlemann, E Stettiner, M Messerschmidt & C Legner (eds.), *Strategic enterprise architecture management: challenges, best practices, and future developments*, Springer Science & Business Media, Dordrecht, pp. 201–227.

Cook, T 2007, 'Electronic records, paper minds: the revolution in information management and archives in the post-custodial and post-modernist era', *Archives and Social Studies: A Journal of Interdisciplinary Research*, vol. 1, pp. 399–443.

Dang, DD & Pekkola, S 2017, 'Systematic literature review on enterprise architecture in the public sector', *Electronic Journal of e-Government*, vol. 15, no. 2, pp. 130–154.

Denscombe, M 2007, *The good research guide for small-scale social research projects*. 3rd edn, Open University Press, Berkshire.

Dikker Hupkes, SD 2009, 'Protection and effective functioning of international organizations. Final report international institutional law; Secure Haven Project', Universiteit Leiden, viewed 28 March 2020, https://openaccess.leidenuniv.nl/handle/1887/14119.

Doucet, G, Gøtze, J, Saha, P & Bernard, SA 2009, 'Coherency management: using enterprise architecture for alignment, agility, and assurance', *Journal of Enterprise Architecture*, vol. 4, no. 2, pp. 27–38.

Duranti, L 2019, 'Trusting records: 20 years of InterPARES research', InterPARES Trust, viewed 28 March 2020, https://interparestrust.org/assets/public/dissemination/Duranti-20yearsofInterPARES-Cuba2019.pdf.

Duranti, L & Rogers, C (eds.) 2019, *Trusting records in the cloud: The creation, management, and preservation of trustworthy digital content*, Facet Publishing, London.

Gong, Y & Janssen, M 2019, 'The value of and myths about enterprise architecture', *International Journal of Information Management*, vol. 46, pp. 1–9.

Greefhorst, D & Proper, E 2011, *Architecture principles: the cornerstones of enterprise architecture*, Springer, Amersfoort, The Netherlands.

Hickson, M 2008, *Research handbook for health care professionals*, Wiley-Blackwell, Chichester, UK.

Hinkelmann, K, Gerber, A, Karagiannis, D, Thoenssen, B, Van der Merwe, A & Woitsch, R 2016, 'A new paradigm for the continuous alignment of business and IT: combining enterprise architecture modelling and enterprise ontology', *Computers in Industry*, vol. 79, pp. 77–86.

Hofman, H 2017, 'The use of models and modelling in recordkeeping research and development', in S McKemmish, A Gilliland & AJ Lau (eds), *Research in the archival multiverse*, Monash University Publishing, Clayton, Australia, pp. 632–658.

International Atomic Energy Agency 2017, 'The agency's financial statements for 2017', International Atomic Energy Agency, viewed 28 March 2020, www-legacy.iaea.org/About/Policy/GC/GC62/GC62Documents/English/gc62-5_en.pdf.

International Atomic Energy Agency 2019, 'Overview', International Atomic Energy Agency, viewed 28 March 2020, www.iaea.org/about/overview.

International Standards Organization 2011, *ISO 30300:2011 Information and documentation – Management systems for records – Fundamentals and vocabulary*, International Standards Organization, Geneva, viewed 28 March 2020, www.iso.org/iso/catalogue_detail?csnumber=53732.

International Standards Organization 2015, 'Resolutions of the 31st ISO/TC 46/SC 11archives/records management meeting, 1–4 June 2015, Beijing, China', viewed 28 March 2020, https://committee.iso.org/files/live/sites/tc46sc11/files/resolutions/N1522%20Resolutions%20of%20the%2031st%20ISOTC46SC11%20meeting%2004-06-2015%205-06.pdf.

International Standards Organization 2016a, *ISO 15489–1:2016 Information and documentation – Records management – Part 1: Concepts and principles*, International Standards Organization, Geneva, viewed 28 March 2020, www.iso.org/iso/home/store/catalogue_tc/catalogue_detail.htm?csnumber=62542.

International Standards Organization 2016b, 'Records management in scope', International Standards Organization, Geneva, viewed 28 March 2020, https://committee.iso.org/sites/tc46sc11/home/projects/published/records-management-in-scope.html.

Iyamu, T & Mphahlele, L 2014, 'The impact of organisational structure on enterprise architecture deployment', *Journal of Systems and Information Technology*, vol. 16, no. 1, pp. 2–19.

Katuu, S 2017, 'TR04: Assessing information systems: facing the challenges of managing records in transactional systems', in 2017 International Seminar – InterPARES Trust, Cape Town, South Africa, InterPARES Trust Team Africa, viewed 28 March 2020, www.researchgate.net/publication/332845611_Assessing_information_systems_Facing_the_challenges_of_managing_records_in_transactional_systems.

Katuu, S 2018a, *TR04: Assessing information systems: a template of analysis – Final report*, InterPARES Trust, viewed 28 March 2020, https://interparestrust.org/assets/public/dissemination/TR04FinalReportJuly2018.pdf.

Katuu, S 2018b, 'Using enterprise architecture as a means of understanding institution technology ecosystems', in V Ribiere (ed.), *ICMLG 2018 16th International Conference on Management Leadership and Governance*, Academic Conferences and Publishing International, Bangkok, Thailand, pp. 130–138.

Katuu, S 2018c, '*The utility of enterprise architecture to records and archives specialists*', paper presented at the 2018 IEEE International Conference on Big Data (Big Data), Seattle, WA, pp. 2702–2710.

Katuu, S 2019a, '*Enterprise architecture– a value proposition for records professionals*', paper presented at the 2019 IEEE International Conference on Big Data (Big Data), Los Angeles, CA, pp. 3116–3125.

Katuu, S 2019b, 'Managing classified records in inter-governmental organizations', in N van der Waag-Cowling & L Leenen, *14th International Conference on Cyber Warfare and Security*,

Academic Conferences and Publishing International, Stellenbosch University, South Africa, pp. 177–188.

Katuu, S 2019c, 'Using enterprise architecture as a template of analysis', InterPARES Trust, viewed 28 March 2020, https://interparestrust.org/assets/public/dissemination/Katuu-CubaEnterprisearchitecture.pdf.

Katuu, S 2020a, 'Enterprise resource planning: past, present and future', *New Review of Information Networking*, vol. 25, no. 1.

Katuu, S 2020b, 'Exploring the challenges facing archives and records professionals in Africa: historical influences, current developments and opportunities', in R Edmondson, L Jordan & AC Prodan (eds.), *The UNESCO Memory of the World programme: Key aspects and recent developments*, Springer Nature, Switzerland, pp. 275–292.

Klareld, A & Gidlund, KL 2017, 'Rethinking archives as digital: the consequences of "paper minds" in illustrations and definitions of e-archives', *Archivaria*, vol. 83, no. 1, pp. 81–108.

Kotusev, S 2016, 'The history of enterprise architecture: an evidence-based review', *Journal of Enterprise Architecture*, vol. 12, no. 1, pp. 29–37.

Kotusev, S 2017, 'Conceptual model of enterprise architecture management', *International Journal of Cooperative Information Systems*, vol. 26, no. 3, pp. 1–36.

Kotusev, S 2018a, 'Enterprise architecture: a reconceptualization is needed', *Pacific Asia Journal of the Association for Information Systems*, vol. 10, no. 4, pp. 1–36.

Kotusev, S 2018b, 'TOGAF-based enterprise architecture practice: an exploratory case study', *Communications of the Association for Information Systems*, vol. 43, no. 1, pp. 321–359.

Kotusev, S 2019a, 'Lecture 1: introduction', viewed 28 March 2020, http://kotusev.com/lectures/Lecture%201%20-%20Introduction.pdf.

Kotusev, S 2019b, 'Lecture 2: the concept of enterprise architecture', viewed 28 March 2020, http://kotusev.com/lectures/Lecture%202%20-%20The%20Concept%20of%20Enterprise%20Architecture.pdf.

Muller, AS 1995, *International organizations and their host states: aspects of their legal relationship*, Kluwer Law International, The Hague, Netherlands.

National Geographic 2019, 'International organizations', viewed 28 March 2020, www.nationalgeographic.org/encyclopedia/international-organization/.

Ooms, D, van den Heuvel, W & van de Walle, B 2018, 'A conceptual framework for civil-military interaction in peace support operations', in K Boersma & B Tomaszewski (eds.), *ISCRAM 2018 Conference Proceedings – 15th International Conference on Information Systems for Crisis Response and Management*, Rochester Institute of Technology, Rochester, NY, pp. 1003–1015.

Raj, P & Periasamy, M 2011, 'The convergence of enterprise architecture (EA) and cloud computing', in Z Mahmood & R Hill (eds.), *Cloud computing for enterprise architectures*, Springer, London, pp. 61–87.

Rao, NA & Simmons, OW 2013, *Koinonia: the requirements and vision for an unclassified information-sharing system*, Naval Postgraduate School, MS.

Riempp, G & Gieffers-Ankel, S 2007, 'Application portfolio management: a decision-oriented view of enterprise architecture', *Information Systems and E-Business Management*, vol. 5, no. 4, pp. 359–378.

Sengsavang, E, Goh, E, Damer, L, How, E, Hofman, D, Michelson, S, Hunter, M, Chicorli, E & Jones, T 2016, 'TR01: Cloud services for international organizations – an annotated bibliography', InterPARES Trust, viewed 28 March 2020https://interparestrust.org/assets/public/dissemination/TR_20161110_CloudComputingForInternationalOrganizations_AnnotatedBibliography_FINAL.pdf.

Shabou, BM, Guercio, M, Katuu, S, Lomas, E & Grazhenskayas, A 2019, 'Strategies, methods and tools enabling records governance in a cloud environment', in L Duranti &

C Rogers (eds.), *Trusting records in the cloud: the creation, management, and preservation of trustworthy digital content*, Facet Publishing, London, pp. 97–116.

Sundqvist, A, Sahlen, T & Andreasen, M 2019, 'The intermesh of records management principles and enterprise architecture: a framework for information governance in the Swedish context', in P Bago, I Hebrang Grgic, T Ivanjko, V Juricic, Z Miklosevic & H Stublic (eds.), *INFuture 2019: 7th International Conference – The Future of Information Sciences*, Faculty of Humanities and Social Sciences, University of Zaghreb, Zagreb, Croatia, pp. 75–85.

Tanner, K 2002, 'Survey research', in K Williamson (ed.), *Research methods for students, academics and professionals – Information management and systems*, Charles Sturt University, New South Wales, Australia, pp. 89–109.

The Open Group 2011a, 'Enterprise continuum', viewed 28 March 2020, http://pubs.op engroup.org/architecture/togaf91-doc/arch/chap39.html.

The Open Group 2011b, 'Introduction', viewed 28 March 2020, http://pubs.opengroup. org/architecture/togaf91-doc/arch/index.html.

The Open Group 2011c, 'Introduction to the ADM', viewed 28 March 2020, http://pubs. opengroup.org/architecture/togaf91-doc/arch/chap05.html.

The Open Group 2012, 'A pocket guide to Archimate® 2.1,' The Open Group, viewed 28 March 2020, https://publications.opengroup.org/g137.

United Nations 2019, 'About the UN: main organs', viewed 28 March 2020, https://www. un.org/en/sections/about-un/main-organs/.

United Nations Architecture Review Board 2013, 'Enterprise architecture roadmap: Report', viewed 28 March 2020, https://unite.un.org/sites/unite.un.org/files/app-desa -header/unitednations-ict-strategy.pdf.

United Nations Department of Global Communications 2019, 'The United Nations system', viewed 28 March 2020, www.un.org/en/pdfs/un_system_chart.pdf.

United Nations General Assembly 2017, 'Ninth progress report on the Enterprise Resource Planning Project: Report of the Secretary General – United Nations General Assembly Seventy-Second Session Agenda Items 136 and 149 on 18th September', viewed 28 March 2020, https://undocs.org/A/72/397.

United Nations Office of Information and Communication Technology 2015, 'ICT strategy', viewed 28 March 2020, https://unite.un.org/sites/unite.un.org/files/docs/unitedna tions-ict-strategy.pdf.

United Nations Office of Internal Oversight Services 2013, 'Activities of the Office of Internal Oversight Services for the period from 1 July 2012 to 30 June 2013', viewed 28 March 2020, https://oios.un.org/resources/ga_report/a-68-337-ar-parti.pdf.

Volgy, TJ, Fausett, E, Grant, KA & Rodgers, S 2008, 'Identifying formal intergovernmental organizations', *Journal of Peace Research*, vol. 45, no. 6, pp. 849–862.

World Bank Group 2016, *The World Bank Group A to Z 2016*, World Bank Group, Washington DC.

World Bank Group 2017, 'Annual report: fiscal year 2017', World Bank Group – Internal Audit, viewed 28 March 2020, http://documents.worldbank.org/curated/en/ 741831513276556078/pdf/WBGIAD-FY17-Annual-Report-AC-App roved-120617-12112017.pdf.

Yustianto, P & Doss, R 2019, 'A unifying structure of metamodel landscape', *Journal of Modelling in Management*, vol. 14, no. 1, pp. 134–152.

8

MANAGING SECURITY CLASSIFIED RECORDS IN INTERNATIONAL ORGANIZATIONS[1]

Ineke Deserno[2] and Eng Sengsavang[3]

Introduction

Organizations are responsible to their members and stakeholders for the safe management and effective exchange of confidential records produced by or entrusted to them. The key principles of this obligation are often stated in the founding treaties or supplementary agreements of international organizations. At the same time, organizations are accountable to stakeholders and to the public for upholding the principles of transparency and access to information about their decisions and activities. These requirements are balanced against privacy and security needs. This chapter argues that the challenges of managing security classified records (SCRs)[4] for international organizations are both ethical and methodological in nature. Ethical considerations are at the root of both access and privacy obligations, and necessarily inform the methodological design of a classified records framework. Many of the challenges of managing SCRs relate directly to the work of information, records, and archival professionals, and call for close coordination with related professionals, such as information security and data protection professionals. Moreover, international organizations are unique players on the global stage. Whether intergovernmental or non-governmental, they regularly handle confidential records related to member states and governments, programme beneficiaries, and diverse types of organizations and entities. Therefore, they operate within a complex and distinct legal and functional space that has implications for the management of security classified records.

In addition to discussing the definition of classified records, the chapter examines the challenges, principles, and policies of managing, protecting, and providing access to SCRs in every aspect of their lifecycle, incorporating records and information management requirements for SCRs. A checklist tool designed to support organizations in developing policies and procedures for managing SCRs is included in Appendix 8.1 of the chapter. A set of minimum descriptive metadata for security classified records is in Appendix 8.2, follwed by categories of roles and responsibilities for managing security classified records in Appendix 8.3.[5]

Sources and background

This study was originally conducted in the framework of the InterPARES Trust study *Managing Security Classified Records in International Organizations* (TR04).[6] The chapter draws on an analysis of records and information security policies of international organizations, as well as a literature review. The literature review includes government sources and articles from security, legal, and archival perspectives. Within the reviewed literature, there is little focus on classified records within international organizations; the literature that does directly address international organizations focuses on a variety of issues, but rarely on the practical aspects of managing SCRs. The gaps in the published work on this topic demonstrate the need for more research and discourse on the topic of SCRs within international organizations.

The sample of policies analysed includes 31 anonymized policies published or updated between 1996 and 2017. The policies belong to 16 anonymized international organizations ranging in size, scope, and type, with 67% forming part of either the United Nations system or the European Union organizations. The organizations are largely located in Europe and North America, with one organization located in Africa. Future studies could expand on the geographical scope and organizational diversity of this initial sample. The organizations are intergovernmental or non-governmental and reflect a spectrum of missions, from humanitarian assistance, development and financial agents, security organizations, and research or domain-specific organizations. The types of policies analysed include information security and/or sensitivity classification; archives and records management; personal data protection; public disclosure and access to information; organizational security; and information technology systems policies.

Defining security classified records

Although seemingly a basic concept, the term "classified records" may be left ill-defined in literature, yet requires clear definition when employed in organizational settings. It is generally understood that classified records, also variously referred to as restricted, confidential, or sensitive records, contain confidential or sensitive information with restrictions about who may see it; for this reason, SCRs are governed and managed differently.[7] However, even within a given organization, the lack of clarity about what constitutes classified records and what does not may cause issues.[8]

Both the policy analysis and literature review show that, on a broad level, classified records are defined as any information regardless of its format that, if disclosed, is deemed to potentially cause a degree of harm − hence the notion of security that attaches to them − and therefore stringent access restrictions and management controls are placed on them. For this reason, SCRs have a separate identity and constitute a body of records that are distinct from public and non-classified records. The majority of policies on SCRs include an internal definition of "classified information," which manifests as ascending levels of security classification.

In many organizations, access to restricted records is not only confined to information that is classified for security purposes. For example, personnel information is also restricted, but for privacy purposes. Security classified records are distinct because of why they are kept restricted. Aftergood indicates that classified records pertain to "that body of information which, if disclosed, could actually damage national security in some identifiable way."[9] At the same time, some organizations may not recognize this distinction in their policies, and handling rules may be the same whether a record is restricted for security or for other reasons of privacy. For a more detailed discussion of this issue, see pp. 182–183.

Security classification levels

The international standard *ISO 27002:2013 Information technology – Security techniques – Code of practice for information security controls* recommends a model of classified information based on an assessment of the impact of unauthorized disclosure of classified information.[10] It states that an information confidentiality classification scheme could be based on four levels as follows:

- Disclosure causes no harm;
- Disclosure causes minor embarrassment or minor operation inconvenience;
- Disclosure has a significant short-term impact on operations or tactical objectives;
- Disclosure has a serious impact on long-term strategic objectives or puts the survival of the organization at risk.[11]

These ISO-suggested levels coincide with the classification categories found in the policies of international organizations, which most often have three or four classification levels. Each level is marked with a security label reflecting the classification level. Although they vary across organizations, commonly referenced levels are:

- Unclassified (internal or official use only);
- Restricted;
- Confidential;
- Secret.

The first category, marked "Unclassified," identifies records that are deemed to have low or no negative impact if disclosed. However, "unclassified" records differ from public information. Unclassified or official records are used for business purposes only. This may include administrative notices on annual leave arrangements, minutes of meetings of internal staff working groups, or a project status report on the implementation of a new system. Therefore, access to these records is internal, i.e., they circulate only within the organization. Often release procedures apply, and access may be further restricted for privacy, management, or commercial reasons. By contrast, public information is information that is intended for public outreach from its creation. This could include web postings, press releases, and annual reports.

The most highly classified records are the most sensitive of the categories, and when records at the highest level are disclosed, there is the risk of a severe impact to an organization, the work of an organization, and/or third parties. Such classified records could, for example, include plans on ongoing humanitarian or military operations.

The policy analysis reveals that international organizations struggle to define the different levels of security classifications in measurable and tangible ways. The duty of assigning a classification level to a record is most often left to the prerogative of the originator, that is, the creator of the record. However, originators may fear repercussions for failing to protect classified information, and may default to over-classifying information.[12] On the other end of the spectrum, records creators may under-classify information, thereby putting at risk diplomatic relations, employees, or those impacted by the activities in question.

The difficulty lies in the fact that it is not possible to predict every situation that may arise from disclosure of a given record, and therefore no precise definition covering every possible situation exists. Appropriate classification decisions therefore rely on the judgement and experience of the originator. However, on matters of judgement, different interpretations or disagreements of the potential impact of disclosure of classified records are always possible, and even likely. Organizations may employ various strategies to address the challenges of classification, which are described on pp. 187–189.

The term "classification" may also refer to the process of applying the designated security classification levels, or it may refer to the security classification levels themselves.

Types of security classified records

The review of the policies shows that the following categories of information always require protection within international organizations, and thus records containing this information are security classified:

- Internal political discussions and negotiations with member states and foreign government/foreign relations information;
- Military plans and operations;
- Information on weapons systems;
- Intelligence information;

- Weapons of mass destruction/nuclear information;
- Scientific, technological, economic matters related to national and international security.

Additional types of SCRs may exist based on the business of the organization.

Other categories of classified records

Classified records are not confined only to information that is classified for security reasons. Personal data and commercial information, though they may be considered distinct types of information, are also confidential, and often classified according to a similar model as classified information for security purposes: that is, based on an assessment of the varying degrees of harm – to a private individual, a company, an organization, or a member state – that would be incurred by unauthorized disclosure. The distinction between SCRs and other kinds of protected information varies among organizations, and is often blurred in organizational policies. For instance, some international organizations make a distinction between sensitive versus confidential information, while others make no distinction at all, even using the term "sensitive" to describe all classified information, so that the term is interchangeable with "classified." In other instances, "sensitive" refers specifically to personal information, which may be classified within an organization's security classified records scheme (for instance, an organization may require that personnel records be classified as Restricted or Confidential).

Aftergood discusses the confusion around the term "sensitive" information: "no one knows what it means. The meaning of 'unclassified' is clear, of course, but the crucial term 'sensitive' is not defined."[13] Is "sensitive but unclassified" information a type of classified information, or something else altogether, and therefore should it be under the same policies with other classified information, or under separate policies?[14]

To add to the confusion, in some organizations the term "sensitive" may be used in combination with "unclassified" or "official use only," and some policies may include procedures for sensitive but unclassified information. Organizations may create special markings for this information to be added to its classification labelling, for example Unclassified – Commercial or Unclassified – Personnel. These markings may exclude such sensitive records from a systematic downgrading or disclosure programme, and imply more stringent access controls and retention and disposition procedures during their entire lifecycle.

In summary, the term "sensitive" often refers to records that are classified for data privacy or legal reasons, rather than for security reasons, and access to them is controlled due to the risk that their release could harm individuals; legal, commercial, management, or political interests of the organization; or interests of other relevant parties. The policies and procedures for managing sensitive but non-security classified records are controlled, and may be either distinct from or the same as those policies and procedures governing the management of SCRs, depending on the organization.

However an organization defines "sensitive," policies should acknowledge the distinction between records that are classified for security reasons and those that are classified for reasons of personal data protection, industrial confidentiality, or other reasons. Organizations should also be clear whether sensitive but non-security classified records are to be handled and managed differently, and how access policies may differ for these records.

Principles, practices, and policies for the lifecycle management of security classified records (SCRs)

A number of principles, practices, and policies can help international organizations to accountably and effectively manage security classified records. These measures are applicable during the various stages in the lifecycle of SCRs, each of which has recordkeeping implications. The following sections provide an overview of the different principles and practices in the management of SCRs, which are typically governed and managed according to a set of interrelated and interreferential policies, guidelines, procedures, and international standards. Aside from policies directly focused on classified information and records management, those addressing topics such as personnel and physical security, information technology systems security, or declassification and public access also play an important role in the management of classified records.

The guidelines below are in part taken from the policy analysis of international organizations, as well as from the standard ISO/IEC 27001:2013 on information security management systems, designed to "provide requirements for establishing, implementing, maintaining and continually improving an information security management system."[15]

Organizational environment

SCRs can be created anywhere in the organization and may be stored in different business systems and repositories across the organization. These records never exist in isolation; they are the product of an organization's decisions and activities. Therefore, the organizational environment in which SCRs are created or received requires attention. The environment consists of the overarching governance framework, including policies and procedures, combined with the tools, processes, and resources dedicated within an organization to manage SCRs. In this context, ISO 27001:2013 stresses the importance of integrating the information security system with core business processes of the organization, as well as its management structure, and calls for the consideration of information security concerns whenever new systems or processes are being designed.[16] Therefore, the definition and execution of the handling and control of classified records should extend not just to the records themselves, but also to their environment, be it a digital system or a file cabinet, and should apply to any point of the records' lifecycle and location within the organization.[17]

Information and records management principles

Although it may seem obvious, it is important to ensure that SCRs are not exempt from normal information and records management policies; in fact, the requirement to maintain the "secrecy" of SCRs implies a corresponding obligation for organizational accountability and transparency vis-à-vis their management. Responsible management of SCRs can have a tangible impact on preventing over- or under-classification, and on promoting systematic declassification and eventual public access to previously classified records. Specifically, it should be clear that SCRs are subject to regulations such as records retention and disposition schedules, file classification schemes, file-naming conventions, and metadata requirements, as well as systematic transfer to archives or accountable destruction, and public disclosure and access policies.

The link to an information lifecycle model not only helps to ensure accountability at all stages in the life of SCRs, but also underscores the fact that SCRs are subject to an organization's information, archives, and records management policies, in addition to information security and other security requirements.

Several international organizations articulate in their policies that classified records must follow records retention and disposition schedules. The link to retention and disposition schedules supports a fundamental understanding that the criteria for permanent retention or destruction of an SCR should be based on its content and value, not on its security classification. Within some organizations, there is a risk that the imperatives of the security community to destroy SCRs may trump the need to preserve classified records based on their permanent value; that is, classified records may be destroyed even though they have lasting historical value. It is therefore essential that the security community embrace the retention schedules developed by records and archives professionals. Stated more directly, international organizations must not destroy classified records that have permanent value. This illustrates a case for the segregation of "duties and areas of responsibility" recommended by ISO 27001, to avoid "modification or misuse" of records.[18] However, this should still be part of a holistic management framework for information security recommended by ISO 27001.

Some policies cite specific qualities of SCRs that should be protected, most commonly confidentiality, availability, and security. The archival concept of a record should also be applied to classified records, to highlight the obligation to maintain not only their confidentiality, availability, and security, but also the qualities of authenticity, reliability, and integrity of records. These obligations ensure organizational accountability and can again be addressed by linking SCRs with an organization's archives, records, and information management policy.

Scope of policies

When creating policies related to the management of classified records, it is important to delineate their scope, which are the topics, assets, and/or individuals and entities that are subject to the policy. The scope of classified records policies should include a clear definition of the information assets covered by the policy, including the types of classified records addressed (e.g., formats; single as well as aggregate units of information; and equipment and systems that process and store classified information); the stages of the lifecycle covered by the policy; and the parties and individuals who are subject to the policy.

Most policies apply to documents created, held, or received by an organization and recorded and/or stored in any format, whether paper, digital, audiovisual, or other. Some classified records policies even include within their scope information that is not recorded, such as spoken information. This highlights the tendency of most policies to conflate content – "classified information" – with the form that the classified information may take – "classified records" – without acknowledging that there is a difference. Indeed, almost all of the policies analysed use the term "classified information" rather than "classified documents" or "records." To bridge this discrepancy, policies should define the terminology they use to encompasses both classified information and classified records, since both the content and the recording of the content in any form need to be protected, and since, as in the example of spoken information, classified content may not be recorded, or may exist in forms for which the concept of "records" has not yet caught up.

Policies should also apply not only to single units of information, such as documents, but also to aggregates of classified information, such as databases, information systems, or registers. It should be clear that policies extend not just to SCRs themselves, but also to their environment. As well as networks that store or process classified records, any physical equipment or classified spaces that store or process classified records, including computers or reproduction equipment, networks, and data storage devices, and media such as servers, should be included in the scope. These may also be covered in other security policies, including IT security policies, all of which should align. The SCR policy should also apply retroactively to SCRs that were classified prior to the establishment of the policy.

There should be comprehensive coverage of the entire lifecycle of SCRs, either in a single policy or in several targeted policies that refer to one another. For example, there may be separate policies for declassification and public disclosure.

International organizations engage various types of individuals under different types of contracts who may come into contact with SCRs entrusted to them. For this reason, the policy should specify that not only regular staff, but all persons employed by an organization under various types of contracts who may handle SCRs (including consultants, project-based hires, etc.) are subject to the policy.

Roles and responsibilities

International organizations take great care to protect SCRs from unauthorized access. The responsibility of each staff member to comply with policies and procedures, including personnel security policies and staff regulations pertaining to confidentiality requirements, should be emphasized. In this context, access to SCRs is restricted to a limited number of employees. Organizations should establish, whenever possible, a personnel security clearance procedure to ensure that employees adhere to fundamental principles of SCR management before they can access SCRs. The purpose of the security clearance procedure is to make a reasonable determination that individuals granted access to classified records are and will remain loyal, trustworthy, and reliable to the organization. The review process determines, among other things, whether the individual has a criminal record, has committed or aided in any act of espionage or terrorism, or is related to a violent or terrorist organization. The procedure consists of a review of personal data and extensive interviews with the employee, their friends, and family. Provided the procedure can be successfully concluded, the employee is given a security certificate. Organizations usually have a revalidation process in place.

Besides a personnel security clearance, organizations may institute a "need to know" clearance procedure. The "need to know" principle is a positive determination that a recipient has a requirement to access classified records in order to perform their professional activities. Prior to handling classified information, employees need to attend information security awareness training and complete regular refresher training.[19] Weaver underscores the importance of information security training by noting that in the U.S., "those who work in the intelligence community endure lengthy instruction on why it is obligatory for those charged with a nation's secrets to properly handle the information and the damage that can ensue from poor practices."[20]

From the above, it becomes obvious that roles and responsibilities as well as access rights for those handling classified records need to be clearly defined and assigned among security-cleared and competent personnel, to ensure accountability and avoid conflict of interests.[21] In areas where a conflict of interest is possible, the responsibilities need to be separated to ensure that "unauthorized or unintentional modifications or misuse" of classified records remain minimal, following the ISO 27001 recommendation for the "segregation of duties" within an integrated management framework.[22]

Roles

In order to support staff who handle SCRs, the roles and responsibilities of various employees should be clearly identified and defined.[23] The necessity to define roles and authority points was illustrated by Schilde[24] and Weaver.[25] Schilde covers the handling of classified records in EU information policy and "the confusion over who has the authority to access, protect, analyze, and disclose EU-classified information."[26] It is critical to hold to the same standards and regulations all those with access to classified records.[27] Policies should define classification authorities who are responsible for classifying records and deciding on the levels of classification. See pp. 207–210 for more on this role. Other key roles include security officers; upper-level management and/or organizational leadership who may have authority to settle classification questions; reclassification and declassification authorities, who may be the same as classification authorities or their successors, or who may be a combination of management, leadership, or committees; and any decision-making bodies such as committees or boards, who have duties related to reclassification or declassification reviews.

The roles of various organizational units that are responsible for different aspects of SCR management, such as IT, human resources, security personnel, legal, and archives and information and records management units should also be clearly outlined and boundaries indicated. Within certain organizations, the highest level or levels of classification may require a different configuration of authorized roles (for example, only upper management or leadership, and not the original classification authority, may be authorized to declassify the most highly classified records), and different procedures and rules may apply to higher levels of classified records. It should be clear that records and information management professionals are responsible for the retention and disposition of SCRs, to ensure that appraisal decisions are not based on the security classification of a record.

Creation and classification of security classified records

Classified records are either created or received by an organization. The act of assigning the correct security level is a crucial step in the classification process, and consists of assessing the degree of negative impact that disclosure of the information would have on an organization's members, personnel, its operations, and its partners. Most policies designate the creator or receiver of the record as the person authorized to decide on its classification.

Strategies for appropriate classification

The pressure to assign an appropriate classification level is heightened by the fact that mis-classification, whether under- or over-classification, has serious consequences. Under-classification results in the creation of records that do not have adequate protection and access controls on them, putting the organization and concerned parties at risk. Over-classification, on the other hand, may impede decision-making and present a barrier to accountability and access to information. Aftergood and Relyea argue that while national security and classification mechanisms are valid tools that serve the public interest, unchecked and arbitrary over-classification hampers accountability of the political process, and prevents informed decision-making by imposing restrictions on information sharing.[28] This insight applies not just to classified records that would not have warranted a classification marking in the first place, but also to classified records that remain classified for longer than necessary.[29]

While acknowledging that it is not possible for anyone to foresee the future, and that classification is an exercise in qualitative judgement based on the experience of the classifier, there are several strategies that organizations may employ to support appropriate classification.

Organizations should put in place training programmes and procedures to help staff and members build a solid understanding of the sensitivities of their information and the associated security classification categories. Providing concrete examples, such as lists of document types and their suggested levels of classification, may be enormously helpful to staff. For example, a typology of documents and their classification levels may suggest higher restrictions for certain types of documents created by the office of certain officials within the organization; or restrictions on categories of documents, such as mission reports, political briefings, military plans, or legal records. Conversely, typologies of documents that should remain unclassified or public may help staff to determine whether a document should be classified at all.

Another strategy, following the example of one organization, is to include situational risks for each degree of harm corresponding to a level of classification. For instance, examples of "exceptionally grave damage" in one organization include the risk of death of an employee or a citizen of a local population; the violation of an individual's medical privacy; or the compromise of security preparations against a terrorist attack. Situational examples could be provided for each level of classification, helping staff to imagine the types of harmful situations that correspond to different security levels if SCRs are leaked.

Risk management principles may also come into play and are cited in several organizational policies, especially policies related to general security. One organization states that the appropriate classification level is determined by the "disclosure risks" of information, based on the magnitude, amount, or kind of damage that could be caused by disclosure. Other measures to ensure that correct security classifications are applied include limiting the number of people that are authorized to classify records, and restricting the types of records that should be classified. In cases of uncertainty, designated higher classification authorities are critical in guiding classification decisions.

Other considerations for the creation of security classified records

When confidential records are received from external sources, many policies state that, where an expectation of confidentiality exists, authorized staff must apply an equivalent or higher level of classification on the record. Possessing the authority to classify records does not automatically give an individual the right to access all SCRs at the same level.

The policy should also clarify procedures for the classification of groups of SCRs. One organization's policy cautions that aggregating classified information may increase the level of classification of the aggregate, above the classification level of any single item in it. The same organization requires that when classifying a group of SCRs, the highest level of classification of any part of the group must be applied to the whole.

It should also be clear whether the organization allows for partial or multiple classification of a document. Some organizations permit different classification levels to be applied to different parts of a record. For example, confidential information may be placed in appendices or other detachable parts, so that the main body of information may be disseminated more widely; conversely, less confidential information may be placed in appendices or attachments and enclosures that may be detached from the classified record. One organization even allows smaller parts of a document to be classified differently, such as a single paragraph. Other organizations require uniform classification of a document, even if different parts of a document have different confidentiality requirements; in the latter case, organizations may require that a whole document bears the highest classification level of any part of it.

Duration of security classifications

The duration of a security classification should be clear from the very point of creation of an SCR. Some policies are vague or not systematic enough on this point, stating only that SCRs are to be classified for only as long as necessary, or for as long as the original classification authority deems it necessary. Such general statements risk encouraging inefficiency and neglect when it comes to declassifying records.

Many organizations define a default classification period for each classification level. Default classification periods of 5, 10, 20, 30, or 50 years may be applied to various levels of SCRs. In some instances, the highest levels of classification are exempt from default classification periods but must be either reviewed at regularly established frequencies, or may be declassified by high-level authorities. Some policies allow the record creator to indicate at the point of creation a classification duration or triggering event, after which a classified document may be automatically declassified, and which may be different from any established default classification period.

Access principles: balancing the need to know with responsibility to share

Access in this section refers to how SCRs may be accessed or otherwise shared during their active life, before the records are declassified and publicly disclosed.

Organizations that produce or receive SCRs need to balance two principles that are equally important. These are the "need to know" and the "responsibility to share." The latter refers to the obligation to make information available and accessible to all those entities that require the information to perform their professional duties. The former refers to limiting the disclosure of information only to those individuals with a "need-to-know." In essence, both principles refer to the same concept, but originate from different points of view.

The requirement to apply the "need to know" principle to SCRs immediately limits the possibility for information sharing. Balancing both principles requires that the originator of the record make a positive determination on information disclosure, considering both the protection and sharing requirements of the information.

Control and handling procedures for security classified records

Marking

The literature and policies underline the need for clearly recognizable and retrievable classified records. This is done through labelling and through pertinent metadata associated with the information item. As may be expected, most policies require that SCRs are clearly marked by the classification authority and the markings should be visible, in whatever form the record appears, including in electronic form. When this is not technically possible, alternative ways of marking the record should be in place.

Some organizations provide explicit labelling instructions. A minimum standard may be defined, such as marking at least the front page of a document, or the front and back of bound materials. In the case when multiple classifications are applied to an integrated SCR unit, each discrete part must be clearly marked with its classification level.

Additional classification markings may be added. These include markings limiting the distribution of a document; restrictions on the use or releasability of information; or indications of the date or event when an SCR may be downgraded or declassified. Containers holding SCRs, such as file folders, storage boxes, databases, or electronic storage devices, should also be clearly marked with the highest classification level of the records they hold.

In several organizations, public records are actively marked "public." Other organizations specify that when documents are not marked, they should be considered internal; in other words, these organizations protect even unmarked documents from public disclosure.

Metadata

Policies should establish a minimum set of required metadata to describe the contents, context, and structure of SCRs, thereby supporting identification, retrieval, access to, and long-term preservation of security classified records.[30] Within electronic systems, the classification level of SCRs should always form part of their metadata. Policies should also distinguish between the security classification of the content versus the metadata of records. For example, organizations should consider whether certain kinds of metadata, but not all metadata of SCRs, should also be security classified. For example, the metadata of highly classified records may itself be actively classified, since even exposing the fact of a classified document's existence, or information about the records such as its title, may pose a risk. Policies should also establish provisions for the retention of audit trail records throughout the lifecycle of SCRs.

Registration

Registration is the process of documenting SCRs created or received by an organization within a centralized information system, or within multiple decentralized information systems. Registration is critical for accountability, serving as a record of the existence of SCRs, and enabling them to be tracked throughout their life, including during transmission and processing, transfer to archives, and destruction.

One organization specifies that documents should be registered when they require an action, follow-up, or response. This applies most clearly to outgoing or incoming correspondence or documents. Another policy states that SCRs must be registered upon receipt, but also before being transmitted. Internal SCRs of an official or final nature should also be registered, such as memos and reports.

Registry systems are accessed and managed only by authorized persons and should comply with an organization's internal security protocols. In the case of multiple registries within the same organization, it is possible that only the central registry may transmit or store the most highly classified records, while subsidiary registries handle lower-classified records. Some organizations have a separate dedicated registry for the highest level or levels of classified records, while not requiring registration of lower-classified records. Procedures such as annual review of all SCRs may be in place. A list of all staff authorized to access or register SCRs should be available.

Physical and technical security measures for registry systems should also be in place and are often outlined in policies. Registry systems should be auditable and should track activities, such as when SCRs have been added, accessed, and transmitted, removed or modified, and by whom.

Transmission/release

Several organizations require that distribution lists be created for transmission of recurring types of SCRs. Distribution lists provide a clear reference of who may receive what kinds of classified records, supporting systematic decision-making and enabling better tracking and auditing of information flow. Policies should establish authorities, such as heads of units or security officers, who are responsible for supporting staff in their decision-making.

As mentioned on p. 190, some organizations outline possible additional markings to further limit distribution or releasability of SCRs. A releasability marking may specify the "release authority" of the information, such as a specific unit or body within an organization, who may authorize further dissemination.

When transmitting SCRs to external parties, there may be specific rules in place. One organization requires a security agreement regulating the release of classified records to non-member states or to other organizations. Another organization requires a data transfer agreement for the transfer of personal data to third parties. Policies should specify whether different rules exist for external versus internal dissemination of SCRs.

The means of transmission of SCRs is, of course, important. Some organizations specify different rules of transmission based on the level of classification. For example, the highest classified documents may be hand delivered only, and email distribution permitted only when necessary, as determined by an appropriate authority. It may be specified that highly classified records must be distributed separately.

Several organizations require that any type of electronic transmission of SCRs must be through cryptographic or other protected means, such as an encrypted USB, an encrypted email attachment, or a file-sharing programme or platform with a strong authentication. However, organizations should ensure that corresponding decryption mechanisms are maintained over time, to ensure long-term access and preservation of SCRs. Electronic media used for transmitting SCRs should also comply with an organization's information technology security policy, be authorized by the relevant authorities, and should undergo regular audits. Policies should establish controls and procedures to ensure integrity and mitigate against corruption or tampering of SCRs, including in automated systems, during internal and external transmission, and in storage.

Storage of security classified records

Storage of SCRs refers to where and how they are kept when "at rest," as opposed to when they are being processed or disseminated in some way. Physical SCRs should be stored securely in locked containers and in physical spaces that are only accessible to authorized staff. Some organizations establish minimum security standards for SCRs. Separate secure storage facilities may be designated for different levels of SCRs. One organization requires that all secure storage facilities are documented in a list. Information security policies should align with an organization's general security protocols, and should include provisions for information security breaches or contingency plans to protect SCRs in emergency situations. Instituting a clean-desk policy that prevents staff from leaving SCRs exposed helps to underline the personal responsibility of each individual for proper handling of SCRs.

Similar to the rules for transmitting SCRs, several organizations require that digital SCRs are stored in encrypted form. However, it is critical that if security encryption or other security mechanisms for digital data are required, then corresponding decryption mechanisms should also be maintained over time, to ensure that SCRs remains legible, whole, and accessible over the long term. Policies should establish controls and procedures to ensure integrity and mitigate against corruption or tampering of SCRs in storage.

The protection of SCRs in digital form should also extend to electronic storage media, including servers, computer equipment, or other media holding SCRs. These should be clearly marked, password-protected, and kept in locked and controlled facilities. Likewise, information systems that store, process, or transmit SCRs should have controls that prevent unauthorized access and protect the integrity of records, and should undergo regular security audits. Ideally, any personal devices such as desktop computers or removable media should not store classified records. SCRs should instead be stored in registries or centralized information systems.

Cloud computing

International organizations may use cloud computing systems to store and process information, including SCRs. Accordingly, policies should extend to SCRs that are not in the physical custody of the organization, but still under the organization's control, including SCRs that are processed and stored using remote third-party cloud computing services. Organizational policies as well as contracts with cloud providers should acknowledge the privileges and immunities of international organizations, particularly the inviolability of their archives and assets. The inviolability principle, typically found in treaties or host agreements of international organizations, protects the archives and assets of international organizations from external interference, wherever their archives or assets are located, unless expressly permitted by the organization. In principle, the inviolability clause is relevant in a cloud computing setting, although it is difficult to enforce in practice.

Classified records should not be stored in public clouds, where information is kept in remote multi-tenancy servers, and organizations have much less control over the environment as well as over contractual terms with the provider. A study by the United Nations Joint Inspection Unit (JIU) notes that different organizations have different "risk appetites" for storing and processing data in the cloud, partially dependent on the sensitivity of an organization's data.[31] If an organization uses cloud computing, classified records should be stored in private or hybrid cloud settings. Specific contractual clauses, including auditing and monitoring requirements, should be instituted to ensure there are adequate guarantees protecting SCRs entrusted to third parties.[32] An important contractual clause would be to specify the location of servers that store SCRs. In a private cloud, the servers may be located on the organization's own premises or in remote single-tenancy (that is, private) servers; in the latter case, there should be a clause specifying where the servers may be stored, in particular within countries where there may be a reasonable guarantee that data will not be subject to government interference. However, the JIU cautions that, "When highly sensitive data and additional layers of control and encryption are needed, extra protective measures may make cloud solutions expensive and, in those cases, potentially unworkable."[33]

Reclassification and declassification of security classified records

Re- and declassification procedures need to be established in parallel with security classification procedures and other information security mechanisms.[34] The act of re- or declassifying records changes or removes a security classification, while retroactive classification adds a security classification to a record that has already been created, potentially removing information from the public domain that was previously accessible.[35] With the removal of security classifications, access control measures also lessen significantly.

Reclassification

Reclassification is the process of either decreasing or downgrading, or increasing the security classification of a record. It can occur either prior to or as part of an organization's default declassification review, or on an ad hoc basis. There may be instances when SCRs need to be reclassified, such as when the potential impact or meaning of certain kinds of information changes, or when records have been inappropriately classified. Downgrading is a type of reclassification that lowers the classification level of a record. This can happen with the passage of time or after certain events that reduce the sensitivity of SCRs.

Organizations should designate an authority who is responsible for ensuring that SCRs are appropriately classified, and who may reclassify records if they are judged to be over- or under-classified. Some organizations do not permit reclassification without the consent of the originator. Organizations may also require that owners of SCRs or the responsible programmes should conduct regular reviews (for example annually), and, based on changes to legal or contractual situations or to the value of information, reclassify if necessary. One organization requires that SCRs at the highest level be reviewed regularly every five years, but the originator may pre-define automatic downgrading before the five-year period, and this must be marked clearly on the document. Similarly, several organizations require that the original classification authority clearly mark any downgrading or declassification actions that are to take place after a triggering event or date. If reclassification takes place, the changes should be noted in a register or in the metadata of SCRs, and recipients of the classified records should be informed.

Declassification

Declassification is the removal of security classifications when records are no longer deemed sensitive. A well-defined system for records declassification is critical for accountability and effectiveness of an organization's classified records programme. Declassification is also a necessary precondition to ensure eventual public disclosure of previously classified records. Kastenhofer and Katuu argue in their analysis of declassification procedures in international organizations that risk-based declassification reviews are the most efficient way to systematically declassify information, based on the premise that in most cases, the justification of classification decreases over time.[36]

There are two broad types of declassification processes, which may be called systematic or ad hoc. Systematic declassification takes place after defined periods of time (i.e., when SCRs have reached their required classification durations) or before or after transfer to archives. There is typically an established process and criteria for reviewing and declassifying records by designated declassification authorities and other actors involved in the declassification process. This requires specific roles, such as a declassification review committee, and designated staff members responsible for overseeing the declassification process, such as the head archivist.

Ad hoc declassification refers to declassification on a case-by-case basis, either when there is an absence of systematic declassification procedures within an organization, or when declassification actions or reviews are triggered by requests for access to SCRs, either by internal or external parties, before they have outlived their required classification periods. Most organizations have a systematic declassification process, while a few only provide for ad hoc declassification, and yet others have a mix of both systematic and ad hoc declassification. Organizations should try to adopt a mixed system of both systematic and ad hoc declassification to ensure efficient and accountable declassification, while also providing for a measure of flexibility by permitting special requests for declassification before the established review periods.

Almost half of the organizations reviewed refer to "automatic declassification" of records classified at certain levels. An equal number of organizations refer to regular or systematic *review* of declassified records, once they have met the established duration periods for classification. This implies that in some organizations, some records may be declassified automatically without the requirement for review of the records, while in some of the same or different organizations, certain SCRs must be reviewed before being declassified, as part of a systematic review procedure.

A few organizations have a system in place for review at regular intervals (e.g., every 5 years) of SCRs that have *not* been declassified following a review. Such policies can help ensure that SCRs do not languish in obscurity beyond a reasonable period and are regularly reviewed for potential declassification. Systematic declassification may also be instituted by requiring declassification either before or after transfer to the archives.

Similar to policies that provide typologies of documents as an aid for classifying records, it may be helpful to provide typologies of documents to assist with declassification reviews or decisions. One organization has provided a list of types of SCRs that may be reviewed after a period of 50 years. Another organization has provided a list of types of information that are exempt from declassification, such as information about intelligence sources. However, organizations should avoid keeping SCRs classified in perpetuity. For the declassification of third-party SCRs received by the organization, the consent of the third party before declassification is often required. Once SCRs have been declassified, they should be clearly marked as such, and the metadata of the SCR should be updated to reflect it.

Public disclosure of declassified records

National as well as international organizations face tensions between the right to information and the need for security. Although much of the discourse around public access to information is expressed in relation to national governments, international organizations are equally accountable for their recordkeeping and should strive for transparency and progressive policies when it comes to declassification and the eventual public disclosure of SCRs.

Hitchens argues that since access to IGO information is "essential to discourse and accountability at the global level," international organizations have an obligation to provide access to their records.[37] Similarly, Roche, who focuses on public access policies at the North Atlantic Treaty Organization (NATO), perceives that as a publicly funded IGO, NATO "has an obligation to its members' citizens of open and honest recordkeeping."[38] This is true of any IGO whose member states pay annual membership fees from national budgets. Nor are non-governmental organizations (NGOs) exempt from public accountability, due to the kinds of records that they handle (e.g., case files) and the actors with whom they engage (including states, individuals, and other international organizations).

Since the latter part of the 1990s, a movement towards transparency in IGOs such as the World Bank (WB), International Monetary Fund (IMF), and the World Trade Organization (WTO) has continued to evolve.[39] The trend includes increased transparency in policy-making and policy reviews, and the establishment of archival access policies within several IGOs.[40] For example, the Archives Transparency Project, an effort by the IMF from 2003 to 2008 to provide archival descriptions for records dating from 1946 to 1988, "effectively creat[ed] the historical archives of the Institution," where previously there had been none.[41] Roche discusses the evolution of access to NATO archives starting from transparency efforts in the 1970s and moving towards the official opening of the archives in 1999, "with tens of thousands of NATO records open to the public for the first time ever."[42] Contemporary efforts at transparency and greater public access to information have manifested in the digitization and availability of archival holdings online,[43] public outreach and communications initiatives, and robust exhibitions and publications showcasing archival holdings at NATO.[44]

Positive as such public access initiatives may be, Roberts cautions that an appearance of transparency may not reflect the realities of access.[45] Invisible barriers to access may be deliberate or unintentional. For example, interviews by Peter Jagnal with researchers and diplomats revealed problems such as poor distribution of documents, IGO secrecy, and insufficient access to IGO databases.[46] It may be difficult to discover the existence of IGO publications, documents, and data files in order to gain access to them.[47] Discrepancies in the stated policies of IGOs versus the realities of distribution systems, bibliographic control, timeliness, and the quality of available information demonstrates a need to close the gap between the ideals of explicit policies and the realities of barriers to access.[48] Within some organizations, "public" records may be nearly impossible to access in actuality.[49] A lack of resources is the main culprit,[50] for example budgetary and workload burdens that are associated with manual review.[51] In particular, the scarce resources and low prioritization given to declassification may hamper the process of opening records to the public.[52] This illustrates the need for automatic declassification procedures.

Another barrier to access is the conception that international organizations are less accountable for their recordkeeping practices than nation states. For example, in 1990, the European Union information policy on access to environmental information gave EU citizens the right to access environmental records produced by any EU member state.[53] However, Hitchens observes that "there seems to be no provision for access to any information which may have been gathered or produced at the EU level."[54] Thus the EU environmental information policy "places the IGO in the role of facilitator for nation states rather than highlighting the IGO's own responsibilities regarding access, consultation, and accountability."[55] This example highlights not only the interconnectivity between IGO and national classified access to information issues, it also highlights the need for international organizations to ensure that there is an explicit system in place for the public disclosure of their own records, including SCRs. This has recently been underscored within a broader context by a 2017 Report of the Special Rapporteur of the Human Rights Council: "While freedom of information policies have been introduced worldwide, international organizations, with a few specific exceptions, have not followed suit"; the report therefore "urges all international organizations, especially the United Nations, to adopt robust freedom of information policies."

Public disclosure policies for declassified records

In order to fulfil the principles of transparency and accountability, clear public disclosure policies are essential for international organizations. A systematic process for public disclosure of records should be in place, including defined duration periods after which records are declassified and become public. Policies should describe the rules for public access to an organization's records, including outlining the type of records that are public and when they are made public.

Some records are created as public documents and therefore are accessible and published immediately. Internal records, on the other hand, are only made public after a defined period of time, such as 20 or 30 years. Public access policies should include a list of records that are considered public and those that are considered internal, and established duration periods after which records are to be disclosed. Certain types of records, such as those containing personal data (e.g., case files, personnel records, etc.), or legal documents, may be subject to longer closure periods. The question of whether partial disclosure of records is permitted should also be addressed.

Policies should specify whether ad hoc requests for access to records that are publicly disclosed is permitted, and if so, there should be an established procedure in place, including a suggested response time by the organization. This procedure should be described in the policy and publicly available. It is within an organization's right to state in its policy that certain kinds of access requests may be refused, for example, requests that are too broad or that would place undue burden on staff time and energy.

Organizations should also clarify whether they distinguish between declassified versus publicly disclosed documents; that is, whether declassified records are publicly disclosed as soon as they are declassified. There should be a process to update the public access permissions of SCRs following their disclosure, and a process to transfer SCRs from their protected environment to an accessible environment following successful disclosure of SCRs for public access. Organizations should also make an effort to actively push and raise awareness about publicly disclosed information to interested parties such as historians, citizens groups, and students.

Digital preservation

As is the case for all permanent records of an organization, it is essential that SCRs are included in the digital preservation policies of international organizations, and that strategies for the long-term preservation of digital records are also applied to SCRs. These include digital preservation actions such as applying checksum functions to ensure data integrity; refreshing (copying from one digital medium to another)[56]; conversion (transforming SCRs from one format or format version to another)[57]; and migration (moving or transferring SCRs from one system to another).[58] If security encryptions or other security mechanisms have been applied to digital SCRs, corresponding decryption mechanisms should be in place to ensure that records are still accessible and legible over the long term. Digital copies and backups should be created for SCRs and kept in secure environments. Any changes to the medium, format, or systems of SCRs should still enable SCRs to maintain their authenticity, confidentiality, reliability, integrity, and usability over time, and should be included in the metadata of SCRs. The digital environment in which SCRs are stored should comply not only with IT security policies, but also with digital preservation, access, and information and records management policies.

Conclusion

In considering the management of security classified records in international organizations, the need for a flexible and multi-disciplinary approach becomes strongly apparent. In order to address the requirements for managing SCRs within an international organization, a solid understanding of the obligations facing international organizations is required. Likewise, an understanding of the different stakeholders involved in managing those records is key. This includes acquiring a common understanding of the terminology used by all professional entities involved. Any programme to manage SCRs in international organizations therefore needs to address the perspectives of different professional domains, including, but not limited to, information security professionals, records managers, lawyers, and information technologists.

The policy analysis shows that, although there are different standards and guidelines available to international organizations, there is a need to harmonize and align the available frameworks across the different professional communities to avoid overlap, compartmentalization, and conflicts of interests. For example, the security community may tend to favour immediate destruction of SCRs, while the records and archives community assesses which records to keep or destroy based on the informational value to the organization, and would hence recommend to keep the information permanently. Records managers and archivists should reach out to other professional communities to raise awareness of the strengths of the information management and recordkeeping policy framework. Furthermore, they should develop strategies to ensure that other professional communities not only understand the relevance of the records management policy and procedural framework of managing SCRs, but also the need to incorporate recordkeeping requirements into future updates and revisions of their policies and practices.

A survey of the literature clearly demonstrates the complexity of balancing the need to protect and the responsibility to share information. In particular, international organizations have competing ethical obligations, including transparency and access to information imperatives, as well as the obligation to protect classified information. To address these challenges, international organizations have institutionalized policies and procedures, specifically in the area of declassification and public disclosure, and initiated transparency projects. These projects are essential to public trust. Recordkeeping plays an important role therein, and records professionals in international organizations should leverage this role by reaching out to senior decision-makers to raise awareness of the importance of records and information management in this endeavour.

On the other hand, decision-makers at international organizations, such as national representatives of member states, should ensure the availability of sufficient and qualified resources and demand better integration and cooperation among different professional communities involved in managing classified records. They should also oversee the development and implementation of a robust policy framework to address the requirements of SCRs. This is particularly important for SCRs in a digital environment, where high volumes of records are generated and reside in a multitude of different digital repositories, and the risk of security incidents is high. The challenges posed by digital SCRs call for an even more robust governance and monitoring framework than already in place for paper records.

Appendix 8.1 Checklist for developing or revising policies for managing security classified information assets[59]

Purpose and scope

This checklist is designed to support organizations in the development or revision of policies and procedures for managing security classified records (SCRs), including digital records, to ensure the reliability, authenticity, confidentiality, integrity, and availability of security classified records and their long-term preservation. The checklist aims to support best management of SCRs throughout their lifecycle: from creation or receipt, active and controlled business uses, to the secondary uses of SCRs, including, where applicable, eventual declassification, disclosure, archiving, or destruction. While various professionals will bring their own respective issues to the table in the process of policy-making, this checklist is not intended to cover comprehensively every one of those issues. Instead, the checklist promotes a long-term approach to SCR management that especially complements information security concerns with those of records management and archival requirements. For this reason, the checklist focuses on protecting the confidentiality of SCRs and managing changes in their classification status, in addition to ensuring that information and records management best practices and procedures are applied to SCRs. It is assumed that organizations managing SCRs already have implemented a general security framework that includes required security clearances for individuals handling SCRs, broad physical and technological access controls, and other organizational security measures.

The checklist is an open tool that may be used by anyone involved in drafting or advising on policies and procedures related to the management of SCRs, for example, administrative; management; information security; information technology; legal; information and knowledge management; and records management or archival staff. Moreover, the checklist is applicable to many different types of organizations that create and handle SCRs, including inter- and non-governmental, governmental, public, and private organizations. The checklist will be especially relevant in the development of policies and procedures that focus on SCRs and their management. In addition, the tool may be useful when developing other types of policies and procedures that impact SCRs, such as declassification, access, and digital preservation policies. The term "policy" is used throughout the checklist to refer potentially to multiple policies and procedures within an organization that address the issues in question. The checklist uses terminology from the InterPARES Trust Terminology Database, and key terms used are defined below. In addition, a minimum set of descriptive metadata for managing and preserving security classified information assets is proposed in Appendix 8.2, and categories of roles and responsibilities are provided in Appendix 8.3.

Background

The checklist is developed from a study of existing policies of 16 international organizations, ranging from large international organizations within the United Nations (UN) structure, to smaller regional organizations in both North America and Europe. The organizations cover a wide range of functions, from humanitarian assistance, development and financial agents, to security organizations and research organizations.

In addition to policies dealing specifically with SCRs, the texts analysed for this checklist include policies for access to information, organizational security, data privacy, and digital preservation. The policies addressed a range of information management issues, such as control and handling, storage and transmission, data privacy, classification and declassification, and public access.

Definitions

Declassification	The process of removing the security classification from a record.
Declassification authority	The person(s) or body(ies) with the authority to declassify a record.
Disclosure	Policies and procedures related to the release of organizational records to parties external to an organization.
Disposition	Records' final destruction or transfer to an archives as determined by their appraisal.[60]
Internal disclosure	Policies and procedures related to the release of organizational records to parties within an organization.
Public disclosure	The process of making a record available to the public.
Reclassification	The process of decreasing or downgrading, or increasing the security classification level of a record.
Reclassification authority	The person(s) or body(ies) with the authority to reclassify a record.
Record	A document made or received in the course of a practical activity as an instrument or a by-product of such activity, and set aside for action or reference.[61]
Security classification authority	The person(s) or body(ies) with the authority to determine the security classification of a record.
Security classification	1. The process of applying designated levels of access control and protection on a record in compliance with organizational policy, including corresponding measures for management and control of the record, based on a security assessment of the degree of negative impact that disclosure of the record would have on the security and interests of an organization, the work of an organization, and/or third parties. 2. The term may also refer to the security classification levels themselves, which vary across organizations, for example Restricted, Confidential, etc.
Security classified record (SCR)	Information, data, documents, or records created or received by an organization or person in any format that is security classified and therefore controlled/managed through specific policies and procedures. In the checklist, we use the abbreviation SCR.
Sensitive but unclassified record (SUR)	A record without a security classification, to which access is controlled due to the risk that disclosure could harm individual, management, political, or commercial interests of the organization or other relevant parties. The policies and procedures for managing SURs are controlled but may be distinct from those policies and procedures governing the management of security classified information records (SCRs).
Withheld date	The date that an SCR considered for downgrading, declassification, or public disclosure is not downgraded, declassified, and/or publicly disclosed.

TABLE 8.1 Checklist for developing or revising policies for managing security classified records (SCRs)

	Question	Y	N	N/A[62]	Notes[63]
1	**Scope and Definition**				
1.a	Does the scope of the policy address the rationale for classifying records not only to protect the organization itself, but also more broadly to protect the work of the organization and third parties for which the organization is accountable, according to its mission and core activities (e.g., case file subjects, programme beneficiaries)?				
1.b	Does the policy provide a clear definition of the records that it covers? For example, does the policy cover SCRs that are created or received by the organization, and in any format?				
1.c	Does the policy specify the stages in the record's lifecycle that are covered, and, if applicable, does it make reference to other relevant policies that cover specific lifecycle stages and/or procedures (such as classification, declassification, reclassification, and public access)?				
1.d	Does the policy enable security classifications to be applied to a single record, a group of records, and a cluster of record groups (e.g., a database)?				
1.f	Does the policy apply retroactively to SCRs that were classified prior to the development of the policy?				
1.g	Does the policy specify the individuals who are subject to the policy (e.g., all personnel who come into contact with SCRs, regardless of their contractual status)?				
2	**Roles and Responsibilities**				
2.a	Are the roles and responsibilities of the parties involved in various aspects of managing the SCRs throughout their lifecycle clearly identified and defined? See Appendix 8.2 for an example of categories of roles and responsibilities.				
2.b	Are the roles and responsibilities of various organizational units that are responsible for different aspects of SCR management (e.g., IT, human resources, security, legal, archives and records management) clearly defined?				

	Question	Y	N	N/A[62]	Notes[63]
2.c.	Is there an information security coordinator within the organization responsible for addressing questions related to SCRs for each phase of the lifecycle?				
2.d	Have all concerned employees (as records creators or users) been informed and trained in order to ensure that they fully understand the SCR policies in place and can confidently perform their own part within the overall framework of roles and responsibilities?				
3	**Creation**				
3.a	Are the levels of information security classifications and the criteria for applying them clearly defined and distinguished?				
3.b	Does the policy specify whether a distinction is made between Unclassified versus Public records?				
3.c	Are guidelines in place to help staff avoid over- or under-classification? For example, is a list of records categories (e.g., intelligence analyses, political analyses, etc.) and the rationale for classifying records categories provided?[64]				
4	**Records Management**				
4.a	In addition to a security framework,[65] are SCRs placed within an information or records management framework? For example, are the organization's information and records management tools applicable to SCRs, such as file classification schemes and records retention and disposition schedules; and are SCRs contextualized within a records lifecycle?				
4.b	Does the policy clearly indicate that the rationale for disposition of an SCR should be based on an assessment of the value of the SCR and/or the procedures defined in the records retention schedule, rather than on the security of the classification?				
5	**Handling and Control**				
5.a	Does the policy establish a link between registration metadata in a classified information register and the SCRs themselves?				
5.b	Does the policy ensure identification and retrieval of SCRs throughout their lifecycle through metadata, marking, registration, transmission, storage, and access procedures?				

(continued)

TABLE 8.1 *Continued*

	Question	Y	N	N/A[62]	Notes[63]
5.c	Does the policy address the security classification of systems that hold or convey classified records, for example registries or electronic records management systems?				
5.d	Does the policy specify whether different rules exist for external versus internal dissemination of classified information?				
5.e	Does the policy provide guidelines for access to/consultation of classified information during its active life?				
6	**Metadata**				
6.a	Does the policy provide sufficient provisions for the preservation of descriptive and technical metadata, including metadata related to security classifications?				
6.b	Does the policy establish a minimum set of metadata for SCRs? See Appendix 8.3 for a recommended minimum set of metadata.				
6.c	Does the policy establish provisions for the retention of audit trail records throughout the lifecycle of SCRs?				
6.d	Does the policy distinguish between the security classification of the content versus the metadata of SCRs? For example, does the policy consider whether certain kinds of metadata, but not all metadata of SCRs should also be classified?				
7	**Information Security**[66]				
7.a	Does the policy address physical security requirements of SCRs such as storage area, personnel, and equipment?				
7.b	Does the policy clearly state that the physical security of classified records should extend to classified records stored in electronic media?				
7.c	Does the policy clearly state that information security requirements should comply with the general security and personnel security policies of the organization?				

Question	Y	N	N/A[62]	Notes[63]
7.d	Does the policy establish controls and procedures to ensure integrity and mitigate against corruption or tampering of SCRs, including in automated systems, during internal and external transmission and in storage?				
7.e	Does the policy address the protection of systems that hold or convey classified information, for example registries or electronic records management systems, through procedures such as security audits?				
8	**Digital Records and Long-Term Preservation**				
8.a	Is the policy applicable to all formats and media, including audiovisual and digital formats?				
8.b	If the policy requires or enables security encryption or other security mechanisms for digital data, are there provisions for long-term access and preservation of the SCRs by maintaining corresponding decryption mechanisms over time?				
8.c	Does the policy cover SCRs not in the physical custody of the organization, but still under the control of the organization, for example SCRs managed using third-party cloud computing services?				
8.d	Does the policy acknowledge changes resulting from the process of copying SCRs from one digital medium to another?[67]				
8.e	Does the policy acknowledge changes resulting from the process of transforming SCRs from one format or format version to another?[68]				
8.f	Does the policy acknowledge changes resulting from the process of moving or transferring SCRs from one system to another?[69]				
8.g	Does the policy cover changes to systems handling SCRs resulting from routine system updates or upgrades?				
8.h	Does the policy address the acknowledged changes to the medium, format, or systems of SCRs with mechanisms that ensure SCRs maintain their authenticity, confidentiality, reliability, integrity, and usability over time?				

(continued)

TABLE 8.1 *Continued*

Question	Y	N	N/A[62]	Notes[63]
8.i	Does the policy ensure that any contractual services engaged by the organization that impact SCRs enable users to be compliant with the policy?				
9	**Reclassification and Declassification**				
9.a	Are the criteria, timeframe, and method for reclassification and declassification of SCRs clearly indicated?				
9.b	Are there both systematic and ad hoc declassification procedures in place to ensure that records are effectively declassified?				
9.c	If your organization distinguishes between declassification and public access, then does the policy reflect that?				
9.d	Is there a systematic process for downgrading and declassification of SCRs after a certain lapse of time?				
9.e	Is there a process to update the access permissions to SCRs following reclassification or declassification of SCRs?				
9.f	Does the policy specify whether an appeals process is in place for unsuccessful downgrading or declassification requests, with clearly defined roles?				
10	**Public Access and Disclosure**				
10.a	Is there a systematic process for public disclosure of SCRs after a certain lapse of time, to ensure that the majority of records do not remain security classified indefinitely?				
10.b	Are the criteria, timeframe, and method for public disclosure clearly indicated?				
10.c	Is there a process to update the public access permissions to SCRs following the disclosure of the SCRs?				
10.d	Is there a process to transfer the SCRs from the protected environment to a more accessible environment following successful disclosure of SCRs for public access?				

Appendix 8.2 Minimum descriptive metadata for managing and preserving security classified records

1   Security classification
2   Classification authority
3   Eligible date for downgrading and declassification
4   Reclassification/declassification date
5   Reclassification/declassification authority
6   Eligible date for public disclosure
7   Public disclosure date
8   Public disclosure authority
9   Withheld date (if applicable)
10 Reasons for withholding (if applicable)
11 Audit trail of persons who accessed the information/document
12 Version history

Appendix 8.3 Categories of roles and responsibilities for managing security classified records

Each of the roles outlined below represents general descriptive designations (e.g., information security coordinators, etc.) related to their functions, and not necessarily their real position titles, which will vary across organizations. Additionally, within organizations there may be more than one person fulfilling a role or fulfilling specific aspects of a role.

Senior management

- Are responsible for the protection of SCRs within the organization. This includes SCRs gathered or generated by the organization, as well as those received from member parties in the case of international organizations;
- Appoints the organization's information security coordinator(s) or ISC(s);
- Approves the organization's procedures and information security classification levels;
- Acts as the final authority on the application of information security classification levels for their area of functional responsibility, in consultation with the ISC(s), in cases of disagreement or uncertainty among staff;
- Coordinates regulatory compliance in the management of SCRs;
- Approves, on a case-by-case basis, any exceptions to this procedure.

Information security coordinator(s) (ISCs)

- ISCs are responsible for all institution-wide information security issues and provide guidance regarding information asset classification and protection. Specific duties of ISCs include, but are not limited to:

- Ensure effective controls for the protection of classified information assets are implemented – technically as well as administratively;
- Support qualified staff and originators (if possible) in determining the level of classification of an information asset;
- Maintain the organization's information security policy;
- Provide assistance for the protection of classified information assets.

Information asset originators

- Classification decisions should be made by staff with knowledge of the contents of the information asset and the classification criteria. In most cases this will be the originator of the information asset.
- The originator is the staff member who creates an information asset (such as a document). This staff member is thus the first person within the institution to encounter the information asset and to determine the proper classification. For example, a staff member drafting a document should make a determination of the classification level based upon its content and the classification criteria.
- In case of uncertainty about the classification level, the responsible supervisor in the hierarchy should be consulted.

Initial classifiers

- The majority of the time the initial classifier is the information asset originator. However, in the situation where the organization receives the information asset, and therefore is not the originator, the receiver within the institution is the initial classifier and must make the classification determination based on the institution's classification definitions.
- The initial classifier could be a staff member receiving information directly from a member party, or could be the archives and records management unit as the initial recipient of official information received.

Information asset stewards

- The institution is the owner of all information assets that are created by its staff. The organization is responsible for ensuring an asset's confidentiality, authenticity, reliability, integrity, and availability.
- The information asset steward (hereinafter referred to as steward) is responsible for the classification and proper handling of the information assets.
- The originator of the SCR may in some cases also be the designated steward. However, in most cases, stewardship is vested in the supervisor of the administrative unit in which the information asset originates.

Authorized derivative classifiers

- In the case of a question or difference of opinion regarding the security classification of an information asset, the authorized derivative classifier is a staff member who is authorized and certified to determine the security classification of an information asset, over and above the decisions of the initial classifier and information asset steward.

- The authorized derivative classifier bases their information security classification assessments on defined organizational guidance and policies.

Declassification and reclassification authorities

- Declassification and reclassification authorities are the issuers of authorized declassification and/or reclassification decisions resulting from the proper enactment of declassification/reclassification policies and procedures of the organization.
- In many cases there will be several parties involved in declassification/reclassification decisions and procedures, such as designated staff members, committee members, and/or member state parties.
- Declassification and reclassification authorities are distinct from any of these roles in that they are authorized to issue the final declassification decision on behalf of the organization. In some cases they may be a committee of representatives rather than a single person or staff member, or they may be a combination of a committee and one or several designated staff members.
- In many organizations, the original classifier may also act as a declassification and reclassification authority.

Users of information assets

- Users of information assets must protect the information asset in accordance with the requirements outlined in organizational policies governing SCRs. This includes the security requirements for handling, storing, marking, protection from unauthorized or incidental viewing, and for reporting security incidents to the ISC.
- Before sharing SCRs with another staff member, the user is responsible for ensuring the recipient is authorized to receive such information and is aware of the protection requirements.
- It is also the responsibility of the users of SCRs to bring to the attention of their supervisors, and the ISC, situations where information is not being adequately protected or where the current procedures do not provide sufficient or consistent guidance.
- Each user is encouraged to raise issues on appropriateness of classification if he or she believes the SCR is not correctly classified.

Records custodians

- The records custodian is a staff member or an organizational unit that has been assigned the responsibility for safekeeping of records, such as recordkeeping and information management staff/units, and information technology staff who have technical responsibility for supporting systems in which SCRs are managed. All records custodians are responsible for complying with relevant records policies.

- This might happen on a temporary or permanent basis. The custodian must ensure that the record is protected in accordance with the requirements set in the relevant policies governing the management of SCRs.

Notes

1 The authors gratefully acknowledge Marie Shockley, Shadrack Katuu, and Julia Kastenhofer for their contributions as part of the research team for the InterPARES Trust study *TR03, Security Classification of Records in the Cloud in International Organizations*, from which Appendixes 8.1, 8.2, and 8.3 of this book are reproduced (with some additions to Appendix 8.1). The chapter is developed on the basis of this study and this work. See Ineke Deserno et al., 2017a, 'TR03 Checklist for developing or revising policies for managing security classified information assets', InterPARES Trust, viewed 13 February 2020, https://interparestrust.org/assets/public/dissemination/TR03-Check list-2-final.pdf; Ineke Deserno et al., 2017b, 'TR03 Security classification of records in the cloud in international organizations: an annotated bibliography', viewed 13 February 2020, https://interparestrust.org/assets/public/dissemination/TR03_20170508_Secur ityClassification_AnnotatedBibliography.pdf; Ineke Deserno et al., 2018, 'TR03 Security classification of records in the cloud in international organizations: a literature review', viewed 13 February 2020, https://interparestrust.org/assets/public/dissemination/ TR03LitReview_SkeletonDraft_24Nov2017v6.pdf.
2 The author is responsible for the choice and the presentation of the facts contained in the publication and for the opinions expressed therein, which are not necessarily those of NATO and do not commit the Organization.
3 The author is responsible for the choice and the presentation of the facts contained in the publication and for the opinions expressed therein, which are not necessarily those of UNESCO and do not commit the Organization.
4 In this chapter, we use the term "security classified records" or "classified records" to refer to all security classified documents or information assets, in any form. From time to time, we may use the term "classified information," which, in this context, is interchangeable with "security classified records" or "classified records." This is in recognition of the fact that (a) particularly in the digital era, the definition of "record" has expanded to include many foreseen and unforeseen forms of permanent records – our use of the word "records" is intended to encompass all these possible forms, including information and data; and (b) most policies on security classified records refer to "information" rather than "records," emphasizing the content rather than the form of classified documents; our use of the word "record" encompasses "information" to acknowledge this.
5 The Checklist for Developing or Revising Policies for Managing Security Classified Records (Appendix 8.1), Minimum Descriptive Metadata for Managing and Preserving Security Classified Records (Appendix 8.2), and Categories of Roles and Responsibilities for Managing Security Classified Records (Appendix 8.3) are reproduced, with some modifications to the Checklist, from: Deserno et al., 2017a.
6 See Deserno et al., 2017a; Deserno et al., 2017b; Deserno et al., 2018.
7 Steven Aftergood, 2013, 'An inquiry into the dynamics of government secrecy', *Harvard Civil Rights-Civil Liberties Law Review*, vol. 48, no. 2, pp. 511–530.
8 Todd B Hooten, 2011, 'How many ways can "classified" be said?', paper presented at *inForum*, Darwin, viewed 15 February 2020, www.yumpu.com/en/document/read/ 43129640/how-many-ways-can-classified-be-said-records-and-information-.
9 Steven Aftergood, 2000, 'Secrecy is back in fashion', *Bulletin of the Atomic Scientists*, viewed 13 February 2020, https://doi.org/10.2968/056006009, pp. 25–26.

10 International Organization for Standardization, 2013b, *ISO/IEC 27002:2013 Information technology – Security techniques – Code of practice for information security controls*, International Organization for Standardization, Geneva, p. 16.

11 Ibid.

12 Herbert Lin, 2014, 'A proposal to reduce government overclassification of information related to national security', *Journal of National Security Law and Policy*, vol. 7, p. 444.

13 Steven Aftergood, 2002, 'Making sense of government information restrictions', *Issues in Science and Technology*, vol. 18, no. 4, p. 26.

14 Ibid; Hooten, 2011; Michael Leyzorek, 1998, 'A missing feature in some records management systems', *Information Management*, no. 32, vol. 4, pp. 46–48; Harold C Relyea & Library of Congress Congressional Research Service, 2008, *Security classified and controlled information: history, status, and emerging management issues*, viewed 15 February 2020, http s://fas.org/sgp/crs/secrecy/RL33494.pdf.

15 International Organization for Standardization, 2013a, *ISO/IEC 27001:2013 Information technology – Security techniques – Information security management systems – Requirements*, International Organization for Standardization, Geneva, p. v.

16 Ibid.

17 Ibid, p. 14.

18 See article A.6.1.2, International Standards Organization, 2013a, p. 10.

19 Ibid, p. 11.

20 John M Weaver, 2017, 'Security of classified information: one standard or many?', *International Journal of Public Leadership*, vol. 13, no. 1, p. 10.

21 International Organization for Standardization, 2013b, pp. 4, 5.

22 Ibid, p. 4.

23 See Appendix 8.3 for an example of Categories of Roles and Responsibilities.

24 Kaija E Schilde, 2015, 'Cosmic top secret Europe? The legacy of North Atlantic Treaty Organization and Cold War U.S. policy on European Union information policy', *European Security*, vol. 24, no. 2, pp. 167–182.

25 Weaver, 2017, pp. 9–12.

26 Schilde, 2015, p. 168.

27 Weaver, 2017, pp. 10–11; International Organization for Standardization, 2013a, p. 3.

28 Steven Aftergood, 2008, 'If in doubt, classify', *Index on Censorship*, vol. 37, no. 4, p. 103; Relyea & Library of Congress Washington DC Congressional Research Service, 2008, p. 26.

29 Aftergood, 2008, p. 103.

30 See Appendix 8.1 for a suggested set of minimum metadata.

31 Jorge T Flores Callejas & Petru Dumitriu, 2019, *Managing cloud computing services in the United Nations system*, report JIU/REP/2019/5, United Nations Joint Inspection Unit, p. 23.

32 For more on cloud computing contract terms, see Jessica Bushey, Marie Demoulin & Robert McLelland, 2015, 'Cloud service contracts: an issue of trust', *Canadian Journal of Information and Library Science*, vol. 39, no. 2, pp. 128–153. For more on cloud computing and international organizations, see Elaine Goh & Eng Sengsavang, Chapter 3 of this volume; Darra Hofman, Chapter 4 of this volume; and Weimei Pan & Grant Mitchell, Chapter 5 of this volume.

33 Callejas & Dumitriu, 2019, p. 23.

34 David A Wallace, 1993, 'Archivists, recordkeeping, and the declassification of records: what we can learn from contemporary histories', *American Archivist*, vol. 56, p. 796.

35 J Abel, 2015, 'Do you have to keep the government's secrets? Retroactively classified documents, the first amendment, and the power to make secrets out of the public record', *University of Pennsylvania Law Review*, vol. 163, no. 4, p. 1037.

36 Julia Kastenhofer & Shadrack Katuu, 2016, 'Declassification: a clouded environment', *Archives and Records: The Journal of the Archives and Records Association*, vol. 37, no. 2, pp. 198–224.

37 Alison Hitchens, 1997, 'A call for IGO policies on public access to information', *Government Information Quarterly*, vol. 14, no. 2, p. 151, viewed 13 February 2020, doi:10.1016/S0740–624X(97)90016.

38 Nicholas Roche, 2015, 'From top secret to publicly disclosed: engaging with NATO's declassified records', *Comma*, vol. 2015, no. 2, p. 55, viewed 15 February 2020, https://doi.org/10.3828/comma.2015.2.8.

39 Charles Eckman, 2005, 'Information classification and access policies at selected IGOs', *DttP, Documents to the People*, vol. 33, no. 2, pp. 23–25; Alison Hitchens, 1997; Alistair S Roberts, 2003, 'NATO, secrecy, and the right to information', *East European Constitutional Review*, vols. 11/12, nos. 4/1, Fall 2002/Winter, viewed 15 February 2020, https://ssrn.com/abstract=1366082.

40 Eckman, 2005, p. 1.

41 Gustavo Castaner, 2014, 'Description of archival holdings of the International Monetary Fund and the project to make descriptions available online', viewed 26 March 2020, www.pokarh-mb.si/uploaded/datoteke/radenci2014/26_castaner_2014.pdf.

42 Roche, 2015, p. 57.

43 Castaner, 2014; Roche, 2015.

44 Roche, 2015.

45 Roberts, 2003, p. 92.

46 Peter Jagnal, quoted in Hitchens, 1997, p. 145.

47 Robert Williams, quoted in Hitchens, 1997, p. 148.

48 Hitchens, 1997, p. 151.

49 Castaner, 2014, pp. 312–314.

50 Castaner, 2014.

51 Eckman, 2005, p. 1.

52 Relyea, 2008; Gill Bennett, 2002, 'Declassification and release policies of the UK's intelligence agencies', *Intelligence and National Security*, vol. 17, no. 1, pp. 21–32; Kevin R Kosar & Library of Congress Congressional Research Service, 2010, *Classified information policy and executive order 13526*, viewed 16 February 2020, https://fas.org/sgp/crs/secrecy/R41528.pdf.

53 Hitchens, 1997, p. 149.

54 Hitchens, 1997, p. 148.

55 Ibid.

56 Also known as "refreshing." See InterPARES 3 Project, n.d., 'Refreshing', *The InterPARES Project International Terminology Database*, online database, viewed 16 February 2020, http://interpares.org/ip3/ip3_terminology_db.cfm?letter=r&term=513.

57 Also known as "conversion." See InterPARES 3 Project, n.d., 'Conversion', *The InterPARES Project International Terminology Database*, online database, viewed 16 February 2020, http://interpares.org/ip3/ip3_terminology_db.cfm?letter=r&term=194.

58 Also known as "migration." See InterPARES 3 Project, n.d., 'Migration', *The InterPARES Project International Terminology Database*, online database, viewed 16 February 2020, http://interpares.org/ip3/ip3_terminology_db.cfm?letter=r&term=501.

59 This checklist and the accompanying Appendixes 8.2 and 8.3 are updated from the original and were developed in the framework of an InterPARES Trust project. See Deserno et al., 2017a.

60 See InterPARES 3 Project, n.d., 'Disposition', *The InterPARES Project International Terminology Database*, online database, viewed 16 February 2020, http://arstweb.clayton.edu/interlex/term.php?term=disposition.

61 See InterPARES 3 Project, n.d., 'Record', *The InterPARES Project International Terminology Database*, online database, viewed 16 February 2020, www.interpares.org/ip3/ip3_terminology_db.cfm?letter=r&term=41.

62 The "N/A" column means "not applicable" or "not known."

63 Use this column for notes, or when there is neither a "yes" nor "no" answer.

64 If the answer is no, consider creating such a list or providing examples of records categories and corresponding security classifications to guide users of the policy.

65 "Framework" refers to the entirety of documents, procedures, and processes that support a given function.

66 The information security standard consulted for this checklist is the ISO 27001:2013 and ISO 27002:2013.
67 Also known as "refreshing." See InterPARES 3 Project, n.d., 'Refreshing', *The Inter-PARES Project International Terminology Database*, online database, viewed 16 February 2020, http://interpares.org/ip3/ip3_terminology_db.cfm?letter=r&term=513.
68 Also known as "conversion." See InterPARES 3 Project, n.d., 'Conversion', *The Inter-PARES Project International Terminology Database*, online database, viewed 16 February 2020, http://interpares.org/ip3/ip3_terminology_db.cfm?letter=r&term=194.
69 Also known as "migration." See InterPARES 3 Project, n.d., 'Migration', *The Inter-PARES Project International Terminology Database*, online database, viewed 16 February 2020, http://interpares.org/ip3/ip3_terminology_db.cfm?letter=r&term=501.

Bibliography

Abel, J 2015, 'Do you have to keep the government's secrets? Retroactively classified documents, the First Amendment, and the power to make secrets out of the public record', *University of Pennsylvania Law Review*, vol. 163, no. 4, p. 1037.

Aftergood, S 2000, 'Secrecy is back in fashion', *Bulletin of the Atomic Scientists*, pp. 24–30, viewed 13 February 2020, https://doi.org/10.2968/056006009.

Aftergood, S 2002, 'Making sense of government information restrictions', *Issues in Science and Technology*, vol. 18, no. 4, pp. 25–26.

Aftergood, S 2008, 'If in doubt, classify', *Index on Censorship*, vol. 37, no. 4, pp. 101–107.

Aftergood, S 2010, 'National security secrecy: how the limits change', *Social Research* vol. 77, no. 3, pp. 839–852.

Aftergood, S 2013, 'An inquiry into the dynamics of government secrecy', *Harvard Civil Rights-Civil Liberties Law Review*, vol. 48, no. 2, p. 511.

Bennett, G 2002, 'Declassification and release policies of the UK's intelligence agencies', *Intelligence and National Security*, vol. 17, no. 1, pp. 21–32.

Bushey, Jessica, Demoulin, Marie & McLelland, Robert 2015, 'Cloud service contracts: an issue of trust', *Canadian Journal of Information and Library Science*, vol. 39, no. 2, pp. 128–153.

Castaner, G 2014, 'Description of archival holdings of the International Monetary Fund and the project to make descriptions available online', viewed 26 March 2020, www.poka rh-mb.si/uploaded/datoteke/radenci2014/26_castaner_2014.pdf.

Callejas, JT Flores & Dumitriu, P 2019, *Managing cloud computing services in the United Nations system*, report JIU/REP/2019/5, United Nations Joint Inspection Unit.

Deserno, I, Sengsavang, E, Shockley, M, Katuu, S & Kastenhofer, J 2017a, 'TR03 Checklist for developing or revising policies for managing security classified information assets,' InterPARES Trust, viewed 13 February 2020, https://interparestrust.org/assets/public/dissemination/TR03-Checklist-2-final.pdf.

Deserno, I, Sengsavang, E, Shockley, M, Katuu, S & Kastenhofer, J 2017b, 'TR03 Security classification of records in the cloud in international organizations: an annotated bibliography,' InterPARES Trust, viewed 13 February 2020, https://interparestrust.org/assets/p ublic/dissemination/TR03_20170508_SecurityClassification_AnnotatedBibliography.pdf.

Deserno, I, Sengsavang, E, Shockley, M, Katuu, S & Kastenhofer, J 2018, 'TR03 Security classification of records in the cloud in international organizations: a literature review,' viewed 13 February 2020, https://interparestrust.org/assets/public/dissemination/TR03LitReview_SkeletonDraft_24Nov2017v6.pdf.

Eckman, C 2005, 'Information classification and access policies at selected IGOs', *DttP, Documents to the People*, vol. 33, no. 2, pp. 23–25.

Hitchens, A 1997, 'A call for IGO policies on public access to information', *Government Information Quarterly*, vol. 14, no. 2, pp. 143–154, viewed 13 February 2020, doi:10.1016/S0740-624X(97)90016.

Hooten, TB 2011, '*How many ways can 'classified' be said?*', paper presented at inForum, Darwin, viewed 15 February 2020, www.yumpu.com/en/document/read/43129640/how-many-ways-can-classified-be-said-records-and-information-.

International Organization for Standardization 2013a, *ISO/IEC 27001:2013 Information technology – Security techniques – Information security management systems – Requirements*, International Organization for Standardization, Geneva.

International Organization for Standardization 2013b, *ISO/IEC 27002:2013 Information technology – Security techniques – Code of practice for information security controls. Geneva, International Standards Organization*, International Organization for Standardization, Geneva.

InterPARES 3 Project n.d., *The InterPARES Project International Terminology Database*, online database, viewed 16 February 2020, www.interpares.org/ip3/ip3_terminology_db.cfm.

Kastenhofer, J & Katuu S 2016, 'Declassification: a clouded environment', *Archives and Records: The Journal of the Archives and Records Association*, vol. 37, no. 2, pp. 198–224.

Kosar, KR & Library of Congress Congressional Research Service 2010, *Classified information policy and executive order 13526*, viewed 16 February 2020, https://fas.org/sgp/crs/secrecy/R41528.pdf.

Leyzorek, Michael 1998, 'A missing feature in some records management systems', *Information Management*, no. 32, vol. 4, pp. 46–48.

Lin, H 2014, 'A proposal to reduce government overclassification of information related to national security', *Journal of National Security Law and Policy*, vol. 7, pp. 443–463.

Relyea, HC & Library of Congress Congressional Research Service 2008, *Security classified and controlled information: history, status, and emerging management issues*, viewed 15 February 2020, https://fas.org/sgp/crs/secrecy/RL33494.pdf.

Roberts, AS 2003, 'NATO, secrecy, and the right to information', *East European Constitutional Review*, vols. 11/12, nos. 4/1, Fall 2002/Winter, viewed 15 February 2020, https://ssrn.com/abstract=1366082.

Roche, N 2015, 'From top secret to publicly disclosed: engaging with NATO's declassified records', *Comma*, vol. 2015, no. 2, pp. 55–65, viewed 15 February 2020, https://doi.org/10.3828/comma.2015.2.8.

Schilde, KE 2015, 'Cosmic top secret Europe? The legacy of North Atlantic Treaty Organization and Cold War U.S. policy on European Union information policy', *European Security*, vol. 24, no. 2, pp. 167–182.

Wallace, DA 1993, 'Archivists, recordkeeping, and the declassification of records: what we can learn from contemporary histories', *American Archivist*, vol. 56, pp. 794–814.

Weaver, JM 2017, 'Security of classified information: one standard or many?', *International Journal of Public Leadership*, vol. 13, no. 1, pp. 9–12.

9

SECURITY CLASSIFICATION AND DECLASSIFICATION WITHIN INTERGOVERNMENTAL ORGANIZATIONS[1]

Shadrack Katuu[2] and Julia Kastenhofer[3]

Introduction

The management of classified information has been a subject of interest in public administration for several decades. Researchers have also explored the management of records in IGOs.[4] However, researchers have not given the management of classified records and archives of IGOs much attention. This chapter will provide an overview of the complexities of security classification and declassification in IGOs by analysing classification categories and declassification procedures. Different facets surrounding security classified information will be discussed, including the consequences of perceptions of secrecy, the practicalities of declassification procedures, and the procedural background necessary for an effective implementation.

IGOs are "entities created with sufficient organizational structure and autonomy to provide formal, ongoing, multilateral processes of decision-making between states, along with the capacity to execute the collective will of their member states."[5] This definition demonstrates the process of interactions within IGOs as well as the possibility of collective outcomes from them.[6] In order to distinguish them from other types of international organizations, IGOs must be established by an international agreement; must have their own separate organs; and must be established by international law.[7] Therefore, IGOs address issues or challenges that transcend national borders, while possessing their own international legal personality.[8] For an IGO, possessing its own legal personality means having an identity that is separate from its members.

Volgy et al. state that IGOs have attributes including "sufficient bureaucratic organization to assure some stability of management," as well as "autonomy in organizational operation and in the execution of the collective will of the membership."[9] Armed with these attributes, IGOs can exercise certain powers as well as enjoy certain rights and privileges.[10] According to Abass, IGOs possess four types of privileges and immunities: "jurisdictional immunity, inviolability of premises and archives, freedom of communication, and immunity relating to financial matters."[11] Issues of classification and declassification of records most closely relate to one of these categories of privileges and immunities: inviolability of premises and archives.

Researchers see inviolability of premises and archives as enabling "privacy and the preservation of secrecy," which is at the foundation of the independence of IGOs and which is required for the fulfilment of their purpose.[12] The inviolability of archives covers all the institution's records, at two levels, at least. In the first instance, inviolability relates to the fact that some national legislation and regulations – such as those related to access to information, data protection, and record-keeping – do not directly apply to the institution. In the second instance, since IGOs maintain their own legal personality, they must develop their own policies and procedures to address the challenges that they face in information classification and declassification. These two aspects demonstrate the need for researchers to understand IGOs in a nuanced manner.[13]

This chapter is closely aligned with Chapter 8 but has a different focus. Chapter 8 is one of the outcomes of a study of security classification of records in international organizations conducted between 2014 and 2018[14] under the auspices of the Inter-PARES Trust Project within the Transnational Team. The study entailed, on the one hand, a review of literature on security classification of records, and on the other hand, a review of policies and procedures of IGOs and other international organizations that relate to security classified information.[15] While Chapter 8 is the synthesis of the research conducted within InterPARES Trust, this chapter focuses specifically on security classification approaches used by IGOs and delves into declassification, which the authors define as the process of removing security classifications.

Purpose of declassification in the context of security classification

Security classification is a formative action with declassification as a process carried out at the end of the record's sensitivity lifecycle (RSL).[16] It is the process by which an institution's employees assess the potential record's content and the context of its creation, and – using formal or informal procedures – determine and place a record within a certain security category depending on the risk of harm to that institution, the individual, or the member state of the institution.[17]

The purpose of security classification is to increase protection of the organization through the restriction of access to information. This is based on the "harm that could result from disclosure, including its level of seriousness and degree of likelihood."[18] The premise of the RSL is that, at the point at which the record is created, if the content or context of the record is sensitive, the record is classified at the level appropriate for the perceived threat and is protected at the requisite level.[19] For this reason, security classification is contingent on the context of classification. If the reason for classifying at a requisite level no longer applies, IGOs need to revisit the classification status to reduce over-classification of information.

Therefore, once a record has a security classification, there should be an expectation that at some point in the future, the security level will change or be removed entirely. For this reason, the record needs to undergo a declassification process, which entails the removal of restrictions from a record based on the premise that the information is no longer sensitive.[20] By this description, declassification is the process of removing security classifications from records based on the assumption that the situation that warranted the initial security classification no longer applies.[21] For an IGO to effectively declassify a record, the institution needs to draw and follow clearly defined procedures.

The reason that information is security classified has a direct impact on how it can be declassified at a later stage. If the reasoning behind the security classification is unknown by the individual that conducts declassification, the steps to be undertaken are much harder, because the thinking behind the classification action can only be presumed. In essence, security classification relies on the motivation for some amount of secrecy. Aftergood states that there are at least three categories of secrecy: genuine national security secrecy, political secrecy, and bureaucratic secrecy.[22] Additionally, Aftergood defines genuine secrecy as "that body of information which, if disclosed, could actually damage national security in some identifiable way."[23]

Since IGOs serve the needs of their membership, they are also obliged to keep some of the information they receive from their members secret. This may include, for example, "design details for weapons of mass destruction and other advanced military technologies, as well as those types of information that must remain secret in order for authorised diplomatic and intelligence functions to be performed."[24] The security of this kind of information is the basis for a secrecy system in the first place, and when it is working properly, this system positively serves the public interest. National security is the most common example of genuine secrecy; however, other categories also warrant secrecy of information – including international relations, ongoing investigations, information provided in confidence, the legal environment, personal information, and policy advice.[25]

The second kind of secrecy is political, which is "the deliberate and conscious abuse of classification authority for political advantage, irrespective of any threat to national security."[26] Even though IGOs are supposed to have autonomy, they tend to feel a certain amount of political pressure.[27] For instance, Annis reports that even though the World Bank touted itself as a knowledge-based institution, its information system remained closed to the outside on the grounds that it had to protect the confidentiality of its discussions with borrowers.[28]

Aftergood suggests that the third kind of secrecy may be the most nebulous and difficult to address.[29] Bureaucratic secrecy is "the tendency of all organizations to limit the information that they release to outsiders so as to control perceptions of the organization."[30] This type of secrecy appears to be the "predominant factor in current classification practice, accounting for the majority of the billions of pages of classified records throughout the government."[31] These categories of secrecy are evident in security classification activities in varied institutions, including IGOs.

However, what makes IGOs unique is the global nature of the institutions, combined with the peculiarity in their individual security classification schemes.

If the reason for classification is made clear during the classification process and documented, such as a specific event that warranted the decision, the declassification decision-making will be facilitated through this contextual metadata.

Security classification in IGOs

Security classification in IGOs has evolved within IGOs in the decades after the Second World War. For instance, Roberts traces the way in which the security classification and handling procedures of NATO evolved from the 1950s to the early 2000s.[32] He argues that inter-governmental collaboration does not lead to greater transparency of information to non-governmental actors.[33]

The Open Society Foundation states that in order to reduce arbitrariness when dealing with classification, it is good practice to institute a formal system of classification.[34] A fundamental pillar in the formal system is structured levels of security classifications. IGOs have used these increasing levels of sensitivity – from no sensitivity to high sensitivity – to warrant different handling procedures for information assets, which should be commensurate with the classification levels with which they are paired.[35] Table 9.1 provides a small sample of the classification levels and the classification titles that a select number of IGOs use to characterize security.[36]

Table 9.1 illustrates that while the titles of classification levels differ considerably among different IGOs, half of them have three levels of information security. The others are Organization 1, which has two levels, and several institutions that have more than three levels, namely Organizations 2, 6, and 8. In addition, it is worth noting that several institutions have nuances even within the same security levels. For instance, Organization 3 has two varieties within the medium sensitivity level, Organization 5 has two varieties in each of its three levels, and Organization 6 has two varieties in its highest security level. Nonetheless, the common thread is the premise that each of these classification levels warrants the level of protection commensurate with the required security level, and the handling procedures tend to be more stringent the higher the sensitivity level.[37] The level of security classification applied to information also has a bearing on subsequent declassification, since the harm derived from disclosure of the information correlates to a higher security marking. The declassifier needs to determine whether information with high security markings can be declassified completely or whether it needs to be reclassified to a lower marking.

Declassification

While security classification in IGOs has been the subject of considerable discussion in the literature, researchers do not discuss declassification as frequently.[38] The only comparable discussion on declassification has tended to be from the experience of nation-states, more specifically from the experience of the U.S. federal government

TABLE 9.1 Classification levels in IGOs

Organization	No Sensitivity	Low Sensitivity	Medium Sensitivity	High Sensitivity
Organization 1	Unclassified		Confidential	
Organization 2	Unclassified	Restricted	Confidential	Top Secret
Organization 3	Public		• Confidential: Internal Use; • Confidential: Restricted Distribution Within the Organization	
Organization 4		For Official Use Only	Confidential	Strictly Confidential
Organization 5		Public	Restricted; Confidential	Secret; Under Seal
Organization 6	Unclassified	Restricted	Confidential	Secret; Top Secret
Organization 7	Unclassified		Confidential	Strictly Confidential
Organization 8	Public	Official Use Only	Confidential	Strictly Confidential

within the English-language literature. Various articles note the cost of classification compared to the scarce resources and low prioritization given to declassification projects.[39] A number of articles trace the different types of classified information and declassification procedures created under U.S. executive orders and statutes.[40] Researchers identify a need to put in place risk-based declassification reviews as the most efficient strategy to declassify information.[41]

In 2010, Kosar noted that in the U.S. federal government there was a backlog of more than 400 million pages of classified records that were 25 years old or older.[42] The situation has become even more dire in the digital age, since U.S. federal agencies create petabytes of classified information annually that quickly outpace the amount of information the government has declassified.[43] For this reason, unless there is a dramatic improvement in declassification processes, "the rate at which classified records are being created will drive an exponential growth in the archival backlog of classified records awaiting declassification."[44]

As stated earlier in this chapter, declassification is the process of removing the security classification from a record based on the assumption that the information is no longer sensitive.[45] Considering the definition of classification by ISO 27001, which includes identifying sensitive content and then appropriately labelling and handling the record, declassification should also include all three activities.[46] Therefore, declassification should entail assessing whether the content requires a lower security classification, ensuring the proper removal of classification labels, and establishing appropriate handling procedures after declassification.

At least one of the motivations that prompted IGOs to consider declassification was the consequential increase in transparency prompted by member states of IGOs. In the 1990s, there was a growing realization that IGOs not only facilitated state policy formation, but also produced information of their own accord and made decisions that affected people in the member states.[47] For this reason, researchers made efforts to access IGO information policies, assessing their transparency and accountability features.[48] In the latter half of the 1990s, several IGOs engaged in a policy review process that increased transparency mechanisms in their decision-making and subsequent documentation processes. This included developing formal access policies for their archives, where "the default classification of most information products was public" and "automatic derestriction of remaining products after a specified timeframe" was established.[49] In order to effectively declassify a record, a clearly defined procedure needs to be implemented and followed. The rest of this section provides an outline of the politics and mechanics of declassification – a declassification schema – and sketches the difference between systematic and ad hoc declassification.[50]

Understanding declassification: the politics and the mechanics

There is a distinct difference between the politics and the mechanics of declassification.[51] The latter identifies the steps and actors involved in the declassification processes. The former constitutes the reasons why information is classified in the first place and explores the legislative and administrative reasons why records should be declassified or remain classified.[52] One such reason is that systematic over-classification causes a backlog of classified records that are waiting to be declassified and overdue for declassification. Over-classification not only hinders information sharing between cooperating nations, but also does so between and within governmental bodies or even between and within the international organizations themselves.[53]

Institutions also have unique nomenclatures for security classification levels that are governed using idiosyncratic regulations across the IGO landscape. This makes any efforts at declassification more complex, and it can reduce the output of declassified material.[54] For example, in the United States, there are three types of classified information: National Security Information (NSI), Sensitive Compartmented Information (SCI), and Restricted Data (RD) or Formerly Restricted Data (FRD). Researchers define each of these based on different legislation or regulations.[55] In Canada, there are two sets of sensitive information, known as classified assets and protected assets. The compromise of both "could reasonably be expected to cause injury," as classified assets could cause injury to national interest, while protected assets could cause injury to non-national interest.[56]

These examples demonstrate the range of issues related to the politics of declassification, from the quantity of classified documents potentially eligible for declassification, to the systems that frame the declassification procedures. By contrast, discussions about the mechanics of declassification relate to the practical processes of how to declassify information. Researchers have observed the considerable impact of the politics of declassification on the mechanics of declassification, but readers should be cognisant of the juridical and administrative contexts in which those observations have been made.[57]

Declassification schema

The Public Interest Declassification Board, an advisory committee established by the United States Congress, states that declassification is "a complex and time-consuming process, typically performed in a culture of caution without much attention to efficiency and risk management."[58] For this reason, we developed six categories that provide a framework of activities that take place during the declassification process:[59]

- *Trigger*: The action that initiates the declassification; may be prompted by stimuli from within or outside the institution;
- *Identification*: The process of distinguishing the records that need to be declassified;
- *Preparation*: The process of organizing the identified records that need to be declassified; entails arranging all the intellectual and physical aids that will assist the process of decision-making;

- *Decision:* The process where a competent authority is presented with records to be declassified and must make an assessment based on predefined declassification criteria;
- *Implementation*: The process where the decision is executed;
- *Notification*: The process where the executed decision is communicated.

While each of these processes has its own challenges, the identification of declassified documents is particularly challenging. Haight argues that it is complicated, not only when identifying documents with security markings, but especially when assessing and identifying sensitive information on documents that have no markings.[60] In large bureaucracies where the identification process is carried out by more than one individual, it is necessary to ensure that there are clear and documented criteria for such security classification assessments on documents with no markings.

Review of declassification procedures

The authors conducted a further assessment on the declassification procedures of five IGOs. These IGOs are anonymized because their declassification procedures are not publicly available documents. The individual institutions shared the information with the authors on the understanding that the confidentiality of the sources would not be compromised. The first analysis determined whether organizations have systematic or ad hoc declassification procedures or both, as shown in Table 9.2.

The second analysis mapped each of the organization's procedures to the six categories of actions, as shown in Table 9.3 for systematic procedures and Table 9.4 for ad hoc procedures

Discussion

Tables 9.2, 9.3, and 9.4 demonstrate that regardless of whether an IGO has systematic or ad hoc declassification procedures or both, the declassification process follows the same six steps. All of the organizations use some form of declassification exemptions to guide their declassification decisions. Declassification exemptions are clearly defined categories of information that are not eligible for declassification during a declassification review. Exemptions differ from information categories that are eligible for declassification since they put the burden on the organization to agree on and clearly state what will not be declassified. This promotes transparency and also inhibits the urge for organizations to keep other (non-exempt) information classified in perpetuity, out of fear that the decision to declassify would expose the organization to reputational risk. Some organizations also allow new or evolving material to bypass the initial declassification exemptions, thereby showing a tendency towards openness.

TABLE 9.2 Categorization of IGO declassification procedures

Organization	Systematic procedure	Ad hoc procedure
Organization A	Triggered after 5, 10, or 20 years; screening against clearly defined exemptions to classification; consultation with the originating unit.	Eligible for records older than 20 years; review by the archives unit/section who has the authority and responsibility to declassify while consulting with the originating unit; all process steps with the archives unit/section.
Organization B	Triggered when the department transfers files to the archives unit/section as part of regular archival processing; the declassification archivist liaises with the originating units; the decision-making power lies with the units.	
Organization C		Requests are pooled by the focus point for public information; the archives unit/section receives all requests, but the decision-making power lies with the originating unit; notification of the decision is by the focal point.
Organization D	Triggered by the public official who coordinates the work on the declassification process and notifies the stakeholders; the chair of the declassification committee assigns a staff member to the declassification case; the implementation lies with the archives unit/section.	
Organization E	The archivist triggers the procedure for records over 30 years old; a declassification report is sent by the Archives Committee to decision-making authorities in the member states; the decision is based on exceptions to declassification.	Triggered by an external request; the decision-making power lies with the member states and the main stakeholders.

TABLE 9.3 Declassification categories in IGOs – systematic procedures

	Organization A	Organization B	Organization D	Organization E
Trigger	Identifying pre-defined record types according to their age	Records transfer by the organizational units	Event-based	Identifying records that are older than 30 years and have permanent historical value
Identification	Records that can be systematically declassified are pre-defined according to information category	Archives staff identify classified records of the records aggregation	Lies with the organizational unit	Same as trigger stage
Preparation	Records identified for potential declassification are checked against exemptions	Records identified for potential declassification are checked against exemptions	Records identified for potential declassification are checked against exemptions	Records identified for potential declassification are checked against exemptions
Decision	Office responsible for providing information access to the public decides	The record-creating unit decides	Declassification authority is assigned by the chair of the declassification committee	Experts in member states come to a decision
Implementation	Office responsible for providing information access to the public implements	Implemented in the archives unit/section	Implemented in the archives unit/section	Implemented in the archives unit/section
Notification	Done through website	Archives unit/section notifies	Archives unit/section notifies	Archives unit/section notifies

TABLE 9.4 Declassification categories in IGOs – ad hoc procedures

	Organization A	Organization C	Organization E
Trigger	Requests for historical records go to the archives unit/section; requests for current information go to the External Affairs Office	Requests go to the External Affairs Office	Requests go to the archives unit/section
Identification	Depends on the age of the records (archives unit/section or External Affairs Office)	Done by the External Affairs Office	Done by the archives unit/section
Preparation	Review of records older than 20 years done by the archives unit/section; records between 5 and 20 years done by the originating unit	Done by the archives unit/section by checking against the exemptions	Done by the archives unit/section by checking against the exemptions
Decision	Archives unit/section makes the decision for records over 20 years old; for younger records the record-creating unit decides	Record-creating unit decides	Experts in member states decide
Implementation	Implemented in the archives unit/section	Implemented in the archives unit/section	Implemented in the archives unit/section
Notification	Through website or – in the case of older records – by the archives unit/section	External Affairs Office notifies	Disclosure notice sent to Committee on Archival Matters

Second, and more generally, whereas systematic declassification procedures put the initiative in the hands of the organization and demonstrate a willingness towards openness, ad hoc procedures show flexibility towards user needs, which may not be served if an organization were only to follow a systematic declassification process. Ideally, an organization implements both to provide the widest cover possible regarding the managed openness of information.[61] Furthermore, the dissection of classification procedures also highlights various aspects of the mechanics of declassification: the reality of implementing declassification procedures, the success of declassification procedures, and the controls necessary for implementation.

According to Eckman, as of 2005 many IGOs did not have systematic declassification, due to budget and workload burdens associated with what had become a manual document-by-document review process.[62] For instance, one cumbersome element required for systematic declassification was "the review of metadata or registry information associated with documentary and archival sources" being information that was "frequently unavailable in electronic form" and therefore being handled in manual fashion.[63]

IGOs have published few studies about how long the process of declassification takes. The only declassification discussions in IGOs relate to the NATO system, and the discussion only tangentially addresses the mechanics of declassification.[64] Many declassification activities are internal to institutions, but the results are indirectly correlated to the number of records that are made public. However, we can learn from national institutions. Among the most common observations in the context of national institutions is that declassification activities take an inordinate amount of time.

As noted earlier, in 2010 Kosar reported that in the U.S. federal government there was a backlog of more than 400 million pages of classified records that were 25 years old or older.[65] If this backlog had to be cleared in a timely manner, declassification would have to happen at the rate of 100 million pages per year.[66] However, an even larger concern relates to information in digital form. The Public Interest Declassification Board noted estimates of the equivalent of at least 5 billion pages of digital information in need of review within the U.S. Presidential Library system.[67] Considering the vast backlog, it may be necessary to develop efficient methods of monitoring and managing all the moving parts of the review and declassification procedures.[68]

While the six categories of declassification activities are a simplification of the processes involved, each step represents a multitude of activities. Declassification is, in fact, a long process. For instance, during the trigger and identification points, staff members within an organization must prepare withdrawal notices with information about which records have been withdrawn and prepared for decision-making activities. Using just the example of hardcopy records in a box, if half the folders in that box contain classified information, the withdrawal processes will take a considerable amount of time.[69] Additionally, records could have more than one provenance, including third-party sources. This is quite common in IGOs that receive a considerable number of classified records from member states or from other IGOs. This means that decision-making processes may require contacting those third parties and receiving their clearances, significantly lengthening the process.[70]

The declassification review process produces mixed results and its success varies considerably according to the subject and timeframe of the records. Haight states, in the context of declassification in the Eisenhower Presidential Library, that popular topics such as the Eisenhower administration's nuclear weapons strategy still contain a large amount of classified material.[71] Only a small percentage of records reviewed for declassification have actually been declassified.[72] Additionally, the success of a declassification request depends on the age of the records considered for declassification – records younger than 30 years are seldom declassified – as well as the geographical area covered in the records.[73]

Declassification review procedures have also been shown to be more effective if an institution establishes both administrative and technical controls. Administrative controls constitute the governance as well as development and promulgation of operational processes and detailed guidance documents. Guidance documents include policy and procedural instructions on all the processes of managing classified information. They may also include security vetting of the staff working with classified records, which is generally more common in national institutions than in IGOs.

Technical controls are necessary to facilitate the handling of classified information by means of technological security regimes, regardless of the information medium. Technical controls include security vaults and special-purpose containers for hardcopy content and identification, cryptography, as well as accountability tools (such as audit trails) for digital content.[74] Without technical controls, the means of streamlined enforcement of declassification review procedures are more cumbersome. Without administrative controls, there is no clearly defined policy basis to implement.

Researchers can glean further insight if the discussion is situated within the wider context of access to information debates. The processes of classification and declassification are often viewed synonymously with that of providing access to records. While the provision of access to records might be an immediate consequence of declassification, this should still be an entirely separate administrative process, as it is managed regardless of whether a record has security classification or not. The only consequence of a declassification action for the record itself should be that the record will be unclassified. Researchers should treat the newly unclassified record like other unclassified records. For instance, a classified record X is 10 years old, and this record is declassified. If the organizational access policy outlines that only records older than 20 years can be accessed by external researchers, the record will remain inaccessible to external researchers for another 10 years.[75]

Another aspect relates to the extent to which an IGO values and protects its records. While declassification does not immediately affect access to records, it does affect the handling procedures of the records concerned. Depending on their security classification level, researchers treat records differently – especially with the increasing levels of intellectual and physical control over individual records. The tendency to understand classified records as being "important" or particularly valuable is therefore another potential reason for systematic over-classification, not only in national organizations, but also in international ones. This means that if a record is classified, not in order to restrict access to it for the safeguarding of persons or agendas, but to ensure that the record is better protected because of its perceived importance for the organization, then the entire concept of security classification has become misused. A security classification marking does not mean that the record is more valuable than other records. Unclassified records are as valuable as classified records.[76]

Conclusion

In this chapter, the authors discussed classification and declassification processes within the context of IGOs. The discussion has demonstrated that the issues are highly nuanced and that, at a very general level, they may follow certain patterns. For instance, an institution might have three or four levels of information security classifications, two types of declassification procedures, and six phases of declassification processes. However, these general patterns – once observed in the context of individual IGOs that have unique mandates and legal characters – may entail unique details that differ from the general patterns. The authors hope these observations constitute a useful complement to the more general analysis in Chapter 8. Both these chapters offer insights for records professionals who may otherwise not have encountered the topics during their formal education and training.[77] Therefore, further research and discussions are necessary on this rich intersection between the management of classified records and the specific context of IGOs.[78]

Notes

1 The authors wish to thank the editors and anonymous reviewers of this chapter for their constructive comments to improve the chapter. The authors gratefully acknowledge the thoughtful readings of previous iterations of the chapter paper by colleagues in IGOs who provided very helpful suggestions and shared their insights.
2 The views expressed herein are those of the author and should neither be attributed to his current employers nor to any of his previous employers.
3 The views expressed herein are those of the author and should neither be attributed to her current employer nor to any of her previous employers.
4 Charles M Dollar, 1986, 'Electronic records management and archives in international organizations: a RAMP study with guidelines', PGI-86/WS/12, UNESCO, Paris; UNESCO, 2018, Guide to archives of international organizations, viewed 26 March 2020, http://web.archive.org/web/20181224193029/http://www.unesco.org/archives/sio/Eng/; Gustavo Castaner, 2014, 'Description of archival holdings of the International Monetary Fund and the project to make descriptions available online', viewed 26 March 2020, www.pokarh-mb.si/uploaded/datoteke/radenci2014/26_castaner_2014.pdf.
5 Thomas J Volgy et al., 2008, 'Identifying formal intergovernmental organizations', *Journal of Peace Research*, vol. 45, no. 6, p. 841.
6 Ibid.

7 Sam Muller, 1995, *International organizations and their host states: aspects of their legal relationship*, Kluwer Law International, The Hague, p. 4.

8 Sander Dikker Hupkes, 2009, 'Protection and effective functioning of international organizations. Final report international institutional law, Secure Haven Project', Universiteit Leiden, viewed 28 March 2020, https://openaccess.leidenuniv.nl/handle/1887/14119.

9 Volgy et al., 2008, p. 841.

10 Eng Sengsavang et al., 2016, 'TR01: Cloud services for international organizations – An annotated bibliography,' InterPARES Trust, viewed 28 March 2020, https://interparestrust.org/assets/public/dissemination/TR_20161110_CloudComputingForInternationalOrganizations_AnnotatedBibliography_FINAL.pdf.

11 Ademola Abass, 2014, 'International organizations', in *Complete international law: text, cases and materials*, New York: Oxford University Press, p. 191.

12 Ibid, p. 99; Sengsavang et al., 2016, p. 57.

13 Shadrack Katuu, 2019a, 'Managing classified records in inter-governmental organizations', in Noelle van der Waag-Cowling & Louise Leenen, *14th International Conference on Cyber Warfare and Security*, Stellenbosch University, South Africa, Academic Conferences and Publishing International, p. 180.

14 Shockley et al., 2017, *Policies for the handling of security classified information in international organizations*, June 7–10, viewed 26 March 2020, https://interparestrust.org/assets/public/dissemination/Shockley_ACAposter.pdf; Ineke Deserno et al., 2018a, 'TR03: Security classification of records in the cloud in international organizations: an annotated bibliography,' InterPARES Trust, viewed 26 March 2020, https://interparestrust.org/assets/public/dissemination/TR03_20170508_SecurityClassification_AnnotatedBibliography.pdf.

15 Ineke Deserno et al., 2018b, 'TR03: Security classification of records in the cloud in international organizations: a literature review,' InterPARES Trust, viewed 26 March 2020, https://interparestrust.org/assets/public/dissemination/TR03LitReview_Skeleton Draft_24Nov2017v6.pdf; Ineke Deserno et al., 2017, 'TR03: Checklist for developing or revising policies for managing security classified information assets,' InterPARES Trust, viewed 26 March 2020, https://interparestrust.org/assets/public/dissemination/TR03-Checklist-2_-final.pdf.

16 Julia Kastenhofer & Shadrack Katuu, 2016, 'Declassification: a clouded environment', *Archives and Records: The Journal of the Archives and Records Association*, vol. 37, no. 2, p. 3.

17 Katuu, 2019a, p. 178.

18 Open Society Foundation, 2013, *The global principles on national security and the right to information (Tshwane Principles)*, Open Society Foundation – Open Society Justice Initiative, viewed 26 March 2020, www.opensocietyfoundations.org/sites/default/files/global-principles-national-security-10232013.pdf, p. 29.

19 Katuu, 2019a, p. 179.

20 Kastenhofer & Katuu, 2016, p. 3.

21 Ibid, p. 5.

22 Steven Aftergood, 2000, 'Secrecy is back in fashion', *Bulletin of the Atomic Scientists*, vol. 56, no. 6.

23 Ibid, p. 26.

24 Ibid.

25 Mark Glover et al., 2006, 'Freedom of information: history, experience and records and information management implications in the USA, Canada and the United Kingdom', ARMA International Educational Foundation, viewed 26 March 2020, www.global-dcc.com/documents/FreedomofInformationinUSUKandCanada-FINA.pdf.

26 Aftergood, 2000, p. 26.

27 Ted Piccone, 2012, *Catalysts for change: how the UN's independent experts promote human rights*, Brookings Institution Press, Washington DC, p. 91; Laryy Attree, Jordan Street & Luca Venchiarutti, 2018, *United Nations peace operations in complex environments*, Safeworld, p. 22.

28 Sheldon Annis, 1991 'Toward a pro-poor information agenda at the World Bank', in *Perspectives on education for all*, International Development Research Centre, Ottawa, p. 27.
29 Aftergood, 2000, p. 26.
30 Ibid.
31 Ibid.
32 Alasdair Roberts, 2003a, 'Entangling alliances: NATO's security of information policy and the entrenchment of state secrecy', *Cornell International Law Journal*, vol. 36, no. 2, pp. 333–334.
33 Ibid, p. 358; Public Interest Declassification Board, 2012, *Transforming the security classification system*, National Archives and Records Administration, viewed 26 March 2020, www.archives.gov/files/declassification/pidb/recommendations/transforming-classification.pdf.
34 Open Society Foundation, 2013, p. 29.
35 Katuu, 2019a, p. 180.
36 Ibid.
37 Roberts, 2003a, pp. 333–334; Public Interest Declassification Board, 2012, p. 9.
38 Roberts, 2003b; Deserno et al., 2018b, pp. 12–13.
39 Kevin R Kosar, 2010, 'Classified information policy and Executive Order 13526,' Congressional Research Services, Library of Congress, viewed 26 March 2020, https://fas.org/sgp/crs/secrecy/R41528.pdf; Gill Bennett, 2002, 'Declassification and release policies of the UK's intelligence agencies', *Intelligence and National Security*, vol. 17, no. 1, pp. 21–32; Alison Hitchens, 1997, 'A call for IGO policies on public access to information', *Government Information Quarterly*, vol. 14, no. 2, p. 145.
40 James David, 2013, 'Can we finally see those records? An update on the automatic/systematic declassification review program', *American Archivist*, vol. 76, no. 2, pp. 415–437; David A Wallace, 1997, 'The public's use of federal recordkeeping statutes to shape federal information policy: a study of the Profs case', University of Pittsburgh.
41 Julia Kastenhofer, 2016, 'Identifying digital records in business systems: the definition of a problem', *Journal of the South African Society of Archivists*, vol. 48, p. 5.
42 Kosar, 2010, p. 17.
43 Public Interest Declassification Board, 2012, p. 3.
44 Ibid.
45 Kastenhofer & Katuu, 2016, p. 22.
46 International Organization for Standardization, 2013, *ISO/IEC 27001:2013 Information Technology – Security Techniques – Information Security Management Systems – Requirements*, International Organization for Standardization, Section A.8.2, Geneva.
47 Robert W Schaaf, 1990, 'Information policies of international organizations', *Government Publications Review*, vol. 17, no. 1.
48 Hitchens, 1997.
49 Chuck Eckman, 2005, 'Information classification and access policies at selected IGOs', *DttP: Documents to the People*, vol. 33, no. 2, p. 23.
50 Michael Pilgrim, 1979, *Proposal for the systematic declassification review of security-classified microfilm*, National Archives and Records Administration, Washington DC; David, 2013, pp. 431–434.
51 Kastenhofer & Katuu, 2016, p. 6.
52 Katuu, 2019a, p. 181.
53 Open Society Foundation, 2013, p. 9.
54 Katuu, 2019a, p. 181.
55 David, 2013, pp. 419–420.
56 Canada Department of Justice, 2019, *Department of Justice guidelines on security for domestic legal agents: protected information and assets. Annex A: Definitions*, Canada Department of Justice, viewed 26 March 2020, www.justice.gc.ca/eng/abt-apd/la-man/security-securite/a.html.
57 Kastenhofer & Katuu, 2016, p. 6.
58 Public Interest Declassification Board, 2012, p. 3.

59 Kastenhofer & Katuu, 2016, pp. 7–8.
60 David Haight, 1989, 'Declassification of presidential papers: the Eisenhower Library's experience', *Provenance, Journal of the Society of Georgia Archivists*, vol. 7, no. 2, pp. 36–37.
61 Katuu, 2019a, p. 186.
62 Eckman, 2005, p. 23.
63 Ibid.
64 Alistair S Roberts, 2003b, *Three patterns in the diffusion of transparency rules*, viewed 26 March 2020, https://ssrn.com/abstract=1439722; Roberts, 2003a.
65 Kosar, 2010, p. 17.
66 Ibid, p. 18.
67 Public Interest Declassification Board, 2012, p. 17.
68 Lynn Scott Cochrane, 1998, 'The Presidential library system: a quiescent policy sub-system', Virginia Technical University, p. 91; Shadrack Katuu, 2019b, 'The utility of visual methods in the research odyssey', in *18th European Conference on Research Methodology for Business and Management Studies*, pp. 164–173, University of Witwatersrand, South Africa, Academic Conferences and Publishing International.
69 Haight, 1989, p. 37.
70 Nancy Kegan Smith & Gary M Stern, 2006 'A historical review of access to records in Presidential Libraries', *The Public Historian*, vol. 28, no. 3, p. 110.
71 Haight, 1989.
72 Ibid, p. 37.
73 Ibid.
74 Shadrack Katuu, 2002, 'Are we information providers or the information police? The uneasy marriage between access and security', in GE Gorman (ed.), *International Yearbook of Library and Information Management 2002/2003*, Facet Publishing, London; Michael E Whitman & Herbert J Mattord, 2012, *Principles of Information Security*, Cengage Learning, Boston, MA, pp. 204–205; Kastenhofer & Katuu, 2016, p. 9.
75 Katuu, 2019a, p. 186.
76 Ibid.
77 Shadrack Katuu, 2020, 'Exploring the challenges facing archives and records professionals in Africa: historical influences, current developments and opportunities', in Ray Edmondson, Lothar Jordan & Anca Claudia Prodan (eds.), *The UNESCO Memory of the World programme: key aspects and recent developments*, Springer Nature, Switzerland.
78 Katuu, 2019a, p. 186.

References

Abass, A 2014, 'International organizations', in Abass, A (ed.), *Complete international law: text, cases and materials*, Oxford University Press, New York, pp. 156–200.
Aftergood, S 2000, 'Secrecy is back in fashion', *Bulletin of the Atomic Scientists*, vol. 56, no. 6, pp. 24–30.
Annis, S 1991, 'Toward a pro-poor information agenda at the World Bank', in *Perspectives on education for all*, International Development Research Centre, Ottawa, pp. 21–29.
Attree, L, Street, J & Venchiarutti, L 2018, *United Nations peace operations in complex environments*, Saferworld.
Bennett, G 2002, 'Declassification and release policies of the UK's intelligence agencies', *Intelligence and National Security*, vol. 17, no. 1, pp. 21–32.
Canada Department of Justice 2019, *Department of Justice guidelines on security for domestic legal agents: protected information and assets. Annex A: definitions*, viewed 26 March 2020, www.justice.gc.ca/eng/abt-apd/la-man/security-securite/a.html.
Castaner, G 2014, *Description of archival holdings of the International Monetary Fund and the project to make descriptions available online*, viewed 26 March 2020, www.pokarh-mb.si/uploaded/datoteke/radenci2014/26_castaner_2014.pdf.

Cochrane, LS 1998, 'The Presidential library system: a quiescent policy subsystem', Virginia Technical University.

David, J 2013, 'Can we finally see those records? An update on the automatic/systematic declassification review program', *American Archivist*, vol. 76, no. 2, pp. 415–437.

Deserno, I, Sengsavang, E, Shockley, M, Katuu, S & Kastenhofer, J 2017, 'TR03: Checklist for developing or revising policies for managing security classified information assets,' InterPARES Trust, viewed 26 March 2020, https://interparestrust.org/assets/public/dissemination/TR03-Checklist-2_-final.pdf.

Deserno, I, Sengsavang, E, Shockley, M, Katuu, S & Kastenhofer, J 2018a, 'TR03: Security classification of records in the cloud in international organizations: an annotated bibliography,' InterPARES Trust, viewed 26 March 2020, https://interparestrust.org/assets/public/dissemination/TR03_20170508_SecurityClassification_AnnotatedBibliography.pdf.

Deserno, I, Sengsavang, E, Shockley, M, Katuu, S & Kastenhofer, J 2018b, 'TR03: Security classification of records in the cloud in international organizations: a literature review,' InterPARES Trust, viewed 26 March 2020, https://interparestrust.org/assets/public/dissemination/TR03LitReview_SkeletonDraft_24Nov2017v6.pdf.

Dikker Hupkes, SD 2009, 'Protection and effective functioning of international organizations. Final report international institutional law, Secure Haven Project', Universiteit Leiden, viewed 28 March 2020, https://openaccess.leidenuniv.nl/handle/1887/14119.

Dollar, CM 1986, 'Electronic records management and archives in international organizations: a RAMP study with guidelines', PGI-86/WS/12, UNESCO, Paris.

Eckman, C 2005, 'Information classification and access policies at selected IGOs', *DttP: Documents to the People*, vol. 33, no. 2, pp. 23–25.

Glover, M, Holsen, S, MacDonald, C, Rahman, M & Simpson, D 2006, *Freedom of information: history, experience and records and information management implications in the USA, Canada and the United Kingdom*. ARMA International Educational Foundation, viewed 26 March 2020, www.global-dcc.com/documents/FreedomofInformationinUSUKandCanada-FINA.pdf.

Haight, D 1989, 'Declassification of presidential papers: the Eisenhower Library's experience', *Provenance, Journal of the Society of Georgia Archivists*, vol. 7, no. 2, pp. 33–53.

Hitchens, A 1997, 'A Call for IGO policies on public access to information', *Government Information Quarterly*, vol. 14, no. 2, pp. 143–154.

International Organization for Standardization 2013, *ISO/IEC 27001:2013 Information Technology – Security Techniques – Information Security Management Systems – Requirements*, International Organization for Standardization, Geneva.

Kastenhofer, J 2016, 'Identifying digital records in business systems: the definition of a problem', *Journal of the South African Society of Archivists*, vol. 48, pp. 1–13.

Kastenhofer, J & Katuu, S 2016, 'Declassification: a clouded environment', *Archives and Records: Journal of the Archives and Records Association*, vol. 37, no. 2, pp. 1–27.

Katuu, S 2002, 'Are we information providers or the information police? The uneasy marriage between access and security', in GE Gorman (ed.), *International Yearbook of Library and Information Management 2002/2003*, Facet Publishing, London, pp. 361–378.

Katuu, S 2019a, 'Managing classified records in inter-governmental organizations', in N van der Waag-Cowling & L Leenen (eds.), *14th International Conference on Cyber Warfare and Security*, Stellenbosch University, South Africa, Academic Conferences and Publishing International, pp. 177–188.

Katuu, S 2019b, 'The utility of visual methods in the research odyssey', in *18th European Conference on Research Methodology for Business and Management Studies*, Academic Conferences and Publishing International, University of Witwatersrand, South Africa, pp. 164–173.

Katuu, S 2020, 'Exploring the challenges facing archives and records professionals in Africa: historical influences, current developments and opportunities', in R Edmondson, L Jordan & AC Prodan (eds.), *The UNESCO Memory of the World programme: key aspects and recent developments*, Springer Nature, Switzerland, pp. 275–292.

Kosar, KR 2010, 'Classified information policy and Executive Order 13526', Congressional Research Services, Library of Congress, viewed 26 March 2020, https://fas.org/sgp/crs/secrecy/R41528.pdf.

Muller, AS 1995, *International organizations and their host states: aspects of their legal relationship*, Kluwer Law International, The Hague.

Open Society Foundation 2013, *The global principles on national security and the right to information (Tshwane Principles)*, Open Society Foundation – Open Society Justice Initiative, viewed 26 March 2020, www.opensocietyfoundations.org/sites/default/files/global-principles-national-security-10232013.pdf.

Piccone, T 2012, *Catalysts for change: how the UN's independent experts promote human rights*, Brookings Institution Press, Washington DC.

Pilgrim, M 1979, *Proposal for the systematic declassification review of security-classified microfilm*, National Archives and Records Administration, Washington DC.

Public Interest Declassification Board 2012, *Transforming the security classification system*, National Archives and Records Administration, Washington DC, viewed 26 March 2020, www.archives.gov/files/declassification/pidb/recommendations/transforming-classification.pdf.

Roberts, A 2003a, 'Entangling alliances: NATO's security of information policy and the entrenchment of state secrecy', *Cornell International Law Journal*, vol. 36, no. 2, pp. 329–360.

Roberts, AS 2003b, *Three patterns in the diffusion of transparency rules*, viewed 26 March 2020, https://ssrn.com/abstract=1439722.

Schaaf, RW 1990, 'Information policies of international organizations', *Government Publications Review*, vol. 17, no. 1, pp. 49–61.

Sengsavang, E, Goh, E, Damer, L, How, E, Hofman, D, Michelson, S, Hunter, M, Chicorli, E & Jones, T 2016, *TR01: Cloud services for international organizations – an annotated bibliography*, InterPARES Trust, viewed 28 March 2020 https://interparestrust.org/assets/public/dissemination/TR_20161110_CloudComputingForInternationalOrganizations_AnnotatedBibliography_FINAL.pdf.

Shockley, M, Deserno, I, Sengsavang, E, Katuu, S & Kastenhofer, J 2017 *Policies for the handling of security classified information in international organizations*, June 7–10, viewed 26 March 2020, https://interparestrust.org/assets/public/dissemination/Shockley_ACAposter.pdf.

Smith, NK & Stern, GM 2006 'A historical review of access to records in presidential libraries', *Public Historian*, vol. 28, no. 3, pp. 79–116.

UNESCO 2018, *Guide to archives of international organizations*, viewed 26 March 2020, http://web.archive.org/web/20181224193029/http://www.unesco.org/archives/sio/Eng/.

Volgy, TJ, Fausett, E, Grant, KA & Rodgers, S 2008, 'Identifying formal intergovernmental organizations', *Journal of Peace Research*, vol. 45, no. 6, pp. 849–862.

Wallace, DA 1997, 'The public's use of federal recordkeeping statutes to shape federal information policy: a study of the Profs case', University of Pittsburgh.

Whitman, ME & Mattord, HJ 2012, *Principles of information security*, Cengage Learning, Boston, MA.

CONCLUSION

Building future networks

Eng Sengsavang[1] and Jens Boel

Technologies are changing so rapidly that the terms we use to describe our times are also constantly shifting to keep pace. The period since the end of the twentieth century to the present day has predominantly been known as the "information age"; but starting from the early twenty-first century, the information age has transitioned into the "digital age." Most recently, in 2019 the UN Secretary-General's High-level Panel on Digital Cooperation (the Panel) has coined a new era, demarcating the period from the 2010s onwards as the "age of digital interdependence."[2] In their report of the same title, the Panel, co-chaired by Melinda Gates and Jack Ma, notes: "While digital technologies have been developing for many years, in the last decade their cumulative impacts have become so deep, wide-ranging and fast-changing as to herald the dawn of a new age."[3] The report describes the concept of digital interdependence:

> The unique benefits and profound risks arising from the dramatic increase in computing power and interconnectivity in the digital age reinforce our underlying interdependence. Globally and locally, we are increasingly linked in an ever-expanding digital web, just as we are increasingly linked, and mutually dependent, in the spheres of economics, public well-being and the environment.[4]

The report suggests that our relationship to digital technologies has undergone a process of globalization, reaching a critical level of interdependence. Not only do we use or even just rely on digital technologies, they are enmeshed into our lives, forming the tissue that connects us all, through our devices, digital networks, and the vast amounts of digital data we produce and consume. The majority of our transactions and activities, both in our personal and work lives, implicate digital technologies in some way.

As we have seen in the Introduction and in each of the chapters of this book, the evolving digital environment has profound implications for recordkeeping[5] processes and will shape the archives of the future. Writing in 1989, the French scholar Arlette Farge described archives as "immeasurable, pervasive like the tides, avalanches, or floods. The comparison with natural and unpredictable flows is far from accidental; the archival researcher is often surprised to evoke this journey in terms of diving, immersion, even drowning ... one meets the sea."[6] Although she is describing French police records of the eighteenth century, Farge's description strikes a chord – possibly a deeper chord – in our age of digital interdependence. The digital sea of information we are now faced with brings new issues and challenges, requiring that organizations adapt to the shifting environment in their recordkeeping practices and policies.

The Panel, convened by UN Secretary-General António Guterres, is part of the UN Secretary-General's Strategy on New Technologies (the Strategy), launched in 2018 "to define how the United Nations system will support the use of [new] technologies to accelerate the achievement of the 2030 Sustainable Development Agenda."[7] The Strategy calls for the establishment of "principles, values, obligations and responsibilities that should guide the design, development and uses of the technologies that are transforming our societies,"[8] based on "the values enshrined in the UN Charter, the Universal Declaration of Human Rights, and the norms and standards of international law."[9] While the Strategy is part of efforts to reform the UN system and is targeted to UN organizations and member states, its goals and the report of the Panel are applicable on a wider level. And although launched more than a year before the onslaught of the COVID-19 pandemic, the aims of the Strategy stand up to recent experience; with the increase in society's interdependence on digital technologies laid bare in an unprecedented manner during the pandemic, its goals appear ever more urgent.[10]

While acknowledging the "incredible promise for human welfare" inherent in digital technologies such as "artificial intelligence, biotechnology, material sciences and robotics,"[11] the Strategy also recognizes that the same technologies "hold the potential to generate more inequality and more violence."[12] For this reason, active efforts to ensure that technological developments incorporate egalitarian goals and human rights principles are fundamental. This also underscores the fact that it is not technology itself, but how technologies are governed and interact within complex human systems, infrastructures, and economies that ultimately determines how they will develop and affect society.

The larger framework of both the Strategy and the Panel is the UN's 2030 Agenda for Sustainable Development and the accompanying Sustainable Development Goals (SDGs). The SDGs set an ambitious programme for achieving concrete goals based on ethical principles in many broad areas. Adopted in 2015 by all UN member states, the SDGs are "a universal call to action to end poverty, protect the planet and improve the lives and prospects of everyone, everywhere."[13] The SDGs establish a 15-year framework in which to achieve 17 defined goals. Among them, Goal 16 defines the objective to "promote peaceful and inclusive societies for sustainable development, provide access to justice for all and build effective, accountable and inclusive institutions at all levels."[14] As part of this goal, ten targets are laid out, among which are target 16.6, "Develop effective, accountable and transparent institutions at all levels," and target 16.10, "Ensure public access to information and protect fundamental freedoms, in accordance with national legislation and international agreements."[15]

Recordkeeping has a significant role to play in achieving both these targets. On a fundamental level, targets 16.6 and 16.10 speak to a particular concept of archives as a public good – which in the twentieth and twenty-first centuries has become the *raison d'être* of recordkeeping – and more specifically, to the "democratic tradition of open archives creating a transparency of politics – an open forum for political decisions."[16] The democratic function of archives, and the link between archives and recordkeeping with transparency and accountability, and with citizens' rights, has a lineage that can be traced to as far back as the archives of the democratic city-state of classical Athens, and later to the French Revolution and to the establishment of the National Archives of France as a public institution. As archivist and scholar Angelika Menne-Haritz observed, archives:

> Make evident the decision-making processes that affect public life and they help guarantee rights, not for the archives holding body, but for the public. That is why we regard it as so self-evident that the right of access is granted by law to every citizen.[17]

The aims outlined in targets 16.6 and 16.10 therefore reflect the purpose of archives and recordkeeping to ensure accountability and transparency from governments, institutions, and other entities, and to guarantee access to information. Alongside these essential developments, recordkeeping theories and methodologies have continued to evolve up to the present day in response to contemporary challenges, as we have seen throughout this book, and to translate concepts of human rights, justice, inclusiveness, accountability, and transparency into professional practice.

Thus in the course of their daily work and to a significant degree, recordkeeping professionals already enact the goals expressed in targets 16.6 and 16.10; and the results of their work, archives, embody the principles therein. The policies, processes, tools, and practices that recordkeeping professionals create and employ to manage an organization's records each contribute to ensuring "effective, accountable, and inclusive" institutions, as well as "public access to information and ... fundamental freedoms." The overall purpose of this work is to ensure that the records of an organization are accountably managed, organized, protected, kept permanently, or destroyed in an accountable way, and made accessible over the long term. For example, records retention and disposition schedules establish which records must be kept permanently or for a set period of time for internal reference, legal, financial, auditing, or long-term historical value; public access policies ensure that staff and the general public have access to records and clear rules for their access; databases, inventories, and catalogues ensure that records and information are searchable, findable, and discoverable; and long-term preservation policies, including, more recently, digital preservation policies, ensure that physical conservation measures and digital preservation strategies are put in place to preserve records permanently.

Another major recordkeeping practice that supports the achievement of targets 16.6 and 16.10 is digitization. The process of digitization represents a literal digital transformation of physical archives from paper and analogue form into digital form. This process is often described as "dematerialization." Notwithstanding the significant financial and human resources, expertise, and labour required to make digitization happen, one could describe the potential effects of this digital transformation as nothing short of miraculous. This is because the digital conversion of archival holdings and collections makes previously hard-to-access – in some cases, outright inaccessible – bodies of records accessible on a global scale, given that the newly digitized "surrogates" are made available through online platforms and databases, and given that the digital divide that still exists can be overcome. Multi-institutional platforms and federated databases also help to increase the visibility and therefore public access to digitized holdings. In some cases, digitization means that, for example, analogue audiovisual archives found on obsolete formats such as 16mm film or reel-to-reel magnetic tape can be enjoyed for the first time since their active period of use decades before. Digitization is also critical in cases where collections are either fragile and suffer from too much handling, or at risk of becoming permanently inaccessible due to physical deterioration, technological obsolescence, poor conservation conditions, or a combination of these factors.

Digitization especially supports target 16.10 of Goal 16 to "Ensure public access to information and protect fundamental freedoms," since it opens access to archives that may otherwise be difficult or impossible to access for individuals due to lack of financial resources, time, or other socio-economic barriers. In another sense, digitization may also be seen as part of a larger effort to bring archives, libraries, and cultural institutions up to speed in the digital era, in order to make use of the benefits afforded by current technologies and to reach broader and more diverse audiences. Since the 2000s, many archives, libraries, and cultural institutions in a variety of institutional settings, including within international organizations, have begun to digitize their holdings and collections. Institutional digitization efforts can range in scale from ad hoc or small to significant projects such as the "Total Digital Access to the League of Nations Archives Project (LONTAD)" by the UN Office in Geneva, or the "Digitizing Our Shared UNESCO History" project by UNESCO.[18] Scholars have also used the terms "large-scale digitization initiatives" or "mass digitization" to describe large projects financed by commercial giants such as Google and Microsoft, or non-profit entities.[19] When digitization projects are accomplished professionally, with due respect for standards and with a long-term preservation strategy, they can be seen as part of the pursuit of the universalist dreams of certain archivists in the 1940s and 1950s. These developed against the backdrop of the disasters for humanity leading up to and during the

Second World War, as well as internationalist cooperation in the 1930s. It is in this context that the historian Emma Rothschild calls mass digitization of archives "a democratization of history, in prospect, and an internationalization of historical sources."[20]

It is clear that more digitization is needed. The COVID-19 pandemic has served to demonstrate the need for digitization in real time, with the closure of physical archives, libraries, and cultural institutions rendering important resources that are only available in physical form suddenly inaccessible. This has affected the ability not only for researchers, scholars, and other professionals to access resources and information; in some cases, it has also prevented organizations from carrying out their work, for example when undigitized official documents are needed for the creation of a budget or report, or for auditing purposes, and yet are physically inaccessible. Undigitized archives therefore represent a significant risk to the smooth functioning of organizational operations. Yet many international organizations and other types of institutions do not have the resources required to fund digitization projects, relying instead on the generosity of member states or external sources of funding. As demonstrated both by current trends in the digital environment and by the COVID-19 pandemic, digitization will continue to be a critical area of growth for the realization of the SDG's Goal 16.

The report by the UN Panel on Digital Cooperation mentioned above also suggests several other avenues for records professionals to contribute to supporting the goals of the SDGs. Several "priority actions" identified by the Panel are extremely relevant to recordkeeping functions. These initiatives would benefit from the expertise of records professionals in the areas of recordkeeping standards, long-term preservation, public access to archives, records retention, privacy and security, and more. For example, records professionals could participate in "the design and application of ... standards and principles such as transparency and non-bias in autonomous intelligent systems" (priority action no. 3C); or "the development of a Global Commitment on Digital Trust and Security to shape a shared vision, identify attributes of digital stability, elucidate and strengthen the implementation of norms for responsible uses of technology, and propose priorities for action" (priority action no. 4).[21]

This is the new context in which archives and records management – and information management, to use a wider concept – must find their place. On another level, for international organizations seeking to respond to the fast-paced digital environment in the aftermath of the COVID-19 pandemic, multilateralism will have to be reinvented. Even before the pandemic, the report by the Panel recommended several priority actions, which are relevant in this respect, among them a shift towards what it terms multi-stakeholderism:

Effective digital cooperation requires that multilateralism, despite current strains, be strengthened. It also requires that multilateralism be complemented by multi-stakeholderism – cooperation that involves not only governments but a far more diverse spectrum of other stakeholders such as civil society, academics, technologists and the private sector. We need to bring far more diverse voices to the table, particularly from developing countries and traditionally marginalised groups, such as women, youth, indigenous people, rural populations and older people.[22]

The Panel thus envisions a more diverse multilateral and multi-stakeholder process. To achieve this complementary multi-stakeholderism, the Panel calls for the UN to "facilitate an agile and open consultation process to develop updated mechanisms for global digital cooperation."[23] Given that governance and management of digital data are central to the challenges identified by the Panel, records professionals should take part in the processes of multi-stakeholderism to come.

Although these new patterns of transnational and transversal cooperation are still to be invented, discovered, and explored, and therefore are very much in the making, some key dimensions can already be identified. More than ever, there is a need for innovation, capacity of transformation, flexibility in working methods and ways of thinking, outreach and openness towards multiple diverse communities, interdisciplinary training and capacity of team-working at all levels, from the local to the global, in an increasingly networked environment. These trends and requirements have consequences for professionals of archives, records, and information management.

As mentioned in the Introduction, for decades most archivists have aimed at facilitating access to their holdings.[24] While doing so they have often built alliances with user communities, such as historians, anthropologists, sociologists, political scientists, and other scholars and students in a wide area of fields. They have also had to convince senior management within their own organizations about the relevance of providing access to a wider public and of using "institutional memory" as a resource for the organization. They have tried to show why and how archives and records and the way they are managed are crucial to strategic requirements and goals, such as programme development, core operations, and accountability and transparency. Now, they can also draw from the framework of the UN SDGs, and particularly Goal 16, to demonstrate how recordkeeping functions align with and support the targets of constructing just societies and protecting fundamental freedoms. The SDGs provide a high-level framework and a powerful mechanism through which recordkeeping professionals can bolster their advocacy and alliance-building work.

As part of their education, future archivists and records managers will need to learn to combine an in-depth knowledge of archives and records management, preservation and access functionalities, including an emphasis on digital dimensions, with a strong understanding of the wider context of political and strategic environments. In order to be successful in their classical mission – organizing, preserving, and providing access – archivists and records managers need to be able to build bridges and links with legal professionals, audit departments, IT divisions, communication and information sectors, and those in charge of strategic planning and decision-making. Educational programmes should prepare them for this by combining a strong professional foundation with contextual training, thereby enabling the future information managers to link their specific technical knowledge with a profound understanding of the purpose of these functions and a capacity to relate to and work with other relevant parts of their respective organizations.

The case studies in this book provide inspiration and examples of how records professionals can adapt to these challenges in practice. This is, for example, the case when it is argued, in Chapter 1, that developing a communication strategy for archives in a transnational environment is essential. Another concrete example of a strategic approach is the proposal in Chapter 6 that information, records, and archives should be managed as part of an integrated system and that an international standard should be designed to support this management. Policy advice also has strategic consequences, for example when it is pointed out, in Chapter 8, that organizations should avoid keeping security classified records classified in perpetuity and that they should actively raise awareness about publicly disclosed information among interested parties such as historians, citizen groups, and students. In the same chapter it is also emphasized that international organizations are accountable for their recordkeeping and should strive for transparency and progressive policies when it comes to declassification and the eventual public disclosure of security classified records. Chapter 9 complements Chapter 8 by establishing an overview of classification and declassification processes within IGOs.

The analysis and discussion in Chapter 7 will hopefully inspire information management professionals to explore the emerging opportunities in utilizing enterprise architecture. The case of data protection within the EU, which is treated in Chapter 2, touches upon essential questions relating to the balance between privacy and other information management concerns. One interesting conclusion is the need to establish internationally recognized common governance principles on artificial intelligence.

Several chapters provide specific advice, including checklists, on recordkeeping in the networked environment. Such guidance is essential for enabling record-keeping professionals to effectively contribute to and have an impact on the strategic policies and goals of their organizations. An example is the recommendation in Chapter 3 that international organizations should apply an interdisciplinary risk-management approach when implementing cloud services, including controls for mitigating risks based on existing standards and risk frameworks. Complementary advice is provided in Chapter 5 with the recommendation that when concluding cloud service contracts, the InterPARES Trust Checklist for Cloud Service Contracts has to be adapted to the specific needs of international organizations, in particular by taking into account existing host country agreements.

The case studies also frame the wider context of archives and records management in international organizations by discussing and analysing key terms. For example, it appears from Chapter 4 that the concept of "inviolability" of records and archives is essential for IGOs. The chapter shows that inviolability is normally established by host country agreements and contractual arrangements, in addition to being, in many cases, included in the foundational documents (such as constitutions) of such organizations. Inviolability of records and archives is rarely guaranteed for international NGOs.

In the Introduction, we defined this book's purpose as double: "To study how recordkeeping in international organizations has been impacted by the extensively networked environment, and to provide, on the basis of case studies, as well as original research and professional experience, some reflections and advice." Some of the key insights and recommendations, which come out of the case studies, are summarized above and many more appear in the individual chapters. However, there are also missing areas, which we hope will be subjects of future research. One of these is recordkeeping within multinational businesses, an area of increasing importance generally, and also from the perspective of international organizations, in particular in the context of multi-stakeholderism. Another area, which is not covered in this book, is international NGOs and their particularities. These organizations are of critical importance, not only because of their number (6,000 compared to 250 IGOs[25]), but also since they cover a wide range of international work, for example in the areas of the environment and human rights. UNESCO and the ICA have in the past taken initiatives to provide NGOs with guidelines that aim at encouraging them to organize their archives, based on the understanding that they form an important part of the record of humanity.[26] We believe that capacity-building for recordkeeping in international NGOs should be a priority for the international professional community and, in particular, for the International Council on Archives.

The questions we have posed in both direct and indirect ways throughout this book centre around what it means to practice a transnational approach to recordkeeping, and how recordkeeping may contribute to improving global and local conditions in specific ways. Along with the recordkeeping challenges analysed in this book, we have also considered how relevant strategies, ethical standards, and principles set by the UN and other international organizations – including frameworks such the UN's 2030 Agenda for Sustainable Development and Sustainable Development Goals, the Strategy for New Technologies, and the High-level Panel on Digital Cooperation – can help to nourish and inform the whys and hows of current recordkeeping directions, practices, and cooperative networks. They also help to bring into sharper focus the current issues and lines of action that are relevant for the work of records professionals, and to which they may contribute. Although seemingly remote from the on-the-ground daily challenges of recordkeeping, global high-level frameworks can act as compelling vehicles – among other means – through which records professionals can achieve their purposes, speak a common language connected to strategic trends within their own institutions and across institutions, and help to ensure, through their work, the protection of rights and equal opportunities. After all, perhaps our best response to current challenges is one that both mirrors and transcends the extraordinary digital networks we have built thus far: a network of mutual commitments and actions inspired by a human-centred vision for our future.

Notes

1 The author is responsible for the choice and the presentation of the facts contained in the publication and for the opinions expressed therein, which are not necessarily those of UNESCO and do not commit the Organization.
2 UN Secretary-General's High-level Panel on Digital Cooperation, 2019 June, *The age of digital interdependence*, viewed 8 May 2020, https://digitalcooperation.org/wp-content/uploads/2019/06/DigitalCooperation-report-web-FINAL-1.pdf.
3 Ibid, p. 11.
4 Ibid, p. 12.
5 In this Conclusion, we base our spelling and definition of "recordkeeping" on that found in the International Council on Archives' *Multilingual archival terminology. Recordkeeping*: "The systematic creation, use, maintenance, and disposition of records to meet administrative, programmatic, legal, and financial needs and responsibilities," Richard Pearce Moses, 2005, cited in InterPARES Trust & International Council on Archives, *Multilingual archival terminology*, 2015, 'Recordkeeping [definition no. 1]', viewed 3 June 2020, www.ciscra.org/mat/mat/term/293. We take a broad interpretation of this definition to include not just records management and archival functions, but also the increasingly overlapping functions of information management.
6 Arlette Farge, 1989, *Le goût de l'archive*, Editions du Seuil, Paris, p. 10. Translation by the authors.
7 United Nations, 2018 September, *UN Secretary-General's strategy on new technologies*, viewed 9 May 2020, www.un.org/en/newtechnologies/images/pdf/SGs-Strategy-on-New-Technologies.pdf, p. 3.
8 Ibid, p. 9.
9 Ibid.
10 The report states explicitly that new technologies "hint at a future of … reduced pandemics," along with a number of other benefits to society. See United Nations, 2018, p. 8.
11 Ibid, p. 4.
12 Ibid.
13 United Nations Sustainable Development Goals, n.d., 'The sustainable development agenda', viewed 2 May 2020, www.un.org/sustainabledevelopment/development-agenda/.
14 United Nations Sustainable Development Goals, 2018, 'Peace, justice, and strong institutions: why they matter', viewed 2 May 2020, www.un.org/sustainabledevelopment/wp-content/uploads/2018/09/16.pdf.
15 United Nations Sustainable Development Goals, n.d., 'Goal 16: promote just, peaceful and inclusive societies', viewed 2 May 2020, www.un.org/sustainabledevelopment/peace-justice/.
16 Angelika Menne-Haritz, 1994, 'Appraisal or documentation: can we appraise archives by selecting content?', *American Archivist*, vol. 57, Summer, p. 531.
17 Ibid, pp. 531–532.
18 See *Total Digital Access to the League of Nations Archives Project (LONTAD)*, viewed 18 May 2020, https://lontad-project.unog.ch/; *Digitizing Our Shared UNESCO History* project website (available until November 2020; the digitized archives will then be migrated to UNESCO permanent repositories), viewed 18 May 2020, https://digital.archives.unesco.org/en/.
19 Oya Y Rieger, 2008 February, *Preservation in the age of large-scale digitization: a white paper*, Council on Library and Information Resources, Washington, p. 4.
20 Emma Rothschild, 2008, 'The archives of universal history', *Journal of World History*, vol. 19, no. 3, p. 401.
21 United Nations, 2018, p. 8.
22 Ibid.
23 Ibid.

24 See also, for a historical overview on developments in archival access up to the early 1980s, Michel Duchein, 1983, *Obstacles to the access, use and transfer of information from archives*, RAMP Study, PGI-83/WS/20, UNESCO, Paris.
25 As indicated in the Introduction, note 3.
26 Armelle Le Goff & International Council on Archives, Section of International Organisations (SIO), 2004, *The records of NGOs, memory to be shared*, Paris. Available via the ICA website, www.ica.org/en/records-ngos-memory-be-shared.

References

Duchein, M 1983, *Obstacles to the access, use and transfer of information from archives*, RAMP Study, PGI-83/WS/20, UNESCO, Paris.

Farge, A 1989, *Le goût de l'archive*, Editions du Seuil, Paris.

Le Goff, A & International Council on Archives, Section of International Organisations (SIO) 2004, *The records of NGOs, memory to be shared*, Paris, viewed 15 May 2020, www.ica.org/en/records-ngos-memory-be-shared.

Menne-Haritz, A 1994, 'Appraisal or documentation: can we appraise archives by selecting content?', *American Archivist*, vol. 57, Summer, pp. 528–542.

Rieger, OY 2008, *Preservation in the age of large-scale digitization: a white paper*, Council on Library and Information Resources, Washington DC.

Rothschild, E 2008, 'The archives of universal history', *Journal of World History*, vol. 19, no. 3, pp. 375–401.

United Nations 2018, September, *UN Secretary-General's strategy on new technologies*, viewed 9 May 2020, www.un.org/en/newtechnologies/images/pdf/SGs-Strategy-on-New-Technologies.pdf, p. 3.

United Nations Secretary-General's High-level Panel on Digital Cooperation 2019, *The age of digital interdependence*, viewed 8 May 2020, https://digitalcooperation.org/wp-content/uploads/2019/06/DigitalCooperation-report-web-FINAL-1.pdf.

United Nations Sustainable Development Goals n.d., 'Goal 16: Promote just, peaceful and inclusive societies', viewed 2 May 2020, www.un.org/sustainabledevelopment/peace-justice/.

United Nations Sustainable Development Goals n.d., 'The sustainable development agenda', viewed 2 May 2020, www.un.org/sustainabledevelopment/development-agenda/.

United Nations Sustainable Development Goals 2018, 'Peace, justice, and strong institutions: why they matter', viewed 2 May 2020, www.un.org/sustainabledevelopment/wp-content/uploads/2018/09/16.pdf.

INDEX